The collected works of Ruqaiya Hasan
Volume 1 Language, Society and Consciousness
Edited by Jonathan J. Webster

every language is a vast pattern-system, different from others, in which are culturally ordained the forms and categories by which the personality not only communicates, but also analyses nature, notices or neglects types of relationship and phenomena, channels his reasoning and builds the house of his consciousness.

Benjamin Lee Whorf 1897–1941 *Language, Mind and Reality*

The Collected Works of Ruqaiya Hasan

Volume 1
Language, Society and Consciousness

Edited by Jonathan J. Webster

Dedicated to the Memory of
Basil Bernstein
1924–2000

who showed us how society permeates
language permeates mind permeates society

LONDON   OAKVILLE

Published by

Equinox Publishing Ltd.
UK: Unit 6, The Village, 101 Amies Street, London, SW11 2JW
USA: DBBC, 28 Main Street, Oakville, CT 06779
www.equinoxpub.com

First published 2005

© 2005, Ruqaiya Hasan, Jonathan Webster

All rights reserved. No part of this publication may be reproduced or transmitted in any form or by any means, electronic or mechanical, including photocopying, recording or any information storage or retrieval system, without prior permission in writing from the publishers.

British Library Cataloguing-in-Publication Data
A catalogue record for this book is available from the British Library.

ISBN 1-904768-33-4 (Hardback)
ISBN 1-904768-34-2 (Paperback)

Library of Congress Cataloging-in-Publication Data

Hasan, Ruqaiya.
  The collected works of Ruqaiya Hasan / Ruqaiya Hasan ; edited by Jonathan Webster.
     p. cm.
  Includes bibliographical references and index.
  ISBN 1-904768-33-4 -- ISBN 1-904768-34-2 (pbk.)
  1. Sociolinguistics. 2. Semiotics. 3. Philosophy of mind. I. Webster, Jonathan, 1955- II. Title.
  P40.H348 2005
  306.44--dc22
                              2004022853

Typeset by Catchline, Milton Keynes (www.catchline.com)
Printed and bound in Great Britain by Antony Rowe Ltd, Chippenham and Eastbourne

Contents

Editor's preface

Introduction   3
Language, Society and Consciousness: transdisciplinary orientations and the tradition of specialisation

Section 1

Editor's Introduction: The sociosemiotic mediation of mind   18
1 Basil Bernstein: an exceptional 1924–2000   21
2 Society, Language and Mind: the metadialogism of Basil Bernstein's theory   48
3 Speech Genre, Semiotic Mediation and the Development of Higher Mental Functions   68
4 On the Social Conditions for Semiotic Mediation: the genesis of mind in society   106
5 Semiotic Mediation and Three Exotropic Theories: Vygotsky, Halliday and Bernstein   130

Section 2

Editor's Introduction: Coding orientations and forms of consciousness   157
6 Code, Register and Social Dialect   160
7 Semiotic Mediation and Mental Development in Pluralistic Societies: some implications for tomorrow's schooling   194
8 Ways of Meaning, Ways of Learning: code as an explanatory concept   215
9 Reading Picture Reading: a study in ideology and inference   228
10 The Ontogenesis of Ideology: an interpretation of mother child talk   256

Section 3

Editor's Introduction: Language and society: conflict or co-genesis?   275
11 The Disempowerment Game: Bourdieu on language   277
12 Bourdieu on Linguistics and Language: a response to my commentators   337

References   354
Index   371

Acknowledgements

'Basil Bernstein: An Exceptional 1924 – 2000' was based on an expanded and revised version of three publications: 'Understanding Talk: Directions from Bernstein's Sociology' in *International Journal of Social Research Methodology*, 2001, vol 4, no. 1, pages 5–9. Courtesy of Taylor and Francis Group; 'Basil Bernstein: An Exceptional' in *A Tribute to Basil Bernstein 1924 – 2000*, edited by S. Power, P. Aggleton, J. Brannen, L. Chisholm and J. Mace, 2002, published by The Institute of Education. Courtesy of The Institute of Education; 'Basil Bernstein 1924-2000: Obituary' in *Functions of Language*, 2000, vol 7, no. 2, pages 279–91. Courtesy of John Benjamins Publishing Co.

'Society, language and the mind: the meta-dialogism of Basil Bernstein's theory' in *Pedagogy and the Shaping of Consciousness: linguistics and social processes*, edited by Frances Christie, 1999, published by Cassell. Courtesy of Continuum International Publishing Group.

'Speech genre, semiotic mediation and the development of higher mental functions' in *Language Sciences*, 1992, vol 14, no. 4, published by Pergamon Press. Courtesy of Pergamon Press, a division of Elsevier Science Publishing Co.

'On the social conditions for semiotic mediation: the genesis of mind in society' in *Knowledge and Pedagogy: the sociology of Basil Bernstein*, edited by Alan R. Sadovnik, 1995, published by ABLEX Publishing. Courtesy of Greenwood Publishing Group Inc.

'Code, register and social dialect' in *Class, Codes and Control*, vol II, edited by Basil Bernstein 1973, Routledge and Kegan Paul. Courtesy of Routledge, Taylor and Francis Group.

'Semiotic mediation and mental development in pluralistic societies: some implications for tomorrow's schooling' in *Learning for Life in the 21st Century: socio-cultural perspectives on the future of education*, edited by G. Wells and G. Claxton, 2002, published by Blackwell Publishers Ltd. Courtesy of Blackwell Publishers Ltd.

'Ways of meaning, ways of learning: code as an explanatory concept' in *British Journal of the Sociology of Education*, vol. 23, no. 4, 2002, pages 537–48. Courtesy of Taylor and Francis Group (http://www.tandf.co.uk).

'Reading picture reading: a study in ideology and inference' in *Language, Education and Discourse: functional approaches*, edited by J. Foley, Continuum, 2004.

'The ontogenesis of ideology: an interpretation of mother child talk' in *Semiotics, Ideology, Language*, edited by Terry Threadgold, E.A. Grosz, Gunther Kress and M.A.K. Halliday, 1986, published by Sydney Association for Studies in Society and Culture. Courtesy of Sydney Association for Studies in Society and Culture.

'The disempowerment game: Bourdieu and language in literacy' in *Linguistics and Education*, 1999, vol 10, no. 1, pages 25–88. Courtesy of Pergamon Press, a division of Elsevier Science Publishing Co.

'Bourdieu on linguistics and language: a response to my commentators' in *Linguistics and Education*, 2000, vol 10, no. 4, pages 441–58. Courtesy of Pergamon Press, a division of Elsevier Science Publishing Co.

It was my good fortune and my privilege to be present in London during the mid-late 1960s when the dialogue took place between Basil Bernstein's Sociolinguistic Research Unit and Michael Halliday's Communication Research Centre. Thanks to the sociological and linguistic insights provided by these seminal scholars, the nature of language – its potential and its power – began to be relatively more visible to me; questions began to take shape, perhaps got better defined over the years.

Ruqaiya Hasan

Editor's preface

What unfolds across the papers in this first volume in *The Collected Works of Ruqaiya Hasan* is a transdisciplinary theory designed to address three interconnected human concerns: language, society and consciousness. The human story is as much told through language as it is about language. The co-genesis of the semiotic and the social demands a theory spanning the biological, the sociological and the linguistic. The theory which emerges in Professor Hasan's works is one born out of the dialogue between Bernstein's semiotic sociology, Halliday's sociological linguistics and Vygotsky's sociogenetic psychology. Left to its own devices, linguistic theory comes across as impoverished, hollow and socially irrelevant, but when enriched through interconnections with other disciplines, it acquires a voice which not only asks the right questions but also speaks to our social conscience.

Choosing to come to terms with what some see only as the shadow[1] that falls between language and non-language, between the semiotic and the social, between the visible and the invisible, Professor Hasan explores the true nature of what is instead a dialectic between the social and the semiotic by which the outside becomes the inside, and the inside reveals itself. Evidence collected from classroom discourse and mother-child talk shows how 'the taken-for-granted nature of the social world' is transmitted through habitual forms of communication, or speech codes, acquired early in life. Codes are the 'the crucial link between the material conditions and the mental life of human beings' (Chapter 1). This notion of code, or 'sociolinguistic coding orientation', as first put forward by Bernstein, is 'difficult to grasp,' notes Halliday, because the phenomena so named 'fall squarely in the problematic middle ground between the system and the instance – between the meaning potential of language and instantiated acts of meaning' (1992/2003). Acknowledging the existence of different coding orientations is a precursor to asking important questions such as 'what is the best way to encourage a dialogue between speakers whose discourse is regulated by different coding orientations?'; 'how can we talk across unshared worlds?'; 'how can a teacher capitalise on the presence of multiple voices in the classroom without creating in any of her speakers either a sense of superiority or a sense of being devalued?'

As present in her consciousness as it was in Bernstein's is 'the need to understand and to reveal the mechanisms whereby the patterns of oppression and often unwitting collusion in oppression maintain themselves in modern progressive societies'. But confronting harsh reality demands hard truth. Bernstein's research into the nature of the pedagogic system not only revealed the fallacy of egalitarian education, 'where the same form of semiotic mediation suits all', but also brought into the question 'widely accepted notions of an individual's discursive freedom'. But the truth is also liberating. The liberating force of literacy as significant pedagogic action is predicated on 'a clearly enunciated conception of a dialectic between the social and the semiotic'.

This first volume in *The Collected Works of Ruqaiya Hasan* lays the theoretical foundation for what follows in a series of seven volumes presenting a selection of unpublished and previously published papers in such areas as:

Semantic variation: meaning in society
Language in education: social aspects
Context in the system and process of language
Describing language: form and function
Unity in discourse: texture and structure
Verbal art: a social semiotic perspective

Her insight into the nature of language, society and consciousness will prompt you to ask the significant questions in your own search for a better understanding of the power and potential of human language.

Note

1   Perhaps along similar lines to what T. S. Elliot describes in The Hollow Men:
    'Between the idea
    And the reality ...
    Falls the shadow'

Introduction

Language, society and consciousness: transdisciplinary orientations and the tradition of specialisation

1 Introduction

Discourse on the interrelations of language, society and consciousness is not exactly a novel enterprise. However, judging from the frequent return to the discussion, it would seem that perhaps the business of describing these relations has not given complete satisfaction. From one point of view, of course, the search for the closure of discourse by the achievement of perfect description/explanation is futile; for though the opposition between structure and process is most probably facile, it has still to be granted that knowledge and understanding are not so much structure as ongoing process: their nature is to remain open to growth and development. This said, there nonetheless remains a question: why has it been so difficult to get these relations 'in place'? What impedes our progress? Two reasons spring to mind at once.

2 Intellectual struggle as conflict of interest

In the first place, our educational traditions have favoured strong boundaries across segregated domains of enquiry and this segregation of specialisms has led to other tangential phenomena. As Bernstein has observed (2000) education is not simply about instruction in some competency; it is also and perhaps more importantly, about the regulation of mental dispositions. The intellectual traditions inculcated by the official pedagogic systems demand not only a mastery of certain conceptual structures in some specific field of knowledge, but in time they also demand an investment of self in the pursuit of the elaboration of those concepts; and eventually, the pursuit of some field of knowledge comes to identify the pursuer. More specifically, in the case of what Bernstein called 'segmental knowledge structures' (Bernstein, 1999; 2000) our identities get shaped not only as 'linguist', 'sociologist', 'economist', or whatever, but also as 'formal/functional linguist', 'structuralist/critical sociologist' and so on. We acquire the ability to produce legitimate discourse in our corner of the chosen field of enquiry; we develop a distinctive language which is designed so as to illuminate the object of our study, but which also acts to deter easy incursions into the field by 'outsiders' whether this consequence is intended or not. This creates an interesting paradox: on the one hand, through these steps, the continuation and possibly the growth of a given field of knowledge is well nigh ensured; but on the other hand, it has the potential of creating and often does create, a sense of allegiance that could be as strong and as much 'above' questioning as are the sacred cows of 'my country, my religion, my language, my culture' and so on. It may come to pass then that the kind of monopolies and hierarchies that we deplore in the management of material capital as some of the worst characteristics of non-egalitarian societies, we embrace without demur in the management of symbolic capital, because the behaviour becomes a 'signifier' of our commitment – because a substantial part of our identity comes to be invested in that very field, from that very perspective!

Not surprisingly, when we attempt to visit a 'foreign' knowledge domain, this entire syndrome can and often does, lead to a certain bias. For example, in the context of the present discussion, the obvious fact that our consciousness, our social organisation and our language are inextricably interrelated, that each plays a major part in our continued existence, that in doing this, they must, of necessity, cooperate with each other – these well-acknowledged facts often get consigned to the back seat; the discourse descends into proving that one's own field of expertise has 'the primary role' in accounting for the most important aspects of human life. Instead of devoting our energies to combating material domination, we get side-tracked into fighting battles for intellectual domination, thus playing the capitalist game whereby gaining a competitive edge on an imaginary or real opponent is an important element in attaining success. Some of these issues are discussed in this volume by reference to a highly regarded sociologist, Pierre Bourdieu, who has without doubt made a valuable contribution to our understanding of the social, but who, nonetheless, displays precisely this attitude when confronting language. So in his writings, along with linguists and their practices as experts in the study of language, language itself gets devalued: it is taken as a surrogate of reality, as nothing but a reflection of social processes (see Chapters 11 and 12). I must add immediately that I have found Bourdieu's work inspirational and insightful in many respects, but admiration for a scholar's contribution is no reason for suspending the activity of reflection and reflection is useful only to the extent that it can proceed from a position of understanding and without fear or favour – in as much as is humanly possible in view of Bourdieu's theory of self-interest.

3 Intellectual struggle in relating distinct domains

But even when scholars are not explicitly engaged in jockeying[1] for a superior position in the pantheon of the sub-fields of the social sciences, a more subtle problem may arise, which constitutes the second reason that impedes our discourse concerning the relations between the three mainsprings of human existence – the semiotic, the social and the mental. To elaborate this point, let me consider here two scholars, namely Whorf and Vygotsky, who have made remarkable contributions to the discourse concerning the relations of the semiotic, the social and the mental: both have argued that society and language play a crucial role in the formation of human consciousness and neither has attempted to devalue the fields to which they do not 'belong'.

Whorf (1956) argued that our habitual ways of thinking have their roots largely in our ways of meaning – our 'fashions of speaking'. From the perspective of ontogeny, what this means is that our modelling of the world owes much to ways of meaning peculiar to the specific language we grow up with; this position resonates with one of his famous contemporaries, Wittgenstein, who claimed that the limits of one's language define the limits of one's world (1953). Whorf went on to present a highly original design for the analysis of meaning in language the potential of which has yet to be fully appreciated by the majority of linguists, who, to my mind, have read Whorf with disdain and discarded him without sufficient reflection[2]. Whorf recognised the dialectic of language and culture, the function of language in giving shape to mental maps of the universe and *'the relation of habitual thought and behaviour to language'*. However, if one were to go to Whorf either to probe in detail the nature of consciousness itself or to discover about the fundamental elements contributing to cultural formations, one would be rather disappointed. The detailed exploration of culture, of principles regulating social practices and of the make up of human mind was not and perhaps could not be, part of the agenda, for Whorf's major interest lay in drawing attention to the pervasive nature of what we learn about the universe through our fashions of speaking in everyday life – what Bernstein (2000 and elsewhere) was to refer to as 'horizontal discourse'; details about how consciousness develops, or how cultures are produced and reproduced with what consequences for the social subject were not his main preoccupation.

In his discussion of the relations of language, culture and consciousness, Whorf appears to have had in mind certain properties of language as 'system'. By contrast, Vygotsky's focus (1978 and elsewhere) was more on language as 'process', how it acts in the development of human consciousness – or, 'higher mental functions'. As a psychologist Vygotsky was interested in the problem of how human minds worked: was learning enabled by some biogenetic attribute, such as intelligence? Were its stages pre-ordained as argued by his eminent contemporaries, such as Piaget? As a Marxist psychologist, Vygotsky believed that the particular kind of consciousness specific to human beings comes from life and this for Marx always meant from *life in society*, just as *human* meant *social*: for Marx consciousness was 'from the very beginning a social product' (1976: 86). Vygotsky identified 'semiotic mediation' as the means whereby a link was forged between the social and the mental. In the chapters of this volume (see especially 3, 4, 5 and 7), I have suggested that when the word 'semiotic' is overwhelmingly identified with the semiotic modality of language – as it is in Vygotsky – then 'semiotic mediation' itself becomes an elegant expression for what language naturally does in discourse. Quite obviously, discourse has a prominent continued presence in human societies; this presence is itself predicated on the unquestionable and massively justifiable assumption that talk between members of the same community makes sense[3] to the interactants. It is this inherent characteristic of the process of language – its ability to act as construer of meanings – that forms the foundation of its role in the mediation of mind. The formation of consciousness, then, owes much to sociosemiotic interactions.

Whorf's concern had been to establish that the lexicogrammatical modes of construing meaning by a specific language are fundamental to the genesis of much of its speakers' 'common-sense' knowledge[4]; these unarticulated belief systems lie below the surface of speakers' consciousness and ultimately regulate the ordinary everyday behaviours of ordinary human beings. There are indications that Whorf believed that if these ordinary everyday belief systems remained unquestioned, they would also permeate the conduct of specialised discourse[5]; but he was mainly interested in everyday habitual fashions of speaking. In fact, his position on language and consciousness is curiously close to Marx's, according to whom 'language is as old as consciousness, language is practical consciousness, as it exists for other men and thus as it first really exists for myself as well' (Marx, 1976: 85). Vygotsky's position is slightly different: when he talks about the contribution of semiotic mediation to the development of mental functions, he is not concerned with the contribution of everyday discourse to human mental activities. His main interest lies in tracing the genesis of esoteric (i.e., specialised) mental activities such as concept formation, logical thinking, logical reasoning – in short the kind of concerns that are central to official pedagogy and on the mastery of which depends educational success: for him the achievement of semiotic mediation was precisely that it enabled these functions.

Naturally, there can be no objection to Vygotsky's foregrounding of this category of mental functions: it is certainly true that they develop 'sociogenetically' and that means via semiotic interactions with other members of one's society. What is more, very often, the development of this specific category of mental functions demands deliberate semiotic mediation – what I have described as 'visible semiotic mediation' (see Chapter 4) – as found for example in pedagogic sites. But a problem arises if this category of mental functions is singled out as 'higher mental functions' and if higher mental functions, in their turn, are said to be 'essentially human' (Vygotsky, 1978), for this series of equations appears tantamount to claiming that, for example, where a certain kind of reasoning typical of Western traditions of education is absent, we have a mind that is 'essentially' not human. If this set of equations is taken as legitimate, then a large part of humanity – in fact the indigenous populations of many non-Western areas of the world – would turn out to be lacking in higher mental functions, thus lacking the quality that makes one essentially human.

One reason why this problem arises in Vygotsky's work is that, like Whorf, he too did not look into the essential elements of the organisation of human societies; nor did he build into his thinking the fact of sociolinguistic variation, something that Whorf took on board at least by recognising the varieties Bernstein was to call 'horizontal' and 'vertical' discourse[6]. Perhaps in the political context of his writing[7] it did not seem important to Vygotsky to ask how social subjects' positioning in society might have any bearing upon the kind of semiotic mediation they are likely to encounter in the many walks of their life, or how the spiral of mental development he postulated might or might not be affected by the subject's starting point. This in turn implies that the relationship between social organisation and the natural process of language, i.e., the social contexts of discourse and their relevance to the nature of discourse, did not engage his attention sufficiently. Vygotsky did much to relate consciousness to society and to language, but he did not manage to reflect in detail on certain important aspects of the last two domains[8].

Summing up this discussion: Whorf was a linguist with a deep sensitivity to the inner structure of language, its relation to meaning construal, which formed the basis of consciousness; he saw meaning as fundamental to cultural life. His writings have enriched our understanding of how a linguistic analysis can illuminate meanings; however, in his writing, the question of the nature of social organisation and the structure of consciousness remained relatively less explored. Vygotsky, as a psychologist, has given us an illuminating account of mental development by rejecting the nature-nurture opposition, by placing the growth of human mind firmly within society, by showing how minds in interaction have greater potential than one individual mind working on its own and by firmly placing mental growth within the most natural of human activities, namely, talk. Several decades later neurological investigations into how our brains develop into minds are confirming that the claims of both these scholars were essentially correct.

But neither Whorf nor Vygotsky can really be credited with getting the relations of language, society and consciousness definitely in place. Each story is incomplete in important respects; and since the pointing out of a 'lack' is typically interpreted as some form of denigration, I want to say quite explicitly that my intention here is not to evaluate but simply to state how things appear to me. And I do this for a reason: I want to say quite categorically that no story about the relations of these three mainsprings of human life is ever likely to be complete. This is not because knowledge never reaches perfection; this is true enough, but it does not prevent 'a state of the art' definitive account. I believe that the obstacle to this enterprise is inherent in transdisciplinary exploration: the story is simply too 'big'; it is too intricate with each field presenting a highly complex organisation; so, in practical terms, even if not logically, it seems improbable that the story could be adequately told by any single scholar. This claim by itself is of no consequence, since one might very justifiably respond that this is why 'specialisation' is favoured, so that each field can be adequately 'covered' by its own experts in their chosen field. At this point, though, it is important to recall the problems that arise precisely from specialisation itself (see Section 2 above). This line of reasoning seems to lead to an impasse: specialisation gives in-depth information, but it can and often does, lead to an insulation from other related areas of human endeavour which may, at best, result in partial information, in un/conscious partiality to one's own field of expertise and at worst in hostility to or neglect of those other areas, as if they bear no relevance to the business in hand. How can this impasse be resolved? My response to this question has been (see Chapter 2) that in order to ensure dialogue between specific knowledge structures we need to rethink what kind of theories are optimally desirable at least in the humanities and in the social sciences, though I would go so far as to claim that the so called 'hard' sciences need to take a hard look at their own achievements in this respect. I raise some of these points below.

4 Theory and transdisciplinary orientation

Our views about the optimal theory for the social sciences have been deeply influenced by the immediate success of physical sciences[9]. It has been generally assumed that the success of science is due to its theory and no doubt this is true; but what needs to be emphasised is that the success of a theory is in direct proportion to how far it respects the nature of its object of study. In a way, talking about theory in this metaphorical vein obscures the fact that what is really at issue is not theories but the persons who design them – how they view their object of study is the really decisive factor. Of course there are certain standard requirements of any viable theory (Hjelmslev, 1961; Matthiessen and Nesbitt, 1996; Halliday, 2002; Bernstein, 2000), but the conceptualisation of the object of study remains the primary consideration. For example, the way we conceptualise language as the object of study determines what we would wish a successful theory of language to model or to explain, to generate or to constrain. If language is conceptualised as a mental organ, then social relations are peripheral; ego-based intuition is more important than experience of living with others. What is to be explained is the formalism, the algorithm, the nature of that which is hard-wired in the brain. Clearly, this perspective has the potential of relating language to only one domain that impinges on human life, namely, biology[10]. However, biological organisms are subject to evolution and evolution itself is activated by contact with physical and social environment. But if it is denied that language as mental organ has evolved adaptively, then even this 'outer' connection is eliminated: language as mental organ becomes autonomous unlike any other part of the human organism, including the brain of which it is supposed to be an organ. A theory describing language conceived in this way is therefore totally 'self-absorbed', completely unrelated to anything else that the speakers do in their lives. I have called such theories 'endotropic' (see Chapter 2).

In the most privileged of the physical sciences, namely physics, theories tend to be endotropic. Certainly the success of physics has been staggering and it has appeared natural for us to wish to emulate such theoretical orientations so that our descriptions of language, cognition etc. may achieve the same degree of scientific validity: this attitude is what Bourdieu pejoratively described as the linguists' devotion to 'scientificity'. I myself have nothing against the search for scientific certainty so long as the object of study permits such certainty: there are many aspects of language that seem to offer complete certainty, such as for example, the fact that social distinctions amongst speakers are homologous with variation in their language use; the fact that all semiotic modalities impinge on the body as an organism, the fact that the speaker's intention does not in and of itself determine the meaning of the words s/he utters and so on. But despite the success of hard sciences, there are serious considerations which suggest that the pursuit of endotropic theories may, in the long run, not be as desirable as traditionally imagined. Precisely because endotropic theories carve out a unitary area of human interest and turn it into a universe sufficient unto itself, they erect a strong boundary between it and other possible human concerns that might be legitimately related to it. This gives the object of analysis a clear definition, something the secret of whose being is enclosed within itself.

This calls to mind Lewontin's description of two distinct theoretical orientations in the field of biology, the 'developmental' and the 'evolutionary'. In the developmental orientation one is really concerned with 'the Platonic typological understanding of nature', where from the beginning, the type is complete within itself and all that is expected is that it will 'develop' much in the manner of a film developing to reveal what has always already been there: 'Development ... is literally an unfolding or unrolling of something that is already present and in some way pre-formed' (2000: 5). Possibly, in the last analysis, endotropic theories 'go with' a high degree of idealisation, dealing with some 'Platonic type'. It is not surprising, then, that the object so studied is bereft of history; all it has is simply a chronology listing the stages in its pre-ordained development. A feature that attracts scholars to endotropic theories is their apparent 'tidiness', the fact that they seem to possess maximal pertinence. Initially, this comes to be taken as evidence of a strong theory, very much 'to the point' – a situation sometimes described as 'not allowing waffle'.

Returning to theories that survive in the field of physics, they are certainly free of waffle; they are to-the-point; and they are parsimonious; and very often their object of study is 'a thing-in-itself'; and, of course, their modelling of the physical phenomena of the universe has been impressive. But perhaps some of the current malaise faced by humanity – the inordinate power to kill large numbers in very short time, or the increasing destruction of the environment – these have most probably arisen because the theories severed connections with all else but the selected area of study in-itself: they prioritised 'pure' research, ignored the fact that the consumers of that research are human beings and did not ask how humanity would be positioned by the impact of the research[11]. But this is exactly what distinguishes endotropic theories: they are indifferent to most information, most aspects of human life because these appear external to the unitary area they take as the object of study, since the latter is complete in itself and has 'nothing to do' with anything else. It is conceptualised as relating to no environment whatever.

Obviously, endotropic theories are the least desirable where the goal is to understand the relations of different areas of enquiry: the furthest an endotropic theory will go here is to tolerate the 'hyphenated' disciplines such as, say, socio- or psycholinguistics, or worse still, text-linguistics, a term which reveals the vacuous concept of 'language' that informed the dominant linguistic theories of the 1960s and 1970s. In retrospect, it was not just a historical accident that these hyphenated 'fields' on the borders of language and some other domain took off just when an endotropic theory of linguistics was at it peak of power and popularity[12]: the advent of these hyphenated fields, in fact, announced the return of the repressed, which declared once again their undeniable centrality! A cursory look at Firth (1957b), Bernstein (1971), Halliday (1978), Whorf (1956), Vygotsky (1978) and many others would have shown that the relations of the social and the semiotic, or of the semiotic and the mental are not one of simple 'contact', but of interpenetration: if language 'is in' society as an indispensable element in its formation, then society itself 'is in' language as an indispensable element shaping its nature; if consciousness develops in society and if the development is mediated through the many semiotic modalities, then consciousness is also a condition for social action, including semiotic action. The relation of this triad is that of co-evolution; their mode of existence is best described as co-genetic. It follows that to understand their co-genetic nature is to understand a very important aspect of the object of study in the 'sciences' of society, of language and of mind, namely, that since they are pivotal to human survival, they must impinge on several domains of human experience: what is or is not done in one domain has repercussions on other domains. But this understanding cannot come through endotropic theories. In Chapter 2 of this volume I suggest that for this we need theories that are *exotropic*.

If the designer of an endotropic theory views the object of study as a universe in itself, as autogenetic, as capable of existing without relation to much else, the designer of an exotropic theory views the object of study as a component in a 'dynamic open system' (Lemke, 1984; 1993). It is thus seen in relation to a number of elements which are implicated in the evolution of the object of study; by its engagement with these elements, the domain of experience under study changes its character and in turn helps change the character of those elements. Certainly language changes to 'suit' the changes in society; but society changes as semiotic interaction takes the place of material interaction. Socially situated linguistic interaction certainly contributes to the creation of forms of consciousness, but the created forms of consciousness intervene in the choice of interactions to be favoured, in the kinds of meanings to be exchanged. This is surely the point about Bourdieu's 'structured structuring structures'. The recognition of each element as relevant to the object of analysis adds a dimension of depth to that analysis. In other words, built into the very concept of what is to be explained, what is to be studied, are phenomena that are seen as the direct outcome of the object's relation to other fields of experience. This as I see it is the basic difference between interdisciplinary and transdisciplinary discourse: the former is a study of domains in contact, the latter, of domains that interpenetrate, one informing the other.

A scholar drawn to such a theory as a means of understanding and resolving some problematic is much less likely to have a hostile attitude to knowledge structures which have grown in the exploration of the related fields of experience, since such relation is constitutive of the fields. Thus I expect that investment in an exotropic theory will not create an identity whose boundaries are impregnable; commitment to one's own area of enquiry will not mean that other areas need to be 'brought down a notch' in importance. It is widely acknowledged that in dialogue between persons a certain amount of goodwill between the interactants is essential for continued discourse. Vygotsky made the brilliant suggestion that a mind in interaction with another extends its potential[13]. I want to suggest here that these observations are also true when it comes to dialogue between theories, which is essentially what transdisciplinary discourse is about. In Chapter 2 of this volume I have referred to such dialogue as 'metadialogue'. What I mean by metadialogue between theories is the ability and willingness of scholars pursuing those theories to cross the barrier of distinct languages of description, the conceptual syntax specific to the individual theories addressing distinct but related objects of study; to think of the various disciplines as coparticipants in the same larger enterprise rather than as competitors in a limited market jockeying for power. This is clearly a possibility where the theories are exotropic, since in such theories, the object of study is not taken as an auto-genetic phenomenon; rather, as I suggest, its genesis, growth and change are accounted for by its relation to other elements of human experience, by its reciprocal engagement with them.

It then comes to pass that cooperation of related areas is what engages such a theorist because it is in this co-action that the answer to most of her/his questions lies. So if we have to go to a linguist to understand language, to a sociologist to understand society, to a neurologist/psychologist to understand brain/mind, we still come to an account of the arena which offers an opening into other concerns. I would suggest that the theories put forward by Whorf and Vygotsky are exotropic in that they recognised the interactive nature of language, society and consciousness and their explanations depend on such interaction. But where these theories were less successful was in meeting a requirement that is built into the making of all theories. As Lemke put it some years ago, a theory is a system of meanings. This means the concepts in a theory are not a 'collection', they are in some sort of systematic relations. Neither Whorf not Vygotsky were allowed enough time to explore the connectivities of concepts in their theories, by following up the implications of some postulated concept, by elaborating ideas, by debating the debatable in their framework. Theories, like languages, demand time to evolve; unfortunately, time is what neither scholar was granted [14]. Two other contemporary scholars come to mind whose theories I would think of as instances of more evolved exotropic theory – these are Bernstein's theory of the social and Halliday's theory of the semiotic. But before turning to these I would make a few comments about exotropic theories.

While it seems quite likely that exotropic theories would offer the best route to understanding the relations of distinct domains of human experience to each other, such theories do invite certain problems. For example, since the object of study in such theories is weakly classified in relation to other domains of human experience, the greatest threat to exotropic theories is the maintenance of their identity – what a theory is the theory of. The safeguard against this lies in the management of the architecture of the theory. Clearly, an exotropic theory could not be a theory of phenomena of distinctly different orders, for the simple reason that the abstractions required to account for one kind of data, one kind of domain, are not, or at least may not be, good for accounting for other kinds of data, other kinds of domain. Although certain fairly basic abstractions might be applicable to data of different domains – an example would be the stratal organisation of the field as with regard to language in SFL and with regard to society in Bernstein's theory (see Chapter 2; also Bernstein, 1996; 2000) – most concepts in the architecture of a theory are designed with the specific attributes of a distinct domain in mind: the possibility of an extensive application of such concepts to all related domains appears quite unlikely.

This is a strong argument for rejecting any claim that the same umbrella theory will work for all related domains. In Chapter 10, I have argued that although the relation between society/culture and language/semiotic modalities is very intimate, it would be wrong to imagine that, for example, describing genres is equal to describing culture: genres/registers have certain properties that culture/society appears not to have and vice versa. What distinguishes an exotropic theory is not that it 'privileges' all data, all fields, to the same extent:

a theory of language is set up to account for how language works, not for the just dispensation of equal status to varied domains of experience. If for example, SFL claims to be a social semiotic theory of language, this does not mean that as an exotropic theory it must allow equal space for the description of both domains as has sometimes been imagined; it simply means that SFL should be a theory which displays the principles that govern the relations of language and society and of language and semiology (for discussion see Chapter 12 of this volume). The demand that a social semiotic theory should describe everything about all semiotic modalities, about aspects of society and also about language is simply an invitation to chaos; what an effort to comply with this demand might lead to in practice is a half-baked description of 'everything', which could hardly be illuminating for any domain. The more evolved exotropic theories such as Bernstein's sociology and Halliday's SF linguistics appear to have maintained their field identity by foregrounding their basic concern, while at the same time taking care to show what interactive relations link their theory to other domains.

5 Two relatively evolved exotropic theories

In Chapter 2 of this volume I have presented my interpretation of Bernstein's theory of the social as an instance of an exotropic theory: the concern this theory foregrounds is a classic problem of sociology. In attending to this problem, Bernstein is able to show how consciousness and language are deeply implicated in the structuring of his explanation. But at the same time, the theory shows how the nature of the social acts on the formation of consciousness itself and how the ways of meaning become regulated by this socially generated consciousness. Note that just like Whorf, Bernstein does not address the details of consciousness and just like Vygotsky, he does not pursue the study of language itself, nonetheless as with Whorf's and Vygotsky's theory, his theory too has a definite place for both. The difference lies only in the extent to which Bernstein is able to 'spell out' these relations (see Chapter 1). The openness of the theory lies in its acknowledgement of the relevance of domains other than that of sociology to his own problematic. The elaboration of the theory, the data it is able to generate and the variations it is able to describe, the ability to specify exactly the ways in which according to the theory language and consciousness enter into the social processes, is the measure of its success as an exotropic theory of the social, *not* of either consciousness or of language. It is the properties of the *elaborated* theory that allow his theory to dialogue with linguistics (see for example Christie, 1999) and with theories of consciousness (see chapters in the first section of this volume); I believe that the latter interaction is very likely to increase, as the study of the sociogenesis of mind as 'personalised brain' (Greenfield, 1997) moves forward: mental dispositions which act on judgment, on reasoning and on affect cannot be ignored in any theory of mind as personalised brain, when the engine for personalisation is the living of life in society. And Bernstein's hypotheses about the logical relations between social positioning, forms of communication and forms of mental disposition certainly offer food for thought in this connection.

Another instance of exotropic theorisation is presented by Halliday's systemic functional linguistics. Here the object of study is language: the basic question is posed in very general terms, namely: how does language work? The answer explores a wide range of phenomena, the description of which can only be briefly touched upon within the confines of this chapter[15]. With the description and modelling of language as its point of departure, SFL approaches its task on two main fronts. Language is first and foremost a semiotic system: as such, it has affinities with other semiotic modalities. One thing in common to all these modalities is that they are resources for meaning. This in turn poses questions: what is the property that permits semiotic modalities to act in this way? How does language differ from other modalities? This leads to the elaboration of the inner structure of language, while at the same time creating lines of connectivity with other modalities (Kress & van Leeuwen, 1996; O'Toole, 1994 and others). Acts of semiosis are inherently social in that as a default they occur in social contexts, in interacting with an other. Thus every naturally produced utterance, every naturally produced text presupposes human relation and human action. Exploration of this line of enquiry brings society into the picture, for a given context of situation is in fact an instantiation of culture as a system. SFL initially postulates two homologous relations to elaborate the relations of language and society: one, the cultural system is to the linguistic system as the situational context is to the process of language, i.e. text/language use; two, the system of culture is to the instantiating context of situation as the system of language is to the instantiating case of language use. The dialectic of language system and language use lies behind the design of language and is the principle of its renewal and continuation over time. Social relations are on the one hand an expression of the subject's social positioning and on the other, they are enacted semiotically. If language is to enact social relations, if it is to construe our experiences of doing, being and saying, if it is to act as the resource for producing connected, coherent discourse which is relevant within and relevant to the situation outside, then its internal design, its meanings and wordings must be so organised as to make this possible.

This line of argumentation took SFL to the incorporation of functionalism, where the functions are themselves at a high level of abstraction. Four such metafunctions are recognised: the 'experiential', the 'logical', the 'interpersonal' and the 'textual'. Unlike Bühler's functions, these metafunctions are not descriptive labels for particular categories of what language is doing in an utterance on any one given occasion; rather they concern what the use of language *always* does on every occasion of talk: the metafunctional organisation of language resonates through the strata of context, semantics, lexicogrammar and the prosodic organisation of phonology. The consideration of discourse in social context opened the door to the study of many registers and through it developed such areas of language study as 'language in education' (Martin, 1985b; Painter & Martin, 1986; Halliday & Martin, 1993), stylistics (Hasan, 1985a) and learning how to mean, i.e., the ontogenetic development of language (Halliday, 2004a; Painter, 1984; Torr, 1997). Exploring the relations of language to social structure and code theory led to extensive research in semantic variation (Hasan[16], 1989; 1992c; 1992b; Cloran, 1994; 1999; Williams, 1995; 2001). This is a very quick indication of the ways in which SFL has established deep and significant relations between the social and the semiotic, as well as between language and other modalities of meaning. However, it is to be noted that what is foregrounded is language: SFL is a theory of language; its main preoccupation has to be with the modelling and exploration of language; but at the same time because language can only exist and find expression in human societies and because within human societies it occurs pervasively with far reaching consequences, the social is a significant element in the explanation of language. There are, therefore, definite locations in the theory where this interrelation between distinct domains has been highlighted. Recent developments in neurological science have begun to indicate the role of society in the development of the human brain and explanations of the make up of human minds are invoking the experience of the living of life as highly significant. For a long period now, SFL has viewed the development of consciousness/cognition as sociogenetic (Halliday, 1975; Halliday & Matthiessen, 1999; Painter, 1999) and recent developments have excited a good deal of interest; Halliday's insight that the interpersonal metafunction is the gateway to the development of human mind is being explored by several scholars (Williams and Lukin, 2004; Thibault, 2004; 2005). It remains to be seen how SFL will utilise the body of knowledge about human consciousness in reference to language system or language process: the current situation is one where the emphasis has been on the crucial role of semiosis in the making of mind. But there is another side to this question: what does a sociogenetically created mind do for language?

6 Concluding remarks

My aim in writing this introductory chapter of the volume has been to argue that only a certain kind of theoretical orientation will succeed in clarifying the interrelations of language, society and consciousness. To affirm the existence of these relations is clearly not enough; nor does it call for every discipline to become a mélange of several distinct concerns. Affirmation of interrelation is not equal to abandoning what Bernstein called theories with strong grammars. A theory with a strong grammar is needed in order to provide viable descriptions of data in any domain. What seems to me to be needed is to show how, at what point in the theory, such transdisciplinary interrelations can be postulated as significant to the field under study, what exactly is the contribution of an 'outsider' domain to revealing the nature of the object of study and in doing so what does it indicate about its own nature. If culture as a system is realisationally related to the system of language, what does this claim say about the nature of language and what does it point to in the make up of a culture? Clearly unless culture was more than what semiosis produces and reproduces, there would be no need to recognise a separate domain; but also clearly, culture, which is certainly related realisationally to the system of language (or even to all semiotic modalities put together) cannot be reduced to semiotic phenomena. A reductive approach portrays the interrelation between domains as that of identity between the disciplines or as one incorporated in the other, as for example in the claim that to describe language is to describe culture, or that consciousness is entirely the gift of language: neither of these positions is tenable. And it is possible that they may do us disservice by limiting our horizons: as Foucault said, the visual is not replicable into the verbal (see Chapter 10 of this volume); the social is not limited to the verbal; the verbal is not a pale shadow of the material. Each has its own specificity, which is as important as its contribution to phenomena of other orders. I would argue that an approach which rejects the existence of any boundaries between, say, these three intimately related phenomena encourages a discourse which is not so much likely to provide clarification, or a reasoned description, as to be the expression of someone's reaction presented as an objective fact of analysis. The difference between analysis and pulling out 'evidence' on the basis of one's intuition needs to be respected even though after a knee-jerk reaction of adulation for a limiting and limited theory – I refer to the cluster of linguistic models spawned by what was known in the 1960s as TG – we are now passing through a stage where all theory is to be suspected. An analysis is something whose underlying principle can be explicitly described, its implications can be discussed, whereas pulling out evidence from the data that seems favourable to one's own stance is a very different kind of enterprise, in which what is presented as a reasoned statement is really a personal preference, because what is being said about this bit of evidence has no basis in an articulated theory of the nature of the domain from which the data has been extracted.

Notes

1. See a discussion of this in Bourdieu and Wacquant (1992).
2. There are some exceptions. See for example Lucy (1985) and Lee (1996).
3. The issue is, rather, how to identify the boundaries of a 'community' where the observation has the probability of being overwhelmingly true. And here Firth's (1957b: 186ff) distinction between speech fellowship and language community is of vital importance (for discussion Butt, 2001).
4. It is interesting to note that this category of 'knowledge' remains unnamed in Bernstein's typology of knowledge structures (Bernstein, 1999).
5. See the last chapters of Whorf (1956).
6. From the point of view of contexts for talk, we may say that the distinction correlates with different spheres of activity: horizontal and vertical discourses are likely to occur in the context of activities in quotidian and specialized sphere, respectively (Hasan, 1999b).
7. Vygotsky's work on semiotic mediation took shape in the early days of the arrival of communism in Russia. Hailed as a new dawn, it was going to create a non-stratified, wholly egalitarian society.
8. One must not forget that Vygotsky's working life lasted approximately one decade!
9. Consider for example Popper (1972).
10. Readers will recognize here the object of study as conceived in Chomskyan linguistics. Interestingly Chomsky (e.g. 1965) short-circuited this relation by relating linguistics, the study of language, to psychology.
11. In making these comments, I am not thinking of reaction at a personal level: once created social institutions come to have a 'will' of their own which is not easy to ignore. It is well known that the scientists working on the bomb in Los Alamos were deeply distressed by the project; but the conventions of 'impartial science' won out. Humanity is paying the price of that scientifically based decision to this day.
12. This is not to suggest that all theories of that era were of this type, but certainly the dominant one was. A notable exception was Pike's Tagmemics as also Sydney Lamb's Stratificational model but neither could be described as dominant.
13. I refer here to his theory of the zone of proximal development.
14. It is interesting to think of Malinowski who in 1923 presented context of situation as something that 'primitive' languages need; it took him 12 years to progress to the point where he recognised that context of situation and culture are central to all languages, whether of primitive communities or advanced ones.
15. See Halliday (2002a; 2002b; 2003; 2004a; 2004b); Halliday and Matthiessen, (1999); Butt (2001); and others.
16. See also Volume 2 of Hasan's *Collected Works*, forthcoming.

Section 1
The sociosemiotic mediation of mind

Editor's Introduction

The papers in this section on the sociosemiotic mediation of mind focus on three interconnected human concerns: consciousness, language and society. No one discipline or theory tells the whole story of human existence as it relates to these three concerns. Instead, Professor Hasan directs our attention to three exotropic theories whose 'interconnections produce a narrative that is much richer than any single discipline could have provided by itself' (Chapter 5, *Semiotic Mediation and Three Exotropic Theories: Vygotsky, Halliday and Bernstein*).

One such exotropic theory was that developed by Basil Bernstein 'whose work spreads over a wide canvas; certainly sociology is its point of departure and its quest but this theory is also about language in society, it is also about the genesis of cognition in society, it is also about the economic organisation of societies; and of course, it is about human relationships'. The first chapter in this section, *Basil Bernstein: an exceptional*, brings together three recently published papers (*Basil Bernstein 1924-2000: Obituary* (2000); *Understanding talk: directions from Bernstein's sociology* (2001); and *Basil Bernstein: an exceptional* (2002). From his studies in the late 1950s into why some children fail educationally to his later work addressing the 'theoretical question of classical sociology: how does the outside become the inside, and how does the inside reveal itself and shape the outside?' (Bernstein, 1987: 563), Bernstein observed that orientation to meanings was crucial in the creation of forms of consciousness. Described by Hasan as a key concept 'in the search for an answer to how the outside becomes the inside and how the inside reveals itself,' *codes* 'were indicative of the form of consciousness created by participation in social practices, which in turn activated the social subjects' sense of relevance, and thus positioned them in some specific relation to how they interpreted the world outside, and how they acted in, and on, it' (Chapter 1).

Comparing Halliday's Systemic Functional Linguistics (SFL) with Bernstein's theory, Professor Hasan notes full agreement with Bernstein on the systemic nature of context, but faults SFL for failing to 'problematise the speaker's recognition of contexts in the way that Bernstein's theory did' (Chapter 1). What Hasan and her colleagues discovered in their study of naturally occurring dialogues between mothers and their young children was 'that speakers' social positioning is the most powerful concept for understanding discourse both its local meanings and its global structure. It is positioning which underlies the invisible level of their communication where the motivational relevancies of communication are located, the latter level in turn underlies their visible communication, and it is this visible communication that linguists describe as discourse' (Chapter 1). What we now realise is that 'the *child* is no longer generic.... the adult agent of semiotic mediation is no longer culturally neutral: s/he is the voice of a distinct ideology' (Chapter 2). Such findings contribute much to helping SFL realise its aspiration to become a truly 'trans-disciplinary theory, which is located at the intersection of semiology, sociology, and psychology' (Chapter 3, *Speech Genre, Semiotic Mediation and the Development of Higher Mental Functions*, 1992).

While acknowledging there are differences in the approaches of Halliday and Bernstein, nevertheless metadialogue is still possible between them because there is 'a reciprocity of concern'. How either addresses its problematic – its conceptual syntax – complements the other. Neither treats its object of study as something impermeable, but instead each 'is cosmoramic, typically embedding its central problematic in a context, where the processes of its maintenance and change originate in its interaction with other universes of experience' (Chapter 2, *Society, Language and Mind: the metadialogism of Basil Bernstein's theory*, 1999). Professor Hasan asks, 'Could any linguistic theory dialogue with Bernstein's sociology? Could any sociology dialogue with Halliday's linguistics?' (Chapter 2). The answer comes down to the distinction between exotropic vs. endotropic theories, and their potential for metadialogism.

Also compatible with the theories of Halliday and Bernstein is Vygotsky's genetic theory of mind which is discussed in greater detail in Chapter 4, *On Social Conditions for Semiotic Mediation: the genesis of mind in society*, 1995. How these three exotropic theories relate to one another is summed up best by Professor Hasan in Chapter 5, where she writes:

Vygotsky contributes to the understanding of our mental life by revealing its deep connection to semiosis; in so doing he anticipates the literature on the dialectic of language and mind: it is this dialectic that is responsible for their co-evolution in the human species. Halliday contributes to the understanding of our semiotic life by revealing its deep connection with society; in so doing, he elaborates on the dialectic of language and society which underlies their co-genesis. Bernstein contributes to the understanding of our social life in modern societies by revealing its inherent connection with consciousness created in semiosis in the contexts of communal living; in so doing, he makes us realise how minds need societies and societies need semiosis to survive, to develop, and to change.

Each approach contributes some insight spanning the biological, the sociological and the linguistic. What Professor Hasan has done is to draw on the insights of each – Vygotsy's sociogenetic psychology, Bernstein's semiotic sociology, and Halliday's sociological linguistics – to develop a theory 'which will specify the social conditions for the semiotic mediation of the human mind' (Chapter 4).

1 Basil Bernstein: an exceptional[1] 1924 – 2000

1 The enduring focus of Bernstein's research

Occasionally in the convention-bound world of academia, there arrives a scholar with sufficient courage and integrity to probe the unpalatable, even in the face of carelessly hostile readings riding high on the wave of popular sentiments: Basil Bernstein was one such. Shunning the allure of rhetoric and committed to a program of enquiry that he had come to regard as necessary for understanding how the so-called progressive societies work, he steadfastly refused to form easy alliances – to climb onto what we have come to know as 'intellectual bandwagons'. Though he never paraded his knowledge, he was a remarkable scholar; and his familiarity with the fields of philosophy, psychology, sociology and areas of linguistics was formidable. This he combined with an irresistible wit and an irony that never stooped to maliciousness. Here is an example: giving the title *Pedagogising Knowledge: studies in recontextualising* to Chapter 3 of the revised edition of his last major publication, Bernstein (2000: 41) begins as follows:

> Titles are worthy of study in their own right, not simply as aesthetic forms, but as signifiers of the play of positions in the intellectual field. Thus it is possible that the title of this paper in the 1950s might well have been *Knowledge and Socialisation: the case of education* with pronounced structural functional overtones. In the 1970s a more fitting title might well have been *Knowledge and Cultural Reproduction* with an Althusserian resonance. But in the 1980s perhaps we would have had *The Pedagogic Construction of the Subject: a technology*, a clear Foucault choice. Today in the 1990s *Knowledge and Subjectivities: a post-modern account* would surely be a winner. My title I admit seems to be somewhat of a compromise...

There is an implicit comment here on fashions in academia, to which he is honest enough to reveal, in an ironic tone, his own ambivalent stance.

Bernstein possessed a fearless imagination, which for the best part of half a century he devoted, with great originality, to the exploration of a question which has sometimes been described as *the* fundamental theoretical question of classical sociology: 'how does the outside become the inside and how does the inside reveal itself and shape the outside?' (Bernstein, 1987b: 563). The reader who, beguiled by the elegant simplicity of this wording, quickly moves forward without further reflection on the reach of this formulation, misses the true spirit of what Bernstein's *oeuvre* has been consistently concerned with. And there is unfortunately no dearth of such readers: they range from the famous to the followers of the famous. So it needs to be pointed out that behind these words is a programme of enquiry with epic proportions that invites an examination of the most essential aspects of human social existence.

A central element of this investigation, ever present to Bernstein's consciousness, was the need to understand and to reveal the mechanisms whereby patterns of oppression and often unwitting collusion in oppression maintain themselves in modern progressive societies. This preoccupation was deepened by his concern with the potential for social change and the potential's many forms of realisation in actual fact. Whatever the realities of some particular element of social organisation that might have formed his immediate concern on any one occasion, these basic preoccupations were always relevant to his enquiry; never far from his sight. The last three decades of Bernstein's research are often perceived as moving into a substantially different direction, but it is my reading that this research into the sociology of pedagogy, a decidedly major contribution for which he is renowned, never abandoned the basic preoccupations with which he began his intellectual journey; even a cursory reading of the major writings in the last decade of his life will substantiate this claim. Thus consider:

> 'Class relations' will be taken to refer to inequalities in the distribution of power, and in the principles of control between social groups, which are realized in the creation, distribution, reproduction, and legitimation of physical and symbolic values that have their source in the social division of labour. This definition draws attention deliberately to the distributive function of class relations, as *this function has been the enduring focus of the research* ... In terms of the particular relationship between class and the process of its cultural reproduction ... what has to be shown is how class regulation of the distribution of power and of principles of control generates, distributes, reproduces, and legitimates dominant and dominated principles *regulating the relationship within and between social groups and so forms of consciousness*. (Bernstein, 1990: 13; emphasis added)

> The substantive issue of ... (this) theory is to explicate the process whereby a given distribution of power and principles of control are translated into specialised principles of communication differentially, and often unequally, distributed to social groups/classes. And how such a differential/unequal distribution of forms of communication, initially (but not necessarily terminally) shapes the formation of consciousness of members of these groups/classes in such a way as to relay both opposition and change.
> (Bernstein, 1996a: 93)

In these extracts, the theme of human experience of the living of life producing consciousness which in turn produces patterns of the living of life, is interwoven with the theme of inequality as a critical aspect of human relation which has so systematically and persistently formed part of all known societies. Naturally, at the initial stage of Bernstein's studies, the research question about the formation of consciousness and the roles of this class-regulated consciousness in the production and reproduction of society had not presented, much less defined, itself in the elegant forms that it took later. The beginnings were humble and the route by which he arrived at this central classic problem is an excellent indicator of the quality of his intellectual engagement with any question that attracted his attention. The milestones on this journey have been recorded by Bernstein himself (1987b; 1990) and attention to the chronology of the original publication of the papers included in *Class, Codes and Control, Volume One: theoretical studies towards a sociology of language* (1971) would support his narrative. One might add that the introduction to that volume together with Chapter 11 of Bernstein 2000 ought to be treated as compulsory reading for all serious scholars of Bernstein's work.

2 The beginnings of early research: codes and consciousness

Bernstein's research began in the best of laboratories – in the direct personal experience of processes typical of a range of workplaces, where some form of knowledge is presented to the young, as an instrument whether for their moral or their material amelioration. He taught the young in different suburbs of London, each of which had one thing in common: by any standard, they would have been seen as less affluent, poor, underprivileged, disadvantaged, working-class, lacking in material capital – call it by the name your ideology finds acceptable. This experience allowed him to witness first hand the working of a crucial part of those mechanisms whereby a differential distribution of knowledge and of consciousness, is brought about in most modern societies: Bernstein pointed to what perhaps many had known without knowing consciously, that the lower the social stratum from which the pupils hailed, the higher the likelihood of their failure in achieving the conventionally valued educational goals. However, the unique observation that Bernstein made on this situation flew in the face of the prevalent academic interpretation of this state of affairs: current wisdom had it that the definitive explanation for the failing students' failure to achieve the desired result was to be found in their level of intelligence as established by the findings of popular IQ tests. Bernstein strenuously and repeatedly drew attention to the systematically ambivalent results of such IQ tests, pointing out that working-class children tended to attain significantly better scores on non-verbal tasks as opposed to the verbal ones. This he interpreted as indicative of the fact that ways of meaning – modes of communication experienced by the pupils – constituted a more critical differentiating factor in the explanation of the results than the pupils' levels of intelligence as established by conventional IQ tests. The roots of educational failure, Bernstein suggested, were to be found not in intelligence, nor in accent or grammar, but in a certain kind of orientation to meanings. He went on to suggest that orientation to meanings was itself a crucial element in the creation of forms of consciousness, in establishing a social subject's sense of what was relevant to the universe in which they lived their lives. This sense of relevance revealed itself in their social practices and crucially through the subjects' 'fashions of speaking' – a Whorfian expression that Bernstein often employed in the 1960s. In other words, long before Vygotsky or Luria became academically fashionable, Bernstein was telling us about the role of semiotic mediation in the formation of human consciousness; naturally, he did not use the Vygotskian formulations and, naturally, being a sociologist, he could not ignore either the variability in semiotic mediation or in the forms of consciousness which it helped mediate: for him semiotic mediation could not be restricted only to the formation of technical concepts valued by official pedagogy, nor could the inequitable distribution of social resources ever be irrelevant to the efficacy of semiotic mediation in the formation of higher mental functions. This, in a very simplified form, is my understanding of the semantics of Bernstein's notion of speech codes as presented to the world in the mid-1970s; this conception of codes, I have argued elsewhere (1973; 1988a), always informed his research on 'elaborated' and 'restricted' code – concepts for which he is most widely known and, for which, thanks to careless 'scholarly' readings, he became so notorious amongst (socio)linguists and educationists!

The concept of code played an important role in Bernstein's enquiries. Code categories as revealed by the various fashions of speaking were worthy of attention precisely because they were active in the formation of consciousness – a precursor to what Halliday and Matthiessen were to describe years later (1999) as 'construing experience through meaning'. For Bernstein the important aspect of modes of communication was not so much what realised them – the sounds or the wordings, which would typically be the main concern for the sociolinguist. Rather, as a sociologist, his focus was on what it was that was realised by code-regulated modes of communication themselves, what constituted their deep meaning. From this point of view, they were indicative of the form of consciousness created by participation in social practices, which in turn activated the social subjects' sense of relevance and thus positioned them in some specific relation to how they interpreted the world outside and how they acted in and on, it. Codes thus were a key concept in the search for an answer to how the outside becomes the inside and how the inside reveals itself. Once these arguments are accepted, the important question naturally becomes: how are codes and their attendant forms of consciousness differentially distributed in human societies? In answering this question, Bernstein drew attention to social relations which were themselves created, maintained and changed through social practices which in turn were epigenetically related to the social agent's positioning in society. The unavoidable implication of this claim is that the overall design of what a social subject might feel inclined to do and actually does do is, to a large extent, responsive to the subjects' location in relation to the production and distribution of the society's resources, which inevitably translates itself into the distribution of power and the fashioning of the principles of control for the preservation of that power. This, Bernstein was always careful to point out, did not mean either a puppet-like existence for the social subjects or a negation of the possibility of change in their orientation to meanings; what was at issue was the overwhelmingly probable forms of social practice. The essential outline of this argument was present in Bernstein's writing as early as the mid-1960s: certainly the 1971 volume of papers establishes the major thrust of the argument, as the following extract shows:

> the particular form of social relations acts selectively upon what is said, when it is said and how it is said ... The different forms of social relations can generate very different speech systems or linguistic codes.
>
> (These) speech systems or codes create for their speakers different orders of relevance and relation. The experience of the speakers may then be transformed by what is made significant or relevant by different speech systems. As the child ... learns specific codes which regulate his verbal acts, he learns the requirements of his social structure. The experience of the child is transformed by the learning generated by his own, apparently, voluntary acts of speech. The social structure becomes ... the substratum of the child's experience essentially through the manifold consequences of the linguistic process. From this point of view, every time the child speaks or listens, the social structure is reinforced in him and his social identity shaped. The social structure becomes the child's psychological reality through the shaping of his acts of speech. (Bernstein, 1971: 144)

The journey of Bernstein's enquiry had begun in 1958 with *Some Sociological Determinants of Perception* – a slender paper of less than 20 pages. The questions he then posed led him increasingly to more important problems in the domain of sociology. The persistence with which he maintained his engagement with the 'enduring problem' of his research bears witness both to the inherent intricacy of the problem and to his scholarly integrity which led him again and again to refine, to elaborate, to modify and to pursue the implications of his own findings. Naturally, along the way, there were changes, not simply in formulation but in the nature of the explanation. For example, in the late 1960s, the tendency for orientation to elaborated and restricted codes was explained by reference to 'personal' and 'positional' family types and 'individuated' and 'ascribed' role types: Durkheim's notions of 'organic' and 'mechanical solidarity' were employed as the basic explanatory concepts for describing the characteristics of social organisation. But before long, Bernstein's explanation moved to a higher level of abstraction. He utilised the notions of 'classification' and 'framing', concepts which were first employed in the analysis of educational transmissions, especially in the management of educational knowledge (Bernstein, 1975a). Underlying the concepts of classification and framing are the distribution of power and the principles of control, respectively. Stated simply, classification is the process of category formation: power lies in the capacity to classify and to define the phenomena of the world – material and social – in terms that suit one's own purposes and relate to one's own ideology.

Bernstein brought sophistication to the concept of 'categories'. Like Saussure's signs, Bernstein's categories are essentially relationally defined: the identity of the categories depends on '... the relations *between* categories' (Bernstein, 1996: 20; emphasis original). What keeps the categories distinct from each other also establishes their identity and points to a division of labour between them, be they categories of gender, race, social practices of various kinds including discourse, or whatever. The integrity of a category is maintained by the insulation between it and other categories and power resides in the insulation of the boundaries between the various categories: 'what preserves the insulation is power' (1996: 21). Classification thus always carries power. The degree of insulation between categories will range from strong to weak, under given conditions: the stronger the boundary, the more assertive the power relation underlying that category. Framing on the other hand refers to the control on the form of the social practice: it is 'about *who* controls *what*' (Bernstein, 1996: 27; emphasis original). For example, in the case of a discourse, framing concerns such matters as who decides what will be talked about, in what order, in what way, at what rate, etc. and also how speakers' discourse will be evaluated. Framing too ranges from strong to weak under specifiable conditions: the greater the control on forms of practice, the stronger the classification. The strength or weakness of classification and framing came to be used as more abstract and more powerful indicators of coding orientations. The concept of coding orientation became inseparable from a subject's sense of what constitutes the legitimate forms of communication in specific contexts: 'The concept of code is inseparable from legitimate and illegitimate communication' (Bernstein, 1990: 15). Whereas in the late 1950s and early 1960s Bernstein's codes were binomial, the use of classification and framing which could vary along the cline of strong-weak, implied a large scope for delicate variation in coding orientation.

As pointed out above, classification and framing are realisationally related to power and control. Therefore, in the final analysis, a logical relation exists between a subject's 'social positioning' and their coding orientation. Codes, as Bernstein maintained, 'are culturally determined positioning devices. More specifically, class-regulated codes position subjects with respect to dominant and dominated forms of communication ... ideology is constituted through and in such positioning' (Bernstein, 1990: 13). By these steps in the argument, coding orientation came to be located by reference to the social division of labour. Thus the later Bernstein (1990: 20) would claim:

The simpler the social division of labour, and the more specific and local the relation between an agent and its material base, the more direct the relation between meanings and a specific material base, and the greater the probability of a restricted coding orientation. The more complex the social division of labour, the less specific and local the relation between an agent and its material base, the more indirect the relation between meanings and a specific material base, and the greater the probability of an elaborated coding orientation. (emphasis original)

The last three decades of Bernstein's research were devoted largely to the sociology of pedagogy. Here he began with the classification and framing of knowledge (1975a) and went on to establish a sociology of pedagogy that has been highly influential internationally[2]. Starting with the widely accepted position that 'education is a relay for power relations external to it ...', he went on to enquire into those characteristics of this relay system which permit it to play this important role in the production and reproduction of societies. His theory of the structuring of pedagogic discourse is an elaborate account of how elements of pedagogic communication are configured to achieve the ends that they do achieve. This 'totalising' statement is deliberate: as Bernstein pointed out (1990: 169) 'The most outstanding feature of educational principles and practices is their overwhelming and staggering uniformity independent of the dominant ideology': deep down, systems of education tend to be the same everywhere. When a lay person thinks of education, their attention moves immediately to the body of knowledge that is packaged into curricula, segmented into presentable units and dispensed by 'trained and qualified' instructors to those who are initially taken to be innocent of these curriculum genres and who, if successful, emerge with a piece of paper that represents some level of 'qualification' with some specific social value. Bernstein's analysis of the educational system certainly took this aspect into account, but it attached equal, if not more emphasis, to certain other far more fundamental features, which constituted the active constitutive rules of the educational system. As for codes so for his sociology of pedagogy, each concept was presented, examined, critiqued and re-presented in a more elaborate form over a period of some 30 years. It is not easy to do justice to this extensive theory in the limited space available here. The interested reader must consult at least Bernstein 1990 and 1996, but to trace the development of his thinking on the system of education requires attention to the entire *oeuvre*. What follows now is a brief and simplified sketch of some of Bernstein's important views on the subject.

3 Bernstein's sociology of pedagogy

First let me introduce the notion of pedagogy itself: if through pedagogy, a social subject acquires some knowledge, some understanding of the ways of being, doing and saying that are viewed as legitimate in the many cultural contexts the subject participates in, then it is clear that there are at least two distinct arenas of such learning: the official and the local. The character of local pedagogy is beautifully summed up by Bernstein when he comments (2000: 199) 'All experiencing carries a pedagogic potential, but all experiences are not pedagogically generated'. Simplifying greatly, the distinction between local and official pedagogy lies in the fact that in local pedagogy the social subject 'learns', whereas in official pedagogy, the social subject is 'taught' according to a deliberately fashioned programme of instruction and regulation: if there is learning, it is intended that it be 'pedagogically generated' in response to the pedagogic practices. Where there is a deliberate programme, there are such considerations as to what should be taught; who are the 'appropriate' learners; in what sequence should it be taught; how should the completion of any stage in sequence be determined; how are those who 'prepare' the material for use in the contexts of official pedagogy located *vis à vis* the complete system of education; and above all, what are the relations of subjects involved in these processes, from the learner to the teacher, from the teacher to the curricula ratifiers and so on and so forth. Bernstein's sociology of pedagogy offers models for the various 'modules' of this complex area. It follows that the term education as used in ordinary discourse refers only to what in terms of Bernstein would form just one part of official pedagogy. According to Bernstein, pedagogic discourse (i.e., any discourse connected with any aspect of educational practices) 'embeds a discourse of competence (skills of various kinds) into a discourse of social order in such a way that the latter always dominates the former' (1990: 183). This claim is formulaically represented as 'ID/RD' (Bernstein, 1990; 1996) – instructional discourse embedded within regulative discourse.

A crucial concept in Bernstein's sociology of pedagogy is that of 'pedagogic device': somewhat analogous to the system of language (see Bernstein, 2000: 26ff), it referred to the entire potential for pedagogic discourse. In other words, all forms of pedagogic communication are instantiations of the pedagogic device, which consists of three interrelated sets of rules:

1   *distributive rules* which distribute forms of consciousness through the distribution of forms of knowledge;
2   *recontextualising rules* which regulate the formation of specific instructional discourse;
3   *evaluative rules* which furnish criteria for legitimate forms of communication.

Pedagogic discourse is always and unavoidably hierarchic. However, the hierarchic position of the 'transmitter' and the 'acquirer' might or might not be visible. This gives rise to the distinction between 'visible' and 'invisible' pedagogy. With visible pedagogy, typically practised in traditional educational institutions, the framing of the discourse is relatively strong. With strong framing the transmitter decides what is to be taught, in what sequence, as well as how the material would be paced and how performance would be evaluated: the acquirer has little or no say in deciding any of these aspects. But precisely because there are set practices, the 'rules of the game' are largely transparent to both parties. In invisible pedagogy, practised typically in 'progressive' schools, the ultimate authority still rests with the transmitter, but the framing of the educational practices is considerably weaker; the acquirers may intervene in the process, but the rules of the game are not transparent except to those who have experience of this particular form of communicative strategy. Typically such pupils tend to come with an experience of participation in the dominating code modalities. So they bring to this pedagogic communication a sense of what would constitute legitimate discourse in the given environment.

The choice between these two types of pedagogy is not free of ideology and it is my reading that at this point the experience of communication prior to schooling – in every day life through local pedagogy – enters logically into the discourse of Bernstein's sociology of education and thus relates it back to the discourse of early coding orientations that the pupils might bring to school. The coding orientation that the pupil brings into the classroom could, at least initially, become the crucial element in deciding how the classroom contexts of pedagogic communication will be recognised: that is, what identity and what value will be ascribed to them. The first move in Bernstein's sociology of pedagogy had been with a paper in the early 1970s on *The Classification and Framing of Educational Knowledge* (Bernstein, 1975a). His last move (Bernstein, 1999) returned him yet again to the continued reflection in the same area. His discussion of horizontal and vertical discourse is, on the one hand, reminiscent of early discussions of the attributes of restricted and elaborated codes and, on the other hand, in my view, represents a major step in establishing a logically argued link between the various categories of knowledge. For example, the characteristics of horizontal discourse bring to one's mind the early pairs such as context dependent vs. context independent, particularistic vs. universalistic, implicit vs. explicit and many other such binomial pairs. The discussion of commonsense knowledge as opposed to knowledge systems construed by vertical discourse recall aspects of early knowledge classification. But as always, return to the 'same' area for Bernstein meant new explorations and, of course, deeper insights. Bernstein (1999) argues that horizontal discourse typically construes 'local knowledge', whereas vertical discourse construes what in official pedagogic sites is considered 'knowledge' proper; these are 'specialised symbolic structures of explicit knowledge'. With vertical discourse, there are two modalities of knowledge construal: (i) hierarchically-organised knowledge structures as, for example, in the sciences and (ii) knowledge structures, each of which has 'a series of specialised modes of interrogation and specialised criteria for the production and circulation of texts, as in the social sciences and humanities'. Bernstein goes on to discuss in detail how these two classes of knowledge differ or resemble each other; how their acquisition criteria differ and how the mode of evaluation of their acquisition differs. In this rich contribution Bernstein opens several avenues of enquiry, dwelling on the implication of the characteristics of the two general classes of knowledge and indicating the value of a diachronic study of the growth and development of both. There was every indication that in this renewed examination of knowledge systems and modalities of their construal, his probings would have added much to our understanding of educational systems, their approved knowledge systems and their pedagogic devices, but unfortunately for us, he was not allowed that time[3].

There are of course many other aspects of Bernstein's sociology of pedagogy that are (with apologies to Bernstein) ignored in this account; here what I want to draw attention to is the fact that this work is sometimes viewed as moving into an area that abandons his earlier concerns. I find this position questionable. It is obvious from his writings that Bernstein saw specific kinds of relations between official and local pedagogy irrespective of the fact that the 'rules' of pedagogic discourse as described in the theory do not apply to acts of local pedagogy[4]. Again, the concepts of classification and framing active in the creation of coding orientation are crucial both to the discourse of codes as well as to any discourse of the pedagogic device, because any instantiation of the latter too is code regulated and underlying the discourse of code is the effort to resolve the same enduring problem. A reading of one of the most outstanding pieces of his writing *The Social Construction of Pedagogic Discourse* (1990: 165ff) will bear out these comments. My own view is, therefore, that even in his sociology of pedagogy there is a continued engagement with the same basic issues of the relations of the division of labour, power, control, communication and consciousness. Bernstein voices the fact of this engagement as follows and note how it echoes his formulations presented at the beginning of this paper in relation to the earlier Bernstein literature:

> to explicate the process whereby a given distribution of power and principles of control are translated into specialised principles of communication differentially and often unequally, distributed to social groups/classes. And how such a differential/unequal distribution of forms of communication, initially (but not necessarily terminally) shapes the formation of consciousness of members of these groups/classes in such a way as to relay both opposition and change. The crucial issue is the translation of power and control into principles of communication which become (...) their carriers or relays (1996: 93)

The last two volumes (1990; 1996/2000) furnish a record of the achievement of this long journey. By this stage what had begun as an examination of a specific social pathology – selective educational failure in modern complex societies – had been transformed into an examination of the principles that underlie the social practice of education *tout court*. In the course of examining the pedagogic processes within modern societies, the conventionally accepted boundary between learning in recognised educational sites – 'official pedagogy' – and learning by and in everyday life – 'local pedagogy' – had been subjected to serious questioning: a non-accidental relation between the two kinds of knowledge had been firmly established. At the same time, the educational system itself had been subjected to an analysis that remains unsurpassed in depth and scope. This progression is typical of how Bernstein worked: arriving at the answer to the question with which he initiated his research programme at any particular stage was not the end of a story; it was always treated as a beginning, an invitation for him to deepen the enquiry further, to question the answer he had arrived at.

His final volume and its revised edition (my favourite) *Pedagogy, Symbolic Control and Identity: theory, research, critique* (1996; 2000) opens yet another new horizon, not unrelated to what had gone before, but enriched by the years of reflection on the turns his research had taken, the problems it had highlighted and the insights it had offered. In producing the sociology of knowledge, as part of the sociology of pedagogy, this volume may fairly be said to provide a framework for the sociology of sociological discourse. Bernstein (1996) presents a concern with the metatheoretical level, pointing to directions for further research. One of his primary concerns was to provide a framework offering analytical categories capable of being operationalised in empirical research:

> A theory must (not only) be capable of providing an explicit, unambiguous description of the objects of its analysis. ... (but it) must (also) ... provide rules for their empirical recognition, description and modalities of their realisation. ... (T)he principle of description ... description derived from the theory, must interact with the empirical levels. ... Ideally, the principles must have the potential of exhausting the possibilities. This means that they have the potential not only of describing imputed regularities to the displays but also of showing their diversities. (Bernstein, 1996: 93)

This volume also contains a critique of today's pedagogic practices that is based on an impressively deep analysis of how elements of the pedagogic device work to collude with power brokers – in our case the sacred cow of 'market forces', which no one administering a university today would dare to question, much less ignore. With uncanny precision, the pages of Bernstein 1996 predict the implications of changes in the socioeconomic domain of our contemporary globalised world for the pedagogue, for the pedagogised as well as for the pedagogy in these high places of learning. There is a huge and significant distance between the very first research question Basil Bernstein had raised in the late 1950s – why do some children fail educationally – and his final concerns: what is the optimal form of a sociological theory which would successfully explain how the outside becomes the inside and how the inside reveals itself and shapes the outside, then what part do local and official pedagogy play in it, how and why – what enables them to do so? The measure of this distance is the measure of Bernstein's unique scholarly achievement.

The final form of the theory Bernstein produced is multi-layered; each layer reaches out to some aspect of social existence which is relevant to his problematic. In this sense his theory is exotropic (Hasan, 1999a). In an exotropic theory there is no place for discipline-based traditional compartmentalisations that carve out areas each strongly classified from the rest. Rather, the theory turns to all those phenomena which form the context of existence for its object of study and which act as a resource for its subsistence. In short, the theory treats its object of study not as something that is impermeable but as an active part of a society's design for living. This might be one reason why comprehensive mastery of Bernstein's theoretical framework is a daunting proposition. No single avenue of approach is the *only* avenue of approach to Bernstein's work: the work spreads over a wide canvas. Certainly sociology is its point of departure and its quest but his theory is also about language in society, it is also about the genesis of cognition in society, it is also about the economic organisation of societies and, of course, it is about human relationships. Even if its major focus in later years is official pedagogy, this focus is not impermeable: it embraces all forms of pedagogy, thus defying the constraints of the institution of education and bringing in the contribution of the experience of living with other social beings. After all, those who are 'into' the classification of official knowledge and who engage in the practices of official pedagogy are still social beings with social relations and with ideologies which speak of their positioning and positioned responses. Given this wide canvas, not surprisingly his theory penetrates into the realms of semiotics, psychology, education and the primary human condition of labour, with all that human labour has historically entailed, particularly the forms of human relations. To each of these areas Bernstein's theory makes a contribution. In the remainder of this tribute to Bernstein, I want to say a brief word about two areas – that of semiotics and that of cognition – both crucially relevant to linguistics, the first because it relates to the question: why does anyone say anything? and the second because it concerns the issue of the relations of language and cognition, such a popular area at present. Let me begin with the domain of semiotics.

4 Bernstein on contexts of talk

Bernstein was almost unique[5] among sociologists in not just paying lip service to the centrality of linguistic processes in the production and reproduction of societies. As indicated in the discussions above, communication has a special place in his theory: it is through communication by various semiotic modalities, but most importantly through language (Bernstein, 1975a) that specifically human societies are given shape and are constantly reshaped. Not surprisingly, communication whether it occurred in everyday life or in the context of official pedagogy was deemed worthy of attention. As his language of description evolved, becoming more rigorous and explicit, he revealed the dialectic of the social and the semiotic, whereby social practice without semiotic input is an impossibility and semiotic practice without its social context is a fiction of the formal linguist's imagination. More specifically, the later Bernstein offered one of the richest accounts of what it is to communicate: why any one says the things they do say. To appreciate the richness and unique contribution of this theory, it is important to place it in the context of how communication, i.e., the use of language in some context of situation, has been typically treated in modern linguistics.

In the dominant linguistics of the 1960s-70s and in some pockets of the discipline perhaps even today, it is taken as axiomatic that in the words of Saussure (1966), in *parole* the individual is the master: speakers can say anything they want and certainly, at least in one sense, the truth of this claim is undeniable. But until quite recently the gulf that divides *can say* from *do say* did not receive the attention it deserved. Implied in this gulf was a paradox: while the freedom of *parole* promised novelty and uniqueness, experience of people talking informed the observer that most discourse is unsurprising, true to expectation and that it does fulfil the promise of originality, but this originality is recognised only by its departure from that which is normally expected: i.e., certain ways of saying 'go with' certain occasions for saying. So there is a problem: what imposes the typical regularity, what predicts the predictability of talk? And what is the degree of precision of these predictions? These questions did not engage many linguists because it called for the study of language in use. This meant studying 'data' and, in formalist wisdom, linguistics that stooped to data even to meet the requirement of observational adequacy was indeed beyond the pale. The situation did not change much until the work of Austin (1962) Searle (1969) and Grice (1975), further flavoured by Garfinkle's ethnomethodology and with Labov's sociolinguistic variation studies, finally legitimised attention to context: context became an acceptable concept.

By contrast[6], systemic functional linguistics (henceforth SFL) fared somewhat better; it borrowed the insights of the anthropologist Malinowski (1923), which were honed further by Firth (1957) into the theorised category of 'schematic construct' for the analysis of meaning in language. The Firthian view of context was further developed by Halliday (in Halliday, McIntosh & Strevens, 1964 and Halliday, 1977a) and colleagues (Gregory, 1967; Hasan, 1973; 1978; 1980). With this developing framework, it was possible for SF linguists to begin to demonstrate that talk and the occasion of talk are systematically related, that it is this relation which offers major explanations for the regularity and predictability of talk. The interest of SFL in what people say was not accidental: it arose from accepting Firth's prescient rejection of what in Bernstein's terms is Saussure's strong classification of *langue* and *parole*. I want to give a very brief indication of what SFL achieved by taking as its object of enquiry both the system and the process of language – both what *langue* potentially enables the speaker to say and what speakers typically do say as *parole*.

Treating context as an element of linguistic theory, SFL proceeded to describe the structure of social context (the 'contextual construct' in terms of Halliday & Hasan, 1985) by reference to the three parameters: (i) field (i.e., social activity), (ii) tenor (i.e., participant relations) and (iii) mode (i.e., means of contact). Any one instance of context is a configuration of some specific values of these three parameters, which Hasan (in Halliday & Hasan,

1985) referred to as 'contextual configuration'. The contextual configuration is critical in the choice of meaning and wording in any occasion of language use. Halliday argued that the structure of language is as it is because the system and process of language are dialectically related (Halliday, 1992): the system is shaped by the process of its participation in talk in the living of life. In support of this argument Halliday (1979a) pointed to the close realisational relation between the three parameters of context and the internal form of language: each contextual parameter has the potential of activating choices typically from some specific areas of meaning and wording. These three specific areas of meanings and wordings – the 'ideational', the 'interpersonal' and the 'textual'– form the resource for the construal of field, tenor and mode, respectively. This prehension between context, semantics and lexicogrammar was taken as proof of the metafunctional nature of language. In the realm of discourse analysis in SFL, context became the crucial explanatory principle for analysing the structure potential of text types, which was said to be activated by the specific character of the configuration of the values of field, tenor and mode[7] (Halliday & Hasan, 1985). This principle permitted a systematic description of the regularities within text types, including their generic structure. It thus appeared as if by approaching context from the point of view of discourse, SFL had arrived at a powerful language of description, which explicated the principles of both the 'regularities of the contextual displays and their diversities'.

SFL was in full agreement with Bernstein on the systemic nature of context whereby 'what counts as context depends not on relationships within, but on relationships between contexts' (Bernstein, 1990: 15). It, however, did not problematise the speaker's recognition of contexts in the way that Bernstein's theory did: contexts in SFL came to have an identity completely independent of the social subjects active within the contexts (and I believe this is true of all other approaches to context spawned since the mid-1970s). Further, at least in some varieties of SFL, notably Martin's 'genre based model' (Martin, 1985a; 1992), field and, in specifiable cases, mode were prioritised as furnishing the activation of the structure of genres, which further underplayed the role of speaking subjects in relating to the occasions of their talk. In my view both these problems have the same origin: how the social subject is conceptualised in relation to context. A survey of literature on the relations of text and context in SFL up to the late 1980s will support the claim that interactants were typically described in terms of their agency, i.e., what they were doing with their language, e.g. salesman-buyer (or to use Ventola's variants Server/Client (Ventola, 1987)); in terms of their relation to each other, both ascribed e.g. mother-child and achieved e.g. expert-novice; and in terms of the social distance between them, i.e., whether and how frequently, the history of their communication had brought them together before and if so in what range of fields, which was intended as a theorisation of degrees of intimacy in interactants relations to each other (Hasan, 1973; 1980)[8]. Put together with Halliday's developing functional grammar, this presented a considerable resource for the description of a text and of the various text types.

But, in the nature of things, the majority of data that SFL linguists analysed came from and represented the sayings of the dominant social class. In fact, the sociological perspective did not penetrate SFL – and as a matter of fact still does not – analyses of discourse, until Hasan and colleagues began to work in the domain of semantic variation (Hasan, 1988; Cloran, 1994; Williams, 1995). Here the data consisted of naturally occurring dialogues between mothers and their young children and it soon became obvious that all mothers do not talk the same way even while engaged in the same activity in some sense of the word 'same' (Cloran, 1994; 1999; Hasan, 2000b). The mothers' sense of what the context is a context for is critically different depending on their social location. To understand why this should be so, we need to consider what Bernstein referred to as the 'invisible' component of communication in the following figure (from Bernstein, 1990: 17):

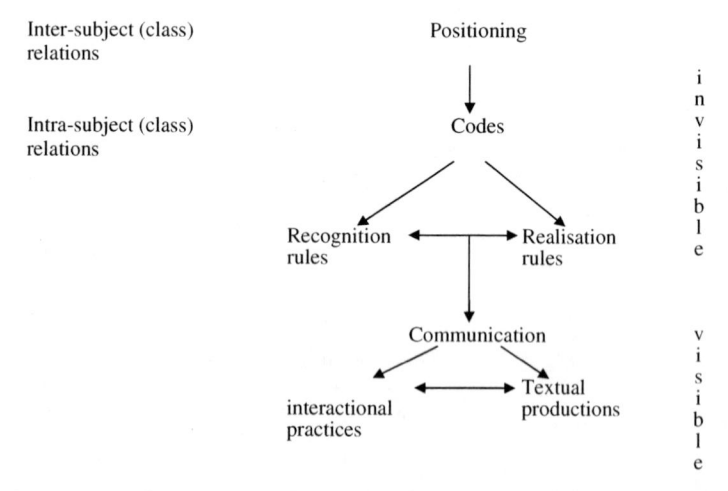

```
Inter-subject (class)              Positioning                    i
relations                              |                          n
                                       ↓                          v
Intra-subject (class)                                             i
relations                           Codes                         s
                                    / | \                         i
                                   /  |  \                        b
                                  /   |   \                       l
                          Recognition ←→ Realisation              e
                            rules     |     rules
                                      |
                                      ↓
                                Communication                     v
                                    /    \                        i
                                   /      \                       s
                              ←→ Textual                          i
                         interactional  productions               b
                           practices                              l
                                                                  e
```

Figure 1.1: The invisible component of communication

Bernstein's code theory problematised the social subject's relation to contexts – how a subject comes to have a sense of what a context is the context for and how the identity of a category of context gets established for social subjects. There are three links in the chain of logical relations that attempt to address this problem: (i) class relations and positioning with the attendant working of the distribution of power and the principles of control; (ii) positioning and codes (to repeat, 'codes are culturally determined positioning devices'); and

(iii) codes and communication (all communication in society is code related; to put it simply, there is no talk that does not speak of the speaker's positioning). Now, if we grant that 'ideology is constituted through and in ... positioning' (Bernstein, 1990: 13) and that positioning implies participation in certain code-regulated ways of being, doing and saying, then we grant that subjects' stance to their universe is being invoked: different orders of relevance inhere in distinct experiences of positioning and being positioned. This, as I understand, is what underlies the invisible component of the diagram; this is where the individual's relation to categories of context is established; this is where the nature of what one typically wants to say and what one would consider appropriate to the occasion of talk, becomes 'naturalised'.

> A code is a regulative principle, tacitly acquired, which selects and integrates (a) relevant meanings ... (b) forms of their realisation ... (c) evoking context. It follows from th[is] definition that, if code selects and integrates relevant meanings, then code presupposes a concept of irrelevant or illegitimate meanings; that, if code selects forms of realisation, then code presupposes a concept of inappropriate or illegitimate forms of realisation; that, if code regulates evoking contexts then again it implies a concept of inappropriate, illegitimate contexts. The concept of code is inseparable from the concepts of legitimate and illegitimate communication and thus it presupposes a hierarchy in forms of communication and their demarcation and criteria. (Bernstein, 1990: 15)

Naturally, this does not mean that prediction could be made about particular morphemes, words, clauses and their structures. Rather, what can be predicted is the orientation to certain categories of meaning; these in their turn would invoke a particular range of wordings. The claim is not that we can say, 'the speaker will produce this here saying', but rather, 'this is the expected habitual predisposition to meanings, this is the picture of this speakers' orders of relevance, so it is highly probable that s/he will be tapping into meanings of this order rather than others'.

It has to be granted that linguists are right to the extent that speakers can say what they want to say, in the sense that there is always the possibility of saying the unexpected. The important question still remains: what is the range of meanings individuals belonging to certain groups habitually and voluntarily mean in the contexts of living their life and why do they prioritise those meanings when the possibilities of making meanings from the point of view of the system of language are infinite? Why do they want to say what they habitually tend to say? By taking the steps described above, Bernstein provides a sociohistorical frame for tracing the genesis of interactants' desires, needs and beliefs. This is in notable contrast to both speech act theory and conversation analysis. In both these enterprises, much discourse flows about interactants' desires, beliefs and needs; the existence or absence of such mental states gets stated as critical to some move or some act. Nonetheless, there is no attempt to explain how these mental states become known to the other party; the basis for the assumption of the intersubjective status, assumed so easily, remains a mystery. It should be obvious that one interactant's desires are irrelevant to communication unless it is possible to argue that the other party has reasonable grounds for recognising the existence of those desires. The ability to project the other's mental set, which is the essence of intersubjectivity, is an essential condition for continued communication. Since typically acts of communication do continue, it follows that normally in everyday discourse, one interactant has the other's measure; at the same time, it is notable that discursive continuity is more likely to occur where the interactants belong to the same/similar social grouping. That is, we have something to say only to those people whose world is familiar and intelligible to us; a Henry Higgins does not engage in casual conversation with an Eliza Doolittle. Of course in linguistics we do discuss shared experience, but like much else, it arrives out of nowhere: it just is. While pragmatists and linguists treat the concept of shared experience as self-evident, it is Bernstein's theory that explains how this shared experience becomes possible, how it is that in the words of Firth (1957a: 186) within one's speech fellowship 'a speaker is phonetically and verbally content because when he speaks to one of his fellowship, he is also speaking to himself'.

For me and for some of my colleagues, Bernstein's theorisation of an individual's relation to contexts was helpful in explaining why given the 'same' social activity such as that of control or sociability or instruction, the texts produced by different groups/classes differ so markedly (Cloran, 1994; 1999; Williams, 1995; Hasan, 1999a; 2000b; 2001a). One group of mothers 'read' almost any context as one for overt control and overt hierarchic relations; the other group translate it into a context for covert regulation of conduct, for the maintenance of invisible hierarchic control and for presenting relatively organised information which re-contextualises elements of specialised knowledge for the young child. The texts that the mothers and children jointly produce differ both in their over-all structure and in their textural qualities, which is not to say that one is better than the other; they are simply doing different things in the same situation.

Currently, the Bakhtinian term 'hybridity' is much in vogue. Of course, at the visible level of communication both the fact of intertextuality and hybridity are naturally visible! In making observations about these phenomena – where they occur, or what form they take – our description has achieved what Chomsky has called 'observational adequacy'. This is an important element in the creation of a theory and in the development of its language of description, but it falls short of explanation, without which no theory is complete. Bernstein's analysis of how subjects are positioned and how they position themselves in relation to the social context of their discourse, offers an explanation of hybridity, or genre-combination (Martin, 1992) in terms of the classification and framing practices of the speaking subjects. In researching mother's everyday talk with their children, my colleagues and I found that speakers' social positioning is the most powerful concept for understanding discourse both its local meanings and its global structure. It is positioning which underlies the invisible level of their communication, where the motivational relevancies of communication are located and the latter level in turn underlies their visible communication; it is this visible communication that linguists describe as discourse. As Bernstein says:

> [A] specific text is but a transformation of the specialised transactional practices; the text is the form of the social relationship made visible, palpable, material ... Further the selection, creation, production, and changing of texts are the means whereby the positioning of the subjects is revealed, reproduced and changed. (Bernstein, 1990: 17)

To put it this way is not to play down the importance of visible talk; it is simply to insist on the complexity of the nature of human talk, whose roots penetrate deep into the design of life in society. Visible communication is certainly what impinges on the other and as such its power cannot be denied. But it is worth emphasising that Bernstein's contribution to our understanding of a social subject's relation to contexts is rich: its potential still awaits exploration by linguists. Whorf (1956: 248) once claimed 'speech is the best show man puts on'. What Bernstein does is to point out that behind this show lies an impressive cast of players, a long history of cultural traditions, the working of institutions, all of them amazingly intricate, but not all of them admirable in what they help perpetuate; yet somewhere in this show there exists the potential for thinking the unthinkable, for change.

5 Bernstein and the concept of the formation of consciousness

Let me turn now to Bernstein's contribution to the relations of language, society and mind – a central theme in the Bernstein literature as argued above. Speaking more accurately, instead of 'language' one should say 'semiosis', i.e., the practice of meaning making by using sign systems of any kind, for Bernstein's interest was in the entire range of social practices, which are obviously realised by many different modes of meaning, not just language. I emphasise language here for two reasons: one, that amongst the many modalities of meaning, an important place was assigned to language by Bernstein himself; and second, that being a linguist, I am partial to the relevance of Bernstein's theory to the study of language as social semiotic. Be that as it may, I would like to say a word here on the place of the formation of consciousness in Bernstein's theoretical framework, for it is the perception of its centrality that leads Bernstein's theory to make connections with both language and cognition. The enduring problem of Bernstein's research was both the problem of social reproduction and of social change – the means whereby these two important forces of all known human societies co-exist, whether one calls them contradictory or complementary is irrelevant at this point; what matters is that if the two forces are co-present then there must be ways and means in the social organisation of human life to support their co-existence. It would be somewhat out of keeping with Bernstein's thinking to take the easy – some might say 'romantic' – way out by placing all responsibility for this with the social subject. Equally, to entirely externalise the processes which lead to reproduction and change from the social subjects' practices would be tantamount to turning the social into a mechanical object. Bernstein took the Marxist position: it is subjects that alter the conditions of existence, but the conditions in which they do this are not entirely of their own making: consciousness comes from life rather than life from consciousness[9]. So far as Bernstein is concerned, as acquirers of this consciousness, the social subjects are always active: the social structure becomes a part of their consciousness by their own *apparently* voluntary social acts. The essentials of the cultural design are semiotically mediated in the course of living: a sociologist who would pay attention to the two polar forces of reproduction and change must attach importance both to the possibility of variability in voices and to the code-regulated recognition and realisation of social contexts.

Bernstein's ideas about the formation of human consciousness resonate well with those of the famous Russian psychologist Vygotsky, whose concept of 'semiotic mediation' and its role in the formation of higher human consciousness are widely acclaimed today. Compare, for example, the extract from Bernstein (1971: 144) with the following from Vygotsky (1978: 57):

> Every function in the child's cultural development appears twice: first on the social level, and later on the individual level; first *between* people (*interpsychologically*), and then *inside* the child (*intrapsychologically*) ... *All the higher functions originate as actual relations between human individuals*. (emphasis added)

Both scholars attach importance to language and to interaction with an acculturated other[10]. But there are crucial differences between Vygotsky and Bernstein. In the first place, Vygotsky (1978) was particularly concerned with the working of semiotic mediation as a means of mediating concepts and knowledge structures which, in terms of Bernstein, are specific to official pedagogic contexts. For Bernstein, despite his brilliant insights into the working of official pedagogy, the scope of semiotic mediation was not limited in this way[11] and, as I pointed out, he saw a systematic relation between the efficacy of semiotic mediation in official pedagogic sites and the experience of semiotic mediation the children bring with them to school. Further 'the child' in Vygotsky remains undifferentiated; whatever the historical rationale for this, the role of social structure and of social positioning is never foregrounded in Vygotsky. It appears as if semiotic mediation would have the same efficacy, no matter what the environment for the interaction.

Certainly one important point Vygotsky was making was the externalisation of thought which accompanies verbal interaction and which is an essential condition for the conscious internalisation and voluntary recall of concepts. Thus he cites the case of children talking around a problem amongst themselves and coming to solve it when any one of them might not have succeeded by working individually (Vygotsky, 1978). This is certainly an important point, which as it were attests to the power of verbal interaction and therefore of semiotic mediation, reminding us of Whorf's comment (1956: 220): 'talk ought to be a more dignified and noble word than "think"'. The spirit of Vygotsky's writing on semiotic mediation and the service to which the concept was put, still imply an important position to semiotic mediation where at least one party was not a cultural apprentice and therefore logically could be said to import into the interactive situation the cultural baggage which always moves with the moving human being. Intimation of any such cultural baggage is absent from the Vygotskian literature. Bernstein's code theory provides an insight into how the same act of semiotic mediation by an acculturated other might have a different significance for persons whose social history is different. The semiotic mediation of concepts specific to instructional discourse may not be unaffected by the historically prior semiotic mediation of orders of relevance through the experience of discourse in everyday life. An exciting scholarly development awaits where the work of these two seminal thinkers can be synthesised to produce a theory of learning which is aware of where the learners are coming from: what are their recognition and realisation rules for the categories of discourse. Bernstein (1996: 5) hoped that 'Education can have a crucial role in creating tomorrow's optimism in the context of today's pessimism. But if it is to do this then we must have an analysis of the social biases in education. These biases lie deep within the very structure of the educational system's processes of transmission and acquisition and their social assumptions'. Whenever in thinking of curricula, methodology, evaluation and so on, we homogenise 'the child', justifying the homogeneity of pedagogic interaction, we contribute to the maintenance of the mythology of egalitarian education, where the same form of semiotic mediation suits all.[12]

6 Bernstein and aspects of Marxist discourse

In the chequered history of reaction to the different phases of Bernstein's research, there has often been a debate on whether or not he was a Marxist. Disdaining such practices of labelling, Bernstein was to point out that they are simply a device for putting scholars and their theories into precategorised boxes, rather like a variety of botanical labelling. Rather than asking whether he was a Marxist bent upon undermining the legitimate structures, or an enemy of the downtrodden, maligning their ways of saying, I feel it is far more relevant to ask: what use did Bernstein make of the Marxist ideas? The answer to such a question is interestingly suggestive. In The German ideology (p. 47), Marx and Engels (1947), asserting the primacy of 'material life-processes' concluded that:

> Morality, religion, metaphysics, all the rest of ideology and their corresponding forms of consciousness, thus no longer retain the semblance of independence. They have no history, no development; but men developing their material production and their material intercourse, alter, along with their real existence, their thinking and the products of their thinking. Life is not determined by consciousness, but consciousness by life.

Marx and Engels claim 'empirical verifiability' for their hypothesis. I suggest that Bernstein picked up the challenge implicit in this view: he not only traced the logical relations that link society and consciousness but also showed how their roots penetrate into the material life-processes of men. In the course of doing this, he transformed the linear dependence into a true dialectic. And the major link in this progression was that of forms of communication which acted as the crucial link between the material conditions and the mental life of human beings which reveals itself in the patterns of day to day living and the institutions that we erect to uphold those patterns. Bernstein was always self-effacing, claiming that his 'approach was too limited to deal with large questions of culture and symbolic control' (2000: xxvi), but this was really because he attached such importance to the exploration of 'the processes whereby symbolic control and its modalities are realised: how power relations are transformed into discourse and discourse into power relations' (ibid.). This was the enduring problem around which decades of research was built and this will be Bernstein's enduring contribution to our understanding of the co-genesis of society, language and consciousness.

7 Bernstein, social class and his critics

As a researcher, Bernstein had deep regard for what Firth described as 'the renewal of connection with experience' (Firth, 1957b: 29). It was not enough to simply talk about code in abstract terms: it was necessary to indicate how it is to be recognised, what is its realisation. The explication of the codes – what activated them, what they produced and how they were themselves realised – became the main preoccupation of work in the Sociological Research Unit under his directorship from 1967 through to the early 1970s. For this work Bernstein came under severe attack. Looking back at the criticism levelled at Bernstein, one is often amazed by the fact that its virulence was in direct proportion to its lack of substance: the less significant the critic's critique, the less it showed evidence of the ability to read with perspicacity, the more vitriolic the attack on Bernstein. So far as I am able to judge, there are three recurrent points of criticism: (i) the validity of the recognition criteria for codes; (ii) the soundness of the empirical basis for the characterisation of the codes and their class attribution, often degenerating into accusations of an immoral bias against the working-classes on Bernstein's part; and (iii) the abstractness and/or difficulty of his writing style.

There is some justification in the claim that the lexicogrammatical criteria which Bernstein cited for the recognition of the two codes posed problems: at that stage it was not easy to show any logical relation between the semantics of the codes and the lexicogrammatical features said to realise them. This much is certainly true. But it has to be appreciated that what Bernstein needed in order to offer better indices of code realisation was a developed semantics; yet this is precisely where linguistics was at its weakest in the 1960s: autonomous syntax ruled the linguists' vision; Halliday's systemic functional linguistics, a framework which had always rejected the postulate of autonomous syntax, had yet to show how wording systemically construes meaning – how semantics and lexicogrammar are 'naturally' related. If Bernstein did not know where to look for the formal realisation of such difficult semantic phenomena as 'decontextualised language' or 'universalistic meaning', the responsibility lay precisely with the linguists whose ideas about the relations of society, meaning and linguistic form were hardly a help, if not outright risible. It was not only dominant linguistics that rejected the very hypothesis of any such relation; even sociolinguists talked of semantics and of social meaning as if these were two different classes of phenomena, ignoring the fact that much of what they called 'social meaning' was actually realised by patterns of language themselves.

As to the semantic characterisation of the codes, this largely fell prey to careless reading. Despite recurrently found passages of the type quoted above (Bernstein, 1971: 144), codes kept being carelessly confused with 'accent' by scholars of even high reputation – the glorified term for it in the dominant sociolinguistics was 'social dialect'. Social dialects, we were told, were different ways of saying the same thing, which is naturally true if 'social dialect' equals 'accent'. Failing to understand Bernstein's arguments about the etiology and nature of code, readers in fact had very little grounds for commenting on its empirical validity – a situation made doubly difficult because of the problematic recognition criteria. Bernstein's code theory made evident why anyone says anything, but to appreciate this one had to accept that ways of saying are also ways of meaning and that dispositions in the choice of meaning are subject to variation, a position that dominant sociolinguistics has strenuously rejected even to this day, ignoring evidence to the contrary (for such evidence, see, for example Hasan, 1989; 1992b; Cloran, 1994; 1999; Williams, 1995; 2001). Not surprisingly Bernstein was accused both of being a Marxist and of being a detractor of the working-class, depending on the ideology and/or the intellectual prowess of the accuser. It may be true that Bernstein's writing is not easy to read; it certainly makes use of many abstractions. To me it seems that the abstractness of his writing was a function of the abstract conceptual realm that his theory explored. Still this is perhaps one criticism with some basis in fact. But difficult writing has not given rise to such concentrated opposition, or such virulent attacks. Besides, amongst his contemporaries, one can easily name at least some considerably more convoluted styles, with equally as abstract concepts and yet they acquired the status of highly favoured masters. The much more relevant point seems to be that though Bernstein recognised political correctness, he had less respect for it than for the integrity of his problem and in consistently drawing attention to the consequences of class-based exploitation he made little concession to the fashions of academia. As he himself points out (Bernstein, 1971: 1) 'I have never been able to contain the thesis in the kernel required for mass consumption'.

Given the wealth of insights into sociolinguistic processes that Bernstein's writing provided, the criticisms appear to be extraordinarily wilful; one is tempted to say they show a lack of academic literacy. So it is interesting to ask why Bernstein's work constantly 'raised hackles'. Here I am inclined to agree with Halliday (1993: 14) that, focused as Bernstein work was on the anatomy of social inequality, he ran head-on into the greatest disjunction of all: 'that a class-supported structure cannot admit the reality of social class'. After all, we who live in class-supported political economies – and this means *all* of us – do collude in the creation and maintenance of the range of classes through which the system sustains itself. Halliday pointed out further that the very notion of speech code is located in the difficult zone between system and instance. I would add also that the idea of code was problematic for another important reason: it went against the widely accepted notions of an individual's discursive freedom, which is dear to middle-class ideology. As Saussure and scholars before him claimed and, as contemporary linguists, philosophers, psychologists and educationists have seen no reason to doubt, the individual is master in matters of *parole*. And along came Bernstein suggesting that the individual's freedom is nothing but a mis-perception on our part; that between an individual's apparently freely produced utterances and the individual's competence over the system of language there lies social structure; that it is the experience of this social structure that functions as the most crucial factor in regulating what someone might choose to say, which part of the language system might be deployed by them, which exploitations will appear normal, what will be the topic of our horrified protest. Naturally our sense of individual freedom is threatened! As Mary Douglas commented (Douglas, 1972) Bernstein had the disconcerting habit of pulling the rug from underneath one's feet.

A biographical note

Basil Bernard Bernstein was born on 1 November 1924 in a migrant Jewish family and was brought up in the working-class ambience of the East End of London, though unlike many of his contemporaries he never wore his social class on his sleeve. After serving in the Second World War, he found a job as a resident worker in Stepney at the Bernhard Baron Settlement, a well known boy's club for disadvantaged Jewish children. He worked at this Settlement for three years and the experience stayed with him for life. It is here that Bernstein became deeply interested in the processes of cultural transmission. In 1947, the last year of his employment at the Settlement, Bernstein joined the London School of Economics for a degree in Sociology. His initial reaction to Sociology was not one of exhilaration, but he was an avid reader and read widely in both sociology and psychology. Unlike many of his contemporaries, Bernstein read generously and with a keen grasp of what was valuable in the literature. If the ideas he encountered interested him, he explored them further by making them work in his framework; denigrating authors on moral, political or personal grounds was not his style. Although at the completion of the Sociology degree, Bernstein enrolled for a higher degree he had to abandon it partly for lack of funds and partly for lack of interest. Having joined a teaching certificate course, he taught at Kingsway Day College as a student teacher and was awarded his post-graduate certificate in education in 1954, when he was appointed to teach at the City Day College. Here was further experience of working with students who neither suited the educational system nor did the system suit them. In the half a dozen years of teaching that Bernstein undertook there, he learned first hand the working of the educational system and found proof in his own innovative work and that of his colleagues of the possibility of successful opposition.

For a couple of years during 1960–61, Bernstein worked as a research assistant in the Department of Phonetics at University College London under Goldman-Eisler, with whom he did his doctoral research. He read Sapir, Whorf, Vygotsky (in translation by Luria), Cassirer and Hughlings-Jackson. Bernstein's work on codes began at about this time and some of the earlier papers included in his 1971 volume were written. Bernstein regarded this stage of life as a formative period in which he 'tried his hand' on ideas and explored areas which enriched his thinking.

In 1963 Bernstein was appointed as Senior Lecturer in the Sociology of education at the University of London Institute of Education, where he stayed until his death. In 1967 he became Professor in the Sociology of Education and at the same time Director of the Sociological Research Unit (SRU), where I had the privilege of working with him for some 18 months.

The high point of Bernstein's career was his appointment as The Karl Mannheim Professor of the Sociology of Education at London University. He retired in 1993 as an Emeritus Professor. Basil Bernstein died on 24 September 2000 a few weeks short of his 75th birthday.

Notes

1 This chapter is based on an expanded and revised version of three publications commissioned soon after Bernstein's death: (1) Understanding talk: directions from Bernstein's sociology. *International Journal of Social Research Methodology* (2001) 4,1: 5–9; (2) *Basil Bernstein: an exceptional. A Tribute to Basil Bernstein 1924–2000*, edited by S. Power, P. Eggleton, J. Brannen, L. Chisholm and J. Mace. London: Institute of Education; and (3) Basil Bernstein 1924–2000. *Functions of Language* (2001) 7,2: 173–201.

2 See for example Morais, Neves, Davies and Daniels (2001).

3 Work in this area is being carried out by several scholars under the guidance of J. Muller (see J. Muller et al. eds, 2004).

4 In fact from this point of view 'local pedagogy' is perhaps a misnomer: it is more appropriately called 'local learning', which may in some social locations contain within it early intimations of pedagogic discourse proper (See Cloran, 1999; Hasan, 2001a), but contains much else, without which any learning whether pedagogically generated or not is logically impossible. This is a vast area of enquiry which awaits further exploration.

5 There is of course Bourdieu (1991) but in my view (Hasan, 1999c) his understanding of language and particularly the relation of language and society is one-

sided and leaves much to be desired. Work awaits that would compare notions of rationality as developed by Bernstein and those developed by Habermas (1973).

6   In this context, one must remember the work of Pike, whose linguistic descriptions were oriented as early as the mid-1950s toward multimodality and referred to situation. Amongst the American anthropological linguists, Hymes and Gumperz were amongst the first to recognise the importance of context to language use.

7   This description applies to the model of discourse analysis proposed by Halliday and Hasan (1976; 1985 etc.).

8   In Martin's model the variant 'social contact' was used instead, to refer to degrees of affect; the basis of affect to the best of my understanding was not specified.

9   The reader familiar with the Marxist literature will recognise the importation of Marxist words and vocables here.

10 I am aware of the tendency in some readers to equate semiotic mediation with cultural mediation. In one sense, semiotic mediation presupposes culture and cannot occur except in the contexts of given cultures. Nonetheless to equate the two is to underplay the essential quality of semiotic mediation which calls for interaction with an acculturated other. This is where the importance of sociohistorically created and maintained human relations comes in: in this sense semiotic mediation is always refracted through these relations.

11 See for example Chapter 2 of Bernstein (2000).

12 See Chapters 4–6 in this volume for further discussion of this topic.

2 Society, language and mind: the metadialogism of Basil Bernstein's theory[1]

1 Introduction

How right was Hjelmslev to point to the invisibility of language! One is surrounded in life by language games of one kind or another, any one of which is capable of exciting a multitude of questions but in actual practice they hardly get asked seriously. Take, for example, one such simple game in my trade of linguistics, that of plucking from thin air any number of imaginary examples of saying. It is amazing how many questions can arise from reflection on this practice. To begin with: if what language does is to correspond to reality, as common wisdom has it, then what sort of reality is it to which language corresponds in such sayings? What are the words and vocables of our language to the world we live in and to the worlds we imagine? Why can we use language to construe imaginary situations and how do these relate to the real ones? Some of these questions I explored early in my apprenticeship (Hasan, 1964), little suspecting the depths of their complexity (Hasan, 1985a; 1995a). Then again, if the imaginable and the sayable hold to each other so closely, one has to ask: what kind of resource is language (Hasan, 1984a) that it can match the flights of human imagination? To do this successfully, its potential must be infinite, which in turn raises another question: if speakers have control over this inexhaustible potential – if they can say anything they like, whenever they like – on what basis do they decide to say one thing rather than another on specific occasions? The practice of producing imaginary examples is in agreement with the belief that speakers are free to say *anything* – and by the same token, *nothing*. After all, we know that unlike animal communication, human use of language is not reflex action. But while granting speakers such freedom of choice in speech shows due respect for their autonomy – for their power as unique individuals to engage dynamically in unpredictable linguistic acts – it is nonetheless a view challenged by the experience of real language use in everyday life. For in real life, more often than not, our sayings merge unremarked into the living of life: they do not draw attention to themselves, simply because, conforming largely to our expectations, they fail to surprise – which is surely one of the prime causes for the invisibility of language. So we need to ask how these shared expectations come about? Who are the sharers? What is the extent of their sharing? How do we specify the limits of our expectations about the sayable, especially when hardly any use of language is identical *word for word* to any other? Then, apart from these questions which arise simply from the practice of giving imaginary examples, there are the examples themselves, most of which in those days invoked the names of John and Mary, names whose popularity has declined only recently by the arrival of (corporate) corpora. Back in the exciting 1960s, though, one met John and Mary on a daily basis, both perpetually engaged in some process or other. So John was in London, or Mary in trouble; they ran and they laughed; they broke the window; opened the door; kissed and killed. And yet, despite this frenetic engagement in so many processes, surprisingly they had no *being* such as, for example, the imaginary Mr Pickwick or even Mr Percival the pelican, in Colin Thiele's *Storm Boy*. Could it be that if *almost anything* can be ascribed to a category, if a category has total freedom in being, saying and doing, then paradoxically such enjoyment of unhampered freedom would dissolve the category itself and deny it identity? Are categories of human agents identified by the nature of their practices, including discursive ones? If so, what are the principles for the distribution of classes of discursive practices to categories of social agents? What has language to do with this distribution and what has such distribution to do with the nature of language?

I am sure that at least some of these questions must have engaged some linguists in the early 1960s, but I must admit in honesty that for my part I did not enter the field of linguistics burning with a desire to pursue them: much worse, like most other speakers, I was in fact oblivious of most. It was my good fortune and my privilege to be present in London during the mid-late 1960s when the dialogue took place between Basil Bernstein's Sociolinguistic Research Unit and Michael Halliday's Communication Research Centre[2]. Thanks to the sociological and linguistic insights provided by these seminal scholars, the nature of language – its potential and its power, its relation to society – began to be relatively more visible to me: questions began to take shape, perhaps got better defined over the years. A general problem fascinated me as I witnessed the metadialogue between the disciplines of sociology and linguistics: what does it take for theories to engage in dialogue? Could any linguistic theory dialogue with Bernstein's sociology? Could any sociology dialogue with Halliday's linguistics? If not, how do we explain this selectivity? This paper is intended as a continuation of reflection on this general problem. I want to ask next in Section 2, what makes it possible for theories to engage in metadialogue? I will then, in Section 3, highlight those design features of Bernstein's theory of the social, which create a space for theories of language and of mind to take a dialogic turn with his theory of the social. But obviously, the continuation of a dialogue requires more than the granting of a turn. So a second question to be raised is that of compatibility: to explore this issue, I will draw attention briefly to a compatible theory of the mind (for discussion, see Hasan, 1995b; Halliday, 1995a; Painter, 1996; Matthiessen, 1993; 1997). This will prepare the ground for examining, in Section 4, what features of the systemic functional linguistic theory enable it to *maintain* a dialogue with Bernstein's theory of the social.

So first, what is metadialogue?

2 On metadialogue

By metadialogue I do not mean to refer to the processes that characterise the iterative cycle of a theory's trial and modification, even though this typically does bring different theories in contact: this is after all the normal mode for the development of a theory still in operation, i.e. not defunct. All living knowledge changes and theories as instances of such knowledge do so too. The use of the middle voice (cf. Halliday, 1994a) here to describe this state of affairs might appear to bestow autonomy on knowledge and theory. So I add immediately that whatever the potential of existing knowledge to guide its own development as in Popper's (1979a) views on World 3, the ultimate active agency for the development of knowledge is indisputably always human. This has implications: for example, the processes of a theory's trial and modification must occur in a human – i.e. social – environment and this invariably means in the context of other (like-)discourses. It so happens, then, that in the process of the modification/development of a theory, its proponents can and often do insert into it concepts that have become familiar to them from other (like-)theories[3]. This simple conceptual adaptation, not to call it appropriation, is as necessary for the life of a theory as breathing for the human organism. In this sense, there are no *absolutely original* theories: rather, absolute originality and human practice are antithetical concepts.

The partial interpenetration of one theory by another in the above manner – call it intertextuality if you like – is, then, not what I mean by metadialogue. A metadialogue, much like an object dialogue, presupposes reciprocity[4] of a positive kind and a necessary condition for theories to engage in dialogue is a reciprocity of concern. To my mind, this does not reside in simply sharing the same problematic, otherwise all linguistic theories would be in dialogue, which is patently not the case. What I mean by this expression is that one theory's mode of addressing its problematic – the conceptual syntax (cf. Bernstein, 1996) in terms of which its theoretical goal is interpreted – complements the conceptual syntax of the other reciprocating theories[5]. I suggest that for this to come about, a theory must conceptualise its object of study as something that in Bernstein's (1977, 1990, 1996 etc.) terms is 'weakly classified'. That is to say, the central problematic is not something enclosed within a sharply defined, impermeable boundary which keeps the impurities and dangers of the outside world at bay. Rather, the object of study is open to external phenomena, which though different in kind from it, still form the context for its existence and act as a resource for its subsistence. Seen thus, theories appear to approximate to two general kinds: (a) *endotropic*; and (b) *exotropic*. Let me elaborate on these terms.

Endotropic theories are centred onto their own object of study, isolating it from all else. The phenomena they attempt to describe are viewed as if they were self-generating, self-fertilising, self-renewing; they are, thus, autogamous with respect to their central problematic. An example would be the conceptualisation of language in Chomskian linguistics, where language as a mental organ is simply a variety of biological phenomena having no connection with anything else, not even biological evolution (Pinker, 1994). This type of strong classification appears to give the object of study an autonomy, which is sometimes interpreted as the source of a theory's strength. Due to its autogenetic conceptualisation of its object of study, the theory can – perhaps, rather shortsightedly – congratulate itself on being free from the intellectual imperialism of other universes of experience explored by other theories, other disciplines: in the eyes of the theory, these have nothing to contribute to the understandings it seeks. However, viewing the central problematic from the perspective of its relevance to human life, this isolation is an impoverishment, not a strength. It is not surprising that the central problematic in endotropic theories appears static and accounts of its history pose problems.

By contrast, an exotropic theory is not confined within the bounds of its object of study. Rather, it is cosmoramic, typically embedding its central problematic in a context, where the processes of its maintenance and change originate in its interaction with other universes of experience. From this point of view, the object of study in an exotropic theory is a component of what Lemke (1984; 1993) calls a 'dynamic open system', changing and being changed by its reciprocal engagement with the other components of the larger system. History is clearly not a problem for such theories: the genesis, fertilisation and change in the object of study are accounted for to a large extent by reference to its relation with the different components of the dynamic open system. As a consequence of this constant exchange, the object of study in exotropic theories appears to be always on the move, presenting a different facet with every change in the observer's vantage point. This apparent absence of a still centre is sometimes misinterpreted as absence of order. Such theories are likely to be viewed with suspicion where there is a low tolerance for attending to a number of simultaneously operating forces which interact with each other. However, it is quite obviously this type of theory that has a greater potential for engaging in metadialogue. I say 'quite obviously' because the exotropic theory is inherently relational: its problematic is at the centre of different kinds of processes and there thus exists a greater chance for reciprocal engagement amongst them.

It is not that the exotropic theory is a theory of everything; rather, it places its object of study in relation to phenomena which though relevant are by definition *different in kind*. Thus if the object of study is, say, human consciousness, then from the point of view of an exotropic theory the relevant phenomena could be human biology, including both evolution and development, the latter implying interaction with environment thus leading to consideration of semiotic exchange, which in turn would implicate social relations amongst interactants[6] and so on. It would be a mistake to think of such a theory of human consciousness as a theory of human evolution, of semiotic interaction or of social positioning[7] and the rest. Rather, it is simply *open* to, i.e. allows dialogue with, theories of these phenomena provided their mode of engaging with their problematic is not in contradiction to its own. At the same time, it has to be emphasised that precisely because it reaches out into so many different domains, the threat of chaos for an exotropic theory is very real and at least two conditions must be met if the theory is to avoid confusion. First, to contain the potential for chaos, the theory's languages of description (see Bernstein, 1996: 134ff on languages of description and the relations amongst them) need to be well-developed. Secondly, because it connects with phenomena of different kinds, its conceptual syntax must not only be able to distinguish amongst the different kinds of phenomena it invokes by way of description/explanation, but it must also be able to specify the relations between these. I suggest that of these two conditions the first is necessary but not sufficient to enable a theory to engage in metadialogue: we do know endotropic theories with highly developed languages of description, which by definition possess no potential for metadialogism. Hjelmslev's (1961) elaborate and elegant linguistic theory comes to mind as a possible example[8]. The necessary and sufficient condition for an exotropic theory's potential for metadialogism is met when its conceptual syntax is so developed that not only does the theory distinguish the different orders of relevant phenomena but it is also able to specify the nature of this relevance. I suggest that it is in specifying this relevance that the theory actually creates locations, interstices, openings – call it what you will – which form the logical points for the theory to address the other components of the dynamic open system.

Hopefully this brief discussion has outlined at least in general terms the conditions for metadialogism in a theory. In the next section, I examine the instantiation of these general principles in Bernstein's theory pointing out its exotropism and identifying the points where it reaches out to other relevant phenomena.

3 Coding orientation: an exotropic theory of the social

It is not necessary for my purposes to present Bernstein's theory of coding orientation in much detail. An account of the elements of the theory can be found in Bernstein's own writings (see especially 1971, 1973, 1977, 1990, 1996), together with comments, critiques and interpretations by others (e.g., Atkinson, 1985, Sadovnik, 1995). I will begin with a brief reading of Figure 2.1.

Figure 2.1 relies heavily on Bernstein[9] and is offered as a representation of my interpretation of just those aspects of code theory which I consider relevant to the present discourse. As the left margin indicates, the figure consists of four specific though related components, three of which have the shape of a hexagon. Each component of the figure represents a different order of abstraction and each displays a number of terms. These terms are in relation to others within the components, while each component bears relation to the others. Together they formulaically sketch specific areas of human experience (for details, see below), brought together in Bernstein's exotropic theory. The theory is able to achieve this end, because it has a strong conceptual syntax as well as a developed language of description, which allows a revealing 'translation' of the entities and relations of one order of abstraction into those of another.

The first component concerns the critical relevant elements in the socio-economic organisation of human conditions of living in society. Labour, as Marx remarked, is an inherent property of human beings, but the way that *division of labour* works out in specific societies is quite another thing: it is not labour as one pleases but typically labour as one must. From the patterns of the division of labour flows the distribution of the wealth of the community, both its *material* and *semiotic capital*. In every society so far known to humans, (the so-called communist regimes not excepted), the distribution of capital has been unequal: some members have greater access to material and/or semiotic capital than others. These relations provide the basis for the formation of social groups, here called *social class*. The position of a social class in community and its access to the community's wealth are homologous. This discussion is not intended as an exhaustive summary account of social organisation; it highlights simply the salient aspects of communal conditions of social life relevant to the discussion of coding orientation.

The nucleus of the coding orientation theory is captured in the relations within and between components (2) and (3). Bernstein (1990: 13) introduces the central problematic of the theory – its 'enduring focus' – as follows:

> In terms of the particular problems of the relationship between class and the process of its natural reproduction, ... what has to be shown is how class regulation of the distribution of power and of principles of control generates, distributes, reproduces, and legitimates dominant and dominated principles, regulating the relationships within and between social groups and so forms of consciousness.

Language, Society and Consciousness

<1>
```
                    division of labour
                   ↙              ↘
         distribution of        distribution of
         material capital       esoteric knowledge
                ↓                      ↓
         access to material     access to symbolic
             resources              resources
                   ↘              ↙
                    class relations
```

<2>
```
                    class relations
                   ↙      ↕      ↘
        distribution of power    principles of control
                ↕                        ↕
           classification              framing
                   ↘                 ↙
                    coding orientations
```

- -

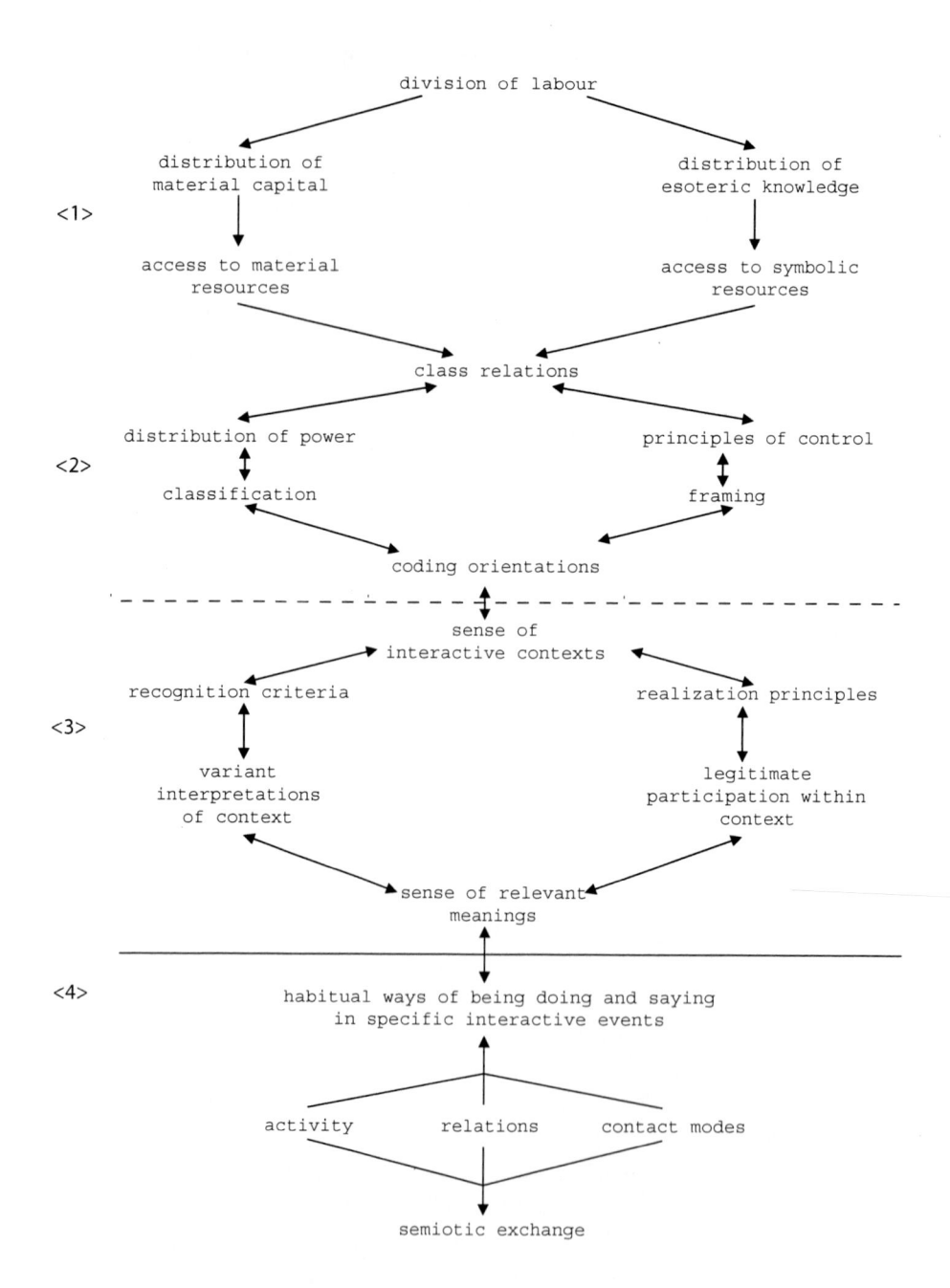

<3>
```
                          sense of
                      interactive contexts
                     ↙          ↕         ↘
        recognition criteria        realization principles
                ↕                            ↕
             variant                      legitimate
         interpretations              participation within
            of context                      context
                     ↘                    ↙
                       sense of relevant
                          meanings
```

<4>
```
            habitual ways of being doing and saying
                 in specific interactive events
                ↙           ↓           ↘
           activity      relations     contact modes
                ↘           ↓           ↙
                    semiotic exchange
```

Figure 2.1 Class, codes and communication: an interpretation (revised 2004)

The relation between social class and the 'distribution of power' as well as 'principles of control' is one of 'realisation', as this term is used in systemic functional linguistics (henceforth SFL): social class is as social class does. The double-headed arrow throughout Figure 2.1 represents a dialectic relation, whereby the distribution of power and principles of control are activated by social class and, their specific 'modality', in turn, construes the identity/value of the social class. The diverging slanting lines from *class relation* to power and control indicate that class relations are realisationally related to both. The double-headed straight arrow between distribution of power and classification represents the realisational dialectic between the distribution of power and *classification* as also between principles of control and *framing*. Classification is the process whereby the categories of human experience of whatever kind are defined. Almost as a metaphor for its exotropic nature, the expressions 'relations within' and 'relations to' have a theoretical significance in Bernstein's theory. A category's relation *to* another is a critical factor in establishing its identity. This is reminiscent of Saussure's ideas on the identity and value of language signs. This attaches significance to the concept of 'boundaries' between categories. To maintain classification, the boundaries between categories must be maintained; they must be kept apart. Control is exerted in the maintenance of boundaries of categories through the process of framing. What is not shown in this diagram is the fact that Bernstein built variation within the workings of classification and framing by recognising a continuum from 'strong' to 'weak': thus either or both could be strong or weak. As Bernstein put it, where classification is strong, there 'things must be kept apart'. Where it is weak, they must be brought together. A brief characterisation of the relations between these terms in Bernstein's own words is as follows:

> Classification refers to the degree of insulation between categories of discourse, agents, practices, contexts, and provides recognition rules for both transmitters and acquirers for the degree for the degree of specialisation of their texts.
>
> Framing refers to the controls on selection, sequencing, pacing, and criterial rules of the ... communicative relationship between transmitters/acquirer(s) and provides the realisation rules for the production of their text. (Bernstein, 1990: 24)
>
> power always operates on the relations *between* categories. The focus of power ... is on the relations *between* and, in this way, power establishes legitimate relations of order. Control, on the other hand, ... establishes legitimate forms of communication appropriate to different categories. Control carries the boundary relations of power and socialises individuals into these relationships ... To summarise ... control establishes legitimate communications, and power establishes legitimate relations between categories. (Bernstein, 1996: 19)

The specific modalities of classification and framing – the calibrated patterns of their strength and weakness – underlie the various *coding orientations*, the last term within hexagon (2). Here at this level of abstraction Bernstein's exotropic theory, brings social order face to face with the politico-economic organisation of society.

If hexagon (2) represents the logical connections between class relations and coding orientations, hexagon (3) explicates the underlying syntax of 'social reproduction', answering the classical question of sociology: 'how does the outside become the inside and how does the inside reveal itself and shape the outside?' (Bernstein, 1987: 563). Here the individual's sociologically necessary experience of coding orientations during the course of the living of life assumes a crucial status: the different social practices in which an individual engages, together with the orders of relevance that experience presents as legitimate during these engagements, create in the individual a *sense of interactive contexts*, that is to say, the experience of living within the speech fellowship (Firth, 1957b) internalises the communal designs for being, doing and saying. In the study of contexts of living, there have generally been two tendencies: one might recognise a 'field' *a la* Bourdieu, which is obviously a large scale concept requiring refinement, or one might talk about relevant context pertinent to specific classes of social practice, something like Malinowski's 'context of situation' developed considerably by Firth and further refined in SFL with special reference to discourse. Bernstein, while recognising the value of both orders of description, takes a different direction, since it is this direction which enables him to show what is meant by the outside becoming the inside and revealing itself in forms of social practice to shape the outside. The individual's sense of interactive contexts is realisationally related to context *recognition criteria* and to *realisation principles* for legitimate practice within given contexts, 'specialised interactional practices' to use Bernstein's terms (1990: 15). Summing up, in the words of Bernstein:

> Recognition rules create the means of distinguishing between and so recognising the speciality that constitutes the context, and realisation rules regulate the creation and production of specialised relationships internal to that context. (Bernstein, 1990: 15)

The specificity of a context – its value and identity – is not given by its own internal structure. Rather, it is a function of relations between contexts[10]. Because the recognition criteria for contexts and the principles for legitimate practices within contexts are acquired in the experience of class regulated coding orientations, one implicit claim in component (3) is that subject's recognition criteria and their realisation principles will vary in keeping with their social positioning. A subject's recognition criteria and realisation principles will be manifested by *variant context interpretations* and *variant participation practices*. The subject's *sense of relevant meanings* 'is' in fact her/his relation to contexts: what a context is the context for, what will count as legitimate behaviour in that context. This sense of relevant meanings is realised in subjects' *habitual ways of being, doing and saying* in specific interactive events.

Before we leave component (3), let me say a word about the dotted line between (2) and (3). This line indicates a qualitative relation between the two components. Bernstein (1990: 17, Fig. 1.3) refers to the area covered by (2) as that which offers an analysis of 'intersubjective (class) relations' and to that covered by (3) as the 'intrasubjective (class) relations' (see discussion of Figure 1.1, Chapter 1). Because of the dialectic of realisation between coding orientations and the subjects' sense of interactive contexts, the concept of coding orientation faces in two directions: coding orientation expressed as the sense of interactive contexts (and their associated practices) is an intrasubjective phenomenon, but its etiology is not entirely intrasubjective. Coding orientations have value only within the environment of intersubjective class relations which regulate the practices of power and control, manifested by the various modalities of classification and framing. Coding orientation is thus a complex concept, having both a social and a psychological dimension. This brings to mind Vygotsky who describes the essential nature of the development of higher mental function as follows:

> Every function in the child's cultural development appears twice: first, on the social level, and later, on the individual level; first, *between* people (*inter-psychologically*), and then *inside* the child (intra-psychologically) ... All the higher functions originate as actual relations between human individuals. (Vygotsky, 1878: 57; emphasis original)

So it is at the logical conjunction of (2) and (3) – coding orientations and the sense of interactive contexts and practices – that Bernstein's theory opens up the possibility of dialogue with a compatible theory of human consciousness. Such a theory is that of Vygotsky's and, more recently, Edelman's (1992) and Dennett's (1991), which explicitly recognise the participation of culture in the formation of consciousness:

> The underlying neural architecture is far from being a *tabula rasa* or a lank slate at birth, ... but it is nevertheless a medium in which structures get built as a function of the brain's interaction with the world. And it is these built structures ... that explain cognitive functioning. (Dennett, 1991: 259)

Unlike Gazzaniga (1993), these scholars do not see consciousness as entirely 'hard wired' – the work of nature alone. Dennett (ibid.) for example borrows Dawkins's (1982) concept of 'meme' as significant cultural ideas, describing the mind as a nest for memes, or as a meme-making machine. But in this account, the relation of individuals to memes as cultural forces is both accidental and unproblematic: memes appear to free-float in the atmosphere and individuals somehow happen to incorporate them. To think of 'interaction with the world' in such general terms is one thing; recognising the specific role of social interaction in the fashioning of individual consciousness is another. Vygotsky took a decisive step in accepting the importance of the 'biogenetic' foundation and at the same time making a more specific claim about the 'sociogenesis' of human mind by introducing the notion of semiotic mediation. It is Vygotsky's concept of semiotically mediated minds that brings his theory close to the 'theoretical question of classical sociology: how does the outside become the inside, and how does the inside reveal itself and shape the outside?' that has engaged Bernstein (1987a: 563) throughout his scholarly career. The acceptance of the view that the cultural reappears in the individual creates a common ground for dialogue between the two theories. However, by ignoring systematic variation in semiotic mediation, Vygotsky tells a simple story. For Bernstein the story is more complex: the varying social relations of class through the varied functioning of their distributive rules ultimately become differentiated internal realities of the differently positioned subjects, shaping differently their notions of the significant and the relevant. *The child* is no longer generic: differently positioned children become the concern; the adult agent of semiotic mediation is no longer culturally neutral: s/he is the voice of a distinct ideology (Hasan, 1989; 1992a; 1992b; 1993; Hasan and Cloran, 1990; Cloran, 1994; this volume; Williams, 1995; this volume). Focusing simultaneously on local and official pedagogic practices, Bernstein's theorisation of 'the social construction of pedagogic discourse' (1990: 165–218) problematises the modifier *higher* in Vygotsky's 'higher mental processes': the essentially hierarchic nature of all knowledge, the positive and high valuation of official knowledge and the logical relations between local and official knowledge, all invite us to question the treatment of the latter as the reference point for measuring the attainment of higher mental functions (consider in this light Luria's explanation (1976) of the logical abilities of the Uzbeks). If between language and its use lies social structure, as code theory maintains, then semiotic mediation is not a neutral and innocent process; it is sociologically sensitive to social phenomena and creates socially differentiated individual minds (Hasan, 1992/2005; 1995b).

Although Vygotsky's theory of the mind ignores social variation as a significant feature of its central explanatory concept, I believe it is still compatible with Bernstein's framework: unlike others such as Popper (1979a) or Gazzaniga (1993) it does not deny the importance of the social; quite the contrary – from the point of view of code theory, the Vygotskian explanation simply does not go far enough. Equally, from the psychologist's point of view, Bernstein's interests bypass the biological altogether. But while the role of the biogenetic in the making of human consciousness does not attract his attention, there is no reason to imagine that such exploration would be incompatible with his theory. It seems important to emphasise that neither theory is a theory of every phenomenon it needs to invoke; instead, the depth of the analysis of such phenomena is governed strictly by the need to explain the central problematic. Both theories have however proved productive because they are open: they allow metadialogue.

I have claimed that the relations within and between the terms of components (2) and (3) form the nucleus of Bernstein's coding orientation theory, because it is here that society and the individual are brought in a dialectical relation through the workings of semiotic exchanges which are themselves sensitive to and which sensitise the interactants to the social foundations of their own social positioning:

> What we are asking ... is how the distribution of power and the principles of control are transformed, at the level of the subject, into different, invidiously related, organising principles, in such a way as both to position subjects and to create the possibility of change in such positioning. The broad answer given by this thesis is that class relations generate, distribute, reproduce, and legitimate distinctive forms of communication, which transmit dominant and dominated codes, and that subjects are differentially positioned by these codes in the process of acquiring them. 'Positioning' is used here to refer to the establishing of a specific relation to other subjects and to the creating of specific relationships within subjects... from this point of view, codes are culturally determined positioning devices ... Ideology is constituted through and in such positioning .. ideology inheres in and regulates *modes of relation*. Ideology is not so much a content as a mode of relation for the realising of contents. (Bernstein, 1990: 13)

Let me turn now to the relations between (3) and (4), as these, particularly the latter, are central to any description of semiotic exchanges. I see this component as closely related to the theory of discourse. This in turn implies relation to the theory of language. Section 4 focuses, then, on these points.

4 A linguistic theory for metadialogue

The basis of communication according to Bernstein is in the intrasubject class relations represented in component (3); but these are themselves a manifestation of coding orientations, which are in the final analysis regulated by social class as the relations of (2) show. Bernstein (1990, see especially Figure 1.3 p. 17) has called this part – i.e. components (2–3) – of the communicative apparatus 'invisible' and that represented in component (4), 'visible'. The solid line between components (1–3) and (4) thus represents the relation of system to instance: if the 'specialised interactive practice' is what is produced in the specific interactive event, then the abstract syntax which generates it is in components (2–3) whose material base is represented in component (1). Component

(4) is, then, the area where actual semiotic exchanges occur; it is here that we come face to face with instances of coding orientations. In this revised version of Figure 2.1, the analysis of context for specific interactive event has been further elaborated into three vectors which are invariably relevant to any instance of social practice, irrespective of whether the activity is semiotic or material; these are (i) the nature of 'activity', i.e., what the interacting subjects are engaged in performing; (ii) the nature of human 'relations', i.e., how the interactants are socially located *vis a vis* each other, irrespective of whether they are co-present or not; and (iii) their 'modes' of contact, i.e., whether the contact is face to face, mediated via some other channel of communication and so on. In Bernstein's theory, the term 'semiotic exchange' – and even 'text' – refers to *all* social practice, not *just* the linguistic ones. However, in the following discussion I shall restrict myself to the linguistic modality alone[11], for reasons which will hopefully become obvious.

One way or another language features in most instances of semiotic exchanges and any viable theory that invokes the concept of semiotic exchange in the resolution of its central problematic creates a space where a compatible linguistic theory might dialogue with it. Code theory creates an explicit location at this point between (3) and (4) where the social and the linguistic can engage with each other. Further, if it is the case that Bernstein's theory makes explicit contact with language in the context of semiotic exchange, then it logically encounters language as instance. This is important for at least three reasons. First, because of the dialectic relation between system and instance (Halliday, 1992/2003), the discourse of instance will carry implications for what specific properties must be conceptualised as inherent to the system, the details of which will depend on what the theory expects the instances to achieve. This in turn furnishes a principle of selectivity whereby only certain linguistic theories may prove capable of maintaining a dialogue with Bernstein's theory of the social. For example, theories which do not recognise text as a linguistic unit, would have little of value to contribute to the working of coding orientation. Second, instances of semiotic exchange and social context are inseparable: a compatible linguistic theory will need to specify systematic, non-*ad hoc* means for relating the linguistic instance to its social context in such a way that it does not negate the relevant elements of the code theory. Finally, since underlying the specialised interactive practices is the subject's sense of relevant meanings and, since it is from the point of view of the relevant meanings that the instances have to be examined, then a linguistic theory will need to have a view of semantics that goes beyond meaning as the representation of 'real reality': real reality is by definition invariable and coding orientations are inherently claims about socially significant variation. I will discuss these closely interrelated issues, but first a comment on the explicit point of contact between code theory and language.

It may be true to say that the code theory comes in contact with language explicitly in component (4) where it finds language mediating as the 'final' act of realisation with a long social history behind it; but if so the significance of the explicit and the implicit in this context needs to be taken into account. If it is supposed that this is the only location for a theory of language to take its turn in its metadialogue with Bernstein's theory of the social, this would be tantamount to putting the world before the word: it would be claiming that the specifically human construal of the social is capable of manifesting itself without language. In my view, this is a misrecognition of the situation[12]. Consider for example components (1–3) in Figure 2.1. If the claim is correct that access to knowledge is a form of capital – symbolic or intellectual capital – then the basis of class relations is already 'coloured' by language: a certain way of examining reality, explaining its parameters and using it as a resource for the exploitation of labour is associated with a group of persons who are socially positioned thus and thus and who by their activities perpetuate the 'invidious' class relations[13]. Intentionality or absence of it is beside the point: in fact the less the intention counts, the more potent the ideology. Further, it is well-nigh impossible to think of classification and/or framing without implicating language[14]. In this sense, Vygotsky certainly had a point: the internalisation of the external requires semiotic mediation and in this semiotic mediation he was right to draw attention to the abstract tool of language as the most pervasive one for manipulating the internalisation of the external. If this is true, then language is already there from the very beginning. I conclude that code theory and semiotic theory – especially linguistic theory – are closely intertwined: code theory attempts to explain the social; the social is inherently (also) linguistic just as the linguistic is itself grounded in the social. We know no language outside human community and we know no human community without language: the Trappist monks are able to give value to absence of language – to silence – precisely because language has presence in the affairs of humans[15]. So then the explicitness of contact between language and society at the conjunction of component (3) and (4) notwithstanding, one must conclude that code theory implicitly brings in language from the very beginning precisely because its explanation of its central problematic invokes semiotic exchange as a crucial concept and the linguistic aspects of interaction are a variety of semiosis. Further what the code theory requires of the instances of semiotic exchange is un-doable without the complicity of language. Moreover, in order for anyone to maintain that instances of language use can achieve what the theory suggests, one must have a particular conception of what the system of language is like. At this point, we have returned full circle to the issues that arise from encountering language as instance, which in my view call for deducing the properties of the system from the characteristics assigned to the instance. First then, what is language as instance expected to achieve in the code theory? To quote Bernstein (1971: 144):

> the particular forms of social relation act selectively upon what is said, when it is said, and how it is said ... [they] can generate very different speech systems or codes ... [which] create for their speakers different orders of relevance and relation. The experience of the speakers may then be transformed by what is made significant and relevant by different speech systems. As the child ... learns specific speech codes which regulate his verbal acts, he learns the requirement of his social structure. The experience of the child is transformed by the learning generated by his own, apparently, voluntary acts of speech ... From this point of view, every time the child speaks or listens, the social structure is reinforced in him and his social identity shaped. The social structure becomes the child's psychological reality through the shapings of his acts of speech.

The experience of participating in exchanges regulated by specific coding orientations translates itself into the subject's psychological reality: the experience of the instance creates the subject's system for linguistic interaction. Codes thus acquire the status of 'culturally determined positioning devices'. 'Ideology is constituted through and in such positioning'; from this perspective, 'ideology is not so much a content as a mode of relation for the realising of contents' (Bernstein, 1990: 13–14). If we adopt the position of the systemic functional linguist, a language instance makes sense by its relation to language system (Halliday, 1992/2003; 1996a; Hasan, 1995a; Matthiessen, 1995). This is not to claim that the system is a constraint or that it fully predicts all features of the performance; it is simply to claim that no matter what the feature of performance, its interpretation invokes the listener's sense of a system. The system is the reference point both for interpreting features that are predicted by the system and for those that are not. As Firth remarked, novelty implies departure from the expected. That an instance of language is related in this way to language system is significant: what the instance is capable of doing must in large part be what the system has built into it as its design features. If instance is able to contribute to the construal of ideology, then this is largely because the system acts as the resource for this. So what does this say about the conceptualisation of language as system for a theory of language which is compatible with code theory?

Elsewhere (Hasan, 1996c), I have drawn attention to the fact that protolanguage is innocent of ideology. This is because, having no level of lexicogrammar, it is a simple pairing of meaning and sound – a relation that comes very close to meaning by naming or by correspondence to external phenomena. I suggest that (Hasan, 1996c: 104–5):

> what makes it possible for human languages to be ideologically saturated is the plasticity of relations between the levels of content and expression ... this plasticity of relations appears impossible where meaning is simply a function of 'correspondence' between a signifier and some 'bit' of extralinguistic

reality ... To be complicit in the creation and maintenance of ideology ... the system of language ... must on the one hand have some resource for construing meanings, and, on the other, ... the meanings construed by language must relate to an extralinguistic reality capable of being contested in some respect or other. In other words there has to exist the possibility of variaiton in how people use the lexicogrammatical resources of their language to construe meanings and there has to exist the possibility of variation in using the semantic potential of language to construe contexts.

Not only does language have to be a multiple coding system where meaning is realised as wording and wording by sound, but at the same time the social context itself is realisationally implicated. It is important to appreciate both the elements of necessity and of freedom in these statements. A subject's linguistic meanings are necessarily construed by the resources of the lexicogrammatical system, but within lexicogrammar itself there is no necessity for the use of this resource rather than some other; such necessity is activated by the meanings to be meant (Hasan, 1995a) and this implies meanings relevant to some occasion of talk. When we claim that speakers can say anything anywhere they like, all we mean is that the resources of the system of wording are not inaccessible to them. However, the orders of meaning that a subject is predisposed to – the semantic aspects of his linguistic *habitus* (Bourdieu, 1991) – are not specified by the grammar: they are code regulated and it is these meanings in the context of that person's positioning that activate the speaker's use of wordings:

> if code selects and integrates relevant meanings, then code presupposes a concept of irrelevant and illegitimate meanings; ... if code selects forms of realisation, then code presupposes a concept of inappropriate or illegitimate forms of realisation; ... if code regulates evoking contexts then again this implies a concept of inappropriate, illegitimate contexts. (Bernstein, 1990: 14)

The necessity is in the relation *between* levels, not *within* a specific level. Speakers' meanings do not pour out independent of their context; their grammar does not unroll independent of their meanings, notwithstanding unexpected occurrences and dynamic moves befitting our unique (dare I say middle-class) individualities. This suggests a systematic relation between these levels – in SFL this relation is known as realisation (Halliday, 1992; 1996a; Hasan, 1995a; 1996; 2000a; Matthiessen, 1995). I believe that the realisational relation between these three strata of linguistic description is a dialectic: thus, for example, context activates meanings and meanings construe context; meanings activate grammar and grammar construes meanings – a principle necessary for showing that 'decontextualised' language is language encapsulating its context, not language independent of social context (see Cloran, 1994; 1999). The realisation relation between phonology and these three strata is criterially different: it is one of conventional association, what Saussure described as the arbitrary bond between the signifier and the signified. Clearly Saussure's notion of language was not presented as multistratal.

If we are to account for how the instance is able to achieve what it is hypothesised to achieve in code theory, it becomes obvious that linguistic theory must be conceptualised as comprising not just the three traditionally recognised strata – semantics, grammar and phonology – but also the stratum of context. Without this, the predisposition towards certain orders of meaning would remain a mystery; and *parole* would appear wilful and disorderly as it did to Saussure. This requirement itself acts as a principle of selectivity on the possibility of metadialogue: to dialogue with Bernstein's theory of the social, the theory of language must extend to and include the concept of social context. Not only this, but it would appear that we have to go further.

A theory for which context is simply a feature of the instance, having no relation to the system itself, poses a serious problem: how/why does a displaced instance of language use construe its own context, to the extent that it does? SFL theory answers this by postulating the principle of metafunctionality: according to Halliday's famous remark, the structure of language is as it is because of the functions language is made to serve in the life of communities. The metafunctional principle resonates through the levels of context to that of wording, as shown in Table 2.1.

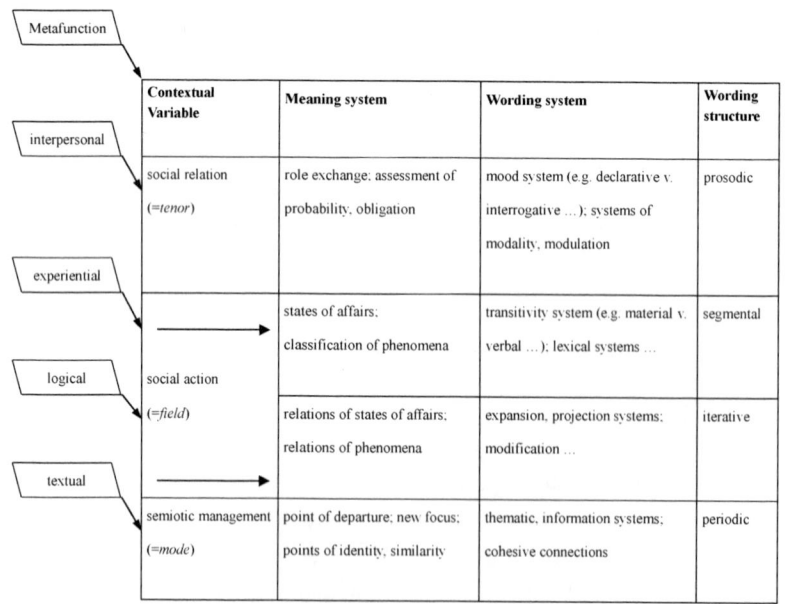

Metafunction	Contextual Variable	Meaning system	Wording system	Wording structure
interpersonal	social relation (=*tenor*)	role exchange; assessment of probability, obligation	mood system (e.g. declarative v. interrogative ...); systems of modality, modulation	prosodic
experiential	social action (=*field*)	states of affairs; classification of phenomena	transitivity system (e.g. material v. verbal ...); lexical systems ...	segmental
logical		relations of states of affairs; relations of phenomena	expansion, projection systems; modification ...	iterative
textual	semiotic management (=*mode*)	point of departure; new focus; points of identity, similarity	thematic, information systems; cohesive connections	periodic

Table 2:1 Functionality in language use and language system

Language in use is able to construe certain aspects of social context, namely:

(i) the field of discourse, i.e., the activity from the point of view of language;

(ii) the tenor of discourse, i.e., the human relations seen linguistically; and

(iii) the mode of contact, i.e., the channel for language transmission. If so, this is because the resources of the system are enabling in precisely these ways and they are so because these aspects of context invariably make a difference to how language will be used.

It is interesting to compare the SFL notion of context of situation with the account of the social underlying Bernstein's view of semiotic exchange as represented in Figure 2.1. Would a compatible theory of language need to develop its view of context so as to encompass the social phenomena as code theory sees it? This is not a question that can be answered within the scope of this chapter, but it is certainly one that SFL linguists might devote attention to. On the one hand in SFL theory today at least two rather different views of context are to be found – that proposed by Martin (1985a; 1992) and that proposed by Halliday (1967; 1991 and elsewhere). Neither of these fully captures the perspective on context found in code theory. On the other hand, there is a view abroad that a social semiotic theory of language such as SFL must necessarily be a theory of culture. I am not convinced that is a tenable position without certain necessary extensions to the model of context.

Returning to context and language use, I am tempted to comment that different coding orientations 'fragment' what from some point of view may be seen as the same register; an example is the register of joint book reading by mothers and children, which is fragmented by systematic variation in coding orientation (Williams, 1999). The variation that Williams is able to demonstrate, which in its broad outlines agrees with the findings of Hasan, Hasan and Cloran, and Cloran (see references above), are variations in coding orientations. This detailed analysis of semantic variation has been made possible by the development of semantic networks as a tool, which is itself a natural extension of the model. There still remains the question whether semantic variation tells the whole story of variation in coding orientations. As Figure 2.1 shows, codes regulate relevant meanings and their organisation within the context of specialised interactive practices relevant to distinct contexts. This implies that a full-scale linguistic study of variation in coding orientation must analyse not simply the elements of messages but also the deployment of messages in texts, probing into variation in textual organisation. Cloran's (1994) development of the notion of rhetorical unit is significant in this respect as it moves from the message to larger constituents of text structure.

Although SFL linguistics needs to develop in specific respects – this as I remarked above is a condition of a living theory – what appears important here is the fact that the concept of language put forward by it is highly compatible with that of code theory. If a theory is known by the descriptions it can generate (Bernstein, 1996), then certainly SFL is a theory, which by virtue of its conceptualisation of the relations of context, meaning and grammar can be interpreted as a social semiotic theory of language.

Notes

1. My thanks are due to Michael Halliday with whom I have discussed issues included in this paper. The responsibility for the views expressed is entirely mine.
2. Later subsumed in the Department of Linguistics, with Halliday as its first Chair and Head.
3. In doing this, they may use the same labels or different ones, they may acknowledge their debt to the other theory or not. All permutations are generously exemplified in the practices of the field of linguistics.
4. Reciprocity does not entail consensus at every point (see discussion of Vygotsky's theory in Section 3) – simply a readiness to grant an opening to a potential interactant. Thus a fight, as opposed to indifference toward a potential interactant, is reciprocal; and although non-consensual, a fight is a dialogue, unlike silence. Nor does reciprocity demand identity of attitude from the interactants. In *agreeing to disagree*, the conflictual reciprocal activity of disagreeing necessarily implies opposing perspectives, which are themselves embedded within the consensual activity of agreeing. This explains perhaps why *agreeing to disagree* is fraught with tension.
5. This relation of complementation between theories is of course variable, occupying a region of delicate tension between, at one end, the appropriation of the concerns of other related disciplines, and at the other, a complete indifference to their existence. The former end ceases to be complementation; it turns into domination. The latter invites solipsism where the concerns of other disciplines cease to exist. A dialogue simply on terms of one interactant is in fact a monologue: it has complete unity of perspective.
6. Vygotsky provides a good example of an exotropic theory of human consciousness; though he does not relate it to the social variable (Hasan, 1992/2005; 1995b), there is no element in the theory to the best of my knowledge which would prevent the consideration of this variable in the context of his approach to mental development. See comments below (Section 3).
7. If the theory of human consciousness attempted to be a theory of genetics, of evolution, of development, of exchange and of social relation, it would cease to be an exotropic theory, whose nature it is to occupy the ambiguous ground between appropriation and indifference (see footnote 5). A theory that claims to explain/describe everything is simply an appropriating, dominating discourse, which treats all else as subservient to its own central problematic. In short, it represents a failure of imagination.
8. The arguments for this claim are lengthy (for some hints see Hasan, 1995a). Very briefly, although Hjelmslev attempts to reach out to phenomena other than language by invoking the notions of purport and connotative semiotic, the relation between language and other phenomena is far from reciprocal in his theory: rather for Hjelmslev everything is subjugated to language. Thus language does not enter here in a dialectic with the social conditions of human existence, changing and being changed by it; language simply construes our sense of the social. This may in large measure be true: most human beings come to know their world the way they do mainly through the processes of language, but this emphatically does not mean that the social can be reduced simply to the linguistic any

more than it is true (cf Bourdieu, 1991; Atkinson, 1985) that the linguistic can be reduced simply to the social (see Hasan, 2000a).

9   I have naturally drawn on my understanding of Bernstein's writing to an extent that specific acknowledgment is problematic. However, see in particular Bernstein (1990: 13–62; 165–218; and 1996: 17–34 and 91–144. I see my Figure 2.1 as directly derived from some of Bernstein's own e.g. his Figures 1.1 and 1.3 (see 1990: 13 and 17 respectively). However, it is important to emphasise that I alone am responsible for the interpretation of the theory and of the figures, without any implication of Bernstein's concurrence with my reading.

10 This is reminiscent of the paradigmatic principle of description favoured by Saussure and developed by Hjelmslev, Firth (1957b) and Halliday (1996a).

11 Even if I were able to talk sensibly of all semiotic modalities, the constraint of space engineered by the publishing trade is severe. My position is that semiotics is *not* coterminous with linguistics. The theory of language is not a theory of everything one can mean in any semiotic modality; it is simply a theory of language as meaning potential: that is complex enough. I would prefer the theory to be exotropic; this means making connections with the relevant environment with the specific purpose of providing insightful descriptions of language as meaning potential. Being exotropic, it would enable a principled invoking of other elements of the dynamic open system and their description to the extent that they are criterial for throwing light on the nature of language as meaning potential. I would argue that if a linguistic theory tries to be a theory of everything, it will be a theory of nothing! From this point of view the fervour of many colleagues to describe the entire culture through linguistics appears misplaced. All socially sensitive linguistics can do is to make explicit the part played by language in the creation, maintenance and change of (certain aspects) of culture and this again is complex enough to keep linguists occupied for decades.

12 See my critique of Bourdieu on language in the affairs of humanity (Hasan 1992/2005). A similar view, presumably historically traceable to Marx's entirely untenable theory of language as superstructure, is taken by Atkinson (1985) when he declares that language is simply an epiphenomenon.

13 The discourse of class is so unwelcome perhaps because as Halliday (1992/2003) points out at some level of consciousness we know that we are all implicated in its creation and its maintenance; perhaps it needs to be pointed out that by the same logic we are also implicated in change. Our reflections and actions 'can have a crucial role in creating tomorrow's optimism in the context of today's pessimism' (Bernstein, 1996: 5).

14 I am not concerned here with the arbitrary valuation of certain categories of language (see debate in Hasan in 2000a). If arbitrary is in opposition to "logical", I question the possibility of arriving at a logic that is in the end not sociological. But this sociologic is not arbitrary where material and intellectual capital is conscripted in the exploitation of labour: it becomes "the" logical way of maintaining control. Language is not cosmetics; it is lethal. If you use it to maintain hegemony, you destroy the other; if you use it to destroy hegemony, you become self-critical.

15 This implies that sociology without an understanding of language tells an incoherent story while linguistics without an understanding of the social is built on sand.

3 Speech genre, semiotic mediation and the development of higher mental functions

1 Introduction

Much can be said in favour of technical terminology, but a title such as mine cries out for translation into 'ordinary, simple' language. So translated, it declares a concern with the role of everyday talk in creating human minds. As a topic, it is perhaps not very highly favoured. As a matter of fact, for most self-respecting linguists, if talk appears at all important it is usually because it can reveal something about language; further, in most scientific linguistic models, it is far more acceptable to argue that mind makes language than that language makes mind. I hope the development of this paper will reveal that an exploration of the relations between the three concepts invoked in the title – 'speech genre', 'semiotic mediation' and 'the development of higher mental functions' – is relevant to some of the foundational issues in linguistic theory. As a first step in the development of this theme, it will be necessary to present an interpretation of the three terms, which are reminders of the intense intellectual activity that characterised the early days of Russian revolution. The term 'speech genre' is used here to invoke the views of Bakhtin (Vološinov, 1986; Todorov, 1984; Bakhtin, 1984; 1986), while 'semiotic mediation' and 'higher mental functions' form important elements in the psychological theory of Vygotsky, whose ambition was to 'create a Capital for psychology using Marx's method' (Lee, 1987: 96).

In order to examine the relevance of these notions to each other and the relevance of the entire debate to the foundations of linguistic theory, the paper is designed to have three movements. The first movement will consist of Sections

2 and 3. In Section 2, I will be concerned with interpreting the two Vygotskian terms. In Section 3, I will point out some residual problems in his conceptualisation of the relation between the two. It has been suggested (Wertsch, 1985c) that Bakhtin's views on speech genre and allied concepts can resolve some of these problems. The second movement of the paper will consist of Section 4, where I will discuss Bakhtin's views in order to ask if they can resolve the residual problems in Vygotsky's approach. In the discussion of Bakhtin's views, it will be seen by those who are familiar with the systemic functional (henceforth SF) model, that there exist many points of similarities between the two approaches. Of course, there are also significant differences. Although from time to time, I shall refer to some aspect of SF linguistics, it is not the aim of my presentation to compare the two approaches, which is a much bigger enterprise and must await another occasion. I shall however draw attention to theoretical problems in the Bakhtinian approach which, in my view, prevent it in its present state, from contributing to Vygotsky's theory. The third and final movement of the paper will identify those features that will be needed in a linguistic theory capable of contributing positively to a clarification of the issues raised in Section 3 with reference to semiotic mediation and the genesis of higher mental functions. This discussion will raise some foundational issues of linguistic theory. Halliday has always maintained (1973; 1974) that the sharp distinction between the intraorganic and interorganic basis of language is intellectually incoherent. The Vygotsky-Luria approach to the genesis of mind in society provides the kind of detailed argument needed to support Halliday's rejection of the above distinction. The other widely accepted antinomy in linguistic theory – Saussure's uncompromising separation of *langue* and *parole* – is seriously questioned by the SF model's view of functionality (Halliday, 1975; Halliday and Hasan, 1989; Martin, 1991; Hasan, 1995a). In general, the Bakhtin-Vološinov perspective on the nature of language supports the SF stance. A functional linguistic theory of the type that SF aspires to be is truly a transdisciplinary theory, which is located at the intersection of semiology, sociology and psychology. The concluding section argues that in the nexus of Vygotsky-Luria, Bakhtin-Vološinov and Halliday, the element lacking is a theory of society such as perhaps that of Bernstein who is able to provide principles for linking semiotic variation with the material social conditions of human existence.

2 Semiotic mediation and higher mental functions

In presenting an interpretation of the two Vygotskian concepts, much of what I say is naturally derivative: for an understanding of these concepts, I have relied on the translated works of Vygotsky (1962; 1978) and Luria (1976) and on the recent growing literature in social psychology (e.g., Mertz and

Parmentier, 1985; Hickman, 1987); I am particularly indebted to Wertsch (1981; 1985a; 1985b; 1985c; 1990; and Wertsch and Hickman, 1987), whose work has made a significant contribution to the revived interest in Vygotsky's ideas. It is important to add though that I alone am responsible for the views expressed here.

To appreciate the importance of the concept of semiotic mediation, we need to understand its role in Vygotsky's theory of psychological development. Some of the important aspects of this theory are highlighted by Wertsch (1990: 64):

> Vygotsky's theoretical vision can be outlined in terms of three general themes that run through his writings:
>
> 1 a reliance on a genetic or developmental method;
> 2 the claim that higher (i.e. uniquely human) mental functioning in the individual has its origins in social activity;
> 3 the claim that a defining property of human mental action is its mediation by tools ('technical tools') and signs ('psychological tools').

By 'genetic' Vygotsky did not mean something inherited in some specific form once for all as in the phrase 'genetic defect'; rather he relates the term to 'genesis' in the sense of origin or growth. Reliance on a genetic, ie. developmental, method in explaining the nature of some phenomenon implies an enquiry into how and why this phenomenon develops the way it does: in the celebrated words of Blonsky 'behaviour can be understood only as the history of behaviour'(quoted in Vygotsky, 1978: 65). According to Vygotsky, mental functioning was not an exception to this principle: if we wish to understand the nature of such higher mental functions as generalisation, abstraction, or the formation of scientific concepts, then we need to understand the trajectory of their development. Within the confines of this paper it is not possible to do justice to all elements of Vygotsky's genetic theory of human mental functioning which covers a wide area (Lee, 1987; Wertsch, 1985b; 1990). I shall restrict myself here simply to the ontogenetic perspective, asking what the role of semiotic mediation is in the development of higher mental functions in an individual.

From this point of view, Vygotsky identified two 'lines' of development – the first, a natural line of development and the second, a social line. Corresponding to these lines of development are two categories of mental functioning: the elementary and the higher. Elementary mental functioning develops along the natural line, while for the development of higher mental functioning, the social line is considered necessary. The two lines are not unrelated; in fact, in human beings mental development results from 'the interweaving of these two lines' (Vygotsky, 1978: 46). By granting the natural line of development a definite status in human psychological development, Vygotsky side-stepped the sterile polarisation whereby either mental functions are biologically given or they are not. Elementary mental functioning, made possible due to the natural line and forming the biogenetic foundation for mental development, is necessary but not sufficient to account for those qualities of mental functioning which are distinctively human. Vygotsky maintained that the uniquely human, higher mental functioning develops along the social line; its roots are to be found in the social nature of human existence. The association between the social line and the higher functioning in Vygotsky's framework is indissoluble. In fact, Wertsch (1985b: 24) points out that 'Vygotsky ... sometimes used the term "cultural" (versus "natural") in place of "higher" (versus "elementary") when describing "mental function"'. Human and social are, thus, closely related terms in Vygotsky's writing, as they are in Marx's work. But what did Vygotsky mean by higher mental functioning?

In general terms, the distinction between elementary and higher mental functioning is qualitative. Four closely related distinguishing criteria for this kind of mental functions are enumerated by Wertsch (1985b: 25):

> (1) the shift of control from environment to the individual, that is the emergence of voluntary regulation; (2) the emergence of conscious realisation of mental processes; (3) the social origins and the social nature of higher mental functions; (4) the use of sign to mediate higher mental functions.

That the four attributes are logically related can be seen from Vygotsky's discussion of the development of memory as an example of a mental function. As an elementary mental function, where it is activated by the natural line of development, memory is:

> characterised by the non-mediated impression of materials, by the retention of actual experiences as the basis of mnemonic (memory) traces ... it arises out of the direct influence of external stimuli ... the entire process is characterised by a quality of immediacy. (Vygotsky, 1978: 38)

By contrast, even in communities lacking advanced technology, human memory may not depend simply on the 'retention of actual experience'. It may be activated by some mediating device such as the use of 'notched sticks and knots'. This particular instance of a mediating device is fairly simple, but the fact of mediation itself has deep implications. According to Vygotsky (1978: 51):

> When a human being ties a knot in her handkerchief as a reminder, she is in essence, constructing the process of memorizing by forcing an external object to remind her of something; she transforms remembering into an external activity ... In the elementary form something is remembered; in the higher form humans remember something.

And although in its potential for mediation, this particular mediating 'tool' is itself quite limited by comparison with, say, writing, its use still shows that human beings in even the most primitive conditions will:

> go beyond the limits of the psychological functions given to them by nature and proceed to a *new culturally-elaborated organisation* of their behaviour ... The central characteristic of elementary functions is that they are totally and directly determined by stimulation from the environment. For higher functions, the central feature is *self-generated stimulation,* that is, the creation and *use of artificial stimuli which become the immediate cause* of behaviour. (Vygotsky, 1978: 39; emphasis added)

The externalisation or voluntary regulation of a mental function is closely related to the possibility of its conscious mental realisation: a process that can be voluntarily regulated can become the object of reflection, of 'intellectualisation'. To take once again the case of memory as a higher mental function, 'to recall means to think' (Vygotsky, 1978: 51). Translating directly from his *Thinking and Speech: psychological investigations* Wertsch (1985b: 26) quotes Vygotsky's view on higher psychological functions:

> [their] basic and distinguishing features are intellectualisation and mastery, that is, conscious realisation and voluntariness.

> At the centre of development during the school age is the transition from the lower functions of attention and memory to higher functions of voluntary attention and logical memory ... the intellectualisation of functions and their mastery represent two moments of one and the same process – the transition to higher psychological functions. We master a function to the degree that it is intellectualised. The voluntariness in the activity of a function is always the other side of its conscious realisation. To say that memory is intellectualised in school is exactly the same as to say that voluntary recall emerges; to say that attention becomes voluntary in school age is exactly the same as saying ... that it depends more and more on thought, that is, on intellect.

Free regulation and conscious realisation require the 'use of artificial stimuli': only 'artificial stimuli' are by definition under the control of the user and can be subjected to intellectualisation and auto-stimulation. But the artificial nature of the stimuli highlights the sociocultural mediation of higher mental functioning. To go back to the knot in the handkerchief, here memory is freely regulated and cannot be attributed to the 'retention' of actual subjective experience. Both the mediating means and the kind of higher mental function mediated by it implicate contexts of human communal living. In explaining the development of such mediated mental acts, it becomes necessary to refer to the sociocultural dimension. If mediated mental functions are by definition higher mental functions, then also by definition, higher mental functions are 'sociogenetic'. Just as free regulation and conscious realisation of mental functions presuppose mediation by artificial stimuli, so also the fact of mediation presupposes sociogenesis: sociogenesis is a necessary attribute of mediated mental functions.

It is difficult to dissociate Vygotsky's notion of 'mediation' from that of 'tools'. In Vygotsky's theory, the tool was transformed from being a simple adjunct of activity to an active principle, contributing to its mental management. He recognised two basic types of mediation on the basis of the kind of tools that served as the means for mediation: mediation by means of 'technological, concrete tools' and mediation by means of 'psychological, abstract tools'. Both sorts of tools lead to a higher level of activity than could be achieved by pursuing simply the natural line of development: the technological tool primarily influences via its effect on the sphere of physical activities; the abstract, via that of mental activities:

> the psychological tool alters the entire flow and structure of mental functions. It does this by determining the structure of a new instrumental act just as a technical tool alters the process of a natural adaptation by determining the form of labour operation. (Vygotsky, 1981: 137)

From this point of view, 'semiotic mediation' could be paraphrased as 'mediation by means of semiosis'; semiosis – the use of sign systems – thus becomes an abstract tool, acting on the mental make-up of the user (Vygotsky, 1978: 40):

> The use of signs leads humans to a specific structure of behaviour that breaks away from biological development and creates new forms of a culturally-based psychological process.

Although Vygotsky was keenly aware of the contribution of other semiotic modalities to higher mental development, semiotic mediation became almost synonymous in his writing with 'mediation by means of semiosis-by-language'. This 'privileging of language', as the situation would be described in the pseudo-revolutionary intellectual discourses of the last few decades, arose from Vygotsky's conviction that amongst the various semiotic modalities, language alone *maximises* the attributes essential for the development of higher mental functions. For example, to go back to memory again, language as an abstract tool permits the free regulation of memory to the greatest degree: this cannot be seriously doubted if we consider the role of writing in this context. But writing is not language's only contribution to the regulation of memory: the conscious realisation of memory is maximally assisted by the internalising nature of language. The use of the sign system 'is a means of internal activity aimed at mastering oneself; the sign is internally oriented' (Vygotsky, 1978: 55). As a mediating means language is far more supple, far more pervasive than any other variety of 'abstract tool'. Amongst all the semiotic systems operative in any community, language alone has the potential of representing the reality that is lived by the members of the community in their everyday existence. That language is active in the creation, maintenance and alteration of all human social institutions is simply one aspect of this potential. The metasemiotic nature of language is another very important factor in its efficacy. The metasemiotic nature of language explains why as an apprentice to culture, the child's access to other abstract tools current in the community depends to such a very large extent on verbal semiosis. This importance of verbal semiosis is not negated even though there certainly exist cultures (John, 1972; Dumont, 1972; Phillips, 1972) where verbal semiosis is sparingly used in actual direct instruction. It is not surprising, then, that verbal interaction, which is itself an expression of social relations, assumes a crucial role in Vygotsky's theory of the development of higher mental functions: by its very nature, everyday talk becomes an active force in the process of acculturation. To quote Vygotsky (1981: 163) once again:

> Any function in the child's cultural (ie higher) development appears twice, or on two planes. First, it appears on the social plane, and then on the psychological plane. First, it appears between people as an interpsychological category, and then within the child as an intra-psychological category. This is equally true with regard to voluntary attention, logical memory, the formation of concepts, and the development of volition. We may consider this position as a law in the full sense of the word, but it goes without saying that internalisation transforms the process itself and changes its structure and functions. Social relations or relations among people genetically underlie all higher functions and their relationships.

This brief discussion leaves out many important elements of Vygotsky's theory, presenting merely the gist of the relation between semiotic mediation and the development of higher mental functions. Before turning to a discussion of the problems in this view, it may be useful to draw attention to some implications that follow from an acceptance of the relationship between these two pivotal concepts.

First, if in the development of higher mental functions, the interpsychological categories precede the intrapsychological ones and if consciousness is another name for higher mental functions, then from a genetic point of view 'the social dimension of consciousness is primary in time and fact. The individual dimension is derivative and secondary' (Vygotsky quoted in Wertsch, 1990: 66). These sentiments are in close harmony with the famous claim made by Marx: 'it is not the consciousness of men that determines their being, but on the contrary their social being that determines their consciousness' (quoted in McLellan, 1975: 40). It is certainly true that individuals have (degrees of) freedom and capacity to control their environment, that they are autonomous in a manner of speaking, so far as their internal psychological processes are concerned. But in the last analysis what actually enables this psychological autonomy, this freedom from dependence on purely external stimuli, is their consciousness in the sense of higher mental functioning and we have seen that the genesis of this consciousness is not to be discovered by looking simply inside the brains of an *isolated* human organism; these origins lie in the external processes of social life characterised by interpersonal interaction. This leads Luria to suggest that 'the Cartesian notion of the primacy of self-consciousness', which assigns a secondary rank to 'the other' must be rejected. The growth of specifically human mental acts presupposes an *other*. To quote Luria (1976: 19):

> The perception of oneself results from the clear perception of others and the processes of self-perception are shaped through social activity, which presupposes collaboration with others and an analysis of their behavioural patterns.

It follows that an individual who has already attained such consciousness should not be confused with the biological human organism. The same point is made very effectively by Vološinov (1986: 34) in the following extract:

> A rigorous distinction should always be made between the concept of the individual as natural specimen without reference to the social world (i.e., the individual as object of the biologist's knowledge and study) and the concept of individuality which has the status of an ideological semiotic superstructure over the natural individual and which, therefore, is a social concept. These two meanings of the word 'individual' (the natural specimen and the person) are commonly confused, with the result that the arguments of most philosophers and psychologists constantly exhibit *quaternio terminorum*: now one concept is in force, now the other takes its place.

The second implication of accepting Vygotsky's views follows partly from these comments. Vygotsky emphasised sociogenesis, but, in doing so, he did not abandon the contribution of the biogenetic foundation in human development. Thus his approach neatly side-stepped the pointless opposition between nature and nurture, individual and collectivity, between the biological and the social. What he postulated in place of these oppositions was a dynamic theory in which the biological and the social are united by a co-genetic logic (Markova, 1990: 14). It is a theory that explains change both in the society and the individual by virtue of the part one plays in the evolution of the other (Vygotsky, 1978: 60):

> The dialectical approach [to the psychological development of humans] while admitting the influence of nature on man, asserts that man, in turn, affects nature and creates through his changes in nature new natural conditions for his existence.

Finally, Vygotsky emphasised the 'empowering' nature of higher mental functions, how they contribute to the evolution of humanity. In this argument, the theme of control over the natural conditions of existence is important as revealed in the following comments (Vygotsky, 1978: 51):

> It may be said that the basic characteristic of human behaviour in general is that humans personally influence their relations with the environment and through that environment personally change their behaviour, subjugating it to their control.

Vygotsky suggests that this empowering human characteristic which represents 'the qualitative leap from animal to human psychology' (Vygotsky, 1978: 57), is at the basis of human evolution (Vygotsky, 1978: 60):

> It is my belief, based upon a dialectical materialist approach to the analysis of human history, that human behaviour differs qualitatively from animal behaviour to the same extent that the adaptability and historical development of humans differs from the adaptability and development of animals. The psychological development of humans is part of the general historical development of our species and must be so understood.

If it is true that what is essentially human in human beings is created by their sociocultural history, it is also equally true that human beings are not simply made by their history; they themselves make their own sociocultural history. We have already seen that this human characteristic of psychological autonomy, which enables control over the environment, itself derives from the internalisation and intellectualisation of those mental activities which are sociogenetic, nurtured largely by semiotic mediation. And when the logical connections that link the arguments in Vygotsky's model are taken into account, he can be heard as suggesting that human evolution and semiotic mediation are related phenomena. These Vygotskian statements foreshadow the idea of 'exo-somatic evolution' which was to be put forward years later by such famous scholars as Popper, Medawar and Eccles, though in a qualitatively different framework where the role assigned to language makes the framework problematic. It is not necessary to elaborate on this point here; it is sufficient simply to note that an acceptance of Vygotsky's views on semiotic mediation and the genesis of higher mental functions implies an acceptance of the role of languaging in human evolution.

3   The problems of semiotic mediation

The above account shows that in its broad outlines Vygotsky's theory of the genesis of mind in society is a powerful means for explaining some of the most serious issues in human and social development. But while in general terms, the role of semiotic mediation in the development of specifically human mental functions as outlined by Vygotsky appears convincing, some serious problems surface as soon as we begin to consider particular cases of higher mental functioning. For example, take the role of semiotic mediation in the development of such higher mental functions as those of categorisation, generalisation, abstract thinking, syllogistic reasoning and so on. These mental functions are so often cited as instances of higher mental functioning that it seems reasonable to think of them as paradigm cases. But if so, then it would seem that we need to be more precise in talking about semiotic mediation: verbal semiosis may be a necessary condition for the development of such functions, but it is not just any kind of verbal semiosis that will necessarily lead to their emergence. Here the discussion of Luria's research in Uzbekistan (Luria, 1976) is particularly relevant. Luria found that different groups of the Uzbek community functioned significantly differently with respect to these specific mental functions, the variation correlating with the absence or presence of 'formal' schooling which subsumes contact with literacy. According to Luria (1976: 48–9):

> Categorical classification involves complex verbal and logical thinking that exploits language's capacity for formulating abstractions and generalisations for picking out attributes, and subsuming objects within a general category ... 'categorical' thinking is usually quite flexible; subjects readily shift from one attribute to another and construct suitable categories. They classify objects by substance (animals, flowers, tools), materials (wood, metal, glass), size (large, small), and colour (light, dark), or other property. The ability to move freely, to shift from one category to another, is one of the chief characteristics of 'abstract thinking' or the 'categorical behaviour' essential to it.

There was no evidence of 'categorical, abstract thinking' amongst those of Luria's Uzbeki subjects who did not have the benefit of formal education and who were functionally illiterate. Luria (1976: 77) comments:

> Every attempt to suggest the possibility of categorical grouping met with protest ... They either disregarded generic terms or *considered them irrelevant*, in no way essential to the business of classification. *Clearly, different psychological processes determined their manner of grouping which hinged on concrete situational, thinking rather than abstract operations which entail the generalizing function of language.* (emphasis added)

The subjects showed a marked tendency for 'concrete situational thinking'. This raises several disturbing questions. First, is 'concrete situational thinking' as much an instance of higher mental functioning as is 'categorical abstract thinking'? If it is not, then, for very obvious reasons, *higher* in the expressions 'higher mental functions' or 'higher consciousness' cannot be equated with *specifically human*, unless the quality of humanity is defined by the ability to think in a particular way. This 'elitist' position is obviously far from the intentions of a psychological theory which would emulate Marx's Capital! If, on the other hand, *both* types of thinking are seen as cases of higher mental functioning, then the two different sorts of psychological processes (if indeed they are two qualitatively different processes) – the one underlying 'concrete situational thinking' and the other underlying 'categorical abstract thinking' – are being hierarchised; the latter kind of thinking is obviously treated as more desirable than the former. I shall not question at this point the rationale for this valuation, but note what is implied with regard to semiotic mediation in accepting the need for the hierarchisation of the forms of higher consciousness.

First, both the more 'valued' and the less 'valued' forms of thinking would have to be accepted as being sociogenetic. Note Luria's unequivocal claim (1976: 79):

> concrete thinking is neither innate nor genetically [i.e., by heredity] determined. It results from illiteracy and the rudimentary types of activity that have prevailed in these [i.e., the unschooled Uzbeki] subjects' daily experience.

Clearly 'concrete situational thinking' is not just an instance of the natural line of development and if its emergence is sociogenetic, then it must be – at least in part – semiotically mediated. This leads to the second implication: the more highly valued 'categorical, abstract thinking' cannot be attributed to 'semiotic mediation' *per se*: rather, its emergence must be attributed to *particular forms* of 'semiotic mediation' – to particular 'fashions of speaking', to use the Whorfian phrase, or to distinct 'coding orientations' as Bernstein would say. These fashions of speaking or coding orientations would be the ones where speakers 'exploit language's capacity' for mediating precisely these sorts of functions and this may be because speakers consider such functions relevant. Third, it follows that there is variation in semiotic mediation. This, in turn, raises two further questions: one, how should that particular variety of semiotic mediation be characterised which underlies the genesis of abstract categorical thinking – what are the internal linguistic attributes of such semiotic mediation? And two, what, if any, is the relation between the material conditions of social existence and variant forms of semiotic mediation? In other words, what underlies the appearance of the internal linguistic attributes that characterise the variant forms of semiotic mediation?

Rational thinking which is said to be based on inference and deduction is also taken to be a higher mental function. Similar problems are encountered when we examine the development of deduction and inference, the classic case of which is said to be syllogistic reasoning. Here is how Luria (1976: 101) describes the nature and function of syllogistic reasoning:

> One of the objective devices that arises in the process of the development of cognitive activity is the syllogism – a set of individual judgments of varying degrees of generality in certain objectively necessary relationship to one another. Two sentences, of which the first ('precious metals do not rust') is in the nature of a general judgment ... while the second ('gold is a precious metal') is a particular proposition, are not perceived by the developed consciousness as two isolated phrases in juxtaposition. A human being whose theoretical thought processes are well developed will perceive these as a completed logical relation implying the conclusion, 'Hence gold does not rust'. This conclusion does not require any personal experience; it is arrived at through a syllogism created objectively by historical experience. A considerable proportion of our intellectual operations involve such verbal and logical systems; they comprise the basic network of codes along which the connections in discursive human thought are channelled.

Luria's subjects were 'exposed' to two categories of syllogisms: syllogisms the content of whose propositions was taken from the subjects' immediate practical experience and those where the content of the propositions was divorced from such experience. The results of this experiment correlated with very finely graded social attributes in the subjects (see discussion Luria, 1976: 113ff). Reporting on one set of results, this is what Luria (1976: 114) says:

> For the non-literate subjects, the process of reasoning and deduction associated with immediate experience follow well-known rules. These subjects can make excellent judgments about facts of direct concern to them and draw all the implied conclusions, displaying no deviation from the 'rules' and revealing much worldly intelligence. The picture changes, however, just as soon as they have to change to a system of theoretical thinking – in this instance, making syllogistic inferences.

Luria cites three factors in explanation of this finding which shows that the non-literate subjects have limited 'capability for theoretical verbal-logical thinking':

[1] mistrust of an initial premise that does not reproduce personal experience ... [2] the unacceptability of the premise as universal ... [3] a consequence of the second ... [the] ready disintegration of the syllogism into three independent and isolated particular propositions with no unified logic and thus no access for thought to be channelled within this system.

It is obvious from the discussion that deduction and inference from the second category of syllogisms – whose propositions are not embedded in the practical experience of the subjects – are thought of as indicative of even *higher* mental functioning. But how do we interpret the inability to relate to any premise that does not 'reproduce personal experience'? What underlies the failure to recognise 'universal facts'? What sort of consciousness do these processes indicate? Could these questions be answered satisfactorily if the defining attributes of that variety of semiotic mediation are identified which underlies the emergence of the valued forms of higher consciousness?

Any attempt to answer the last question turns us inevitably to Vygotsky's views about language. And although it is important to discuss both his views on the system of language as the potential and on that variety of language which selectively actualises precisely that part of the potential which underlies the emergence of the valued forms of higher consciousness, I shall argue that for Vygotsky's framework it is language use that is absolutely crucial. This is because in Vygotsky's approach, interpersonal languaging – social speech – forms the fulcrum of semiotic mediation. To begin again by quoting Wertsch (1985c: 53ff), who identifies two apparently 'opposing tendencies' recognised by Vygotsky as basic to 'the organisation and use of human language':

> On the one hand, language has *the potential to be used* in abstract, decontextualised reflection. This led to the study of concept development, categorisation, and syllogistic and scientific reasoning, and to a focus on the decontextualisation of the 'meaning' of words. On the other hand, there is a side of linguistic organisation rooted in contextualisation ... Vygotsky considered the ways in which the structure and interpretation of utterances depend on their relationships with their extralinguistic and intralinguistic contexts ... this aspect provides the foundation for an account of inner speech and the notion of 'sense'. (emphasis added)

In discussing Luria's research, we have already seen that what is at issue is not 'the *potential* of language to be used in abstract decontextualised reflection'. Rather, the valued higher mental functions develop only if this potential is *actualised* in verbal interaction. It is, of course, necessary to demonstrate that such a potential inheres in language as a system, but this demonstration cannot explain the genesis of the actualisation of any part of the postulated potential. The crucial question is when and why does it appear relevant to speakers to 'exploit language's capacity for formulating abstractions', for categorisation, syllogistic reasoning and so on. One must mention here Vygotsky's repeated references to pedagogic discourse as one type which could be perhaps viewed as maximising the possibility of developing the higher mental functions in the pupils. But against this claim, we must also remember that the actual mental development of pupils, in this sense of mental development, is subjected to evaluation; that the rate of educational success for pupils, according to repeated findings, is not the same; and that variation in levels of educational success correlates typically with the pupils' social positioning. Why should this be so? And what aspect of semiotic mediation in pedagogical contexts could be cited as a possible explanation for this differential outcome in mediating the development of mental functions?

In the literature, a distinction is made between the concrete context-bound use of a word to refer to something that is physically present to the senses, as a child might say *horse* when a horse is present. This is using the linguistic sign as a 'signal'. This contrasts with the use of the linguistic sign – the word – as a 'symbol'. The word is said to be used as a symbol when the meaning structure underlying the linguistic sign is so well internalised by the speaker that s/he can use it to recount, to pretend, to hypothesise – in short, s/he can use it 'in displacement'. It seems to me that four closely related points need to be made here.

First, the move from signal to symbol is a significant step in learning how to mean (Halliday, 1975; Painter, 1984), as it turns the sign into a creative 'tool' rather than one which is constrained to 'correspond' to or 'reproduce' a concrete reality existing in the here and now of the speech situation. Thus the identification of this feature as important in the development of mental functions appears fully justified.

Secondly, the emergence of this stage in the child is a classic example of the 'interweaving of the two lines' of development (Vygotsky, 1978: 46); the internalisation of the specific meaning structure of the word in the child relies no less on sociogenetic foundations (Malinowski, 1923; 1935a; Painter, 1984) than on the biogenetic ones. The specific character of the meaning structure internalised by the child is a major step in the creation of that intersubjectivity which makes communication possible between the child and her 'speech fellowship' (Firth, 1950/1957: 186ff).

Thirdly, by the same tokens, to speak as a normal adult is to have arrived at this stage of using the linguistic sign as a symbol. No matter how far a particular group of Uzbeki fell from the standards of 'abstract thinking' as defined in Vygotsky and Luria, their use of the linguistic sign could not have been a signalling use; it *had* to be a symbolic use in the definition of the term offered here, for such use is a *condition* of all adult communication. Any examination of language use even in the most primitive communities, irrespective of how primitiveness is defined, would reveal that the sign system of language is used symbolically by normal adults everywhere. It is on this basis that 'displacement' has been recognised as an inherent quality of the linguistic sign system.

Finally, it follows from this that if all language use presupposes 'decontextualisation' of word meaning – as this situation is sometimes described – then 'the decontextualisation of the 'meaning' of words' *by itself* cannot be responsible for the emergence of the *valued* higher mental functions, repeatedly mentioned by Vygotsky-Luria. Since the quality of 'decontextualisation' of word meaning is ubiquitous, this quality must underly both the less and the more valued higher mental functions. The Uzbekis used language signs as symbols, no less than did the famous scholars of their time who used the Uzbekis as subjects in their experiments. As Wertsch (1985c: 55) points out:

> the Vygotsky-Luria argument ... concerns the *process of reflecting on decontextualised word meanings*. The 'latent or potential content of speech' (Sapir, 1921: 15) is a necessary but not a sufficient condition for this form of abstract reasoning to appear. (emphasis added)

The 'process of reflecting on decontextualised meanings' has to be seen as *a specific kind of social process*, a particular kind of language use, as for example in certain cases of classroom discourse (Butt, 1989; 1985/1989), or in explaining the steps in problem solving. The results of my research in Australia (Hasan, 1989; 1991; 1992a; 1992b; Hasan and Cloran, 1990) indicate that engagement in this kind of language use is the prerogative of a speaker's privileged socioeconomic position in the wider community. In the context of such complex communities as the capitalist democracies of today, it becomes problematic then to even relate this social process directly to the 'sociocultural history' of a speech community as a whole. What would it mean to say that the sociocultural history of the working class mother in Australia is less evolved than that of the middle class mother? That this explains why the working class mother's higher mental functions, her consciousness, are less evolved by comparison with the the middle class mother? It seems to me that the Vygotsky-Luria framework for the sociogenesis of mind calls not only for a more sophisticated theory of language as suggested by Wertsch; it also needs a sophisticated theory of social organisation.

Suppose it is granted that what underlies the genesis of higher mental functions is reflection on decontextualised meanings of the verbal sign and the readiness to use language to construe experience which is not simply remote from one's actual personal experience but might even run counter to it. Even so, it is clear that what we are talking about here are *qualities of language use*; these qualities are, as it were, permitted – not demanded – by the inherent nature of the language system. So, in identifying the 'desirable' variety of semiotic mediation by languaging, it is not a question of what there is in the system of language, but rather of how that system is deployed. And we may formulate a general rule here: how a linguistic system is deployed is never a simple question of manner; it is, rather, a question of the social situatedness of speakers and their speech process – who is talking to whom and why. In order to be able to intellectualise the social situatedness of the varieties of verbal interaction, what we need is a theory of social context. In Vygotsky's work this necessary element of the theory of language is virtually absent. Certainly Vygotsky does mention some specific contexts of talk, eg. the pedagogic contexts of the classroom, peer interaction, adult-child interaction, but the attributes of the talk situation identified by him will be found to be incidental to his concern with whatever specific kind of mental activity is under discussion. Moreover as Wertsch points out Vygotsky's analysis of language focused most often on the unit word and its characteristics. The natural unit for semiotic mediation is not the word, but text/discourse – language operational in a social context (Halliday and Hasan, 1989).

Obviously the analysis of forms of semiotic mediation would stand to gain if the concepts of text and context in relation to each other can be utilised. It is to achieve this goal that Wertsch turns to Bakhtin's notion of 'speech genre'.

4 Speech genre and semiotic mediation

Over the last two decades, Bakhtin's views on the nature of language have attracted a good deal of attention. Particularly his concepts of 'speech genre', 'intertextuality', 'social language' and 'ideologically based communication' are cited as making a much needed contribution to linguistic theory. Though I shall touch briefly on all of these concepts, my main concern in this Section will be with the Bakhtinian views on speech genre, in the discussion of which I shall rely largely on his work, *The Problem of Speech Genres* (1986). I shall refer also to Vološinov (1986), especially with respect to the ideological basis of human consciousness and communication, though recognising Todorov's cautionary comments (1984: xii) against assuming authorial identity between the two. It may be true that *Marxism and the Philosophy of Language* was not penned by Bakhtin, but surely the principles of intertextuality and dialogism would make it closely related to his views. This exclusive reliance on Bakhtin-Vološinov's writing is not to deny the contributions of other scholars to the interpretation of these authors views; it is simply that this would introduce a dimension of complexity to which the scope of this paper cannot do justice. The bond of intertextuality also links Vygotsky and Bakhtin, though perhaps not so closely as Bakhtin-Vološinov. I do not know that the two former scholars were specifically aware of each other's work, but without doubt the themes of one are to be found also in the works of the other: as Bakhtin might say each epoch has its own concerns, its own web of intertextuality and the contemporaneousness of these scholars makes it likely that their writings would be mutually complementary. In what follows, I shall first present an account of Bakhtin's concepts; each such presentation will be followed by a critique in an attempt to evaluate the explanatory and descriptive power of the Bakhtinian framework. This will furnish the basis for answering the main question: would Bakhtin's concept of speech genre, utterance, intertextuality, social language etc. successfully resolve those problems in Vygotsky's framework that were outlined in closing the last section.

From this point of view, the perspective on language adopted by Bakhtin promises well. He is deeply committed to the importance of *parole* – language as it is actualised in verbal interaction, making a sharp distinction (1986: 67) between 'utterance as a unit of speech communion' and 'the units of language (words and sentences)'. For Vygotsky's theory of mental development language use is more relevant than language system. Further, as pointed out by Wertsch (1985c; 1990), one of the problems in Vygotsky's discourse on semiotic mediation is that he often describes the nature of semiotic mediation in terms of words; Bakhtin's commitment to utterance as the natural unit of verbal interaction could be valuable in providing a means of examining the crucial characteristics of that variety of semiotic mediation which leads to the emergence of the valued kinds of higher mental functions. Not only is Bakhtin concerned with utterance as a whole, but he is able to suggest a means for classifying utterances by linking them to his notion of speech genre. This is how Bakhtin (1986: 60) introduces the concept of genre:

> All the diverse areas of human activity involve the use of language ... the nature and forms of this use are just as diverse as are the areas of human activity ... Language is realised in the form of individual concrete utterances (oral and written) by participants in the various areas of human activity. These utterances reflect the specific conditions and goals of each such area not only through their content (thematic) and linguistic style, that is, the selection of lexical, phraseological, and grammatical resources of the language, but above all through their compositional structure. All three of these aspects – thematic content, style, and compositional structure – are inseparably linked to the *whole* of the utterance and are equally determined by the specific nature of the particular sphere of communication. Each separate utterance is individual, of course, but each sphere in which language is used develops its own *relatively stable types* of these utterances. These we may call *speech genres*. (emphasis as in original)

It is obvious from this extract that the two terms 'utterance' and 'human activity' are closely related: both appear criterial to the discussion of speech genre. 'We speak only in definite speech genres, that is, all our utterances have definite and relatively stable typical forms of construction of the whole' (Bakhtin, 1986: 78). As a term, 'speech genre' might be paraphrased as 'utterance type' – 'utterances and their types, that is, speech genres' (Bakhtin, 1986: 65). It follows that every 'concrete utterance' is an actual instance of some speech genre. Such concrete utterances belong to 'various spheres of human activity and communication' (Bakhtin, 1986: 62). This line of reasoning argues that there exists a definite relation between utterances, utterance types and spheres of human activity. So what does the term 'human activity' refer to?

One point that is obvious from the longer extract given above (Bakhtin, 1986: 60) is that human activity is relevant to utterance since it is 'reflected' or it 'determines' both the wording and the compositional structure of the utterance. If so, then another term for 'human activity' might be 'social situation' since this is precisely how social situation too is said to act on utterances: 'The immediate social situation and the broader social milieu wholly determine – and determine from within, so to speak – the structure of an utterance' (Vološinov, 1986: 86). The deep relationship of human activity or social situation to utterance is again and again pointed out by Bakhtin-Vološinov. Consider for example the following claims:

> The organizing centre of any utterance ... is not within but outside – in the social milieu surrounding the individual being. Only the inarticulate cry of an animal is really organised from inside the physiological apparatus of an individual creature ... even the most primitive human utterance produced by the individual organism is, from the point of view of its content, import, and meaning, organised outside the organism, in the extra-organismic conditions of the social milieu. Utterance as such is wholly a product of social interaction, both of the immediate sort as *determined by the circumstances of the discourse, and of the more general kind, as determined by the whole aggregate of conditions under which any given community of speakers operates.* (Vološinov, 1986: 93; emphasis added)

The social 'situation shapes the utterance, dictating that it sound one way and not another' (Vološinov, 1986: 86). This relationship between the utterance and the social situation is also viewed dialogically: 'language enters life through concrete utterances (which manifest language) (sic!) and life enters language through concrete utterances as well' (Bakhtin, 1986: 63). As instances of speech genres, utterances that are shaped by situation, act as a bridge between the history of society and the history of language: 'Utterances and their types, that is, speech genres, are the drive belts from the history of society to the history of language' (Bakhtin, 1986: 65).

Such comments make it very clear that human activity *alias* social situation should have a crucial role in a theory of utterance and utterance types, i.e., in the theory of speech genre. It is interesting to note then that the concept of social situation is breath-takingly wide and inclusive – this is certainly the case if we take Vološinov (1986) as indicative; but, at the same time and, quite paradoxically, the notion of social situation remains underdeveloped both in Vološinov and in Bakhtin. What I mean by this is the marked absence of a schema of any sort which might give the terms 'social situation' and 'social milieu' a tangible quality, making it obvious what would count as elements of social situation and why. Using the terms in Vygotsky's theory, one might say that the concepts are not sufficiently 'intellectualised'. However, their complexity is quite obvious. Vološinov (1986: 47) himself accepts the need for their clarification:

> the fact of the matter is that the organised social milieu into which we have included our complex [spheres of reality – physical, physiological, and psychological, see p. 46; *loc. cit.*] and the immediate social communicative situation are *in themselves extremely complicated* and involve hosts of multifaceted and multifarious connections, *not all of which are equally important for the understanding of linguistic facts* (emphasis added)

A developed theory of social context would at least have two attributes: one, it would explain the principle whereby the immediate social situation is related to social milieu and two, it would specify the composition of social situation itself, making salient those of its significant elements which are relevant to the understanding of the linguistic facts as they impinge on utterances and utterance types. Ideally, the theory would attempt to specify the *principles* by virtue of which the elements of the social situation happen to be related to the wording and the compositional structure of the utterance (types). If these steps are not taken and the notion of context is allowed to remain 'elastic' – i.e., theoretically underdeveloped – if individual elements of situation are deployed adventitiously to 'explain' the nature of the wording and/or the structure of concrete utterances wherever, whenever they suit the analyst's purpose, then clearly this would create descriptive problems (Firth, 1957c; Cook, 1990). This kind of theoretical elaboration is lacking in Bakhtin-Vološinov; and since they provide no clear criteria for making judgments, the reader is left to infer from a scattering of their comments what they might consider the relevant elements of the social situation; inevitably, such inferences contain lacunae. For example, a category of speech genres is said to be 'extremely varied depending on the *subject matter, situation, and participant*' (Bakhtin, 1986: 60; emphasis added). But in such comments it is not clear whether 'subject matter' is a part of 'human activity', whether it is at the same level of abstraction as the next two terms 'situation' and 'participant', whether 'situation' is inclusive of 'participant' or simply on par with it and in what way these two relate to 'human activity'.

The element of social situation that is emphasised most often in both authors is the interpersonal one. Thus (Bakhtin, 1986: 70):

> These genres [i.e., speech genres] are so diverse because they differ depending on the situation, social position, and personal inter-relations of the participants in the communication.

Here 'social position' and 'personal interrelations of the participants' in effect refer to the interpersonal aspect of the social situation. Consider again (Bakhtin, 1986: 95):

> Both the composition and, particularly, the style of the utterance depend on those to whom the utterance is addressed, how the speaker (or writer) senses and imagines his addressees, and the force of their effect on the utterance. Each speech genre in each area of speech communication has its own typical conception of the addressee, and this defines it as a genre.

Two further extracts on this topic, this time from Vološinov (emphasis added):

> the forms of signs are *conditioned above all by the social organisation of the participants* involved and also by the immediate conditions of their interaction. (Vološinov, 1986: 21)

> ... to observe the phenomenon of language, both the producer and the receiver of sound and the sound itself must be placed into the social atmosphere ...After all, the speaker and the listener must belong to the same language community – to a society organised along certain particular lines. Furthermore, our two individuals must be encompassed by unity of *the immediate social situation*, i.e., they must make contact, as one person to another, on *a specific basis*. Only on a specific basis is a verbal exchange possible ... (Vološinov, 1986: 46)

Here in the first extract the context of the discussion makes it quite clear that the 'forms of sign' should be read as 'forms of utterance'. Turning to the second extract, it seems that the 'social atmosphere' is the 'social milieu', since it appears to be equated with language community and societal organisation. The speaker and the listener need also to 'be encompassed by the unity of the immediate social situation'. Are, then, the 'two individuals' elements of the immediate social situation? Or do they come together in a pre-existing social situation as actors come together upon a pre-arranged scene on the stage? And what is 'a specific basis'? Is it another word for social situation, or is it an element therein? To ask that concepts such as human activity, immediate social situation and the relation of these to social milieu should be clarified is not just a pedantic demand. These concepts are needed so that we may establish whether the claims being made about the determination of the utterance by social situation are indeed tenable and, if so, what is the nature of those concepts and arguments that are offered in support of the claim. If the concepts of human activity and utterance are to be used in explicating how different forms of semiotic mediation differ from each other, we shall certainly need this degree of explicit clarification. But, without denying the richness of Bakhtin's writing, it has to be conceded that this kind of explicitness will be hard to find in his writing.

Let me turn now to the concept of utterance in Bakhtin's discussion of speech genres. The term 'utterance' is used in Bakhtin (1986) in at least two senses. It is the 'natural unit' of verbal interaction, corresponding to 'discourse' and/or 'text'; secondly, it is also used to refer to a unit that is much closer in its sense to a 'turn' as in turn-taking in dialogue. It is only in the first sense that utterance type and (speech) genre are exchangeable terms as is evident from the following locutions: 'the novel is a secondary (complex) utterance' (Bakhtin, 1986: 62); 'concrete utterances (written and oral) belong to various spheres of human activity and communication: chronicles, contracts, texts of laws, clerical and other documents' (Bakhtin, 1986: 62); and so on. From this view of the utterance, we are moved to another conception of the term. Deploring the linguists' 'imprecise' use of the word 'speech', which might stand for 'the speech process', i.e., speaking, or for 'the individual utterance', or for 'an entire long indefinite series of such utterances, or a particular speech genre' as in 'he gave a speech' (Bakhtin, 1986: 70), Bakhtin comments that these confusions 'result from ignoring the *real unit* of speech communication: the utterance' (Bakhtin, 1986: 71):

> Speech is always cast in the form of an utterance belonging to a particular speaking subject, and outside this form it cannot exist. Regardless of how varied utterances may be in terms of their length, their content, and their compositional structure, they have common structural features as units of speech communication, and, above all, quite clear-cut boundaries ... The boundaries of each concrete utterance as a unit of speech communication are determined by a *change of speaking subjects*, that is, a change of speakers. Any utterance – from a short (single-word) rejoinder in everyday dialogue to the large novel or scientific treatise – has, so to speak, an

> absolute beginning and an absolute end: its beginning is preceded by the utterances of others, and its end is followed by the responsive utterances of others (or, although it may be silent, others' active responsive understanding, or, finally, a responsive action based on this understanding). The speaker ends his utterance in order to relinquish the floor to the other or to make room for the other's active responsive understanding.

I have quoted extensively to reveal the basis of my claim that Bakhtin's use of the term utterance is ambivalent. It is of course ingenuous to claim, as Bakhtin does by implication, that there is no ambivalence, that in actual fact utterance in the sense of a turn in a dialogue and in the sense of a text/discourse is the same thing at the deepest level of analysis. It seems that Bakhtin is aware of the problematic nature of his claim; he argues at some length in its support (Bakhtin, 1986: 75-6):

> Let us turn to the real-life dialogue ... this is the simplest and the most classic form of speech communication. The change of speaking subjects (speakers) that determines the boundaries is especially clear here. But in other speech communication as well ... the nature of the boundaries of the utterance remains the same.

> Complexly structured and specialised works of various scientific and artistic genres, in spite of all the ways in which they differ from rejoinders in dialogue, are by nature the same kind of units of speech communication. They too are demarcated by a change of speaking subjects, and these boundaries, while retaining their *external* clarity, acquire here a special internal aspect because the speaking subject – in this case, the *author* of the work – manifests his own individuality in his style, his world view, and in all aspects of the design of his work ...

> The work, like the rejoinder in a dialogue, is oriented toward the response of the other (others), towards his active responsive understanding ... Like the rejoinder in the dialogue, it is related to other work-utterances: both to which it responds and which respond to it. At the same time, like the rejoinder in the dialogue, it is separated from them by the absolute boundaries created by a change of speaking subjects.

> Thus the change of speaking subjects ... is the first constitutive feature of the utterance as a unit of speech communication ... [a] second feature, which is inseparably linked to the first ... is the specific *finalisation* of the utterance.

There are, however, serious difficulties in maintaining this ingenuous claim of deep identity between a complete text/discourse and a dialogic turn, which could simply be part of a text/discourse. Let us ignore, for the moment, the problems of self-contradiction in maintaining on the one hand that different genres allow different degrees of discretion for 'reflecting individuality' (Bakhtin, 1986: 63) and, on the other, claiming that authorial individuality is an ever-present feature of all utterances. Reliance on the 'imprint of individuality' – even if this were equally available to all utterance types – is hardly likely to distinguish one utterance/text from another *where the same author is concerned*. And while there are certainly many advantages in viewing the entire *oeuvres* of an author as one unified utterance/text, this will equally certainly pose problems for genre typification: the notion of genre demands a clear articulation of the principles which will define and distinguish the boundaries of individual utterances – in the sense of text/discourse – one from another. As I have claimed before, Bakhtin is well aware of these problems and he offers 'three indicators of the *wholeness* of the utterance' which will apply to both senses of the term 'utterance'. He reiterates that what gives an utterance its identity as an utterance is 'subject neither to grammatical nor to abstract semantic definition' (but note first indicator below!) (Bakhtin, 1986: 76):

> This finalised wholeness of the utterance, guaranteeing the possibility of a response ... is determined by three ... factors that are inseparably linked in the organic whole of the utterance: 1. semantic exhaustiveness of the theme; 2. the speaker's plan or speech will; 3. typical compositional and generic forms of finalisation.

The 'possibility of response' on which Bakhtin relies almost implicitly, is itself a double-edged sword in his framework. To Bakhtin's credit, unlike most scholars, his view of response and understanding are truly dynamic – as such, they are, certainly, an ongoing feature of the dialogue. In a dialogue then the possibility of response must characterise both 'utterance' in the sense of individual turns (or even parts thereof) and 'utterance' in the sense of (a substantial fragment of) the over-all verbal interaction. How else could one account for a 'retrospective' response? Since admirably, in Bakhtin, response is not a uniquely situated phenomenon, since it is an ongoing quality of engagement in the speech process, the 'possibility of response' is indeed incapable of acting as a criterion for boundary demarcation, since such dynamic response is ever-present. Turning to the three factors enumerated above, each one of these remains equally vague (see Bakhtin's discussion, 1986: 77ff) to an extent that makes it quite doubtful that they could be actually used effectively for the recognition of utterance boundaries. As I see it, the reasons for this vagueness have to do with the lack of theoretical development. This point can be elaborated, by stating exactly what sort of relations are missing from Bakhtin's genre theory.

First, take the theorisation of the relation between context and text. I have already commented on the pretheoretical status of the notion of social situation. Since social situation and the wordings and compositional strucutre – that is to say, generic strucutre – of utterance/text are so closely related, it is reasonable to suppose that the three indicators of 'the finalised wholeness of the utterance' mentioned above can be clarified by reference to social situation: indeed, in the SF model, this issue has been debated and developed for some time (Hasan, 1978; 1984b; 1995a; Ventola, 1984; 1987; Martin, 1985a; 1992; Gregory, 1988). But to do this successfully, it is necessary to know the specific details of what may be the significant elements of the social situation and which element is related to which aspect of the utterance. What are those aspects of the social situation to which is related the semantic exhaustiveness of the theme in an utterance/text? Could it be the nature of the social activity i.e., the 'field of discourse', to use SF terminology (Halliday and Hasan, 1989)? What is that quality of the speech process that allows us to 'embrace, understand and sense the speaker's speech plan or speech will, which determines the entire utterance, its length and boundaries'? And a similar question can be asked also about the basis on which we 'guess' the genre 'from the very first word' uttered by the speaker. Bakhtin (1986: 78) reiterates the nexus between utterance and the social situation:

> the choice of a particular speech genre ... is determined by the specific nature of the given sphere of communication, semantic (thematic) considerations, the concrete situation of the speech communication, the personal composition of its participants, and so on.

But as I have said before such assertions are pretheoretical; they cannot provide the foundation for a viable description. What Bakhtin passes over as 'the speech process' is a functionally organised configuration of linguistic meanings. This configuration addresses the extra-linguistic situation on the one hand and the linguistic form – grammar, lexicon, intonation – on the other. A viable description has to find some means of bringing together these distinct orders of abstractions.

This brings me to the second point: the Bakhtinian framework has no apparatus for distinguishing different orders of abstraction, much less for relating them to each other on a principled basis. Although such words as 'manifestation', 'actualisation', 'realisation', 'expression' etc., are used by Bakhtin-Vološinov, this use remains informal. To explain the relations between social situation, utterance/text and the 'units of language' such as words, phrases, sentences, we need to recognise 'stratification' and 'realisation' as formal concepts in the descriptive model (Halliday, 1992; Hasan, 1995a). This would allocate different orders of abstraction to different strata and yet permit them to be linked by realisation to each other. Bakhtin's claim that utterance/text cannot be described in terms of words, phrases and sentences is echoed in SF (Halliday, 1977a; Halliday and Hasan, 1989). Utterance/text is not *made up* of sentences, phrases etc; rather, it is *realised* as sentence(s), phrase(s) etc. This realisational relationship (see for discussion, Halliday, 1992) links context, text and lexicogrammar (Halliday and Hasan, 1989; Martin, 1991; Matthiessen, 1992; 1995). Just as a text realises its context, similarly it is itself realised by the lexicogrammatical units of language. It seems to me that some consistent means of linking the social situation and the language of the utterance – i.e., what the utterance manifests and what manifests the utterance – is a necessity in the theory of genre. Assertions about the nature and attributes of utterance/text will tend to create a 'mystification', unless they are grounded in the social and the verbal systems. If 'stylistic effect', almost as a rule, is not produced by the functioning of the categories of the system of language in context, then by implication its source is mysterious and in explaining its appearance, we may need to appeal to something akin to the individualistic subjectivism, which Bakhtin so categorically rejected as having no basis in reality. Like most linguists Bakhtin appears to think that appeal to the system of language can be made to explain the actualisation of *only* those categories which conform to the system, replicating the norms exactly. However, as Firth (1950/1957) pointed out, divergence, originality, individuality in language use cannot be described coherently except by relation to the language system operative in some social context.

Bakhtin-Vološinov are incisive critics of the approaches in linguistics that they described as 'abstract objectivism' and 'individual subjectivism'. They advocate a linguistics committed to the analysis of whole utterances in the speech process. However, in supporting the linguistics of *parole*, they are inclined to underplay the importance of *langue*. Superficially this may appear to be a corrective step, but in fact it simply replicates the Saussurean situation in reverse. With Saussure system was everything: with Bakhtin, process is everything. Neither stance can support a dialectical approach; both are monological. A third sense in which I find Bakhtin's framework theoretically underdeveloped is precisely its inability to relate language process to language system. Naturally I am not implying that Bakhtin-Vološinov are unaware of the fact that speech process creates, maintains and alters the system so that the system is always 'becoming', always being 'renewed'. In fact we owe some of the most illuminating comments to Bakhtin-Vološinov on the relation of *langue* and *parole*. Consider the following comments by Vološinov:

> From the standpoint of observing language objectively, from above, there is no real moment in time when a synchronic system of language could be constructed. (Vološinov, 1986: 66)

> ... the constituent factor for the linguistic form, as for the sign, is not at all its self-identity as signal but its specific variability; and the constituent factor for understanding the linguistic form is not recognition of the 'same thing', but understanding in the proper sense of the word, i.e., orientation in the particular, given context and in the particular, given situation – orientation in the dynamic sense of becoming and not 'orientation' in some inert state. (Vološinov, 1986: 69)

There is abundant proof in their writing that Bakhtin-Vološinov are fully aware of the importance of *parole* as 'an essential factor in the history of language' (Vološinov, 1986: 61); 'speech genres are the drive-belts from the history of society to the history of language' (Bakhtin, 1986: 65). So I am not suggesting that Bakhtin is unaware of the fact that 'process becomes system'; rather, I am claiming that in Bakhtin's framework, *there exists no apparatus for modelling this symbiosis of process and system,* for explaining how it is that process *could* become system. Vološinov (1986: 67) asks a rhetorical question in order to reject a particular conception of language system:

> Does language really exist for the speaker's subjective consciousness as an objective system of incontestably, normatively identical forms? ... Is the mode of being of language in the subjective speech consciousness really what abstract objectivism says it is?

> We must answer this question in the negative. The speaker's subjective consciousness does not in the least operate with language as a system of normatively identical forms. That system is merely an abstraction arrived [at] with a good deal of trouble and with a definite and practical focus of attention. The system of language is the product of deliberation on language and deliberation of a kind by no means carried out for the immediate purpose of speaking.

It would seem that the 'verbal consciousness of speakers has ... nothing whatever to do with linguistic form as such or with language as such' (Vološinov, 1986: 70). He goes on to suggest that:

> for the consciousness of a speaker of a language, the real mode of existence for that language is not as system of normatively identical forms. From the viewpoint of the speaker's consciousness and his real-life practice in social intercourse, there is no direct access to the system of language envisioned by abstract objectivism. (Vološinov, 1986: 71)

Here I would make three points. First, according to Bakhtin-Vološinov, both speaking and understanding are constituted ideologically. But does this imply that for communication to occur, the community of speakers capable of engaging in verbal interaction must subscribe to (largely) the same ideology? This is problematic, if for the simple reason that social domination requires verbal intercourse with the dominated (Hasan, 1986). Besides, if speaking and understanding are constituted by a single ideology, how do we explain the creation of such sophisticated utterances as Dostoevsky's novels? Thus there has to be some qualification, some elaboration of the notion of ideologically governed speaking and understanding. I believe I am right in saying that this qualification and elaboration would throw into question some of the views expressed by Bakhtin-Vološinov on the verbal consciousness of speakers.

The second point is closely related to this. If the need for recognising not one but several co-existing ideologies is granted, then we have to grant also that in the speakers' consciousness there must be a representation of some kind of language system which permits a wider play for intersubjective objectivity: there has to be some response to the other co-existing ideologies in the same social milieu, even if it is to contest, to resist, to engage in a struggle. What would this language system be like, the representation of which in the verbal consciousness of the members of the wider community is essential for the necessary presupposition of intersubjective objectivity? What would be the attributes of a system of this kind? How is this system activated in the speech process?

This brings me to the third point: in their disdain against language system, Bakhtin-Vološinov always seem to operate with the same conception of language and linguistics which they have already given us grounds for rejecting. It is as if linguistics, language system were immutable realities, which no amount of reasoned debate could hope to alter. When Vološinov (1986: 78) claims:

> Formal, systematic thought about language is incompatible with living, historical understanding of language ... The structure of a complex sentence ... is the furthest limit of linguistic reach.

or when Bakhtin (1986: 72) declares that:

> The relations among whole utterances cannot be treated grammatically since, we repeat, such relations are impossible among units of language, and not only within the system of language, but within the utterance as well.

both authors are implicitly operating with the same conception of language system and of language study, that same authoritarian sense of grammar, which can be traced back to antiquity: Saussure's was simply the most persuasive voice commending these views early this century. But what if the Saussurean conception of language system itself is erroneous, as Bakhtin-Vološinov have already argued? What if, ideational meaning (Bakhtin's 'thematic content') is not the only meaning to be considered integral to the system of language? What if, the system of language is functionally organised as suggested by Halliday? And grammar is concerned with describing not only single (complex) sentences but with the description of utterance/text? What if the system of language is inherently variable? Through their brilliant analysis of why linguistics should not be construed the way it is, why the system of language with which we function could not be the way it is said to be in Saussurean linguistics, Bakhtin-Vološinov tantalisingly take us so far, but they abandon us at the end of their negative polemics. They do not provide any set of relations which would explain how speech process can intervene in the internalisation of the living, variable, valuated system of language that they wish to attribute to the speakers' verbal consciousness. In fact Bakhtin (1986) is vehement that evaluation of linguistic phenomena cannot be ever explained by reference to language system. But he could be quite wrong; it can be argued that the textual and interpersonal metafunctions are part of the potential of language (Halliday, 1973; 1977a; Lemke, 1992; Matthiessen, 1992). Bakhtin-Vološinov do not tell us what a linguistics model needs to be like in order to account for the conception of language as implied by their views; instead they simply denounce that same system whose fictitious nature calls for its rejection. Language use and language system as needed to support their conception of language use are thus not anchored together in their theory. How, then, should we interpret the claim that 'behind each text stands a language system' (Bakhtin, 1986: 105), except as a trivialisation of the notion of system as potential.

One of the most valuable contributions made by Bakhtin (1984; 1986) to our understanding of the speech process is via the constellation of notions that revolve around his conception of *understanding* as an integral element of the speech process. Bakhtin rejected 'fictions' such as that of a speaker who actively produces speech and the listener who passively understands it. To him understanding and responding are two aspects of the same activity: 'understanding is inherently responsive' (1986: 68); the responsiveness may be manifested in different ways, one of these being responsive speaking. But if one possible form of responding is speaking then this is tantamount to claiming that responsive speaking should be treated as the active form of understanding. This is a critical conclusion for it implies that the boundary between understanding and speaking is tenuous – the two could be seen as symbiotic:

> all real integral understanding is actively responsive, and constitutes nothing other than the initial preparatory stage of a response (in whatever form it may be actualised). And the speaker himself is oriented toward such an

actively responsive understanding ... any speaker is a respondent to a greater or lesser degree. He is not after all the first speaker, the one who disturbs the eternal silence of the universe. (Bakhtin, 1986: 69)

To speak is to be located sociohistorically by virtue of your participation in all those speech processes in which you have ever engaged. We can already begin to see the genesis of the notion of 'intertextuality' in these claims. If an utterance is a response to some utterance(s) and if all saying has some generic identity or other, then it follows that each saying is intertextually related to (some) sayings (at least) in that genre within that area of social existence. 'The speaker is not the biblical Adam' (Bakhtin, 1986: 93). This is true not only with respect to generically differentiated vocabulary, but with respect to the entire speech process (Bakhtin, 1986: 91):

> Any concrete utterance is a link in the chain of speech communion of a particular sphere ... Utterances are not indifferent to one another, and are not self-sufficient; they are aware of and mutually reflect one another ... Each utterance is filled with echoes and reverberations of other utterances to which it is related by the communality of the sphere of speech communion ... Our thought itself – philosophical, scientific, and artistic – is born and shaped in the process of interaction and struggle with others' thought, and this cannot but be reflected in the forms that verbally express our thought as well.

Virtually the same sentiments are voiced by Vološinov (1986: 72):

> Any utterance – the finished, written utterance not excepted – makes a response to something and is calculated to be responded to in turn. It is but one link in a continuous chain of speech performances. Each monument carries on the work of its predecessors, polemicising with them, expecting active, responsive understanding in return. Each monument in actuality is an integral part of science, literature or political life. The monument, as any other monological utterance is set toward being perceived in the context of current scientific life or current literary affairs, i.e., it is perceived in the generative process of that particular ideological domain of which it is an integral part.

These ideas are potentially relevant to the problems I have identified in Vygotsky's framework. Can they be employed for explaining the existence of variant forms of semiotic mediation which may be said to underly the genesis of variant forms of mental functions, variant forms of consciousness? It is at this point that we need to turn to Bakhtin's ideas about social language and the ideological basis of communication. To quote two extracts from Vološinov:

> Signs can arise only on *interindividual territory*. It is territory that cannot

be called 'natural' ... signs do not arise between any two members of the species *Homo Sapiens*. It is essential that the two individuals be organised socially, that they compose a group (a social unit); only then can the medium of sign take shape between them. (1986: 12)

The only possible objective definition of consciousness is a sociological one. Consciousness cannot be derived directly from nature ... ideology cannot be derived from consciousness. Consciousness takes shape and being in the material of signs created by an organised group in the process of its social intercourse. The individual consciousness is nurtured on signs; it derives its growth from them; it reflects their logic and laws. The logic of consciousness is the logic of ideological communication, of the semiotic interaction of a social group. (1986: 13)

It is here that Bakhtin-Vološinov and Vygotsky-Luria most closely share a common ground and it is in the idea that members of different social groups might experience different forms of verbal interaction that the heterogeneity of semiotically mediated consciousness could find a 'rational' explanation. Language seen socially is discourse specific to a particular stratum in society, defined by some social attribute such as class, profession, race, gender, or age. At any one point in the history of a community, there might exist many such 'social languages'. This amounts to saying that the natural experience of language is in the form of specific dialects, specific registers/genres and specific codes displaying distinct semantic orientation. Moreover members belonging to distinct social groups experience a different subset of these varieties and this expereince actively shapes their own verbal consciousness or their own ways of saying and meaning. It is these habitual fashions of speaking – and coding orientations to meanings – that mediate specific forms of human consciousness. The three elements of such an argument are summed up by Vološinov (1986: 21):

1: ideology may not be divorced from the material reality of sign ...;

2: the sign may not be divorced from the concrete forms of social intercourse ...;

3: communication and the forms of communication may not be divorced from the material basis.

What we need now to give substance to these claims about linguistic varieties, about differing experiences of intertextuality, about ideologically constituted limits on speaking and understanding, is a theory that will specify why human communities stratify, why sub-groups are created, how members are 'recruited' in a sub-group, why they tend to stay there despite the fact that 'objectively' speaking membership in a sub-group might not be advantageous and why or how these social relations might ever change. As before behind the fascinating and perspicacious analyses of language phenomena offered by Bakhtin-Vološinov, we will not find the kind of theoretical precision which would assist in an empirical enquiry of the kind that is needed.

The sociosemiotically constituted human consciousness, the sociohistorical nature of verbal semiosis, the heterogeneity of voices, the centrality of utterance as the unit of social interaction, the recognition of the centrality of social situation and milieu – these elements are indeed potentially important in the clarification of some of the problematic themes found in Vygotsky-Luria. If my reading is correct then it does seem rather improbable that this potential of the Bakhtin-Vološinov framework could be fully actualised. This is because its concepts and relations lack the kind of precision that is needed for a definitive study of the problems. The principles along which the Bakhtinian explanations might proceed are clear; what is not clear is the nature of the very constructs which are to be used in the explanation.

I should add, before leaving this debate, that my reading is partial and derivative; it is limited by my own inability to experience directly the literature relevant to the Bakhtin-Vološinov positions. But even so, perhaps one could justifiably place some of the responsibility with Bakhtin, who himself commented that:

> in my work there is also considerable incompletion, incompletion not of thought but of its expression ... My penchant for variation and a plurality of terms to name the same phenomenon. The multiplicity of perspectives. The convergence with the distant without any indication of the intermediate links. (Quoted in Todorov, 1984: xii)

5 Mind, society and language: foundational issues

My critique of Vygotsky and Bakhtin is actuated by an interest in a positive outcome. I am not so much concerned with what was lacking in Vygotsky and/or Bakhtin's frameworks simply to record the negative fact of some lack in their theory. My approach has been to accept most of the theoretical and pretheoretical statements made by these two great scholars, while at the same time trying to understand how the questions raised by these 'incompletions' in their accounts can be answered and what would these answers imply with regard to the foundations of a linguistic model. I can hardly do better than repeat Bernstein (1990: 168), with apologies for introducing minor changes to his comments made in a similar but different context:

my criticisms should not be read as acts of dismissal. The criticisms should not be considered as part of a methodology of disposal; a field procedure for the displacement of theories of others. The concern here was to show what such theories and approaches presuppose, and, perhaps, inadvertently, what cannot be addressed as a consequence of the form the theories take.

In this final section of the paper, I turn to the questions posed by the Vygotskian approach. I will try to outline what is implied for a linguistic theory in any attempt to provide viable answers. Let me begin, then, by stating clearly three assumption, which are based on the acceptance of Vygotsky's arguments and of Luria's findings in Uzbekistan:

Assumption 1   The sociogenesis of higher mental functions entails semiotic mediation using language as the mediational means;

Assumption 2   within the same speech community, variant forms of higher mental functioning exist all of which are sociogenetically produced;

Assumption 3   it follows from 1 and 2 that in every speech community, there must exist variant forms of semiotic mediation using language as the mediational means.

These assumptions carry certain implications attention to which has already been drawn in the course of the discussions in Sections 3 and 4; but it may be useful to briefly summarise them here once again.

1   Since all sociogenetically produced higher mental functions are semiotically mediated by language, whatever language attributes are cited as important to semiotic mediation of any kind whatever, must refer to properties such that the system of language is capable of 'supporting them'. This includes the potential of language to refer to phenomena not present to the senses in the here and now of speech; it includes the inherent efficacy of language in the classification of phenomena, in the definition of experience, in concept formation, in enabling metalinguistic reflection and so on. The potential for being used in these ways inheres in all human languages, irrespective of whether and/or how habitually which of these potentials might be deployed. Human languages are not 'primitive' in the sense of not being capable of being used for some purpose or other. It follows that in a viable linguistic theory language must be viewed as an inexhaustible resource, such that the system of language itself is infinite, while the texts already instantiated by it are finite (Halliday, 1992).

2   The notion 'semiotic mediation' properly understood is 'participation in language use'. Since language use is a sociohistorically situated (convergent or divergent) instantiation of (some features of) the system of language, any account of semiotic mediation must involve an analysis of language as code and language as behaviour in social contexts (Halliday, 1984a). To be able to describe the details of semiotic mediation, the linguistic theory must postulate three orders of abstraction: language system, language use and the social context. This in turn means that such a theory must provide a coherent set of relations between these orders of abstraction. Notions such as those of genre, intertextuality and ideological basis of communication pertain to the general theory of semiotic mediation as such, in that no accounting of any form of semiotic mediation is at all possible without these postulates.

3   Semiotic mediation as conceptualised above makes meaning the most central concept of linguistics. By definition these meanings are *linguistic* meanings and they are not limited to word meaning; the meaning of language in use is not a sum of the meanings of individual words, phrases and sentences. A viable theory of linguistics will need to explain how participants construe the meanings of their own interaction when using language; whether these meanings are related in any way to the social context which includes the participants' experience of interaction; whether the forms – the lexicogrammar – of a language is related to the meanings being construed. It will be seen that a theory which attempts to explain the activation, construal and on-going interpretation of meaning in language use will need to recognise the Whorfian notion of cryptogrammar as central to the description of linguistic form.

Let me reiterate also the three basic questions posed by the existence of variant forms of semiotic mediation below:

Question 1   How can the fact be explained that within 'the same' wider community there exist variant forms of human consciousness and of semiotic mediation?

Question 2   What does a linguistic theory need in order to describe those linguistic features which distinguish the variant forms of semiotic mediation, one from another?

Question 3   What is the basis for assigning some value to some particular form of semiotic mediation and its corresponding human consciousness?

To take the first question first, the explanation for the existence of variant forms of semiotic mediation cannot really be given in terms of Bakhtin's notion of linguistic heterogeneity: the recognition of heterogeneity is simply another way of saying that the possibility of the existence of variant forms of semiotic mediation exists. What is needed is an explanation for the genesis of heterogeneity, the presence of distinct 'voices', different fashions of speaking. Following Marx's lead, Bernstein (1971; 1982; 1987a; 1990) explains the existence of distinct forms of semiotic mediation by relating them to the material conditions of social existence, which act on human action and relation, thus affecting and being affected by the forms of consciousness. Bernstein's explanatory base is more specific than the 'large' expression 'sociocultural history', but appears to add substance both to Vološinov's maxim (1983: 21) that 'communication and forms of communication may not be divorced from the material basis' as well as to Marx's claim that:

> In the social production of their life men enter into definite relations that are independent of their will ... The sum total of these relations of production constitutes the economic structure of the society ... to which correspond different forms of consciousness. The mode of production of material life conditions the social, political, and intellectual life processes in general. It is not the consciousness of men that determines their being, but on the contrary, their social being that determines their consciousness. (Quoted in McLellan, 1975: 40)

These relations of production which constitute the economic structure of the society, translate themselves into the relations of power and control via practices of division of labour in society, thus entering into everyday human life as differential privilege of access to social processes and different structures of human relation. Bernstein suggests a relation between material basis and orientation to meaning – i.e., coding orientation (Bernstein, 1982: 310). The more specific and local the relation between an agent and the material base, the more direct the relation between meanings and (this) specific material base; what appears relevant is itself local relations. Conversely, the less specific and local the relation between the agent and the material base, the less direct the relation between the meanings and the specific material base. The experience of languaging in the former segment of the community is critically different from that in the latter. On the basis of their social positioning, infants are 'recruited' as apprentices to 'different spheres of human social existence' each of which stands in some specific relation to the distribution of power and control: to the extent that their material base is different in the ways specified above, to that extent their experiences of discourse are diverse and variant forms of consciousness are created (Bernstein, 1971: 144):

the particular forms of social relation act selectively upon what is said, when it said, and how it is said ... [they] can generate very different speech systems or codes ... [which] create for their speakers different orders of relevance and relation. The experience of the speaker may then be transformed by what is made significant or relevant by different speech systems. As the child ... learns specific speech codes which regulate his verbal acts, he learns the requirements of his social structure. The experience of the child is transformed by the learning generated by his own, apparently, voluntary acts of speech ... From this point of view, every time the child speaks or listens, the social structure is reinforced in him and his social identity shaped. The social structure becomes the child's psychological reality through the shapings of his acts of speech.

It seems obvious that Bernstein's explanations would apply to the results of Luria's research in Uzbekistan. There is a crucial difference between Bernstein's account of semiotic mediation and that which one finds in Vygotsky or Bakhtin. In Vygotsky's account it seems as if all that is needed for the genesis of a particular form of higher mental functioning is 'contact' with a particular fashion of speaking, a specific kind of language use. With Bakhtin the ever-enlarging circle of intertextuality implies almost unlimited access to any voice; it is not clear at what point, why and how the material basis and the forms of communication constrain this pervasive intertextuality. By relating the distribution of power and control to the regulation of social interaction and personal experience, Bernstein's approach is able to provide answers to these questions. The specific relations he has postulated can begin to explain why different sections of the wider community might have different patterns of engagement in social processes, why there would be different orders of relevance, or different interpersonal relations. Moreover through his theory of socialisation – which is in fact a theory of how different forms of consciousness are produced – Bernstein is able to explain why pedagogic discourse is one thing for one set of learners and another for another set. The concepts of 'official' and 'local pedagogy' (Bernstein, 1990: 179ff) become a means for showing how 'social milieu' enters into 'immediate social situations', and vice versa. Both Vygotsky and Bakhtin need a theory of societal organisation – a framework that explains why human activities take this form here and another form there; why access to human activities is not universal in any community; and how in the creation of consciousness both the socialised and the socialising parties make an active contribution.

How are these facts relevant to a linguistic theory? Consider the earlier claim that a viable theory will need to bring social context, language use and language system in relation to one another. A sophisticated sociological theory will provide a 'good' account of those aspects of societal organisation by reference to which it can be surmised who will engage in what sort of social activities, what would be the quality of their interpersonal relations, or their access to means of semiotic management. It would identify viable principle(s) to account for significant variation in social action, by relating this variation to variables with fundamental function in the management of the community's life. Such a theory will clearly tell us about those elements which are indispensable in conceptualising the relation between the wider context of culture and the more immediate context of situation. Judgments about relevance are judgments about meaning. If social contexts act on speakers' ideas about what is relevant, then they also act on what is meaningful. The need to explicate the relation of context to meaning and of meaning to wording is further reinforced as a desirable goal of any linguistic theory that would aspire to describe semiotic mediation. Moreover, if as Bakhtin-Vološinov imply the system of language is always 'becoming', always being 'renewed', there can be only one source of this renewal – and that is in language use. From this point of view, whatever impinges upon language use, whatever functions as an active principle in explaining the character of language use, needs to be incorporated in the larger design of the linguistic theory, for it is only then that it can be coherently brought in relation with the system of language. If the notion of context is important to linguistics, linguistics needs to understand the sociological basis of both who recognises what as a context and who engages in which contexts.

Turn now to the second question. If semiotic mediation is centrally concerned with meaning, it seems very probable that the characterisation of variant forms of semiotic mediation will be semantic in character. But this use of the term 'semantic' is very far from what passes as semantics in linguistics in general. Traditionally, in linguistics the conception of meaning is limited; all meaning is just 'cognitive', 'referential', or 'experiential'. Semiotic mediation takes the form of text in context; therefore the notion of semantics has to be rich enough in linguistics to be able to account for 'text-ness', for how meanings and wordings realise the generic identity of some communication. By the same token, a linguistic theory must be able to account for the interpersonal meanings construed in a verbal interaction. The limited notions of meaning which linguistic models have seen it fit to operate with, break down each time they confront the reality of human communication as it occurs in social contexts. This is not because by some inevitable *fiat* linguistics is concerned with language system and language system cannot be used for explaining any of these phenomena as Bakhtin-Vološinov imply. It is only because the ideas about language and about linguistics propagated by formalist models are inadequate. They need revision. And this revision would require a recognition of language as a resource for meaning – for construing our experience, for enabling the construal of complex relations, for expressing interpersonal meanings and for enabling meanings that will construe coherence, both within the communication and between that communication and its social context (Halliday, 1985a; Halliday and Hasan, 1989; Martin, 1991; Hasan, 1995a). Where language is seen as a resource, the theory can represent the form of a verbal interaction as choice of meaning in social context, thus being able to account for variation as well as similarities between texts and contexts.

Finally, to turn to the last question, which has the least direct relevance to the theory of linguisitcs: what is the basis for assigning value to forms of semiotic mediation? Why are some forms of human consciousness considered more desirable, others not? This issue relates very closely to the genesis of variation in semiotic mediation. One possibility is to limit the scope of the reference of the expression 'semiotic mediation', so that it refers only to that kind of language use which is instrumental in the creation, transmission and internalisation of scientific concepts, of mathematical operations, of decontextualised reflection – in short only to what Vygotsky-Luria typically presented as instances of higher mental functioning. This will pose certain problems. For example, the boundary between scientific and everyday concepts is not crystal clear and Vygotsky certainly accepts this. Moreover, if this is how semiotic mediation is to be understood, then a simpler equivalent for that kind of use of language is 'official pedagogic discourse' (Bernstein, 1990) or 'instructional registers'. There are, however, communities where at least some members have never experienced such discourse. It would therefore be necessary to dissociate the notion of semiotic mediation from the genesis of human consciousness, for obvious reasons. This makes the theory far less powerful, leaving the role of language in the construction of everyday experience completely undescribed. It also creates another serious problem: is semiotic mediation to be referred to as semiotic mediation only if it is successful in producing this specific sort of consciousness? or is it simply a label applied to language certain semantic properties? If the former, then semiotic mediation in the sense of official pedagogic discourse would be semiotic mediation for some but not for others (Bernstein, 1971; 1990). If it is the latter, then it has acquired a rather static character and it would not necessarily enter into the discourse of the sociogenesis of higher mental functions. These are serious problems. And it has seemed to me nearer Vygotsky's usage to think of semiotic mediation as 'learning through the mediational means of language in use', without making the nature of that which is learnt criterial to the definition of the term.

But this solution brings us back to the problem of valuation, for valuation of variant forms of consciousness – and hence of semiotic mediation – does exist. I suggest that essentially the valuation of the variant forms of human consciousness is irrational. I agree with Marx when he says that 'the ideas of the ruling class are, in every age, the ruling ideas' (quoted in Bottomore and Rubel, 1976: 93) and the ways of meaning and saying – the form of human consciousness – we consider desirable are those that belong to the power group, whoever they may be and whatever their source of power. However, the valuation is *rationalised* by appeal to our ideas about what counts as human evolution, or what is construed as human progress. Those ways of meaning and saying which appear to contribute to 'control over environment', to the subjugation of resources for our own use and benefit, thus knowledge which enables such control – these things are said to lead directly to human progress. This is to forget two things. First, that as Whorf once said 'we do not know that civilisation is synonymous with rationality' (Whorf, 1956: 81); it is possible that there are other measures of progress than those cherished in the dominant western ideology. Second, even if this view is accepted, it must be recognised that everywhere the actual utilisation of such knowledge so as to lead to the actual control of the environment, so as to subjugate the resources, depends upon labour of the kind where the agent's relation to the material base is highly localised. Given the organisation of our societies, this segment is as essential for progress as those who display the more valued forms of higher mental functioning. The valuation of the variant forms of human consciousness is thus quite invidious, especially in societies such as ours whose economic structure depends upon stratification.

Before closing this paper, it should be added that Vygotsky's approach to the development of human mental functioning presents a paradigm that linguistics might well learn from. Like the elementary mental functions, it is likely that the elementary forms of human semiosis have a biogenetic foundation. The early presymbolic and earliest protolanguage (Trevarthen, 1979; Halliday, 1975; Shotter, 1978; Newson, 1978) might be regarded as forms of human semiosis which develop along the natural line. The complex structures of the adult language are laid on this foundation, but the emergence and evolution of human language as we know it, is inconceivable without sociogenesis. And sociogenesis takes us to the social, which is itself construed through semiosis. Herein we have in a nutshell the complexity of linguistics. Theories of language have to strive to explore this challenge.

4 On the social conditions for semiotic mediation: the genesis of mind in society

1 Introduction

How is it that human beings typically develop the ability to interpret their environment, to reflect on it and to act on it with an understanding that leads to some degree of foresight? What enables them to transform themselves from simply biological organisms into social beings capable of participating in the living of life so that not only their interpretations but also their reactions and actions are seen as meaningful by others around them? The explanatory principle invoked in response to such questions has often been in terms of the human mental equipment. As a matter of our birthright, suggests this response, we are endowed with a mental organ so designed that it makes us develop in just these ways. But this response, in turn, raises an important question. Exactly how far in detail does the effect of the natural *design* extend? Would the correct analogy here be that of a time-bomb, destined to explode, in the fullness of time, into a specific kind of activity, all significant details of which are essentially predictable except for certain quite unimportant minutiae? Or, to go to the other extreme, is human mind an empty receptacle to be filled by experience – what Popper (1979b: 60-66) in his pejorative description of commonsense learning refers to as 'the bucket theory of mind?'

In the history of academic discourse, this kind of polarisation has occurred from time to time, turning the two positions into something of a caricature which because of its very absurdity is arguably not so dangerous. What is more persistent and less easy to counteract because of its taken-for-granted nature is the frequent assumption that the two positions are logically mutually exclusive. If human mind is *natural*, then it cannot be *social*; if it 'belongs to' the *individual*, then it could not 'belong to' the *collectivity*. This shows, perhaps, a befitting deference to the ancient law of contradiction, though it appears to ignore an equally valid axiom: opposites tend to depend on each other; it is this interdependence that secures them their identity. It was the great achievement of Vygotsky (1896-1934) to point out that the specifically human aspects of mental functioning can be explained convincingly only when the natural and the social are considered in relation to each other from the point of view of their role in the making of mind: The minds of individuals have not been known to develop except within human societies; and even within societies, physiologically damaged brains have not been known to follow the same developmental trajectory.

The aim of this chapter is to make a contribution to the approach inaugurated by Vygotsky's pioneering work. To achieve this end, in Section 2, I will begin by presenting a brief account of Vygotsky's theory of the 'genesis of human mind'. Human mind for Vygotsky is a developing phenomenon; it moves from elementary, less evolved functions, having a biogenetic foundation, to higher, more evolved functions, with a sociogenetic foundation. The active agent in this developmental move is the process of 'semiotic mediation' – an expression which, in effect, captures the deep meaning of social interaction. In this way the theoretical framework lays a firm foundation for bringing together the natural and the social. However, I will draw attention, in Section 3, to certain problems with reference to the notions of higher (more evolved) mental function and semiotic mediation, both of which are critical to the theory. I will argue that the implications of these concepts have not been explored in sufficient detail, leaving certain residual problems unresolved. The nature of social interaction and so of semiosis, cannot be studied or understood in isolation from the social environment in which it occurs. Where semiotic mediation is interpreted as the agency of meaning in the evolution of minds, the question arises whether all persons in a given society are so positioned as to engage in all varieties of acts of meaning? Whether ways of meaning in a society are entirely invariant? And whether all types of exchange of meaning lead to the evolution of the same categories of higher mental function? These questions cannot be answered without theorising the notion of society itself. This in turn calls for a sociological theory such as, for example, that of Bernstein, who is able to provide principles for linking semiosis to the material conditions of social existence. This theme will be developed in Section 4, where Bernstein's views on the relation between social interaction and social structure will be briefly described, to show how these insights might resolve some of the problems in Vygotsky's framework. There is an urgent need for a theory of human cognition which recognises both its biogenetic and sociogenetic character. Vygotsky set out to satisfy this need through his genetic theory of the mind. However, this theory does not do justice to the *socio* in the sociogenetic. It is important for such a theory to be aware of the social evaluation of certain forms of semiosis, to enquire into the origin of such evaluation and to recognise variation in forms of semiotic mediation as a manifestation of the principles underlying certain kinds of social structures. This might shed a somewhat different light on *higher* in *higher mental function*, revealing the active intervention of the collectivity in the making of individual minds.

2   The development of mental functions

The three general themes recurring in Vygotsky's theory of psychological development are pointed out by Wertsch (1990: 64) as follows:

1: a reliance on a genetic or developmental method;

2: the claim that higher (i.e., uniquely human) mental functioning in the individual has its origins in social activity;

3: the claim that a defining property of human mental action is its mediation by tools ('technical tools') and signs ('psychological tools').

Vygotsky used 'genetic' to refer to processes pertaining to the origin or growth of a phenomenon; 'genetic', 'developmental' and 'historical' are thus used as close synonyms in his theory, as are 'mind', 'consciousness', 'cognition' and 'psychological/mental function/ activity/behaviour'. Reliance on a genetic method in explaining human cognition thus implies an enquiry into the history of mental behaviour. To understand the nature of such higher mental functions as generalisation, abstraction, or the formation of scientific concepts, one needs to understand their developmental trajectory. In Vygotsky's framework, this trajectory can be viewed from two complementary perspectives: the phylogenetic and the ontogenetic. The account of mental development presented here is restricted to the ontogenetic perspective only.

Vygotsky believed that an enquiry of this kind must recognise two lines of development – the natural and the social. The natural line of development relies on the biogenetic foundation. On this foundation are based the elementary functions of the mind such as early forms of memory. It is implied that the biogenetic foundation is universal to the human species and constitutes a necessary condition for the development of human cognition. However, by itself it is not sufficient to account for those qualities of mental functioning which are distinctively human. According to Vygotsky the uniquely human, higher forms of mental function have a sociogenetic foundation: they develop along the social line in the much more important sense that in their origin and growth, social interaction with an acculturated *other* plays a critical role. Vygotsky (1978: 46; original emphasis) rejects the idea of any sharp discontinuity between the biogenetic elementary functions and the sociogenetic higher ones.

Within a general process of development, two qualitatively different lines of development, differing in origin, can be distinguished: on the one hand the elementary processes, which are of biological origin and, on the other, the higher psychological functions of the sociocultural origin. *The history of child behaviour is born from the interweaving of these two lines.*

Despite the 'complicated, qualitative transformation of one form of behaviour into another' (Vygotsky, 1978: 19), the genetic perspective implies that the elementary and the higher functions are simply distinct moments in the history of cognitive development. Given this complex relation of identity and difference, it is important to be clear what distinguishes the two forms from each other – on what basis the moments are recognised as distinct. Vygotsky identified four closely-related features to distinguish the higher functions from the elementary. First, there is an essential difference in how the stimulus-response relations are structured in the two kinds of mental activities (Vygotsky, 1978: 39):

> The central characteristic of elementary functions is that they are totally and directly determined by stimulation from the environment. For higher functions, the central feature is self-generated stimulation, that is, the creation and use of artificial stimuli which become the immediate cause of behaviour.

In higher mental functions, behaviour is mediated via some 'artificial stimuli' and this implies control over stimulation – individuals do not have to depend on the environment. By contrast, in elementary functions, behaviour is dependent upon specific features of the environment over the production of which the individual has no control. Taking memory as an example, Vygotsky provides (*loc. cit.*) a more concrete illustration of this difference:

> One [type of memory], dominating in the behaviour of non-literate people, is characterised by the non-mediated impression of materials, by the retention of actual experiences as the basis of mnemonic (memory) traces. We call this *natural memory*... it arises out of the direct influence of external stimuli... the entire process is characterised by a quality of immediacy.

This contrasts with 'other types of memory' which is mediated, an evidence of which can be found even amongst non-literate people, lacking advanced forms of technology. To quote Vygotsky (1978: 39) again:

> The use of notched sticks and knots, the beginnings of writing and simple memory aids all demonstrate that even at early stages of historical development humans went beyond the limits of the psychological functions given to them by nature and proceeded to a new culturally-elaborated organisation of their behaviour... we believe that these sign operations are the product of specific conditions of social development.

But control over mediating means is not the only secret underlying the self-regulation of higher mental activity: The use of mediating means has far reaching consequences for the structuring of the mental activity itself; this becomes obvious from Vygotsky's ideas about intellectualisation and internalisation of mental functions.

The second characteristic of higher mental functions is mediation itself: Higher mental functions are always mediated. In fact, mediation is a condition for the 'shift of control from environment to individual' (Wertsch, 1985b: 25) for it is only where there is mediation that it makes sense to talk about self-regulation and internalisation of a mental process. Internalisation is a complex process, passing through various stages. An example provided is the child's *grasping movement* which is a physical activity, initially entirely 'external'. As a physical act it is empty of any social content. When this external activity of the child is responded to as if it were a 'gesture of demand', its character begins to change. It ceases to be just physical activity. Instead, through the interpersonal process of interpretation, it begins to emerge as a sign. Finally, the signing potential of the activity is internalised by the child. Because of the 'interpersonal' process, it acquires the status of a sign on the 'intrapersonal' level (Vygotsky, 1978: 55-7). An external activity is thus transformed into an internal one. Thus mediation may occur via a concrete tool, a primitive example of which is the notched stick, the knot in the handkerchief, or it might be effected via abstract tools, through the use of a sign system such as gesture or verbal language. In either case the mediation acts on the individual's mental structure itself.

The third characteristic is implicit in the nature of mediation. Higher mental functions are always sociogenetic. Their nature is social not in the simple sense that they are tool-mediated and tools are social *in themselves*. Rather the cultural, interactional process is a necessary element for conceptualising something as a mediating means, no matter whether these means are concrete or abstract. Vygotsky (1978: 57) emphasises the cultural nature of sociogenesis:

> Every function in the child's cultural [i.e., higher] development appears twice: first, on the social level, and later, on the individual level; first *between* people (*interpsychologically*), and then *inside* the child (*intrapsychologically*). This applies equally to voluntary attention, to logical memory, and to the formation of concepts. All the higher functions originate as actual relations between human individuals.

It is in this way that elements of what 'belongs to' the *collectivity* enter a mind that 'belongs to' an individual and 'the outside becomes the inside' (Bernstein, 1987a). The fourth and perhaps the most important characteristic of higher mental functions, is their 'intellectualisation' – a characteristic that is sometimes also referred to by such expressions as 'conscious realisation' or 'conscious awareness'. In Vygotsky's framework this feature characterises the highest forms of mental activities, some instances of which are the formation of scientific concepts, generalisation, abstraction etc. In the development of such mental activities, semiotic mediation by means of language plays a central role. Moreover, for intellectualisation to take place, language must operate as a symbolic system rather than as a signalling device tied to the immediate physical context. Finally, the intellectualisation of functions and their voluntary regulation are intimately related. Thus Wertsch (1985c: 26) translates Vygotsky as claiming:

> At the centre of development during the school age is the transition from the lower functions of attention and memory to higher functions of voluntary attention and logical memory… the intellectualisation of functions and their mastery represent two moments of one and the same process – the transition to higher psychological functions. We master a function to the degree that it is intellectualised. The voluntariness in the activity of a function is always the other side of its conscious realisation. To say that memory is intellectualised in school is exactly the same as to say that voluntary recall emerges; to say that attention becomes voluntary in school age is exactly the same as saying… that it depends more and more on thought, that is, on intellect.

It would appear then that what is in common to, for example, memory as elementary mental function and memory as higher mental function, is their historical relation, reflected in the shared nomenclature. But despite sharing the same name, the two stages of the development of 'this same thing' are not just the same thing. Vygotsky (1978: 51; emphasis original) expressed this epigrammatically by saying: 'For the young child, to think means to recall; but for the adolescent, to recall means to think'. If higher mental functions are uniquely human, constituting 'activity that is absent even from the highest species of animals' (Vygotsky, 1978: 39), then it follows that the essence of humanity lies in 'mediation' – the harnessing of the universe as a means for mental activity – and this presupposes 'sociogenesis'. This sociogenetic mediation of the mind is a quality unique to human beings.

Let us turn now to 'semiotic mediation'. It is already clear that mediation cannot be dissociated from the idea of tools. However, in Vygotsky's theory, the idea of tool became an explanatory principle. Seen in relation to human cognitive development, it is not simply an adjunct of an activity, as was the celebrated stick in the hands of the problem-solving ape; instead it was transformed into an active principle, contributing to the internal management of mental activity. Vygotsky (1981: 137) used the effect of 'technological, concrete tools' in the sphere of physical activity to explain by its analogy the contribution of 'psychological, abstract tools' to the sphere of mental activity:

the psychological tool alters the entire flow and structure of mental functions. It does this by determining the structure of a new instrumental act just as a technical tool alters the process of a natural adaptation by determining the form of labour operation.

Semiotic mediation is mediation by means of abstract tools. Such tools come to have the status of sign; they are semiotic tools in that they mediate meanings and it is as mediators of meaning that they assist in the internalisation and conscious realisation of a mental activity. Sign systems are abstract tools, mediating by means of semiosis and this *mediation by means of semiosis* achieves its effect by changing the very basis of mental functions – by acting on a subject's mental make-up (Vygotsky, 1978: 40):

> The use of signs leads humans to a specific structure of behaviour that breaks away from biological development and creates new forms of a culturally-based psychological process.

Among the sign systems, Vygotsky assigned the highest status to language, so that semiotic mediation became almost synonymous in his writing with *mediation by means of semiosis by means of language*. To him, of all the semiotic modalities, it was language that *maximised* the attributes essential for the highest forms of mental activities. Signs, in general, are internally oriented and serve as 'a means of internal activity aimed at mastering oneself' (Vygotsky, 1978: 55), but language is the more so because of its potential for 'decontextualisation'. If the intellectualisation of scientific concepts calls for systematisation, it is notable that this systematisation is almost identical to the taxonomies in the linguistic sign system itself. Language is most pervasive in representing aspects of a community's everyday existence and it alone is metasemiotic. This is why as an apprentice to culture, the child's access to other abstract tools current in the community depends to a very large extent on verbal semiosis. These characteristics of language allow it to play an active role in the creation, maintenance and alteration of all human social institutions. So not surprisingly *verbal* interaction is taken as the paradigm case of *social* interaction. The use of language in *interpersonal* interaction, semiotically mediates *intrapersonal mental dispositions*. In Vygotsky's words (1978: 24-5; emphasis original):

> *the most significant moment in the course of intellectual development, which gives birth to the purely human forms of practical and abstract intelligence, occurs when speech and practical activity, two previously completely independent lines of development converge.* Although children's use of tools during their preverbal period is comparable to that of apes, as soon as speech and the use of signs are incorporated into any action, the action

becomes transformed and organised along entirely new lines... the child begins to master his surrounding with the help of speech. This produces new relations with the environment in addition to the new organisation of behaviour. The creation of these uniquely human forms of behaviour later produce the intellect and become the basis of productive work: the specifically human form of the use of tools.

This closes my account of Vygotsky's views on higher mental functions and semiotic mediation. Though it is far from doing justice to the richness of his framework, it hopefully furnishes all the information relevant to the major problems I wish to raise. However, before turning to these, let me point out three important implications of Vygotsky's dynamic theory of mental genesis (see Hasan, 1992/2005 for more detail). First, if in the development of higher mental functions, the *inter*psychological categories precede the *intra*psychological ones, then so far as the adult mind is concerned 'the social dimension of [specifically human] consciousness is primary in time and fact. The individual dimension is derivative and secondary' (Vygotsky in Wertsch, 1990: 66). These sentiments echo Marx's famous claims that the essence of humanity is its sociality and that 'it is not the consciousness of men that determines their being, but on the contrary their social being that determines their consciousness' (in McLellan, 1975: 40). This is not to imply that individuals act like puppets; thanks to the intellectualisation and self-regulation of their mental functions, they are certainly free to act as they wish. But this freedom is qualified at the very source by the social fashioning of the individual's ideas about relevance, the structuring of their mental disposition, which underlies both the choice and the execution of actions. It is this realisation that led Luria to suggest that 'the Cartesian notion of the primacy of *self*-consciousness' must be rejected. Like Mead, he found that the conception of self presupposes that of the *other* (Luria, 1976: 19):

> The perception of oneself results from the clear perception of others and the processes of self-perception are shaped through social activity, which presupposes collaboration with others and an analysis of their behavioural patterns.

Second, while Vygotsky emphasised sociogenesis, he by no means ignored the contribution of the biogenetic foundation. Wisely shunning the sterile opposition between nature and culture, individual and collectivity, biological and social, he articulated a dynamic theory whose aim was to provide an explanatory analysis of the processes of mental development, not by simply describing the features of some given stage but by returning to its source and reconstructing all the significant points in its development. In agreement with Blonsky's claim that 'behaviour can be understood only as the history of behaviour' (in Vygotsky, 1978: 65), he devised a genetic methodology, which invites a dialectical approach: The biogenetic capital is shaped by the operation of mediated activities which lead to internal organisation, enabling a qualitatively different form of mental activity, wherein the biogenetic capital has not disappeared but keeps being transformed. 'Development,' claimed Vygotsky (1978: 56) 'proceeds not in a circle but in a spiral, passing through the same point at each new revolution while advancing to a higher level'.

Finally, Vygotsky's theory explains change both in the individual and the society by revealing through its analysis the part that one plays in the evolution of the other (Vygotsky, 1978: 60):

> The dialectical approach [to the psychological development of humans] while admitting the influence of nature on man, asserts that man, in turn, affects nature and creates through his changes in nature new natural conditions for his existence.

Keeping in mind attacks on the poverty of historicism (Popper, 1957) and the critique of the determinism of sociocultural explanations (as if that determinism is more reprehensible than biological determinism!), it is important to point out that the theme of control over the natural conditions of human existence is well thought out in Vygotsky's theory as revealed in the following comments (Vygotsky, 1978: 51):

> It may be said that the basic characteristic of human behaviour in general is that humans personally influence their relations with the environment and through that environment personally change their behaviour, subjugating it to their control.

Vygotsky suggests that this specifically human characteristic which represents 'the qualitative leap from animal to human psychology' (Vygotsky, 1978: 57) is at the basis of human evolution (Vygotsky, 1978: 60):

> It is my belief, based upon a dialectical materialist approach to the analysis of human history, that human behaviour differs qualitatively from animal behaviour to the same extent that the adaptability and historical development of humans differs from the adaptability and development of animals. The psychological development of humans is part of the general historical development of our species and must be so understood.

These Vygotskian statements more than foreshadow the idea of 'exo-somatic evolution' which was to be attributed several years later, somewhat ironically, to Popper – perhaps the most unsympathetic critic of the historical approach to mind and society. Note though that in his qualitatively different framework, where the role assigned to language and social learning is jejune, the idea of exo-somatic evolution poses severe problems. To rescue its coherence, Popper would need to revise his ideas about language as also those about the nature of knowledge in society.

3 Semiotic mediation and higher mental functions: some problems

While in general terms, the role of semiotic mediation in the development of specifically human mental functions as outlined by Vygotsky appears convincing, some serious problems surface as soon as we begin to consider particular cases of higher mental functioning. For example, take the development of such functions as those of categorisation, generalisation, abstract thinking, syllogistic reasoning and so on. These are so often cited as instances of higher mental function that it seems reasonable to treat them as paradigm cases. But if they are indeed the paradigm cases, then we need to be more careful in talking about the social and the human as synonymous terms; we need to understand the social conditions for semiotic mediation in relation to the development of higher mental functions. In developing these themes, a quick look at Luria's research in Uzbekistan (Luria, 1976) is particularly relevant.

Luria found that different groups of the Uzbek community differed from each other significantly with respect to certain higher mental functions. Following is Luria's (1976: 48-9) account of such functions:

> Categorical classification involves complex verbal and logical thinking that exploits language's capacity for formulating abstractions and generalisations for picking out attributes, and subsuming objects within a general category... 'categorical' thinking is usually quite flexible; subjects readily shift from one attribute to another and construct suitable categories. They classify objects by substance (animals, flowers, tools), materials (wood, metal, glass), size (large, small), and colour (light, dark), or other property. The ability to move freely, to shift from one category to another, is one of the chief characteristics of 'abstract thinking' or the 'categorical behaviour' essential to it.

The variation across the groups in respect to these functions correlated with the absence or presence of 'formal' schooling which subsumes contact with literacy. There was almost no evidence of 'categorical, abstract thinking' amongst those of Luria's Uzbek subjects who did not have the benefit of formal education and who were functionally illiterate. Luria (1976: 77; *emphasis added*) comments:

> Every attempt to suggest the possibility of categorical grouping met with protest... They either disregarded generic terms or *considered them irrelevant*, in no way essential to the business of classification. *Clearly, different psychological processes determined their manner of grouping which hinged on concrete situational, thinking rather than abstract operations which entail the generalizing function of language.*

One critical question raised by this result is: despite being a 'different psychological process' is 'concrete situational thinking' as much an instance of higher mental function as is 'categorical abstract thinking?' If it is not, then, this in the light of the significance of the term *higher* raises some problems. Recall that such mental development was claimed to be *specifically human*. Although this formulation does not make the ssevolution of the higher mental functions a *defining* characteristic of humanity, it does claim by implication that while all human beings have the potential, only some actually achieve this level of development. This raises two vexing questions. First, under what conditions is the potential for higher development actualised? It would be absurd to suppose that the reason for the absence of higher mental function in the Uzbeks is the total absence of any semiotic mediation. No matter what the level of their mental evolution, in the Uzbeks' living of life 'speech and practical activity' must have converged, giving rise to that 'significant moment in the course of intellectual development which gives birth to the purely human forms of practical and abstract intelligence' whereby 'new relations with the environment' and 'new organisation of behaviour' are produced in human subjects (cf. Vygotsky, 1978: 24 quoted above). The Uzbeks must have used language as a tool in their practical activities, as Malinowski's (1923; 1935a) account of other technologically primitive societies would suggest. If despite some semiotic mediation, the Uzbek intellect did not evolve beyond a certain level, then clearly this development could not depend on semiotic mediation *per se*. Second, does the degree of mental development hierarchise human beings? Were the Uzbeks lesser human beings because they did not achieve a particular level of mental evolution? The 'elitism' implicit in an affirmative response is obviously far from the intentions of a psychological theory which would emulate Marx's Capital, as Vygotsky wished to (Lee, 1987: 96)!

But perhaps we are going against the intentions of a developmental theory in saying that 'concrete situational thinking' of the type the Uzbeks displayed is not a higher mental function. In a developmental theory, there logically have to be different levels of development. The Uzbek's 'concrete situational thinking' is perhaps higher than some forms of elementary functions. Consider Luria's claims (1976: 79):

concrete thinking is neither innate nor genetically [i.e., biologically] determined. It results from illiteracy and the rudimentary types of activity that have prevailed in these [i.e., the unschooled Uzbeks] subjects' daily experience.

This supports the claim that 'concrete, situational thinking' is not just an instance of the natural line of development based on biogenetic foundation. And since it is sociogenetic, it is likely to have been semiotically mediated, but the formulations suggest that it should be seen as lower than categorical, logical thinking. So the problem of hierarchisation still remains. The higher the mental function the more valued it appears to be. Does the high value placed on higher mental functions *logically* inhere 'in the nature' of those functions? What criterion is used for determining how valuable a mental function is and to whom? Then there is the second set of problems, which arises from the close connection between higher mental activity and semiotic mediation. If there are variant forms of consciousness, then variant forms of semiotic mediation must exist. The more highly valued 'categorical, abstract thinking' must be attributed not to semiotic mediation *per se* but to *a particular form* of 'semiotic mediation' – to a particular 'fashion of speaking', to use the Whorfian phrase, or to a distinct 'coding orientation' as Bernstein would say. What are these particular forms of semiotic mediation like? Are they, too, valued more highly? If so, why?

Luria's attempt to account for the patterns of rational thinking amongst the Uzbeks might be taken here as implying certain answers. The results of this enquiry too were similar to those reported above. Since rational thinking is said to be based on the development of deduction and inference, the classic case of which is syllogistic reasoning, let us see how Luria (1976: 101) describes its nature and function:

> One of the objective devices that arises in the process of the development of cognitive activity is the syllogism – a set of individual judgments of varying degrees of generality in certain objectively necessary relationships to one another. Two sentences, of which the first ('precious metals do not rust') is in the nature of a general judgment... while the second ('gold is a precious metal') is a particular proposition, are not perceived by the developed consciousness as two isolated phrases in juxtaposition. A human being whose theoretical thought processes are well developed will perceive these as a completed logical relation implying the conclusion, 'Hence gold does not rust'. This conclusion does not require any personal experience; it is arrived at through a syllogism created objectively by historical experience. A considerable proportion of our intellectual operations involve such verbal and logical systems; they comprise the basic network of codes along which the connections in discursive human thought are channelled.

Luria's subjects were 'exposed' to two categories of syllogisms. Syllogisms the content of whose propositions was taken from the subjects' immediate practical experience and those where it was divorced from such experience. The results of this experiment correlated with very finely graded social attributes of the subjects (see details in Luria, 1976: 113ff). Reporting on the set of results pertaining to his 'non-literate' subjects, Luria (1976: 114; emphasis added) claimed:

> For the non-literate subjects, the process of reasoning and deduction *associated with immediate experience follow well-known rules*. These subjects can make *excellent judgments about facts of direct concern to them and draw all the implied conclusions, displaying no deviation from the 'rules' and revealing much worldly intelligence*. The picture changes, however, just as soon as they have to change to a system of theoretical thinking - in this instance making syllogistic inferences.

Luria cites three factors in explanation of his finding that his non-literate Uzbek subjects have limited 'capability for theoretical verbal-logical thinking':

> [1] mistrust of an initial premise that does not reproduce personal experience... [2] the unacceptability of the premise as universal... [3] a consequence of the second... [the] ready disintegration of the syllogism into three independent and isolated particular propositions with no unified logic and thus no access for thought to be channelled within this system.

Note that these explanations do not problematise his subjects' mistrust of non-subjective experience, or their reluctance to consider the universal. Luria simply emphasises that deduction and inference from the second category of syllogisms, whose propositions are not embedded in the practical experience of the subjects, indicate even *higher* mental evolution – perhaps the highest. This 'disembedded thinking' has been celebrated by philosophers, e.g. Popper (1979b); psychologists, e.g. Donaldson (1978); educationists, e.g. Olson (1977), as the *sine qua non* of intellectual *finesse*. I postpone asking why this should be so, since the answer would take us to a consideration of fairly constant elements in the Western ideology of knowledge, to our interpretation of the term *progress* and to the concepts of what might be taken as the ultimate goal of human evolution. Let me simply ask: In a genetic theory of mental development, how should one interpret an individual's inability to relate to premises that do not 'reproduce personal experience?' What underlies the failure to recognise 'universal facts?' What sort of consciousness do these processes indicate? I have by now asked a goodly number of questions arising from Vygotsky's views on the sociogenesis of consciousness. Let me summarise these under three general headings:

1 Identification of the valued form of semiotic mediation. Given that there are varieties of semiotic mediation, *how would the theory characterise that variety of semiotic mediation which is associated with the genesis of the most highly valued variety of mental function*?
2 Genesis of variation in forms of semiotic mediation and human consciousness. Given that different levels of mental function and varieties of semiotic mediation exist within the same sociopolitical community, *how does the theory explain the existence of this variation*?
3 Valuation of variants. Given the unmistakable impression that some forms of mental development are better than others, *how would the theory explain this valuation*?

It is usual to judge theories, by reference to what has been actually achieved through their use, but perhaps a more sympathetic approach would be to ask not what has actually been done, but what it is possible to do within the limits of the theory as it stands? My discussion shows that Vygotsky did not actually recognise – much less did he address – any of the problems outlined above. But this is less important than the question: Can the explanations we seek be found within the limits of the Vygotskian framework? Let me take the first question cited above to explore the possibilities that lie in the theory.

If semiotic mediation is mediation by means of semiosis by means of language, then it is reasonable to suppose that Vygotsky's views about language will be particularly relevant to any attempt to answer a question about the characterisation of valued forms of semiotic mediation. Simplifying somewhat, the two complementary perspectives for examining language are *language as system, as the potential for meaning* and *language as process, as the actualisation of meaning in use*. Recalling Vygotsky's insistence on the primacy of the *inter*personal over *intra*personal in the internalisation of semiotically mediated mental functions, it would seem that it is the process aspect of language – its use – that would form the fulcrum of semiotic mediation. So, for example, what is at issue is not the *potential* of language for being used in rational thinking, deduction, generalisation, abstraction and so on; the question is when and why do speakers *actually exploit* these capacities of language in their own processes of interaction? It is, of course, necessary to show that the system of language does have the potentialities being postulated, but this is a necessary, *not* a sufficient condition for their actualisation. In identifying the valued variety of semiotic mediation, it is not simply a question of what there is in the system of language, but rather of how that system is deployed, which of its potentialities appear relevant to whom, when and why. And, in this respect, it is important to emphasise that why the linguistic system is deployed the way it is, is never simply a question about language; rather; it is a question about the social situatedness of speakers. In order to be able to intellectualise the social situatedness of talk, what we need is a theory of social context which will explain what brings humans together, how and in what relation to each other in their speech and their practical activities. Without such a theory the details of semiotic mediation cannot be described; and if the description itself is problematic, it would be equally problematic to specify systematically the defining characteristics of variant forms of semiotic mediation.

In Vygotsky's theory, this necessary element whereby language and social processes are brought together is virtually absent. Certainly Vygotsky does mention some specific contexts of talk, e.g. the pedagogic contexts of the classroom, peer interaction, adult-child interaction, but these are used as commonsensical categories without any theoretical elaboration. The manner of their use leaves a good deal to be desired. Take, for example, his repeated references to pedagogic discourse. There is an unmistakable sense that this type of discourse maximises the possibility of developing higher mental functions in pupils. It is as if *each and every* pupil will 'read' the teacher in the same way; the teacher's language use will have the same cognitive consequence for all pupils. But this assumption is open to question. The educational systems have their own assessment practices for evaluating their pupils' cognitive development. While all pupils are 'exposed' to the same teacher talk, not all succeed equally well. Variation in levels of educational success correlates typically with the pupils' social positioning. Even if it is argued that the assessment practices of the educational system do not evaluate cognitive development in Vygotsky's sense of the term, it cannot be gainsaid that the efficacy of language in mediating meaning does not rest with the speaker alone. The addressee's orientation to what is being said is just as important. The non-theorisation of social context in Vygotsky's framework has the consequence of simplifying the concept of social interaction. The speaker and the listener become 'culturally non-specific' (Bernstein, 1990: 48); the range of verbal and practical activities lack contextual specialisation as if anyone can say or do anything anywhere anytime. Disappointingly, but not surprisingly, no concept of text develops. Word, or at best words in systemic sense relation, remain the unit of analysis in semiotic mediation. But it is clear that the relevant unit for semiotic mediation is not the word; it is text/discourse – language operational in a social context (Halliday and Hasan, 1989). What all this amounts to is that the perspective of *language as process actualising meaning* is effectively absent in Vygotsky.

As to his view of 'language as system', it may explain why language should be seen as the primary means for semiotic mediation, but it cannot account for variant forms of semiotic mediation. Either the characteristics of *a specific* language, or of human language *universally*, are such that no use can avoid them, in which case distinct groups of Uzbeks would not differ from each other; or the characteristics are capable of appearing in some uses but not in all, in which case the fact that they '*are* in the system' is quite irrelevant for explaining variation in semiotic mediation. The qualities of language as system which Vygotsky identified as important are such that no human language is known to lack them and no adult use can avoid them (for discussion, see Hasan, 1992/2005). So they cannot be invoked in the identification of the highly valued forms of semiotic mediation. Appeal to principles of abstract classification, preoccupation with decontextualised meanings, reflection on inferential relations – these and other such features are to be found in particular kinds of language use. The results of my research in Australia and that of my colleagues (Hasan, 1989; 1991; 1992a; 1992b; Hasan and Cloran, 1990; Butt, 1989; Cloran, 1989; Cloran, 1994) indicate that engagement in this kind of language use is the prerogative of a speaker's privileged social position. But as I have pointed out, Vygotsky's framework contains no theory of language use in social context and it has no systematic means of making any observations about the social positioning of speakers and addressees. It is not simply that variation in semiotic mediation has not been explained in this sociogenetic theory of mental development; the fact of the matter is that within the limits of that framework it is impossible to explain it. I have argued elsewhere (see Hasan, 1992/2005) why importing the Bakhtin-Vološinov notion of 'speech genre' into the Vygotsky-Luria framework as suggested by Wertsch (1985c; 1990) may not resolve the problem. Nor does it help to appeal as Luria did to the 'sociocultural history' of a speech community in order to explain why its members use language the way they do. In the context of such complex communities as the capitalist democracies of today, it becomes problematic how the term 'community' or 'sociocultural history' should be interpreted. For example, what would it mean to say that the sociocultural history of the working class mother in Australia is less evolved than that of the middle class mother? and that this explains why the working class mother's higher mental functions, her consciousness, are less evolved by comparison with that of the middle class mother? It seems to me that the Vygotsky-Luria framework for the sociogenesis of mind calls not only for a more sophisticated theory of language as suggested by Wertsch; it also needs a sophisticated theory of social organisation. I turn below to the consideration of a theory of social organisation – that of Bernstein's – which I believe can answer the three questions raised above.

4 Social conditions for semiotic mediation

Although, unlike Vygotsky, Bernstein is not concerned with examining specific historical stages in the development of human consciousness, like Vygotsky he has always been concerned with relations between the individual and the collectivity. Bernstein (1987a: 563) identifies the central project of his theory as a continuing engagement with the 'general theoretical question of classical sociology: *how does the outside become the inside and how does the inside reveal itself and shape the outside?*' This is an ambitious project, which, since its inception in the 1960s, has grown steadily in depth, spelling out in greater detail the elements of the dialectic between the *inside* and the *outside*. This preoccupation with the dialectic between the mental and the social makes Bernstein's framework relevant to other sociogenetic models such as those of Wittgenstein's, Mead's, Whorf's, Bateson's and Halliday's and, of course, Vygotsky's. There is, however, another factor underlying the similarity of perspective between Vygotsky and Bernstein. In different ways, the work of both scholars takes note of the Marxist analysis of social phenomena. My concern here is not with all elements of Bernstein's theory. I shall briefly discuss only those elements of the theory which are particularly relevant to the three questions raised in the last section. Since the questions are logically related to each other, the answer to one foreshadows the answer to the other two. It is difficult to dissociate the genesis of variant forms of consciousness and of semiotic mediation from the characterisation of the latter since they are logically implicated in the genesis of consciousness; and it has been suggested that it is their origin that largely explains their differing valuation in society. So let me take the second question first: *how can we explain the existence of variant forms of semiotic mediation and of human consciousness in 'the same' community?*

Bernstein answers this question by developing a system of logically related concepts, which at the most abstract level refer to the relations of the social division of labour and at the most concrete level to the variant forms of communication, thus exploiting multiple levels of abstraction in order to create explicit links between the 'macro' and the 'micro' of social organisation. The facts of the most abstract level – the social division of labour and its internal social relations – find their expression in the distribution of power and the principles of control, which in turn, regulate the relationships *within* and *between* social groups – both their categories and their interactional practices. The relationships *within* and *between* social groups underlie their distinct forms of communication and the distinct forms of communication are essential to the creation, transmission, maintenance and change in distinct forms of consciousness. In turn, these forms of consciousness in members of the social groups in a community enact the relations of the social division of labour, thus completing the dialectical revolution. Despite unavoidable simplifications, this is the outline of the relations between the various levels of the theory as I understand it. To my knowledge, the technical term 'semiotic mediation' is not used by Bernstein; however, the relevance of the concept in the creation of human consciousness is very clearly indicated. Consider the following extract from an early work (Bernstein, 1972: 473):

> the particular form of a social relation acts selectively upon what is said, when it is said, and how it is said... different forms of social relation can generate very different speech systems or communication codes... different speech systems or codes create for their speakers different orders of relevance and relation. The experience of the speaker may then be transformed by what is made significant or relevant by different speech systems. As the child learns his speech, or... learns specific codes which regulate his verbal acts, he learns the requirements of his social structure. The experience of the child is transformed by the learning generated by his own apparently voluntary acts of speech. The social structure becomes, in this way, the substratum of the child's experience essentially through the manifold consequences of the linguistic process. From this point of view, every time the child speaks or listens, the social structure is reinforced in him and his social identity shaped. The social structure becomes the child's psychological reality through the shaping of his acts of speech.

Since the social relations and the entailed forms of communication are so central to the theory, we need to ask how does the theory model the genesis of social relations, their regulation of the 'speech systems or codes' – the different principles for the use of language which become the means for the variant modes of semiotic mediation? Bernstein answers these questions by reference to the levels of abstraction in his theory. The concept of social relation cannot be divorced from that of the social division of labour: they are two sides of the same coin, but the social relations internal to the division of labour vary according to the nature of the latter. Where internal to the social division of labour in society are class relations, there inequalities arise in the distribution of power and the principles of control. And as implied by the systematic relations of the concepts in the theory, these inequalities in the distribution of power and in the principles of control necessarily implicate the forms of interaction and so the forms of consciousness. Bernstein (1990:13) claims:

class relations generate, distribute, reproduce, and legitimate distinctive forms of communication, which transmit dominant and dominated codes,... subjects are differentially positioned by these codes in the process of acquiring them. 'Positioning' is used... to refer to the establishing of a specific relation to other subjects and to the creating of specific relationships within subjects. In general, from this point of view, codes are culturally determined positioning devices. More specifically, class-regulated codes position subjects with respect to dominant and dominated forms of communication and to the relationships between them.

Thus a part of Bernstein's answer to the first question is that what we see as 'the same' community is riven by conflict. The theory models the processes whereby class relations intervene in the kind of ways indicated in the above extract. The principles of the distribution of power are manifested in the regulation of the relations between and within social categories – including categories of social subjects. The identity and value of a social category is given by the social practices of that category in relation to other categories of the same order. It is these specialised practices which both make it distinct from other categories and constitute its inner nature. The more specialised the practices of a category, the clearer its identity and value – i.e., the place it occupies – within the social system. Bernstein uses the metaphor of 'voice' to refer to the speciality that is constituted by a category's specialised practices. A category is knowable by its voice to the extent that this voice is distinct from that of other categories. To maintain the specificity of a category is to maintain insulation across the voices of distinct categories. Bernstein uses the term 'classification' to refer to the processes that create and maintain the insulation of one category from another, keeping their specialisation distinct. The practices of classification call for power (Bernstein, 1990: 24):

> the insulation maintainers must have power and the conditions to exert it. Thus insulation presupposes *relations of power* for its creation, reproduction, and legitimation...*Power relations position subjects through the principles of the classification they establish.* If power relations are regulated by class relations, then class relations position subjects through the principles of classification they establish.

The strength of classification forms a *cline* i.e., a continuum. At one extreme, classification may be maximally *strong*, at the other, maximally *weak*: the *stronger* the classification, the more unambiguous a category's position *vis a vis* the others, whereas the *weaker* the classification, the less sharp the boundaries between categories and the more integrated the social practices. If the strong end of the cline keeps things – social groups, classes of objects, social contexts

– apart from one another, then the weak end brings them together (Bernstein, 1987a; 1990). The voice of a category – its specialisation – is enacted in its social interaction: this enactment constitutes the *message* of the category. The form of the message is shaped by the pacing of social interaction – what degree of control *vis a vis* each other the categories have in the development of the interaction. Variation in pacing is thus regulated by the principles of control. The processes of the principles of control are known as 'framing'. If classification is concerned with the *what* of communication, framing is concerned with the *how*. The strength of framing, like that of classification, is conceptualised as a cline. 'Strong framing' leaves the pacing of the interaction within the discretion of the dominating category, while with 'weak framing' the pacing is shared by the interacting categories. The etiology of a subject's coding orientation can be traced to the nature of that subject's experience of social categories as they are refracted through the practices of classification and framing. In other words, through the processes of the distribution of power and of the principles of control, the voice and message of a social category are translated into specific kinds of acts of meaning and participation in such acts of meaning is the means of the acquisition of coding orientation. The variant coding orientations will semiotically mediate the form of consciousness that is the expression of a subject's relation to her social positioning. I suggest that the steps I have just described are the very steps whereby a social subject is *ideologically formed.* Ideology is not something that can be separated from the relations of power and control as experienced in forms of communication which are active in generating forms of consciousness.

What the above account shows is that the theory logically relates the speaking subject's socially (re)produced consciousness with the principles governing that subject's fashions of speaking. The coding orientation, with its antecedent logical relations, forms the invisible mainspring for the visible forms of communication. From this point of view, a given text – language operational in use – is 'the form of the social relationship made visible, palpable and material' (Bernstein, 1990: 17). The social relationship, which is linked, in the last resort, to the relations internal to division of labour in a society, 'activates' forms of communication, which forms of communication, can be used to 'construe' the social relations (see Halliday, 1992 for an interpretation of these terms). And as in the case of language system, so also in the case of the social system, process is the environment for renewing, maintaining and changing the system. As Bernstein (*loc. cit.*) says 'the selection, creation, production, and changing of texts are the means whereby the positioning of subjects is revealed, reproduced, and changed'. (It should be added that by 'text' Bernstein does not mean simply verbal texts.) We thus have in Bernstein's model, a theory of social context and of discourse, both embedded within a theory of social structure. The theory can thus answer the question about the genesis of variant forms of communication by linking them to the subjects' social positioning, in which positioning the subject's experience of communication is an active element, as it is in the formation of her consciousness.

Let us turn now to the first question. What can Bernstein's theory tell us about the distinct forms of communication associated with distinct coding orientations? The answer has already been implied in saying that participation in distinct codes – its active and receptive experience – furnishes the subjects' ideas of relevance – what meanings will appear significant, deserving of the speakers' and listeners' attention. Bernstein (1990: 20) states his general hypothesis as follows:

> The simpler the social division of labour, and the more specific and local the relation between an agent and its material base, the more direct the relation between meanings and a specific material base, and the greater the probability of a restricted coding orientation. The more complex the social division of labour, the less specific and local the relations between an agent and its material base, the more indirect the relation between meanings and a specific material base, and the greater the probability of an elaborated coding orientation.

When the social conditions encourage an orientation to restricted coding, the meanings that typically appear most relevant are those which relate relatively more directly to the material base; they tend to relate to the local contexts, for it is the local contexts that impinge more directly on the living of life. Thus Luria's 'concrete situational thinking' could be a feature of a variety of restricted coding. By contrast, with elaborated coding, the meanings that typically appear relevant are not in direct relation to the material base; the subject's relation to the material base of the social division of labour is itself not direct. Supra-local meanings appear relevant; decontextualised language will be favoured. Generalisation and abstraction could assume importance. The voice and the message of a social category are logically related to that category's social positioning, but the nature of this voice and message and, so of positioning, is knowable only through the acts of semiosis. Taking verbal semiosis as the paradigm case, distinct social positionings imply distinct experience of languaging. The broad lineaments of these differences across distinct forms of semiotic mediation can be easily outlined. But such characterisation can neither be offered nor verified by examining atomic elements of language e.g. words, word groups; they pertain to the disposition of the discourse as a whole. Further, there are no rigid criteria translatable into the empirical researcher's favourite '*x* occurs' vs. '*x* does not occur'. Instead, the semantic features that differentiate the distinct coding orientations have to be presented in terms of probabilities (on this perspective see Halliday, 1992/2003), as demonstrated in my studies of semantic variation (see earlier references and some details in Halliday, 1995b). One problem that has to be kept in view in specifying such characteristics is the Janus-faced nature of discourse. Two apparently contradictory properties are common to all instances of human discourse. First, discourse is an effective means for change, which implies the appearance of the unexpected – this is the unfamiliar, unconventional aspect of talk. Second, discourse is a means of maintaining the current programs of the social conditions of existence, which implies the appearance of the expected – this is the recognisable, conventional aspect of discourse. To characterise the features of variant forms of semiotic mediation, we need a theory that links social structure and discourse, showing how the one lives by the other, unchanged and changing at one and the same time. I suggest that in Bernstein's theory we do have a model that most closely approaches this ideal. Further through its elaboration of the notion of 'pedagogic discourse' it is able to show how the *official* and *local pedagogic practices* can be described using essentially the same theoretical apparatus that I have attempted to bring to attention. In Bernstein's theory there is no glorification of the higher mental functions, as the term is used in Vygotsky and Luria. This is so because it is impossible to dissociate higher mental function in this sense of the term from the reproduction of dominating voices and messages which are relayed in official pedagogy via teacher-pupil talk or in local pedagogy through adult-child talk in the dominating social categories.

This leaves us with the final question. Why are the different levels of higher mental function evaluated differently? I believe Bernstein's answer is implicit in his approach to the earlier two problems and echoes a Marxist view. The forms of mental activity to which societies invariably attach greater value are those which characterise the power groups in a society, whatever the source of their power. This brings us back to the dominating and dominated codes, suggesting that the ways of meaning typical of the dominating codes are also inevitably seen as the best ways of meaning and thinking in a society. Let me add immediately that in saying this Bernstein is simply stating what *is* the case, not what he thinks *should be* the case. But in agreeing with Bernstein, there still remains an important question. Are there no *logical* reasons for better valuing such higher mental functions as those of abstraction, generalisation, deductive reasoning, disembedded thinking, etc? Are these functions valued highly *only* because they are associated with the dominating codes? Or are they valued because they are the ultimate point in the programs of the development of the human mind, necessary for subjugating the environment? These questions throw long shadows and it is my conviction that neither the sociology of knowledge nor its philosophy, neither the science of cognitive development nor of physics have pursued these questions. This may be because no matter how we answer these questions, the answers are immensely disquieting and they certainly mock the facile pseudo-revolutionary postures of many academics today.

5 Concluding remarks

Hopefully the above discussion shows that a sociologically sophisticated theory of the relationship between forms of semiotic mediation and development of human consciousness is able to resolve some of the problems that inhere in the Vygotsky-Luria approach. The virtue of Bernstein's theory is not that it recognises variation in semiotic mediation. After all, Vygotsky's close contemporaries, Bakhtin-Vološinov, too recognised its existence in their notion of linguistic heterogeneity, as did Marx before them. But it is one thing to talk vaguely about the effect of sociocultural history (cf. Luria), or of ideological and material basis (cf. Bakhtin-Vološinov), or the social being of men (cf. Marx) and it is quite another thing to provide an elaboration of the theoretical steps whereby social structure, social interaction and individual's minds enter in a dialectic that can be described as a theory of the sociogenesis of human consciousness. Bernstein's theory does precisely this and is therefore essential to an understanding of the workings of certain aspects of the Vygotsky-Luria project. However, it should be emphasised that in making these comments I am not asking for the Vygotsky-Luria approach to be replaced by that of Bernstein's: this would strike me as a rather simplistic solution to a situation that calls for a much more complex research program.

To describe this program, let me turn to another Vygotskian concept – that of the 'zone of proximal development' (Vygotsky, 1962; 1978 etc.). Just as the potential of a mind is not revealed by looking at what that mind is capable of in isolation from other minds, so it would seem to me that the potential of a theory is not capable of being judged in isolation. Theories too must be observed in interaction before we can judge their zone of proximal development – what they are capable of doing given a cooperative environment. We need Vygotsky for the creative way he integrates the biogenetic with the sociogenetic. This aspect of the human mind is scarcely mentioned in Bernstein's theory and, though the omission is understandable, it is not one that a theory of mind can tolerate. On the other hand, we need Bernstein for the meticulous and deep description of the meaning of sociogenesis. No theory of human mind can do without this element. But since sociogenesis implies semiosis, we cannot stop at this point. Just as Vygotsky's theory cries out for a deeper understanding of the social, so Bernstein's cries out for a deeper understanding of the semiotic. And given the place of language in semiosis, this calls for an understanding of language. Just as sociogenesis without a theory of society leaves a good deal unsaid, so code regulated semiotic mediation without a theory of linguistic meaning defies description. And just as not all theories of society would equally successfully complement Vygotsky's sociogenetic theory of the mind, so not all theories of language will equally successfully complement Bernstein's theory of the production and reproduction of society. Only a powerful theory of language – one where language is not viewed as an epiphenomenon of the social – would succeed in complementing this theory. Social interaction – typically, talk – is what all aspects of social organisation, including the relations of social division of labour, turn on. How does this happen? In offering its explanations, sociology in general bows in the direction of language but considers it as extraneous. By contrast, Bernstein's model does not – in fact *cannot* – treat language as extraneous. This sociological theory compels us to explore the theoretical connections which span the biological, the sociological and the linguistic, combining the insights of Vygotsky's sociogenetic psychology, Bernstein's semiotic sociology and Halliday's sociological linguistics to arrive at a theory which will specify the social conditions for the semiotic mediation of the human mind.

5   Semiotic mediation and three exotropic theories: Vygotsky, Halliday and Bernstein

1   Introduction

In this paper I want to weave together the story of three specialisations. Since each represents a large area of scholarship, the story will have to be selective, weaving together simply some fragments from each. The moral at the heart of the story is that disciplines have arisen in the service of maintaining and changing human life, an essential precondition for which is understanding human life. Because the concerns of human life are interconnected, therefore, in order to appreciate the nature of one concern, you must have some idea of how the others function in relation to it. To be useful, the disciplines logically must be permeable. This in turn says something about the very nature of theory, for in the end it is theory that supplies the foundation for the structure of specialist disciplines. As Bernstein pointed out (2000: 91ff) it is after all theories that explicitly and unambiguously identify the object of study, build the conceptual syntax for revealing its nature and provide the language of description so that all instances may be described in a way that permits us to understand them adequately. The three human concerns whose interconnectedness forms the focus of my story are: consciousness, language and society. The fragments that I choose to foreground from these specialist disciplines represent the work of authors who I believe would welcome an enterprise such as mine: they are Vygotsky, Halliday and Bernstein, respectively. Let me begin then with consciousness, since, as some might maintain, this is where all stories regarding human life begin.

2 The genesis of consciousness: a Vygotskian perspective

In this and the following section, I will present some fragments from a theory of consciousness that has deservedly received much attention during the last two decades. The theory is associated with the name of Vygotsky (1962; 1978), who introduced its crucial features during the early days of Russia's communist revolution. At this point, two comments about this theory appear appropriate: first, in my view, the richness of the theory derives to a large extent from Vygotsky's readiness to make connections with other areas of human concern, such as the biological, the educational, the social and particularly the semiotic and, within the semiotic, particularly the linguistic. Secondly, in as much as the theory is open to some serious critiques, this too derives from the fact that other possible and equally important connections are either missed or are not robust enough. In the course of this discussion I hope to elaborate on these points more fully. So far as Vygotsky's theory of consciousness, my main interest lies in the concept of semiotic mediation. This is not simply because my work has mostly concerned a sub-field of semiotics, namely, linguistics; it is because the concept of semiotic mediation plays a crucial role in Vygotsky's theory of the development of human consciousness. Vygotsky firmly believed that human behaviour can be understood only as the history of that behaviour and, in his account of the sociogenesis of certain forms of human consciousness, semiotic mediation is a critical factor. The broad sweep of Vygotsky's vision included both phylogenetic and ontogenetic perspectives on mental activity. For my purposes the latter perspective is arguably more relevant. I want to examine the role of semiotic mediation in the ontogenesis of consciousness.

Vygotsky postulated two 'lines' for the genesis of human mental activity: the natural line and the social or cultural line. The natural line enables elementary mental functions, while the social line is active in the genesis of the higher mental functions. Vygotsky was careful to point out that the two lines of mental development do not simply run a parallel course; rather, according to him, the specific nature of human consciousness is the product of the 'interweaving of these two lines'. The natural line is where, for all normal humans, mental activity begins: this level of activity Vygotsky referred to as 'elementary mental functions' or sometimes simply as 'natural' mental functions. These represent the initial levels of mental development in human beings and act as the biogenetic foundation on which more advanced mental activity can be built. Vygotsky argued that the qualities specific to human mental functions are not manifested in the make up of the natural mental activities; rather, they are introduced into mental functions through the intervention of the social line, which transforms the early natural functions into a higher level of mental activity. An excellent example of the relation of the two lines of mental development is provided by Vygotsky (1978: 51; emphasis added) in the following extract:

> when a human being ties a knot in her handkerchief as a reminder, she is in essence, constructing the process of memorising by forcing an external object to remind her of something: *she transforms remembering into an external activity... In the elementary form* [of mental action] *something is remembered; in the higher form humans remember something.*

The process of remembering is not unknown to the natural line; it exists in all normal human beings, who are biologically designed to remember. But when the social line enters the scene through the action of tying a knot as a deliberate reminder for recall, the nature of the mental process changes. The remembering subject now gains control on the activity of remembering, which is no longer dependent on environmental triggering. In this sense reminding oneself by tying a knot, a humble enough action, is a sociogenetic mental process: it is socially mediated. Remembering as an elementary mental process is a serendipitous activity triggered by a chance encounter of a stimulus presented by environment. Reminding oneself purposefully and consciously by the mediation of some instrument that is within one's control is a higher and different order of mental function: as Vygotsky put it 'to recall [in this sort of context] means to think' (1978: 51). Below are Vygotsky's views on higher mental functions presented in his own words (as translated by Wertsch, 1985b: 26):

> [their] basic and distinguishing features are intellectualisation and mastery, that is, conscious realisation and voluntariness.

> At the centre of development during the school age is the transition from the lower functions of attention and memory to higher functions of voluntary attention and logical memory... the intellectualisation of functions and their mastery represent two moments of one and the same process – the transition to higher psychological functions. We master a function to the extent that it is intellectualised. The voluntariness in the activity is always the other side of its conscious realisation. To say that memory is intellectualised in school is exactly the same as to say that voluntary recall emerges; to say that attention becomes voluntary in school age is exactly the same as saying... that it depends more and more on thought, that is, on intellect.

By this brilliant illustration of how human mental development spirals from what is given by nature into something qualitatively different and of a higher order by the intervention of the social, Vygotsky was able to show the continuity between the physical and the social aspects of human life in relation to human consciousness. He thus neatly side-stepped the sterile debate, which is being actively pursued even to this day about whether human consciousness is given by 'nature' as the Cartesians would have it, or by 'nurture' i.e., by society as Marx so eloquently argued. Faced with this either/or proposition, Vygotsky simply opted for both, thus enriching his field by recognising the complexity of its object of enquiry. This was a remarkable achievement, particularly when it is recalled that Vygotsky took this stance in the heyday of Piagetian psychology and at a time when the enormous influence of Pavlovian psychology was by no means spent. In the realm of the production of knowledge, we are much given to applauding originality without perhaps fully appreciating its true nature. Let me suggest that, contrary to conventional wisdom, originality does not really refer to absolute novelty, to a freshness uncontaminated by past endeavours by others. In the context we have in mind, it consists in perceiving new connections amongst already existing concepts and structures. Originality is therefore very much like Vygotsky's higher mental functions, a sociogenetic phenomenon.

3 Semiotic mediation in the development of mental functions

If the development of a characteristically human mind equals the emergence and growth of higher mental functions, and if higher mental functions are characterised by 'conscious realisation' and 'voluntary control', a pertinent question is: where do these two characteristics arise from? Vygotsky's response is again brilliant in the acuteness of observation that it reveals. Voluntary regulation and intellectualisation call for the 'use of artificial stimuli': it is only such stimuli that are under human control, and this is an essential condition for their manipulation. Ultimately, then, the growth of voluntary control and conscious regulation can be traced to the fact of mediation by artificial stimuli. To quote Vygotsky (1978: 39; emphasis added):

> [human beings] go beyond the limits of the psychological functions given to them by nature and proceed to a *new culturally-elaborated organisation* of their behaviour... The central characteristic of elementary functions is that they are totally and directly determined by stimulation from the environment. For higher functions, the central feature is *self generated stimulation*, that is, *the creation and use of artificial stimuli which become the immediate cause of behaviour.*

For 'use of artificial stimuli' read 'use of tools': the notion of tools is crucial to the process of mediation. Tools are artificial stimuli, not given by nature but created by human beings in the course of their social life and this has important implications. To clarify the significant contribution of tools to human social existence, Vygotsky used an analysis of physical activities as his point of departure. He pointed out that in performing labour, human beings use 'technological' or 'concrete tools' and, as everyone knows, in the practical sphere, mediation by tools changes the very nature of human physical performance, making possible achievements that would otherwise have remained out of reach. The structuring of human labour is altered through this mediation and eventually it affects the very nature of the environment in which we live[1]. Vygotsky argued that, from the point of view of mediation by social stimuli, mental activities are analogous to physical labour: as a form of human labour, they too reach higher levels through mediation by artificial stimuli; their structure too changes and in time they too affect the environment in which we live. The only difference is that in this case, the tools are 'abstract', 'psychological' and 'semiotic', hence the term 'semiotic mediation'. In Vygotsky's words (1981: 137), the mediation of mental activities by means of semiotic tools:

> alters the entire flow and structure of mental functions. It does this by determining the structure of a new instrumental act just as a technical tool alters the process of a natural adaptation by determining the form of labour operation.

We may thus paraphrase the term semiotic mediation as 'mediation by means of semiosis', that is, by the use of sign systems which act as an abstract tool in changing the character of human mental activity. According to Vygotsky (1978: 40):

> The use of signs leads humans to a specific structure of behaviour that breaks away from biological development and creates new forms of culturally based psychological processes.

Now, semiotic acts are acts of meaning, and meaning can be construed by various semiotic modalities, of which language is only one instance. But in his discourse on the concept of semiotic mediation, Vygotsky (1962; 1978; 1981) attached significantly greater importance to language than to other modalities of meaning, so that in the Vygotskian *œuvre*, the phrase 'semiotic mediation' has come to stand for 'mediation by means of the linguistic sign'. In assigning this crucial place to language, Vygotsky was acknowledging his conviction that amongst the various semiotic modalities language alone maximised the qualities that are necessary for something to function as a psychological tool capable of mediating the development of the mind. A Bourdieu (1991) might sneer that this view of language is simply a signifier for linguistic imperialism, but those who have actually worked with language might better understand the point Vygotsky is making (Sapir, 1921; Firth, 1957; Whorf, 1956; Hjelmslev, 1961; de Saussure, 1966; Halliday, 1975; Donaldson, 1992; Deacon, 1997; Hasan, 1992/2005; 1999c): of all the semiotic modalities only language at once defies time, is capable of being reflexive, classifies reality, construes communicable human experience and articulates the many voices of a culture with equal facility, which is not to say that by its internal nature, it determines their social privilege, or that other modalities make no contribution. These qualities of language are relevant to its capacity for acting as an effective abstract tool and nowhere is this more evident than in the formation of the growing child's consciousness. It is here that the social nature of the semiotic tool assumes great importance. Here is Vygotsky again (1978: 25):

> Prior to mastering his own behaviour, the child begins to master his surroundings with the help of speech. This produces new relations with the environment in addition to the new organisation of behaviour itself. The creation of these uniquely human forms of behaviour later produce the intellect and become the basis of productive work: the specifically human form of the use of tool.

Further, to say that tools are artificial is to say that they are inherently social. If language is an abstract tool for semiotic mediation, it follows that language too is a social phenomenon. This implies that sedimented in language are traces of human social activities and social relations; from which it follows that in using and learning language, children learn their culture (Halliday, 1980). The contribution of the social to the child's cognitive growth is central to Vygotsky's discourse of semiotic mediation (Vygotsky, 1981: 163):

> Any function in the child's cultural [i.e., higher] development appears twice, or on two planes. First it appears on the social plane, and then on the psychological plane. First it appears between people as an inter-psychological category, and then within the child as an intra-psychological category. This is equally true with regard to voluntary attention, logical memory, the formation of concepts, and the development of volition.... it goes without saying that internalisation transforms the process itself and changes its structure and functions. Social relations or relations among people genetically underlie all higher functions and their relationships.

4 Semiotic mediation: an analysis of the concept

As the last two sections have indicated, Vygotsky's concept of semiotic mediation has an enormous reach. One might expect a crucial element of a psychological theory to make contributions to the conventionally recognised areas of psychology such as the origins of human behaviour, the nature of learning, the role of intelligence in learning, and the development of consciousness. Vygotsky's concept of semiotic mediation addresses all of these concerns, but it also goes beyond them: it links the development of consciousness to semiosis – and specifically to linguistic semiosis – and it links the specifically human aspects of our practical and mental life to our sociohistorical contexts. With the introduction of the concept of semiotic mediation, the canvas of

Vygotsky's theory expands: it becomes broad enough to locate the relations of mind, language and society. Vygotsky was, unfortunately, not allowed time to develop the many threads of intellectual enquiry that the concept adumbrated, but even during his brief working life, the concept was used in remarkable researches (see, Vygotsky, 1962; 1978; Luria, 1976; Wertsch, 1985b). The last three decades have seen a steady growth of scholarship around the concept. Nonetheless, it seems to me that the concept has itself not been fully interpreted, with the result that its impressive reach across the many concerns of human life has remained invisible. In this section I will attempt to deconstruct the concept by using insights from systemic functional linguistics (henceforth, SFL). I will then go on to briefly indicate which aspects of the concept have been developed in more recent scholarship.

It does not need to be pointed out that the noun *mediation* is derived from the verb *mediate*, which refers to a process with a complex semantic structure involving the following participants and circumstance that are potentially relevant to this process:

1 someone who mediates, i.e., a mediator;
2 something that is mediated; i.e., a *content/force/energy* released by mediation;
3 someone/something subjected to mediation; i.e., the '*mediatee*' to whom/which mediation makes some difference;
4 the circumstances[2] for mediation; viz.,
   (a) the means of mediation i.e., *modality*;
   (b) the location i.e., *site* in which mediation might occur.

These complex semantic relations are not evident in every grammatical use of the verb, but submerged below the surface they are still around and can be brought to life through paradigmatic associations i.e., their systemic relations: we certainly have not understood the process unless we understand how these factors might influence its unfolding in actual time and space. To begin with the first element, when we say *tools mediate*, we are using the verb *mediate* in the same way as the verb *drive* in *this car drives well*. In the world of our experience we know that the initiative and the active agentive power is not with the car or the tool; thus in the case of material mediation, the initiative and the active power lies in the one who is responsible for the *use* of tools to mediate. In other words there must be some conscious *mediator* (1). To say that a tool mediates is to say that someone uses it to impart some force or energy to the business in hand: this is the *content* of mediation (2). With technological tools the content is material; what is imparted is material force/energy. With an abstract tool, the energy is semiotic; it imparts some semiotic force. The content/energy to be imparted is directed towards something/someone; it has a destination. The technological tools direct the energy to the process of labour being carried out by the mediator-labourer; the abstract tool is directed toward an other who is addressed by the mediator-speaker and in this sense semiotic mediation is an inherently interactive process: there must be a conscious *mediatee* (3). The extracts in the last section show that Vygotsky is keen to draw attention to the interactive nature of semiotic mediation. This is where the concrete and abstract tools differ in a crucial way: the participation of a conscious other, which is a condition of mediation by the abstract tool, alters the nature of the process. We can still maintain that the mediator has the initiative and active power to impart the semiotic/semantic energy, but here the user/mediator has far less control on what happens to this mediated energy: the mediator may impart semiotic energy, but the mediatee may or may not respond to its force, or respond to it in a way not intended by the user. At the heart of semiotic mediation there is this element of uncertainty. Notably, this is not a fact that to my knowledge has ever been brought to attention in the Vygotskian literature: semiotic mediation in the Vygotskian literature appears to always act felicitously. Finally the circumstances of mediation (4) are also important. By referring to the tool as material or semiotic, we have already introduced the different means by which mediation occurs: with the semiotic tools, the *modality* of language is crucial (4a). Finally there is the question of the spatio-temporal location of mediation: what are the *sites* in which mediation becomes a possibility (4b). I want to suggest that notwithstanding the role of inner speech in thinking, the necessary environment for semiotic mediation is discursive interaction, which logically brings in train all those social phenomena which impinge on the occurrence of discourse.

This discussion has very likely appeared tedious in its details. But in my view, precisely because these tedious details have not been the object of reflection, the full potential of semiotic mediation to human life has remained hidden and, at the same time, its problematic nature has failed to be recognised (for some discussion see Hasan, 1992/2005; 1995b). In the majority of the scholarship that centres around the concept, the concern has been typically with (2) i.e., the content and with (4b) i.e., the site of *semiotic mediation*: what does it mediate, and what is the environment in which it mediates. To be more accurate, the question of content has been treated as non-controversial: the term semiotic mediation as used in the literature could be said to be an abbreviation for *semiotic mediation of such higher mental functions as logical reasoning, logical memory, concept formation and problem solving etc., by means of the modality of language*, as if the mediating power of language is restricted only to these phenomena. As I have remarked elsewhere (Hasan, 2002) the normal condition of the use of language is for it to mediate something: the question is what are the range of mental structures that are mediated by language, where and when. Certainly, language does play an important role in mediating the genesis of the above mental functions; but this does not exhaust the description of its mediational powers. What we need to recognise is that wherever there is language in use, i.e., discourse, there is semiotic mediation going on. From this perspective, the overwhelming experience of semiotic mediation that each and every member of a society encounters is that which occurs in local sites i.e., in the ordinary, everyday living of life, for to say that the site for semiotic mediation is discourse is to say that the site is social life; whatever else the experience of social life might or might not have, there must always be for mentally normal human beings, an experience of interaction with others in the daily living of life. To those of us who know our Bernstein and our Halliday well, it is in this context that language mediates the most fundamental element of our mental life: it produces in us an unfailing sense of what the world is like in which we live. Through semiotic mediation in this discursive environment, we come to recognise the legitimate, acceptable, sensible ways of responding to objective and subjective phenomena in our socially defined universe. It is through this category of semiotic mediation that we internalise our concepts of relevance, and thus of 'rationality', and 'normality': this is where mental habits are created and nurtured. And these dispositions, these habitual ways of engaging mentally – or not, as the case may be – are, as Bernstein has argued since the mid-1960s, pertinent to a subject's perception of what is worth attending to and in what way. Through semiotic mediation in local environments we learn ways of being, doing and saying which are intelligible to others in our speech community.

The above comments clearly indicate that the limits on the content of semiotic mediation are not determined purely by the inherent characteristics of language: the equally, if not more important, element is the environment in which mediation is encountered[3]. The nature of this element is not universal, for access to environment is socially regulated (see discussion below). In recent literature the environment of semiotic mediation (4b) has attracted a good deal of attention and I shall briefly discuss this aspect of the structure of the concept in the concluding paragraphs of the next section. Elements (1) i.e., mediator and (3) mediatee have received scant attention as social beings (see, however, Axel, 1997), though arguably these relations are crucial to the claim of the sociogenesis of mind (more discussion to follow). When it comes to the circumstance of means (4a), Vygotsky had a good deal to say about the nature of the modality, i.e., language (more discussion follows). In recent literature, Wertsch (1985c; 1991) has drawn attention to some problems in Vygotsky's conception of language. In the following section, I will look more closely into those fragments of Vygotsky's theory which concern specifically the position of language in relation to mind. Perhaps the best way to approach this question is through Vygotsky's ideas on the development of thought and language in the growing child, for it is in this context that he presents his views on the social basis of the sign, on the nature of language and on the role of language in the development of concepts, which as I remarked above, is often foregrounded in the literature as the main achievement of semiotic mediation.

5 Semiotic mediation: language in the making of mind

Vygotsky was, of course, very familiar with the work of Stern, Bühler and Piaget, the three major psychologists whose writing in the field of child development had already engaged much contemporary attention. There is, ironically, no indication that he knew about the writings of another contemporary, the anthropologist, Bronislaw Malinowski, whose work on child language development (Malinowski, 1923), though slender, resonates quite well with Vygotsky's own sociogenetic approach. What is striking about both is their insistence on the centrality of meaning and on the crucial role of society in the ontogenesis of meaning making in the infant. Both these issues are foregrounded in Vygotsky's critique of Piaget. Piaget claimed that the early activity of the child 'is unquestionably egocentric and egotistic. The social instinct in well-defined form develops late' (Piaget, 1924: 276). In support of this claim Piaget cited his observation that the early conversation of children was 'egocentric', not 'socialised'. Thus, according to Piaget, the young child at first talks mostly about himself and only to himself, and has no active discursive involvement in the addressee. The intersubjectivity that forms a necessary condition for normal adult discourse is, in Piaget's view, absent from the young child's speech. Vygotsky disagreed; he suggested (1962: 19) instead that:

> The primary function of speech, in both children and adults, is communication, social contact. The earliest speech of the child is therefore essentially social. At a certain stage the social speech of the child is quite sharply divided into egocentric and communicative speech.... Egocentric speech emerges when the child transfers social collaborative forms of behaviour to the sphere of inner-personal psychic functions.... When circumstances force him [the child] to stop and think, he is likely to think aloud. Egocentric speech, splintered off from general social speech, in time leads to inner speech, which serves both autistic[4] and logical thinking.

Note that Vygotsky uses 'communicative' rather than Piaget's term 'socialised', since for Vygotsky all speech is social in any event. Whereas for Piaget the sequence of mental development in the child is first non-verbal autistic thought, then egocentric thought and speech, then finally socialised speech and logical thinking, for Vygotsky with his sociogenetic perspective, the sequence is predictably different: first social communication, then egocentric speech, and then arising from the latter what Vygotsky called inner speech in which the child thinks aloud. This is in keeping with Vygotsky's thesis that the true direction of mental development is not from the individual to the social, but from the social to the individual.

The question naturally arises: what did Vygotsky mean by social 'communication' or social speech, particularly in infancy, where there is quite obviously no recognisable natural language? It is my understanding that there is no satisfactory answer to this question in Vygotsky's work who simply remarked in passing (1962: 7) that:

> understanding between minds is impossible without some mediating expression... In the absence of a system of signs, linguistic or other, only the most primitive and limited type of communication is possible. Communication by means of expressive movements, observed among animals, is not so much communication as a spread of affect. A frightened goose suddenly aware of danger and rousing the whole flock with its cries does not tell the others what it has seen but rather contaminates them with its fear.

In fact, the question of social communication in the first weeks of an infant's life was to be answered several decades later by scholars such as Trevarthen (1977), Shotter (1978), Bullowa (1979) and others. Their empirical studies revealed intricate patterns of social communication mediated by gestures between mothers and their weeks old infants, thus vindicating Vygotsky's views on the primacy of social communication. It should be added immediately that the gestures these scholars studied were not simply *expressive movements*, in other words infant communication can not be treated simply as *social contact or as a spread of affect*; according to the scholars, some sort of understanding was at issue and the gestures became systematic remarkably early. Whether one would call them a system of gestural signs or not depends on how one understands the terms 'system' and 'sign'. I will return to Vygotsky's notion of linguistic sign shortly, but first let me pause a little at the above extract.

I am particularly arrested by the last sentence, an analysis of which would suggest that for Vygotsky communication equals telling someone something that in all likelihood they had not known before. Central to this interpretation of communication is, in terms of Bühler (1990), the concept of 'reference' or 'representation' – part of what Halliday (1978) was to refer to as the experiential function of language. Halliday's own case study of a child's language development (1973a; 1975) showed quite clearly that before the emergence of mother tongue, the child is able to perform a number of communicative functions, using what has become known in linguistics as 'protolanguage' – child tongue as opposed to mother tongue. However, the majority of these early functions (from nine to about 15 months of age) were interpersonal such as getting people to do things, greeting them, expressing dis/pleasure, demanding attention or satisfaction of bodily needs and so on (see Halliday, 1975: 148-55). There is also evidence for the ontogenesis of imaginative play in the child; however, even right into the early mother tongue stage, the child was not able to 'talk about' some particular state of affairs to any one who was not already familiar with it. Halliday's findings were replicated by two other case studies (Painter, 1984; Torr, 1997). The hallmark of protolanguage is the absence of grammar; each 'utterance' stands as a whole for one function, and to say that there was no grammar is to say that the utterance was not analysable into constituent units. While there may occur utterances in the later stages of protolanguage that seem to sound just like a familiar word from the mother tongue, this is not a word or phrase in the true sense for the word: its function is different from that of the word – perhaps, it is what Vygotsky meant by the primitive function of word as 'signal'. The emergence of grammar and of the informative, i.e. (proto) experiential function, coincide with entry into the mother tongue, and both require time to establish themselves. But all three children gave unmistakable evidence of what Vygotsky would have called 'intellectual activity'; possibly this is what Vygotsky meant by prelinguistic thought (Vygotsky, 1962: 44).

A few things need to be noted at this point: first, studies such as those cited above both in prespeech and in protolinguistic communication support Vygotsky's claim that the first communicative acts of the child are social; this favours the view of language as a socially-developed system. Secondly, by implication, Piaget's scheme of developmental sequence is brought into doubt: to the extent that thoughts do not think themselves (cf. Vygotsky, 1962: 8), they must implicate available forms of experience. It is obvious the child, through his acts of communication, already has some experience of the social. So autistic thought could not be the first stage of his mental development. This supports an early start for the sociogenesis of human mind. Third, if we accept that at this early stage the child is communicating, then we have to grant also that the term communication has a wider reference than just telling someone something that they might not have known before: the child's communication could not be dismissed as a genetically programmed 'spread of affect', but at the same time it would be absurd to suggest that the child is 'telling someone something' in the sense of recounting or debating on an experience. Nor could we claim that communication depends on the availability of words and this is where Vygotsky's own position appears unclear: is the protolinguistic child communicating, or is he not? If he is not, then his early mental activity could be autistic as Piaget claimed; if he is communicating, then clearly communication is possible without words and we must grant that preverbal meanings exist.

An understanding of the nature of language shows that the emphasis on word as the *sine qua non* of language and the function of language to tell someone something stem from the same source: in terms of SFL theory, they are both directly related to the meanings and wordings of the experiential function, respectively. But it is only in adult language use that referring to events and entities, telling someone something in this sense, overshadows the other functions of language, namely, the interpersonal and the textual: so it is in the adult use of language that the experiential function comes into its own. And the reason most scholars have attached greater importance to the referential/experiential function of language is precisely because popular views of language are typically based on the observation of adult language. Vygotsky was not an exception to this rule and like most psychologists, he too attaches greater importance to the experiential and logical functions of language – what in SFL is known as the ideational metafunction. This does not sit well with his insistence on the primacy of the social. It is this privileging of the ideational metafunction that has given Vygotsky's notion of semiotic mediation its selective reading, whereby it is almost exclusively linked to what Vygotsky called higher mental functions of logical reasoning, concept formation, etc. These are mental activities much valued by the official pedagogic systems of the western cultures.

Let us turn now to Vygotsky on words and meaning. The unit of linguistic analysis that appears to have had the greatest significance for Vygotsky is word: in fact he seldom if at all mentions any other linguistic units. The word was the ideal form of a sign. The importance of the word lies for him in the fact that it refers not to some specific concrete entity but to a generalisation and a generalisation is a unit of thought. Thus word meaning represents a union of thought and language, giving us the molecules of verbal thought. The early months of a child's life when he engages in prespeech or protolinguistic communication are also what Vygotsky describes as the child's pre-intellectual stage. He believed that entry into the mother tongue is possible only when the child's intellect has achieved a certain stage of development. The 'two objective unmistakable symptoms' (Vygotsky, 1962: 43) of this stage are (1) that the child becomes curious about words, wanting to know the 'name' of everything; and (2) as a result there is a rapid increase in the child's vocabulary. This is when 'speech begins to serve the intellect and thoughts begin to be spoken', and 'speech which in the earlier stage was affective-conative begins to enter the intellectual phase' (Vygotsky, 1962: 43). The case studies by Halliday (1975), Painter (1984) and Torr (1997) agree with Vygotsky's position to the extent that the development of the heuristic function in all three subjects occurred at about 15 months and prior to this the child's protolinguistic communication had been largely affective-conative. However, all three linguists also note that entry into the mother tongue is heralded by the emergence of grammar; the child's utterances become analysable and *this is not simply because the child has now more words*: all three case studies indicated that the combination of one word with different intonation patterns created different message meanings. To understand this phenomenon one must understand the true meaning of the word 'grammar' and its power in the construal of meaning. It would seem that for Vygotsky, linguistic meaning was the sum of word meanings; grammar had no role to play so far as meaning was concerned.

Despite this shortcoming, which was not at all unusual for Vygotsky's *milieu*, his views on word *per se* were far from naive. He recognised the various states in the process of its mastery, tracing its trajectory in the life of the growing child from its function as just a signal when it stands for an object present to the senses, to the point where it functions as a symbol, a classifier of reality, dealing in generalised classes rather than signalling entities *in praesentia*. It is when the word acts symbolically in this way that it can be used to refer to decontextualised phenomena and achieves the power to function as an abstract tool in the processes of concept formation. The latter, according to Vygotsky, is a complex and lengthy process requiring the simultaneous development of various mental faculties: Vygotsky maintained that every factor in the process is indispensable, but the ability to use words as symbols to refer to phenomena that are not present in the here and now of communication is crucial (1962: 59; emphasis original):

> [we] must... view concept formation as a function of the adolescent's total social and cultural growth, which affects not only the contents but also the methods of his thinking. The new significative use of the word, its use *as a means of concept formation* is the immediate psychological cause of the radical change in the intellectual process that occurs on the threshold of adolescence.

While recognising the separate lines of the initial development of language and thinking in the child, Vygotsky affirmed repeatedly their interdependence in the higher stages of development. Thus (Vygotsky, 1962: 153; emphasis added):

> The relation between thought and word is a living process; thought is born through words. A word devoid of thought is a dead thing; and a thought unembodied in words remains a shadow.... Thought and language, which reflect reality in a way different from perception, are the key to the nature of human consciousness. *Words play a central part not only in the development of thought but also in the historical growth of consciousness as a whole. A word is a microcosm of human consciousness.*

It would be wrong to suggest that Vygotsky was unaware of other aspects of language. On the contrary, his sophistication is quite impressive. But side by side with acute observations, we come across views which are disappointing. The majority of these arise from his elevation of word as the sole meaning maker, which, for example, led him to suggest, at least by implication, that grammar/syntax is antithetical to meaning. Thus discussing inner speech, Vygotsky (1962:145) remarks:

> With syntax and sound reduced to a minimum, meaning is more than ever in the forefront. Inner speech works with semantics, not phonetics.

This simply reveals a confusion on Vygotsky's part: linguistic meaning is not antithetical to grammar and phonology; as SFL literature has argued, units of meaning can only take shape, they can only have the status of semantic units by virtue of their relation to lexicon and grammar on the one hand and context on the other. Interestingly, elsewhere in the same volume (see pp 143-4) Vygotsky offers an extract from Dostoevsky to illustrate how the meaning of the same word changes with change in the intonation pattern and intonation pattern is of course very much a unit of description at the level of sound. However, this apparent contradiction should not surprise us, because the change in meaning in this Dostoevsky example is affective rather than significative; in terms of SFL the meaning change is interpersonal, not experiential and we have seen that for Vygotsky meaning is overwhelmingly a matter of the signification of words. It is true that Vygotsky is not alone in this predilection: the idea that meaning resides in words and that grammar is simply a matter of form is typical of thinking about language even amongst linguists; the only exception are a handful of anthropologically oriented scholars such as Malinowski (1923), Whorf (1956), Firth (1957) and more recently some functionalist scholars. The importance assigned to referential, representational or experiential meaning – call it what you will – is the inevitable legacy of the belief that linguistic meaning resides solely in words.

Vygotsky (1962: 146) also discusses though briefly the role of context and co-text in meaning construction:

> A word in a context means both more and less than the same word in isolation: more because it acquires new content; less, because its meaning is limited and narrowed by the context. The sense of a word ... is a complex, mobile and protean, phenomenon: it changes in different minds and situations and is almost unlimited. A word derives its sense form the sentence, which in turn gets its sense from the paragraph, the paragraph from the book, the book from all the works of the author.

But in the Vygotskian literature on semiotic mediation, there is no engagement with discourse or with context specifically in relation to that concept, though in other contexts Vygotsky did produce excellently insightful discussions of text, especially literary ones (Vygotsky, 1971). I will conclude this section by drawing attention to certain major contradictions in the Vygotskian discourse on semiotic mediation. Most of these arise from (1) how language as system is conceptualised and (2) how language is shown, or more accurately *not shown*, to function as a *means* or modality for semiotic mediation. I suggest that any viable account of the nature of language as a means for semiotic mediation must approach it from two inherently interdependent perspectives: that of system and that of process. In the first perspective, the issue is to determine the internal nature of language as a system of signs: what is its semiotic potential, how do we explain the capacity of language for being used to meet so many human needs and, above all, what is the relation between the system – the way that language is – and the process of language – the way that it is actually used. In the second perspective, the issue is with the use of the system of signs: what is the actual semiotic behaviour of speaking subjects; the concern is with who actually says what, where, why and to whom; how are discourses structured and why in some particular manner. There is a tension between what members of a community *can do* with their language, i.e., the potential of language as system, and what they *actually do* with it, i.e., its situated deployment in a process. We have to recognise that although in material terms it is the speaking subject, who as Saussure pointed out, is the 'master' in *parole*, nonetheless the semiotic voice of the master has much in it that has been mastered in social interaction and this internalisation of the communal comes about because of the ubiquity of semiotic mediation. In understanding semiotic mediation, both perspectives on language are important: the systemic potential spells language's power for sociogenesis; the actual process would indicate the content of semiotic mediation in which a mediatee has participated.

The above comments on language are presented by way of an introduction to the first contradiction in the Vygotskian discourse: *semiotic mediation by means of language entails language use, but the Vygotskian framework has no theory of language use* (Wertsch, 1985c; 1991; Hasan, 1992/2005; 1995b). Language in use is text/discourse, call it what you will; in relation to semiotic mediation text/discourse has no place in the Vygotskian writing as has been pointed out by Wertsch (1985c; 1991). Wertsch suggests that this lack could be complemented by Bakhtin's theory of speech genres. However, I have argued in some detail (Hasan, 1992/2005) that though Bakhtin's views concerning speech genres are rhetorically attractive and impressive, the approach lacks, in terms of Bernstein, both a developed conceptual syntax and an adequate language of description. Terms and units at both these levels in Bakhtin's writings require clarification. Further, the principles that underlie the calibration of the elements of context with the generic shape of the text are underdeveloped, as is the general schema for the description of contexts for interaction. A second suggestion for complementing the lack in the Vygotskian approach has been to locate semiotic mediation in social cultural activities. The notion of activity had already been introduced by Vygotsky in his late work (Minick, 1997). It was developed further by Leontiev and a good deal of work has been done in this area in recent years (see for detail Leontiev, 1978; Wertsch, 1981; Cole, Engeström and Vasquez, 1997; and Engeström, Miettinen and Punamäki, 1999). Space does not permit detailed discussion, but in my reading, activity theory is concerned with specifying the significant attributes of situated social practices. Thus while Wertsch had recommended discourse, activity theory appears to recommend something comparable to context as a site for semiotic mediation. But to the extent that all discursive practices are social practices, the theory of text in context can be taken as a sub-category of activity theory and so logically on the one hand the scope of activity theory should be wider than that of a theory that is able to account just for discursive contexts, and on the other hand, the two should be compatible. However, activity theory on the one hand displays no interest in the role of talk in the performance of an activity and, on the other hand it is heavily biased in favour of the experiential function; it, therefore, chiefly concerns itself with concepts relating specifically to non-verbal actions. These are concepts such as goal, motivation, purpose, action, outcome etc., what SFL would consider as elements in the 'field of discourse' – a component in the social context for text. However, this bias is unhelpful in describing the social practice of discourse, whose complexity requires a theory that goes beyond action into interaction since the selection, management and outcome of action/field depends so heavily on what SFL calls 'tenor of discourse', i.e., the social relations and the positioning of the interactants. Further, the nature of semiotic and material contact between the discursive participants i.e., their 'mode of discourse' is an important consideration in understanding the shaping of discourse. The true nature of the process of semiotic mediation cannot be elaborated if any of these aspects of the use of language is ignored.

The second contradiction in Vygotsky arises directly from his views on language as system. For Vygotsky *the history of the development of linguistic meaning is social, but meaning itself is representational/experiential*. He wishes to stress the role of language in the sociogenesis of higher mental functions, but the only meanings he finds of interest are the meanings that do not directly relate to interpersonal relations. Talk of language as a system of symbols capable of decontextualised meaning does in no way alleviate the problems inherent in this situation. There can be no quarrel with Vygotsky on the centrality of meaning to the process of semiotic mediation, but as I have pointed out above, in his work the concept of meaning turns out to be remarkably one-sided. His orientation to experiential meaning goes hand in hand with an absolute preoccupation with word meaning because sense and reference relations are in fact experiential. So convinced is Vygotsky of the contribution of word to the making of human mind that he ignores his wonderful insights into thematic movements in text and role of context (see Vygotsky, 1971) all of which appear as if irrelevant to semiotic mediation. That most of Vygotsky's contemporaries held comparable views on the nature of language is indisputable; but unlike Vygotsky they were not making claims for the sociogenesis of the mind. It is sad that the work of contemporaries such as Mead (1934), Whorf (1956), Malinowski (1923) and Vološinov (1973) seemed never to have come to his notice. Whorf and Malinowski both emphasised the value of grammar in the construal of linguistic meaning. Further, Whorf's views on the role of language in habitual thinking and in the fashioning of certain aspects of cognition are compatible with Vygotsky's. Mead and Vološinov emphasised the importance of language to human relations. All these emphases are important to understanding semiotic mediation.

The problems with Vygotsky's view of language system go beyond language as the mediating tool to the heart of the content issue – what it is that language mediates. So far as Vygotsky is concerned, as a system language is exclusively representational/ideational. The social relations and the social situatedness of semiotic mediation cannot be handled by a system of this kind and it should not surprise us that the only achievement of semiotic mediation to which the Vygotsky literature refers is in line with his concept of the language system as exclusively ideational. As I have commented above, the elaboration of what Vygotsky meant by higher mental functions, on the one hand gives us a selective reading of the achievements of semiotic mediation by means of language and, on the other hand, presents a view that could be accused of being highly 'elitist'. Higher mental functions, the quintessential artefact of semiotic mediation according to Vygotsky, are characteristically human. So how do we interpret results such as those Luria obtained in his Uzbeki research where adult subjects failed in certain contexts to do successful logical reasoning, inference making and generalisation? Surely these subjects used language as *symbol* for this is a condition of adult language use (for discussion, see Hasan, 1992/2005). We note that all the mental activities that fall under the rubric of higher mental functions appear to be based in the ideational function of language: it is the ideational function of language to construe technical concepts, logical and inferential relations, entailments of states of affairs and so on. And the higher mental functions constitute a condition of success in the official pedagogic systems, where their mastery is, in the words of Bernstein, privileged and privileging. With regard to his Uzbek subjects Luria suggested that the absence of higher mental functions was due to the lack of schooling in his subjects, as if the lack of schooling, i.e., failure to 'benefit' from official pedagogy, is a simple matter of physical access to official pedagogic discourse, as if education is not an arena where the social class struggle is fought everyday, with the odds heavily stacked against the dominated members of society. If we accept Bernstein's claim that official pedagogy 'articulates the dominant ideology/ies of dominant groups' (1990: 66), then it would appear that higher mental functions are the monopoly of the members of the dominant groups. This is an extraordinary turn for a psychological theory which had aspired to match Marx's *Das Kapital*! It comes to pass for two reasons. First because in Vygotsky the potential of language is limited, excluding everything except ideational phenomena and second because the Vygotsky literature entirely ignores what I have called 'invisible semiotic mediation' (Hasan, 2002): mediation that occurs in discourse embedded in everyday ordinary activities of a social subject's life. In this way, the literature on semiotic mediation ignores the genesis of mental dispositions, the social subjects' culturally learned sense of what matters in life. And yet there is every reason to suppose that these mental attitudes are critical in the success or otherwise of 'visible semiotic mediation', which acts as an instrument in the genesis of the so called higher mental functions.

These reflections on Vygotsky's views on language have brought the story of the genesis and development of human consciousness face to face with another discipline, that of linguistics. But like other disciplines, linguistics represents diverse approaches and ideologies. The fragment of the discipline of linguistics that I would weave into this story and to which I made reference above is taken from SFL, since on the one hand the roots of this theory are as much in Marxist thinking as those of Vygotsky's psychology and, on the other hand, SFL arguably offers the most developed approach to language which would bring together in a coherent way the system and process of language and provide insightful descriptions of both. It offers a functional view of language, where language is seen as inherently multi-functional and all functions are equally essential to it as system and as process; focus on both the ideational and the interpersonal functions of language within the frame of the textual would lend useful insights into the story of the sociogenesis of human consciousness. SFL has a well-articulated theory of meaning construal which, on the one hand, links meaning to social context and, on the other, to the formal patterns of language, including the systems of grammar and phonology, so it goes beyond word without abandoning attention to it. It is not accidental that the views of Halliday and Vygotsky on child language and thought development are so close: both are, in the end, looking at the power of language and its role in fashioning acculturated minds: the difference between the two is that as a linguist Halliday is able to theorise the nature of language as possessing a richer potential. Unlike the approach of formal linguists, SFL takes the position that language development in the child is essentially learning how to mean (Halliday, 1975) and, as linguistic meanings are social, child language development consists of 'learning language, learning through language and learning about language' (Halliday, 1980). This view is obviously compatible with the Vygotskian approach. Highly relevant is the fact that Halliday and his colleagues have demonstrated how the development of the experiential is, as it were, embedded in the interpersonal. The first experiences of a baby are filtered through the social context (Hasan, 2001b); the child feels the other before s/he is able to address the other. And in addressing the other, relation precedes information: much before there can be any exchange of information, the child-adult communication first positions them *vis a vis* each other as persons with affect, as beings in some social relation. These perspectives from SFL would, I believe, weave a coherent story when combined with Vygotsky's narrative.

Finally, the third contradiction in Vygotsky I would draw attention to here is closely related to the last one: *speech, Vygotsky maintained, is social; semiotic mediation is social. But when it comes to the process of mediation, it appears to be curiously a-social.* Vygotsky's is a theory that would celebrate the social foundations of mental development, while disregarding almost completely if not entirely the role of language in enacting social relations, as well as the relevance of social relations to mental development. Of the four elements of the semantic structure of the process of mediation (see analysis of the concept in last section above), *it is the mediator and the mediatee (i.e., 1 and 3) that are crucial to the socially situated quality of semiotic mediation: these are also the ones that are least foregrounded in the Vygotskian literature.* The child after all is not just a repository of mental functions; through the living of life in community, s/he is first and foremost a social person. But in the discourse on semiotic mediation, the mediator and mediatee remain socially innocent; the acculturated adult mentioned sometimes in connection with semiotic mediation remains in Bernstein's terms, 'culturally non-specific' and neither participant seems to be located in the social structure, which in no way appears to impinge on their life. Semiotic mediation can only occur in the course of cultural activities involving speech and sites for semiotic mediation are not 'free for all'; access to them is specialised by categories of subjects, as Bernstein has argued (see next section for more detail). It is in this respect that in his description of the drama of mental growth Vygotsky's *dramatis personae* remain 'flat characters'. To breathe life into them, to make them three dimensional, we need to weave another discipline into this story and that is the discipline of sociology, specifically the sociology of Bernstein.

6 Semiotic mediation and the sociogenesis of mind: a Bernsteinian view

In invoking Bernstein's sociology, my aim is not to present or comment on the sociology of Bernstein as such: to do that would be like carrying coals to Newcastle! What I want to do is precisely what I have done for SFL: to weave fragments of a fragment of the discipline of sociology into one story, namely the story of the sociogenesis of human consciousness by means of semiotic mediation. The way I propose to do this is to refer back to my analysis of the concept of semiotic mediation and ask: does Bernstein's sociology have a significant contribution to make to the various elements of the concept. If so, how? What element of his code theory allows us to better understand this or that aspect of the concept of semiotic mediation?

But perhaps it would be best to begin by first establishing the fact that the *idea* of semiotic mediation, though not the *label* itself, has been an important part of Bernstein's theory of the social. As early as 1965 (reprinted 1971: 144; emphasis added), Bernstein pointed out that:

> speech systems or codes create for their speakers different orders of relevance and relation. The experience of the speaker may then be transformed by what is made significant or relevant by different speech systems. As the child learns his speech... he learns the requirements of his social structure. The experience of the child is transformed by the learning generated by his own, apparently, voluntary acts of speech. *The social structure becomes, in this way, the sub-stratum of the child's experience essentially through the manifold consequences of the linguistic process. From this point of view, every time the child speaks or listens, the social structure is reinforced in him and his social identity shaped. The social structure becomes the child's psychological reality through the shaping of his acts of speech.*

This extract bears witness to the fact of mediation through the modality of language. Unlike Vygotsky, Bernstein does not talk of language as one undifferentiated system, but the fact that from the beginning, code varieties are recognised, does not negate the fact that the mediational power of language is critical to code theory. The content of semiotic mediation in the above extract is clearly not the same that attracted Vygotsky: Bernstein is concerned with the internalisation of the social structure, rather than with the principles for the production of officially approved orders of knowledge, but whether it is the internalisation of the former or of the latter, the means are the same: in both cases semiotic mediation is the means. The issue of mediation is implicit in the 'general theoretical question of classical sociology' that Bernstein's theory posed itself: 'how does the outside become the inside, and how does the inside reveal itself and shape the outside' (Bernstein, 1987a: 563). Bernstein's theory set itself the task of answering this question over four decades. During this period, understandably, the theory went through developmental cycles, but whatever the language of description the importance of semiotic mediation in the achievement of this explanation remained the same. Bernstein's contribution to the sociology of pedagogy is immense and he is rightly recognised for this contribution, but for me as a linguist, there is no discontinuity between the early Bernstein and the late: Bernstein's œuvre remains steadfast in regard to his commitment to semiotic mediation. Here is one of the most recent Bernstein statement on the concerns of his theory (2000: 91; emphasis added), which confirms this claim:

> The substantive issue of the theory is to explicate the processes whereby a given distribution of power and principles of control are translated into specialised principles of communication differentially, and often unequally, distributed to social groups/classes. And how such an unequal distribution of forms of communication, initially (but not necessarily terminally) shapes the formation of consciousness of members of these groups/classes in such a way as to relay both opposition and change. The critical issue is *the translation of power and control into principles of communication which become (successful or otherwise) their carriers or relays.*

I now want to turn to the semantic structure of the concept of semiotic mediation, to pick up the discussion where we left it last, namely the mediator and the mediatee (1 and 3). The concept in Bernstein's sociology that appears to me most relevant in understanding the social identity of persons is that of social positioning. Bernstein (1990: 13) used this concept to 'refer to the establishing of a specific relation to other subjects and to the creating of specific relationships within subjects'. What is important about the concept of positioning in Bernstein's writing is its place within the system of his theory. At the risk of repeating what is familiar to you, positioning is ultimately grounded in the most fundamental concepts of any theory of sociology that would attempt to describe a modern society. In the conceptual syntax of Bernstein's theory, positioning is realisationally related to the concept of codes, codes to distribution of power and principles of control and the latter to the class division of society which realise the basic foundational concepts of division of labour and of capital. This is a firm grounding for the concept of positioning but, it does not yet specify the full architecture of the theoretical frame in which this concept is embedded. Here is Bernstein's elaboration (1990:13-14; original emphasis):

more specifically, class-regulated codes position subjects with respect to dominant and dominated forms of communication and to the relationships between them. Ideology is constituted through and in such positioning. From this perspective, ideology inheres in and regulates modes of relation. Ideology is not so much a content as *a mode of relation* for the realising of content.

I read this as a claim that positioning is realisationally related to class-regulated codes, which are themselves realised as dominant and dominated forms of communication. If a person's ideology is constituted through and in such positioning, then we are claiming that there is a logical relation between a subject's social positioning and the mental dispositions, habits of the mind, the orders of relevance which they bring to bear on whatever they encounter in their social life: there exists an ineluctable relation between one's social positioning, one's mental dispositions and one's relation to the distribution of labour in society. In the universe of Bernstein's sociology there are no socially innocent humans. By these steps it is revealed that semiotic mediation occurs always and only within the frame of the social experiences of the mediator and the mediatee. This fragment of Bernstein's theory not only complements a lack that we noticed in Vygotsky's account, it also allows us to see the greater complexity of the concept.

In arguing above that Bernstein's theory is from its very beginning committed to the notion of semiotic mediation, I have already indicated Bernstein's preoccupation with the content of semiotic mediation: what is it that is produced by the energy released by semiotic mediation. As a sociologist, the object of study for Bernstein is society: how does society reproduce itself, how does it change, what are the principles of its organisation and how did society come to be organised the way that it is, i.e., its history. Semiotic mediation in Bernstein's theory plays an important role in answering these questions. Vygotsky paid closest attention to the product of what I have called visible semiotic mediation (Hasan, 2002) – the conscious discourse aimed at mediating a specific category of reasoning, a certain range of technical concepts and a particular relation to the physical phenomena of the world whereby the world is classified and categorised in a certain way. By contrast, Bernstein paid very close attention to invisible semiotic mediation (Hasan, 2002) especially in the early stages of his scholarship – how the unself-conscious everyday discourse mediates mental dispositions, tendencies to respond to situations in certain ways and how it puts in place beliefs about the world one lives in, including both about phenomena that are supposedly in nature and those which are said to be in our culture. The early work on code theory[5] at its abstract level indicated very clearly the primacy of invisible semiotic mediation in a person's life: code-regulated discourse is not treated as simply the regulator of cognitive functions; it is also central to the shaping of 'dispositions, identities and practices' (Bernstein, 1990: 3): the results of Luria's research with the Uzbeks would not have caught Bernstein's theory by surprise! But Bernstein's theory does not stop at this point: it goes on to present a description of the semantic properties of language use which are essential to the quality of semiotic mediation. By the time the theory reached its apex around the late 1980s, Bernstein had already introduced and elaborated certain concepts such as those of classification and framing, pointing out the potential of their variation. This allows us not only to analyse acts of semiotic mediation, i.e., discourses from the point of view of the relation between the mediator and the mediatee, but also how the classification and framing of pedagogic knowledge is not a simple matter of 'socially innocent' semiotic mediation.

We noted earlier the interest in the question of the site of semiotic mediation (element 4b) (see last two sections). Here Bernstein would be in agreement with Wertsch, that the environment for mediation is social practice, which of course includes discourse. However, to affirm simply the significance of social practice or to produce one homogeneous general schema of what is important in the structuring of social practice is not sufficient, because given the 'same' context, different segments of a society do not necessarily engage in the 'same' actual social practices. Bernstein argued that what from some point of view might be thought of as the 'same' context could elicit different practices from persons differently positioned. Bernstein postulates (1990: 16ff) pertinent concepts to show how this comes about. Socially positioned subjects, through their experience of and participation in code-regulated dominant and dominated communication, develop rules for recognising what social activity a context is the context for and how the requisite activity should be carried out. Participation in social practices, including participation in discourse, is the biggest boot-strapping enterprise that human beings engage in: speaking is necessary for learning to speak; engaging with contexts is necessary for recognising and dealing with contexts. This means, of course, that the contexts that one learns about are the contexts that one lives, which in turn means that the contexts one lives are those which are specialised to one's social position. Empirical research carried out by Hasan (1989; 1992b) Cloran (1994; 1999) Williams (1995; 1999; 2001) supports these observations: eating a meal with a child may be an occasion for the elaboration of information on life and death, or on food chain (Hasan, 2002) in one family, but in a differently positioned family eating a meal may be a significantly different kind of activity. What kind of contexts will act as the site for the production of what kind of content by semiotic mediation becomes a question of who the speaker and the addressee are, socially speaking, that is to say, what is their social positioning and what is the pattern of their participation in the classification and framing of social practices. For some subjects, mundane everyday activities furnish a context for the recontextualisation of official pedagogic discourse; for others the contexts of official pedagogic discourse are simply not relevant. Bernstein certainly does not share Luria's easy faith in the beneficial consequences of semiotic mediation in official pedagogic sites, because between the mediation and the internalisation of mediated concept lies the social history of the active agents, i.e., the mediator and the mediatee. This is not to say that Bernstein counts out the possibility of change, or the role of pedagogy in it. As the conclusion to Bernstein (2000: 189; emphasis added) points out:

> the transmission/acquisition systems the thesis projects do not create copper etching plates in whose lines we are trapped. Nor are the systems, grids, networks and pathways embedded in either concrete or quicksand. The transmission/acquisition systems reveal and legitimate the enabling and disabling functions of power relations which they [i.e., the systems] relay and upon which they rest. Attempts to model the internal principles of such transmission do not make them eternal. *Such analysis may show the poles of choice for any set of principles and the assemblies possible within those poles. It calls attention to the selective effects of transmission, their social costs and the basis for change.*

To reveal the *set of choices, the assemblies of possibilities* is all we can ask of a theory; to understand *the effects of transmission, their social cost and the basis for change* is to understand how to make our actions, perhaps, more effective. The relevance of Bernstein's theory of the structuring of pedagogic discourse to the working of semiotic mediation in the distribution of knowledge cannot be emphasised too much.

On the question of the modality for semiotic mediation, Bernstein's early code theory relied on traditional available descriptions of language. Bernstein himself did not engage, unlike Vygotsky, in any research on the internal structure of language. And although in talking about codes, his emphasis had always been on meaning, it was impossible to find any framework for the semantic analysis of language in use that could be deployed as a heuristic device for the identification of the crucial characteristics of the elaborated and restricted codes. The analysis of data in the early stages, in terms of word classes and grammatical categories such as logical connectives etc., was not well-received. With hindsight, it seems that the fault was not so much in the patterns identified; it was largely in the inability of linguists to produce a framework which would relate meaning and wording on a systematic basis. The collaboration of Halliday and Bernstein produced interest in early semantic networks (Halliday, 1973a; Turner, 1973), but this was a completely uncharted territory and required much spade work before it could become a viable tool for linguistic analysis[6]. Bernstein withdrew from the linguistic analysis of codes, but of course he could not withdraw from semiosis. His codes are described as the regulators of meaning: 'code selects and integrate relevant meanings'; it therefore 'presupposes irrelevant and illegitimate meanings... The concept of code is inseparable from the concepts of legitimate and illegitimate communication' (Bernstein, 1990: 14). To talk of code was to be involved with meaning practices. And Bernstein had an extraordinary sense of the prehension between the social condition and a specific range of semantic patterns that the social condition would logically select from. Ironically as he withdrew from analysis grounded in linguistic form, his contribution to our understanding of language in use rose to a much higher level. Later Bernstein, in the discussion of the pedagogic device, in the elaboration of rules of recontextualisation, in the development of vertical and horizontal discourse, in the working of the classification and framing in discourse has left a legacy the full scope and value of which we have yet to work out. It is a challenge to semantic analysis to show how these phenomena manifest themselves in the lexicogrammar of a language. What is most relevant at this point is the fact that since these concepts relate to language in use, to discourse as social practice, they are directly relatable to the working of semiotic mediation from the point of view of how the modality performs what it actually does.

7 Conclusion

To present a reasonably coherent account, the story of the sociogenetic development of human consciousness has required fragments from three different disciplines. In weaving these threads together into the fabric of this paper, my aim was not to criticise this scholar or that for 'inadequate theory'; rather I wished simply to emphasise that essentially human, which is to say social, phenomena are complex and stories around them are long; this distance cannot be covered by the movement of one discipline. In beginning with Vygotsky, it is his narrative that became the point of departure; its lacks were identified and other fragments from other disciplines were found that could fill the gap. But one could have started with Halliday or with Bernstein and one would have found lacks in both. This is not because Halliday's linguistics is not good enough, or Bernstein's sociology is inadequate, any more than that the lacks mean that Vygotsky's theory is invalid: it is simply that any story which has for its theme the conditions of human existence is bound to remain incomplete within the bounds of one discipline because the concerns of human life are interconnected. Perhaps the best we can hope for in a theory is that it should be exotropic, that is to say, that as a theory it should embed its object of study in a context where the processes of its evolution, stability and change can be seen to originate in the interaction of the object of study with other universes of human experience (Hasan, 1999a). In fact all three theories I have examined here are exotropic in this sense. And together their interconnections produce a narrative that is much richer than any single discipline could have provided by itself. Vygotsky contributes to the understanding of our mental life by revealing its deep connection to semiosis; in so doing he anticipates the literature on the dialectic of language and mind: it is this dialectic that is responsible for their co-evolution in the human species. Halliday contributes to the understanding of our semiotic life by revealing its deep connection with society; in so doing, he elaborates on the dialectic of language and society which underlies their co-genesis. Bernstein contributes to the understanding of our social life in modern societies by revealing its inherent connection with consciousness created in semiosis in the contexts of communal living; in so doing, he makes us realise how minds need societies and societies need semiosis to survive, to develop and to change. In today's political atmosphere, Bernstein, read properly, would reveal the pathology of capitalism, whereby our exosomatic evolution, hard won through the working of the higher mental functions Vygotsky celebrated, appears to be leading us towards a large-scale extinction of the other in the interest of protecting our boundaries and maintaining our control.

Notes

1 In this argument which Vygotsky developed in the elaboration of his phylogenetic perspective (Vygotsky, 1978), we have the precursor to Popper's idea of exo-somatic evolution (Popper, 1979a) – that is, the characteristic of the human species to evolve not by somatic adaptation to environment but by altering the environment so that it suits the human body.

2 I ignore the full range of circumstances e.g. circumstance of manner as in *mediate skilfully* etc.

3 Jean Lave's interesting discussion on the relation of 'performance and situation' (Lave, 1997) is relevant at this point, though the emphasis is different.

4 There is good reason to believe that Vygotsky's use of the term *autistic* does not refer to the now well known pathological condition, but rather to a marked subjectivity of interpretation.

5 Much remains to be reinterpreted in Bernstein's early work, where in my reading the heuristics of code theory so savagely attacked were the outcome of a semantically poor linguistics. Even if one accepts that Bernstein's prose is at best complex, its reading by scholars does no credit to their literacy skills!

6 It took SFL some time to elaborate its conception of language as a multistratal system, with a 'natural' realisational relation between the levels of lexicogrammar and semantics. With the metafunctional hypothesis, context assumed a crucial role in the process and system of language. Halliday's pioneering work (1973) in the description of message semantics, was eventually pursued by Hasan (1983: mimeo). A substantial system network of message semantics, it has been used in the analysis of everyday talk to identify distinct code modalities (Hasan, 1989; 1992/2005; 1992b). It has been further extended by Cloran (1994) and Williams (1995).

Section 2

Coding orientations and forms of consciousness

Editor's Introduction

In the first paper in this section, *Code, Register and Social Dialect* (1973), Professor Hasan argues for the existence of 'specifiable correlations between language and elements of social structure' (Chapter 6), whose causal, rather than incidental, nature is most clearly demonstrated in the semantic structure of language, in its meaning structure. Her basic thesis is that ways of saying and meaning cannot be separated from ways of living. As Professor Hasan puts it (Chapter 6):

> Language is used to live, just as social structure is used to live. This introduces a complexity in the description of language and argues for a weakening of boundaries between various systems for communication. The exhaustive description of language is an ideal, which may perhaps never be achieved, but there will certainly be much *less* chance of its being achieved if language is separated from the living of life totally.

The specific internal formal patterns which distinguish the linguistic varieties according to user (i.e. dialects, whether temporal, social and geographical) cannot be used to explain the basis of their own social correlates; in this sense dialect studies relate some manifest linguistic pattern to some manifest social attribute of the dialect speaker. Contrasting this with code variation, Professor Hasan highlights the explanatory power of Bernstein's code theory to bridge the gap between language and non-language by mapping social elements onto semantic ones. Similarly, in the study of variation by use, i.e. register, Professor Hasan suggests that attention to the semantic level might be more fruitful than reliance on 'frequency ... of individual patterns'. The elements of meaning most relevant to register distinction would be 'text-wide'.

Chapter 7, *Semiotic Mediation and Mental Development in Pluralistic Societies: some implications for tomorrow's schooling* (2002) continues the theme of the causal relation between ways of meaning and ways of living by exploring those factors that play a role in the semiotic mediation of concepts in the learning situation. These may include 'the learners' mental disposition, their readiness to engage in the appropriation of some concepts rather than others, as well as the mode of negotiation they habitually bring to the learning situation. This idea is further developed in Chapter 8, *Ways of Meaning, Ways of Learning: code as an explanatory concept*, where Bernstein's code theory is again identified as 'a powerful resource for examining the complex interplay of the factors active in the formation of consciousness and the unequal distribution of knowledge'.

On the one hand, learning does not begin at school – the child brings to school a previous history of discursive participation, which 'will help the child decide what is to be considered relevant by way of information, and how information is to be framed'. On the other hand, it is at school where 'the business of learning is 'institutionalised', and there develops 'a particular kind of discursive experience, a particular form of consciousness' (Chapter 8). Because children differ in their previous histories, some will be advantaged – 'the middle-class child coming to school finds herself in a crucially different situation: the discourse in the classroom is reminiscent of that at home' (Chapter 9, *Reading Picture Reading: a study in ideology and inference*, 2004), others will be disadvantaged because their previous experience 'has not already paved the way to accepting classroom discourse as legitimate' (Chapter 9). Egalitarian education remains as elusive as ever, not just because there exist different ways of saying and meaning, but also because these differences continue to be exploited by the dominating segments of society for their own benefit. As Professor Hasan explains (Chapter 7):

> The challenge is that those for whom the educational system is ostensibly designed bring many voices into the classroom, but even a cursory look at the classroom practices reveals that it privileges one single voice. This happens to be the voice of the more powerful segment of the society. Those who do not recognise this voice cannot truly participate in the specialised discourse of knowledge production and must strive on their own to master this other epistemic dialect.

Section 2: Editor's introduction 159

In Chapter 10, *The Ontogenesis of Ideology: an interpretation of mother child talk* (1986), Professor Hasan looks at how the ideology of woman's work is transmitted through mother-child talk. Over the course of casual conversation, mothers present themselves and their work to their children, offering a revealing look into 'the system of ideas that surrounds the work women do in the privacy of their homes'. What Professor Hasan describes is 'a constellation of linguistic patterns', working in concert with other semiotic systems, and thus articulating the ideology of womans work: while every woman is at once an instructor, a labourer and a companion, providing emotional support to her child, she herself undervalues the worth of her own work. Based on the evidence from her data, Professor Hasan concludes that 'the ontogenesis of ideology occurs early, if the ideology is to take hold. And the mechanisms for this ontogenesis are the habitual forms of communication, wherein the taken-for-granted nature of the social world is transmitted'.

6 Code, register and social dialect

1 Introductory remarks

The main aim of this paper[1] is to examine the notions 'code', 'register' and 'social dialect'. Each of these categories is without doubt relevant to the field of sociolinguistics; at the same time, their recognition adds valuable dimensions to theories regarding the nature of language. The examination of these concepts, therefore, raises issues which appear to be of fundamental importance both to sociolinguistics and general linguistics.

I start with the assumption that there exist specifiable correlations between language and elements of social structure. The nature of the correlations may vary in given cases but what is basic to the assumption remains true and may be formulated as follows. Language is primarily a social phenomenon; despite the fact that some of man's biological attributes play a decisive part in the acquisition and subsequent use of language, it remains the property of social man rather than that of animal man. This gives rise to the possible hypothesis that aspects of social structure would be reflected in language. Such an assumption forms the very basis of social-linguistics. Although accounts of coherent theories and methodologies for this field are conspicuous almost by their absence, the literature does vindicate the above hypothesis.

I sympathise with Fishman's view that sociolinguistics is probably a misnomer for what goes on in the field (Fishman, 1970). The label may suggest that sociolinguistics is a matter of applying linguistic techniques to the study of language placed in some socially significant context. No doubt it is true that more and more sociolinguists are at present employing the techniques for the description of language evolved by linguistics; none the less this does not appear to be the significant characterising factor. What seems to be central to sociolinguistics studies is not that linguistic techniques are employed; it is rather that he structure of language is related at various levels of abstraction to social structure. It is, perhaps, not often recognised that such study, where it is explanatory, is of theoretical significance to general linguistics, extending its scope in a manner which has potentially far-reaching consequences, not only for the description of some of the essential properties of human language, but also for a study of the patterns of language acquisition by members of given communities and sub-communities. The relationship of sociolinguistics and general linguistics is such that one may find it difficult indeed to draw a definite boundary line between the two. Does the work of the functionalist linguists of the Prague School represent one or the other? One would like to be able to answer that it represents both in that it relates the structure of language to social elements and at the same time provides a model for the description of language in general and of a language in particular.

Perhaps it needs to be pointed out that although the bulk of literature in linguistics is currently concerned with some aspect of the writing and construction of grammars, general linguistics itself cannot be equated with grammar even where the word is used to cover other aspects of the internal patterning in language than just syntax. Instead of going into a detailed discussion of the scope of general linguistics, I would here refer to Firth's *A Synopsis of Linguistics Theory 1930-55* (1957a) as presenting one of the most catholic and systematic brief accounts of the concerns of general linguistics. On this particular issue Firth's views are generally shared by other linguists. Within the same general tradition, may be mentioned names such as Sapir (1921), Whorf (1956), Pike (1954) and Firth's own colleagues and students.

Firth maintains that 'linguistics accepts speech and language texts as related to the living of, and therefore to the 'meaning' of life, and applies its theory and practice as far as it is able, to the statement of such 'meaning' in strictly linguistics terms if the problem is dispersed by analysis at a series of congruent levels'. Firth's use of the word 'meaning' has been criticised by linguists (Lyons, 1966; Langendoen, 1968). I am not concerned in this paper with an evaluation of the Firthian concept of 'meaning'; but as the discussion of the three concepts code, register and social dialect continues, it will be seen that the question of meaning in language, as opposed to meaning in individual items constituting the entries in the lexicon, indeed, cannot be handled adequately except by dispersion at a series of congruent levels of analysis; moreover, some of the levels of analysis may not be identified entirely by reference to the formally recognised components of syntax, lexicon and phonology. It would appear that underlying Firth's view of meaning is the assumption that a given linguistic utterance is capable of conveying a composite of different types of meanings rather than just one type. There seems to be no *a priori* reason for suggesting that, say, the content-meaning of an utterance is *ipso facto* more important or more deserving of attention in a verbal interaction than its affective meaning. As users of language, we would seem to take into account all the components of the meaning of an utterance and our response appears to be conditioned by the totality of the meaning rather than by any one particular component.

This concern with the meaning of a linguistic event, in the wide sense of the word 'meaning', provides the Firthian schema with one of the justifications for a binary distinction in the study of language in general. Language can be studied formally and it can be studied institutionally. The formal study of language is concerned with the network of relationship obtaining amongst the 'bits' of a given language, whereas the institutional study of language places it in relation to some circumstance of the speech community. It should be added that the segmentation between the two types of studies is not as discrete as the above statement might suggest. Indeed were that the case, it might be taken as argument for regarding either the one or the other but not both as the 'proper concern' of general linguistics.

2 Social dialect

Aspects of the formal study of language are of peripheral interest to this paper. I turn my attention then to institutional linguistics, which studies language in relation to some circumstance of the speech community. At the risk of over-simplification, I shall restrict myself here to the brief examination of only three of the generally accepted categories of institutional linguistics. These are *'etat de langue'*, 'geographical dialect' and 'social dialect'.

The assumption in each case is that a language L has (or 'is a sum of') some varieties a, b, c ...; that a, b, c ... all share certain formal features which justifies their being regarded as instances of L; that the variety La has certain formal features (or a pattern of formal features) belonging to it exclusively; by virtue of these La is differentiated from Lb, from Lc ... Thus, in order to be accorded the status of varieties of L, each of the categories a, b, c ... *must* simultaneously be alike and different from others in respect to some specifiable formal properties. The differences between a, b, c ... can be correlated with some extra-linguistic factors, to which reference has been made earlier under the general label 'some circumstance of the speech community'. In the case of *'etat de langue'*, a term much in use since Saussure, the difference is correlated with time; in the case of geographical dialect, with space and, in the case of social dialect, with some social attribute of the speech group in question. Of these, the last is of special interest to the discussion; the first two are referred to in determining the nature of the category of social dialect.

Halliday et al. (1964) define dialect thus:

'Each speaker has learnt ... a particular variety of the language of his language community, and this variety may differ at any or all levels from other varieties of the same language learnt by other speakers ... Such a variety, identified along this dimension is called a dialect'. Geographical dialect is a variety of language determined by 'who you are' and, 'in general, 'who you are' for this purpose means 'where you come from'.

If geographical dialect may be defined thus, by analogy social dialect may be defined as a variety differing at any or all levels from other varieties of the same language according to 'who you are', where 'who you are' would mean 'what social class you belong to'.

There are problems in the measurement of nominal social class membership. These problems arise out of the question of the range and the weighting of attributes which are considered as demarcation criteria. However, a parallel may be found in the case of geographical dialects, where a variability in the demarcation may result from a variation in the delicacy of focus. We may, for instance, recognise both a Scottish dialect and a Glaswegian one, where the latter is subsumed in the former. Similarly, we may recognise a social dialect A, spoken by members of a social group defined by reference to its members' income level. If, with reference to, say, the education of its members, the same social group can be sub-divided into sub-groups 1, 2 and 3, and if, corresponding to these sub-groups, further distinctions within dialect A can be established, then we would have at least three social dialects pertaining to sub-groups, further distinctions within dialect A can be established, then we would have at least three social dialects pertaining to sub-groups 1-3. The relationship of the latter to A would be the same as that of Glaswegian to Scottish. Just as Glaswegian is a more specific instance of the broader category 'geographical dialect: Scottish', so social dialects pertaining to sub-group 1-3 would be more specific instances of the broader category 'social dialect: A'. Social parameters, such as those of income, education and occupation etc., may be used individually or in combination to define the boundaries of given social groups; the larger the number of attributes combined to define a social group, the more specific the social dialect pertaining to the group will be.

Geographical and social dialect may thus be seen as roughly parallel descriptive categories of institutional linguistics. In both cases, the linguist's approach is essentially the same: the identity of the dialect is defined by those of its formal properties which distinguish it from other dialects of the same general category. The search for language-external factors correlating with the distinctions in formal properties is based upon the assumption that consistent patterns of formal variation do not occur randomly; that if there exist different varieties of the same language, then some extra-linguistic factor(s) will indicate in general terms the boundaries of their operation.

It is to be noted in this context, that normally in the study of dialectology, the manifest in language is related to the manifest in non-language. If one asks: why does a particular person speak a particular social dialect, the answer in all likelihood would be that he has an affinity with a particular social group. The question is seldom answered or even asked: why does a particular social dialect differ from another just in these specific respects? This, it appears, happens because the extra-linguistic factor(s) correlating with the distinctions are regarded as only incidental to, but not constituting an explanation of, the specific peculiarities. There being no true causal connection between the dialect boundaries and their respective extra-linguistic correlates, at least in theory the possibility is to be granted that one may, for instance, be a native of Glasgow without possessing a Glaswegian dialect; similarly, one may belong to a particular social group with a particular income level and education, without possessing the social dialect said to pertain to the group in general. This is related to the observation that the identity of a dialect is crucially defined by reference to its distinctive formal properties, not by the extra-linguistic factors as such. Consequently the geographical and social provenance of a speaker does not, in itself, constitute an argument for his membership in a given dialect community. In the mouth of a born Londoner, Glaswegian still remains Glaswegian; it does not become Cockney.

Thus the internal formal patterns of a dialect, be it temporal, geographical or social, are studied purely descriptively; they are not related in any specific manner to 'the living of life' by the speech community in question. This characterisation of dialect is not presented as a criticism of dialectology in general. The aim is simply to throw some light on the nature of the category 'dialect'. Indeed, the patterns of the formal levels by reference to which the identity of some dialect is established do not appear to be directly relatable to the 'living of life', except in some restricted areas of the structure of its lexicon, and more doubtfully, in some aspects of its syntax. Dialects, whether they correlate with time, space or social attributes of the speech community, remain a descriptive category, relating the manifest to the manifest. While the boundaries of the dialect will always correlate with some extra-linguistic factor(s), the latter cannot be used to predict the absence or presence of the formal patterns defining the identity of the dialect. The relationship between the two is not of logical dependence or concomitance but of simple co-occurrence.

3 Code

Having characterised dialect thus, we may inquire if Bernstein's category of code could be regarded as parallel in its nature to that of social dialect. Two outstanding differences between the two immediately draw attention to themselves: while the extra-linguistic factor(s) correlating with social dialect are incidental, those correlating with code are said to be causal; if the relationship between the two in the former case is simply that of co-occurrence, the relationship between the two in the case of code is that of logical dependence, which presupposes co-occurrence. Second, while social dialect is defined by its characteristic formal properties, the code is defined by its semantic properties[2], thus involving the consideration of the formal levels only indirectly. That is to say, it can be argued that the semantic properties of the codes can be predicted from the elements of social structure which, in fact, give rise to them. This raises the concept code to a more general level than that of language variety; indeed, there are advantages in regarding the restricted and the elaborated codes as codes of behaviour, where the word behaviour covers both verbal and non-verbal behaviour. In the present paper, however, the notion code is discussed mainly in its capacity of controlling verbal behaviour.

Bernstein maintains that 'these two codes, elaborated and restricted, are generated by a particular form of social relation. Indeed, they are likely to be realisation of different social structures' (1969). It would appear that the aspects of social structure most relevant to the definition of codes are those which relate to the principle of social organisation.

The concepts mechanical and organic solidarity can be used to indicate the emphasis within a society of one form of social integration rather than another. Organic solidarity is emphasised wherever individuals relate to each other through a complex interdependence of specialised social functions. Therefore organic solidarity presupposes a society whose social integration arises out of *differences* between individuals ... Mechanical solidarity is emphasised wherever individuals share a common system of beliefs and sentiments which produces a details regulation of conduct. If social roles are achieved in organic solidarity, they are assigned or 'ascribed' in mechanical solidarity (Bernstein, 1967).

To simplify, the identity of the members of societies characterised by mechanical solidarity can be stated adequately in answer to the question 'what is x?' whereas in those characterised by organic solidarity, the question must take the form 'who is x?' In the former case the identity is stated in terms of some recognised ascribed social role; for example, x may be father, boss or neighbour. In the latter case the identity is completely stated only when some individual characteristic of the member in question is stated in addition to his recognised social role, thus rendering him unique.

For obvious reasons, the form of social integration plays an important part in how a child is socialised. Bernstein approaches the question of socialisation through four contexts which he considers to be critical, in that at the level of primary abstraction they exhaust the areas in which socialisation takes place. These have been discussed in various writings by Bernstein and may be listed as follows (1970a):

The regulative context – these are authority relationships where the child is made aware of the rules of the moral order and their various backings.

The instructional context where the child learns about the objective nature of the objects and persons and acquires skills of various kinds.

The imaginative context (or innovating) where the child is encouraged to experiment and re-create his world on his own terms and in his own way.

The interpersonal context where the child is made aware of affective states – his own and others.

According to Bernstein, the difference between the forms of social integration will be naturally manifested in the verbal and non-verbal behavoiur of the participants – the socialiser and the socialised – in all these four contexts. Although more work has been done on the first two contexts (Cook, 1972; Bernstein and Henderson, 1969; Brandis and Henderson, 1970; Robinson and Rackstraw, 1972; Turner; Turner and Pickvance, as well as Robinson, 1973), implicit in these studies are certain predictions regarding the last two.

In social structures integrated by mechanical solidarity, the institutional and the communal is predominant, the unique meaning of the individual being less relevant. This is a way of saying that any possible set of situations is, as it were, largely precategorised by reference to communal beliefs and reactions. Consequently an alternative interpretation of a situation by reference to some specific attribute of a participant or some specific characteristic of the total event will be normally neither sought nor offered. The general propensity to view situations and the participants of the situations simply in terms of the communal precategorisation, presupposes the propensity not to analyse – much less to question – the principles underlying a category. The emphasis is not on this aspect; rather it is on the process whereby a certain category is manifested. This attitude extends itself not only over the characterisation of the moral order but also over the world of personal relations and concrete objects. Some of the consequences of these propensities for the four critical socialising contexts can be predicted in general terms.

In the regulative context, a situation may be characterised morally in absolute terms: 'that's wrong/ that's naughty', without conceding the possibility that the individual's intent might not have been 'wrong' or 'naughty'. The emphasis is on punishment, verbal or non-verbal. If any appeals occur, they are likely to be made by reference to the positional status of the participants: 'your dad told you not to do that/boys don't play with dolls'. In the instructional context, an object or phenomenon is characterised by reference to what it does and/or how it does it. To be sure, this does not mean that the underlying principles may not be internalised; simply that characteristically, an explicit formulation of the controlling principles will not be forthcoming. In the interpersonal context, the positional orientation of members functions as a restraint, both upon the exploration of the bases of interpersonal interaction and the explicit verbal formulation of the affective states. Since there is a general lack of awareness regarding the controlling principles and the abstract properties of form, in the imaginative context this may lead to a greater freedom for fantasy which is likely to be less constrained by the logic of organised objective facts or by the explicit conventions of artistic form. Innovation in the world of objects – as distinct from artistic creativity – is likely to be tied down to the level of 'doing' and is not expected to arrive at the level of 'explaining the doing' in terms of the underlying principles.

The above is only a highly simplified and brief account of how membership in a certain type of social structure may affect the living of life in the crucial socialising contexts. Persons, objects, situations and their interaction – phenomena round which the living of life revolves and which in other types of social structures might be the object of scrutiny and analysis – are here less likely to be questioned; they are filtered mainly through the communally recognised beliefs and attitudes. In this manner of living, a lot is taken for granted. The beliefs and attitudes of the members of the community are seen generally as unambiguous, forming part of a largely known paradigm. This is the kind of society in which the 'general' is raised above the 'particular', the common above the specific and the 'we' above the 'I'. Bernstein has pointed out that the restricted code 'emerges where the culture or sub-culture raises the 'we' above the 'I'' (Bernstein, 1969). It is assumed that the language which constitutes the verbal realisation of the restricted code of behaviour will display certain semantically characterisable features which are expected to be reflected at the formal levels of syntax, lexis and most probably phonology. The justification of these assumptions can be provided in the following terms: meanings are social and are therefore affected by the characteristics of a social structure. In the description of languages, components of meanings are said to form units of the semantic level; the formal patterns which occur in any verbal interaction are activated by the semantic components underlying them. Thus, if any crucial characteristic of meaning can be predicted by reference to the nature of codes, then it follows that prediction regarding the possible crucial formal patterns can also be made (Hasan, 1971).

In societies which are integrated by organic solidarity, the differences between individuals are of crucial importance; their recognised social role does not overshadow their personal attributes which are utilised in the achieving of the role. By the same token, special parameters of given situations cannot be ignored. Thus no sets of situations are precategorised totally or irrevocably; there is always the possibility that, despite the overall acceptance of communal beliefs and attitudes, some specific attribute of a participant or some specific parameter of a situation will be taken into account, allowing a modified interpretation. The readiness to modify a category presupposes the readiness to separate the elements constitutive of a category. It indicates an attitude which is basically analytic, although the details of the reasoning behind the analysis may be totally or partially wrong when considered from a technical point of view. That is to say, it is not being implied that the members are here 'scientific' or 'knowledgeable' in the technical sense of the word; simply that they have an attitude of scrutiny towards persons, objects and situations.

Again, such an attitude is generally reflected in the crucial socialising contexts, both in the verbal and the non-verbal behaviour of the participants. In the regulative context, the emphasis is upon the inner regulation of the person and this is achieved mainly through the greater use of the verbal elaboration of meanings as they focus upon the interpersonal and intrapersonal (for details regarding this point see Bernstein, 1971a). In the instructional context, an object, phenomenon or skill will be characterised not only by reference to what it does and how it does it but also by some explanation regarding the underlying principles (for details see Robinson in this volume). In the interpersonal context, the orientation to differences between individuals and the general concern with the motivation and the personal affects of participants leads to a scrutiny of the bases of interpersonal interaction, with the implication that the attributes whereby the individuals are rendered unique are likely to be explicit. This constant scrutiny and analysis fosters an awareness of the abstract properties of form with an emphasis on what might be described as the recognised 'objective realities'. In the imaginative context, fantasy is likely to be conditioned by the knowledge of explicit aesthetic frames, while in the innovation of objects the level of explaining the doing can be reached in explicit terms – again without any implication that the explanation would be necessarily correct. It is clear that in this manner of living not much can be taken for granted. The possibility of ambiguity is greater since the status of persons, objects and events is generally not seen in terms of their ascribed functions. The specific, therefore, over-rides the general; the personal, the communal. Elaborated code emerges from this type of society. The language that constitutes the verbal realisation of the elaborated code of behaviour can again be characterised semantically, again with the implication that the possible range of crucial formal patterns can be stated by reference to the crucial characteristics at semantic level. As varieties of a language, the verbal manifestations of these two codes – the restricted and the elaborated – will differ from each other in respect to certain mutually exclusive formal patterns. If this assertion could be proved false, then there would be no case for regarding the codes as responsible for leading to varieties in language.

Though the above account is brief, it is hoped that it clarifies the relationship between the social elements and the verbal realisations of the two codes. Members of different types of societies use different codes; ultimately, the codes differ linguistically in some particular respects only because they reflect the two modes of the living of life. It may be best to elaborate upon this comment by discussing one particular example. It has been shown that in the use of language controlled by the restricted code, there is a much higher frequency of exophoric reference (Hawkins, 1969). So far the statement does not appear to be very different in nature from the statement that in Cockney English, the initial 'h' is 'dropped'. This difference emerges only when we concern ourselves with a reasoned explanation of the phenomena referred to in the two seemingly parallel statements. While it is difficult to find any reason why the phenomenon of 'dropping the initial h' should occur in Cockney but not in the suburban dialects of London, the higher frequency of exophoric reference in the variety of language controlled by restricted code can be explained. Although this explanation involves a complex set of arguments, it will be useful to examine it in brief.

The information encoded in an exophoric item is available to an immediate participant of the situation (Hasan, 1968). It is perhaps important to point out that one does not acquire the status of participant in a speech situation by simple physical presence at the moment of verbal interaction. Rather, the status is allowed to one if one is in possession of the relevant parameters of the situation which motivate the speech. The use of exophoric reference generally implies an assumption on the speaker's part that the hearer knows what the communication is about in general. Characteristically, exophoric references occur frequently where such an assumption can be made; characteristically, such an assumption can be made only where the possibility of ambiguity is not very high. It has been pointed out above that in sub-cultures which give rise to the restricted code a lot is taken for granted and ambiguity is generally not anticipated. This is one of the factors which accounts for the predominance of exophoric reference in the variety of language controlled by the restricted code.

It is important to realise that the high frequency of the exophoric reference, by itself, is not a crucial characteristic of this variety of language alone. That is to say, there are varieties not necessarily controlled by the restricted code, in which the frequency of such reference may be equally high. However, the formal patterns to be found in the variety controlled by the restricted code will display a 'semantic compatibility' which arises from the deep meaning of the code. For example, consider another prediction related to the observation regarding the preponderance of exophoric references in the language controlled by the restricted code. This prediction maintains that the structure of the nominal phrase will be predominantly simpler in the variety under discussion; in other words, fewer modifying parameters will be selected to set aside the entity modified. Moreover, where the modifying parameters do get selected, they will tend to belong to certain semantically classifiable sets. Now, the formal elements 'modifier' and 'qualifier' are the encoding means of differentiation of any kind as applied to any category of person, object or event; it is through these that the uniqueness of an entity may be made explicit in language. The larger the number of parameters of differentiation, the higher the frequency of the modifiers and the qualifiers would be; the more varied the bases of differentiation in the nature of an entity, the wider the set of items which could perform the function of modification.

It has been noted earlier that in the type of societies which give rise to the restricted code, specific attributes of persons, objects and events are less likely to be emphasised or raised to the level of verbal explicitness; here the positional attributes would be emphasised more characteristically. This allows us indirectly to state the limits imposed upon the parameters of differentiation: if differentiation is to be made in terms of positional attributes for, say, persons, then the sets of items covering the semantic fields of sex, age and social role would be more relevant. The limitation on the parameters of differentiation lowers the possibility of complexity in the nominal phrase, since complexity is here merely a function of the selection of modifier and qualifier elements in permissible structures. To this may be added a fact discussed above – namely, that explicit encoding of meaning is not the primary concern of communicative acts here, since ambiguity is generally not anticipated. These two facts considered in conjunction provide sufficient explanation for the comparative simplicity of the nominal phrase in the variety under discussion. At the same time, the above discussion serves to clarify the meaning of the phrase 'semantic compatibility' as applied to characteristic formal patterns, diagnostic of a variety. Further, the discussion of these examples indicates how meanings may be affected by the characteristics of a social structure and how this may in turn affect the formal patterns of the language used by the members of the society.

In the above discussion the speakers making habitual use of a particular code have been identified by reference to their membership in different types of social structures, characterised by specific types of social integration. However, it would be rare, if not impossible, to find a contemporary society which is totally monolithic in its social integration. This would imply that in most contemporary industrialised societies, the two codes would exist side by side, since the social conditions giving rise to them would do so. Thus there exists the possibility the one and the same person may have access to both codes at once, using them in different contexts. However, given the genesis of the codes, it follows that every person in a society must have access to the restricted code, while social conditions may be created due to the complex interrelations between industrialisation, social class and education, whereby effective access to the elaborated code may become the prerogative of one class through its forms of socialisation and access to education (Bernstein, 1971a). That effective access to elaborated code may be restricted, under certain social conditions, only to one class may give rise to the idea that the term 'code' is just another label for what has been known as 'social dialect'. The results of the work carried out in the Sociological Research Unit, under Bernstein's guidance, have indicated a tendency to an orientation to the restricted code on the part of the working-class population, whereas the middle-class population appears to be oriented to the elaborated code (Brandis and Henderson, 1970; Gahagan and Gahagan, 1970; Hawkins, 1969; see also Cook, and Turner and Pickvance 1973). However, it would be a misinterpretation of this correlation of code orientation with social stratification to argue from it that the term 'code' and 'social dialect' stand for the same concept. Note that access to the restricted code by all members of a society is not only allowed for in practice but it is essential in theory. It is true that one and the same person may have access to two social dialects; this would be, however, something determined largely by chance. There is nothing in the nature of the social dialects as such which demands that every member having access to one particular dialect should also have access to another particular one. Where access to codes is concerned the hypothesis that every member of a society would have access to the restricted code, whether or not he also has access to the elaborated code, is ultimately based upon the nature and origin of two codes; the validity of this hypothesis depends upon the validity of the sociological arguments underlying the very genesis of codes.

The nature of codes differs from that of social dialects in other important respects. In the case of all three types of dialects discussed earlier – the temporal, the geographical and the social – the defining linguistic characteristics of the varieties are said to be located at the encoding levels of syntax, lexis and phonology. In the case of codes, however, the distinctive characteristics can be stated more powerfully and economically by referring to the level of meaning; it is not so much the formal patterns but rather the semantic structure of a message that is under focus when the latter is examined in relation to codes. Moreover, keeping the genesis of the codes in view, one may meaningfully raise the question: if different social strata show a tendency to use different codes in the same social contexts – such as the four crucial socialising ones – what sociological explanation for this may be found in consonance with the theory of codes? This is an interesting question, the answer to which would probably involve a consideration of the structure of power and the control of knowledge in society (Bernstein, 1971b). it will be noted that such questions cannot be asked meaningfully with reference to the social dialects, for there does not appear to be any true causal relation between the defining formal characteristics of a social dialect and the social factor correlating with it.

Being an explanatory sociolinguistic concept, the code is likely to have implications both for the field of sociology and that of linguistics. The concept may be used to throw light on questions important to both these parent fields. Consider, for instance, the question of change and stability, which is crucial to any sociological theory. A sociological theory must provide some hypothesis, not only about how societies change, but also how they continue with their essential characteristics. Bernstein has used the concept of code to put forward a hypothesis regarding stability in society. He postulates a bi-directional relationship between codes of communication and elements of social structure. As the earlier discussion has shown, different forms of social relationships determine what orders of meaning will have relevance for members entering into these different relationships. This in turn determines the kind of communication code to be employed. Stripped to its bare essentials this is the view taken by many linguists, that language reflects, albeit indirectly, the speech community which makes use of it for the living of life. Epigrammatically, society fashions language as it is.

The above is one direction of the relationship between social elements and codes of communication. The other direction points to a factor leading to stability in social structures. Bernstein maintains (1965) that:

> the social structure becomes the developing child's psychological reality by the shaping of his act of speech. Underlying the general patterns of his speech are ... critical sets of choices, preferences from some alternatives rather than others, which develop and are stabilised through time and which eventually come to play an important role in the regulation of intellectual, social and affective orientation.

The origin of these statements can be traced back to the famous Whorfian hypothesis that language creates the orders of perception and the relevance of patterns in terms of which the so-called world of objective reality is segmented by a speech community. Thus, according to this view, reality is relative and the specific shape of its segmentation is determined by the characteristics of the language one speaks. Epigrammatically, language fashions society as it is.

In the context of the present discussion, the relevance of these general comments is as follows: it may be maintained that orientation to a particular code implies a particular kind of experience and attitude on the part of the speaker, making him sensitive to just those aspects of social relationships which underly the use and the origin of the code in question. Thus the code of communication created by a particular form of social relation also perpetuates this same form of social relation by sensitising the speakers to just these particular social meanings. This naturally raises the question of how the structure of a society admits of any change. Change in social structures can obviously emerge from varied factors, most of which need not concern us here. The factor relevant here is Bernstein's notion of change in the orientation to code. He allows the possibility that orientation to code can change for members. However, this change is not simply a matter of making the member learn certain aspects of the grammar and lexicon of the language; it entails no less than a change in his social identification (Bernstein, 1970b). A prerequisite of change in orientation to code that the member may be enabled by some agency to perceive forms of relevance and meaning other than those to which he is sensitised by his own code orientation. This in turn entails that he should enter into some forms of social relation other than those which underly the genesis of the code to which he is already oriented. The relevance of this hypothesis to the entire education system is obvious: educational failure may not be as much a result of the pupil's inability to master the concepts, as that of the educational system which fails to establish any relevance between these concepts and the pupil's living of life, especially where the life in school is not a simple extension of life outside.

The relevance of language to social identification has some rather interesting implications for the acquisition of language. No doubt there is some biological attribute in normal humans which enables them to learn language. However, it seems highly improbable that this learning is triggered off simply by the possession of the biological attribute. The motive is furnished by the strongest urge of all – the urge for identification and placement in a social system as a member of a community. An infant remains an animal organism for a surprisingly short period of his life and I am suggesting that from very early infancy the learning of communication is simply grasped as a means of learning about one's identity in some social unit. Language being the most efficient medium of communication – and probably the most explicit means of social identification – receives attention in this capacity. A child learns to speak not because otherwise he could not get his mother to give him his bottle, his rusk or his teddy or whatever – these are comparatively low level pragmatic functions of language, although their value for sheer physical survival is great. He learns language because he is a social animal and his relation to society is determined for him most effectively by the mastery of the verbal system of communication.

The claim is then, that if Bernstein's hypothesis is correct, a child exposed physically to human language which is never placed in any social context, so that it does not symbolise forms of social relation, will not learn the language, despite his biological language-acquisition device. An experiment can be suggested – which for humane reasons could not be undertaken: a child exposed to human language only through a tape-recorder would not learn human language, since this stream of noise would be in no way related to his living of life and therefore would have no specific social meaning. He may be able to utter strings of noises which sound like the human language to which he is exposed, but they will not have the essential characteristics of relevance and flexibility. Unlike the learning of walking, running and jumping, the learning of language is a social phenomenon, much like the learning of non-verbal salutation. In all cases the possession of some biological attribute makes the actual operation possible; it is only in the latter two cases that the possession of the biological attribute alone is not enough.

Recently in linguistic theory, the notion of 'competence' has been introduced (Chomsky, 1965) as determining the area of language that a linguistic model must be able to account for. Very simply, competence is an idealisation of the speaker's knowledge of language – the description of a language should at least be able to specify explicitly what the speaker knows – perhaps only implicitly – about his own language. It should be clear that the word 'speaker' as used in such statements is an abstraction, resembling in many respects the notion of *langue* in linguistics and of 'conscience collective' in the field of sociology. In order to bear any relevance to the purpose for which the notion of 'competence' is introduced originally, the speaker in these cases *must* be the 'ideal speaker'. The mythical nature of the 'ideal speaker' is made abundantly clear when considered in the light of Bernstein's views regarding the relationship of codes to social relations. If his hypotheses regarding the origin and function of codes are correct, then it follows that the social relations underlying and determining some of the characteristics of the total meaning system of one code are not the same as those social relations which underly and determine some of the characteristics of the total meaning system of one code are not the same as those social relations which underly and determine the meaning structure of another one. The implication is that for members with access to only one code, at least some of the meanings of the other codes are filtered through their own code. The 'ideal speaker' even as a theoretical fiction is, therefore, an impossibility in sociolinguistics. His recognition presupposes the existence of a member who can enter into all forms of social relations simultaneously – which is an impossible proposition in sociology. It may be relevant to remark here that the rituals of a social group to which one does not belong appear often meaningless in the absence of technical sophistication.

A logical conclusion of Bernstein's views about the relevance of social elements to codes would be that all meanings are social – what the members can mean is determined by society. Bernstein is not alone in holding this view; ignoring the many sociologists and anthropologists, one could cite names from linguistics such as those of Boas, Bühler, Firth, Halliday, Pike, Sapir and Whorf who have all supported the hypothesis – implicitly or explicitly – that meanings in language cannot be arrived at without reference to society, since they are in the first instance generated by society itself. The various forms of systems of communication only provide the means whereby the totality of social meaning can be encoded and thus made available for transfer to other members. I would suggest that the social origin of meaning would argue strongly for the need to establish a point of contact between elements of social structure and that level of a communication system which is concerned with the meanings that can be encoded through the symbols of the said system of communication. If this premise is granted, it may have interesting implications for the study of language. Here, the level concerned with meaning is generally known as the semantic level. In both the systemic and the stratificational models for the description of language, the semantic level is regarded as the highest language-internal level, bearing a dynamic relation to the encoding levels of syntax, lexis and phonology. In any particular language interaction, the selection of specific categories from the latter three levels is motivated by the selection of certain semantic components (Hasan, 1971). This view explains the basis of selection from amongst the totality of formal-phonological patterns available to a speaker; it cannot, however, explain what motivates the selection of particular semantic components in any given instance. In view of the social origins of meaning, it is perhaps not far-fetched to suggest that the answer to this question will lie in relating the semantic level to elements of social structure (Halliday, 1971b). Most linguists would agree that the semantic level bridges the gap between language and non-language; there are, however, not very many hypotheses as to how the bridging of the gap takes place. It is being suggested here that perhaps a large part of this bridging would consist in the mapping of the social elements onto the semantic ones.

If the origin of meanings is social and if there are various forms of systems of communication, at least in theory the possibility has to be granted that the meaning potential of any one form of system of communication may not be identical with that of any other. Moreover, the meaning potential of any one form of system of communication may not be identical with that of any other. Moreover, the meaning potential of one particular communication system will always form only a part of the totality of meanings available to the society. Thus, the verbal system of communication may be seen as having communicative control over only a part of the total social meaning potential and there may be some advantage in remembering that verbal systems of communication do not have the sole monopoly of encoding meanings. In any given situation, various forms of communicative systems may be employed side by side and often it may not be possible to state definitely that the realisation of a particular component of meaning was achieved solely through some symbol(s) of one and only one particular communicative system. The meaning of a comment with a smile is the function of the interaction of the smile with the comment; this meaning can be realised neither by the verbal symbols nor by the smile alone. Where one's primary concern is the study of meanings communicated in a particular instance, it may be necessary to weaken, if not to disregard, boundaries between the verbal and the non-verbal means of communication. These comments may be taken as a plea for considering human behaviour as a unified whole, in which the verbal and the non-verbal merge in the process of what can only be described as the natural living of life. If in the interest of greater clarity, we choose to study some instance of human behaviour in its different aspects, separating each aspect from the others, it is desirable not to lose sight of the fact that the unit itself is greater than its own individual segments and that the meaning of the unit as such cannot be stated if any of its segments are ignored.

It is hoped that the above discussion would justify the claim that code is a 'key concept'; it is productive in that it leads outside itself. With the help of the concept one may raise questions and one may throw light on matters that do not form part of the concept as such.

4 Register

I have made an attempt earlier to show that code as a concept lies on a level different from that of social dialect and that the two cannot be considered as different labels for the same thing. This is equally true where the pair 'code' and 'register' is concerned; the terms are far from being synonymous.

Register is a variety of language differing at any or all levels of form from other varieties of the same language, 'distinguished according to use' (Halliday et al., 1964). A particular register is said to be characterised by reference to some syntactic, lexical or phonological patterns; that is to say, register varieties differ language-internally by virtue of distinctive formal patterns, such that the totality of distinctive patterns for one particular register is not identical with that of any other register. To this extent they resemble temporal, geographical and social dialects, as well as varieties controlled by the different codes. So far as linguistics is concerned, no category of dialect, code or register can be recognised unless it differs from another category at the same level of abstraction in respect to some formal properties, in a consistent manner. The difference between registers and dialects lies in the fact that, but for a few immaterial exceptions, the distinctive formal patterns characterising a dialect cannot be shown to be motivated by the circumstance of the speech community correlating with it. By contrast, but for a few immaterial exceptions, the distinctive formal patterns characterising a particular register can be shown to be motivated by the factors which correlate with register distinction.

These factors can be studied under two main heads: those which form the relevant parameters of the situation giving rise to the use of language and those which arise from the nature of the channel through which language is transmitted. The latter is often referred to as 'medium'. One may question whether it is justifiable to separate the medium from what it is a medium of. Although it is difficult to think of any other medium for human language, I believe I am right in saying that none the less it is an accident that the transmission of human language takes the channels that it does. In essence the symbolic property of the system 'human language' is independent of the medium of its realisation. A practical and, perhaps weaker, argument in favour of the separation of the verbal symbolic system from its medium may be found in the observation that individual formal patterns of a language seem to vary according to variation in medium – we do not speak as we write and often foreigners sound strange, not because their language is ungrammatical, but simply because they have failed to master this distinction. I believe that no contradiction is involved in maintaining that the symbolic system *qua* a symbolic system is independent of the medium while holding the view that different individual bits of the system have a tendency to correlate with different forms of the medium. Somewhere in the acquisition of language, members of a language community, which possesses both basic media, do gather an awareness of the difference between spoken and written language. In most cases they are able to tell from the language, dissociated from its original context, whether it was produced orally or not. Clearly, extreme case of either such as 'trespassers will be prosecuted' and 'what with one thing and another I wasn't able to make it to the party' will be recognised without any difficulty, though there can arise complications, some of which are discussed below in the discussion of medium.

The total set of factors correlating with the varieties of register can be listed briefly as follows:

Subject-matter of discourse.

Situation-type for discourse.

Participant roles within discourse.

Mode of discourse.

Medium of discourse.

It is assumed that the factors listed above can vary independently, so that any combination of an instance of any is possible. If upon further study it can be shown that some factor listed above independently is in fact a function of some other factor(s), then the former would have to be subsumed in the appropriate category. Thus if it can be shown, for example, that the situation-type fully determines the subject-matter of the discourse, then there would be no need to consider subject-matter as an independent variable, since the specification of the situation-type in this would be tantamount to the specification of the subject-matter as well. Neither originality nor empirical substantiation on a large scale is claimed for the selection of these factors as relevant to register variation. The factors are largely derivative of the account presented by Halliday et al. (1964) (see also Ellis and Ure, 1969) and the only justification for their present arrangement is intuitive; they seem to me to be both independent of each other and important to register variation.

It may be just as well to add in what sense the word 'independent' is being used here. I recognise that the independence of the listed factors is not absolute. That is to say, in actual fact the selection of specific subject-matter may present a fairly reliable basis for the expectation that it would be embedded in specific situation-types. If we take the subject-matter of linguistics, it is highly probable that this particular subject-matter will be embedded in a situation-type which could be labeled generally as 'informative', the exposition of hypothesis/evaluation of hypotheses/comparison of hypotheses etc. being more specific instances of the general situation 'informative'. And it would be rather unlikely to use the subject-matter of linguistics to flatter or to provoke, but neither is totally ruled out and instances of both can be found in linguistic literature. Thus, although specific instances of specific factors may be shown to 'go together' normally, conforming to the pattern of expectations, this co-occurrence is not necessarily predetermined. It is in this sense that I regard the factors as independent of each other. Certain general statements can be made. For instance, the more technical the subject-matter, the less likely it is that it would be embedded in a situation-type involving the arousal of personal reactions; the more institutionalised the situation-type, the less likely it is that the impersonal mode of discourse would be used. These generalisations have a certain degree of validity as they are based on an intuitive understanding of the social meaning of the categories involved; on the other hand, for the examination of a particular case, these generalisations are not of primary interest, only the actual is significant.

One general point seems worth making here before I embark upon a discussion of the factors listed. It has been too readily assumed that the easiest and most valid form of describing the linguistic characteristics of registers is to state the frequency or likelihood of individual patterns or of their combinations. I would suggest that it might be advantageous to specify the characteristics of given registers by reference to some high-level semantic component. For instance, two semantic components common to all sale situations would be the denigration and the desirability of the object of sale. Admittedly the situations would be somewhat different in societies where bargaining is customary as opposed to those where the fixed price rule obtains, but it seems to be true in both that certain semantic components are functions of the situation-type and the participant roles within the discourse. The characterisation of registers by reference to some high-level semantic components would have at least three advantages. In the first place, the description of registers need not be tied down to the specification of individual sets of items or their combination occurring within a particular variety – the presentation of such an inventory seems to me to be almost impossible to achieve. Consider the examples below:

1   It certainly is lovely but it's expensive

2   It *is* expensive but it's unique, made by our own exclusive craftsman.

In most societies – and particularly in those where bargaining is customary – (1) would be a possible statement by a buyer and (2) by a seller. The interesting point to note here is that the two are not different ways of saying nearly the same thing. Despite the use of the item *expensive* in (2), what stands out is the relative cheapness of the item which is an argument for its desirability, while in (1) the item *expensive* has its standard dictionary meaning. One is saying: it is expensive because of some desirable attribute(s) and therefore cheap: the other, that it is expensive despite the attribute(s) and therefore not worth the expense. No item-inventory could handle such features for the simple reason that they are not the property of individual items but of items of often different levels in combination. What distinguishes the two statements is the fact that one denigrates 'it' while the other stresses the desirability.

It is often difficult to know what value to assign to the relative frequencies of items occurring within a text when it is a question of allocating the text to some specific register. If the text is long, there seems to be no explicit criterion for concentrating on certain items rather than on others. I am suggesting that the postulate of a high-level semantic component provides a justification for picking out those items of the encoding levels which are pertinent to the encoding of the said semantic component. I would further suggest that the realisation of these high-level semantic components is not 'localised' but that it is likely to be dispersed over the text as a whole. Less technically, the register allocation of a text is impossible without understanding the meaning of the text and I am suggesting that within the meaning of the text there are constellations of meanings which are crucial to the identity of registers; these are the very meaning constellations to which I have referred as the high-level semantic components of the text.

Further, the statement of points of similarity and dissimilarity amongst different register varieties may be made easier by this approach. What Davies says (Davies, 1969) regarding the formal patterns of a text on chemistry may be true only of a particular sub-type of chemistry texts. I would doubt that the grammatical structures whose frequency he considers to be crucial to chemistry texts upon Taylor's findings (Taylor, 1968) would be crucial to chemistry texts in pedagogical situations where the participant roles are school-teacher and young pupils; one only needs to look at a school-book of chemistry – or to listen to a teacher in the class – to realise that the density of attributive and locative clauses is not a function of the subject-matter alone. At the same time, the kind of propositional relations cited by him as a property of this register are not specific to it alone – they will be found equally in texts of the same tenor on other physical sciences, if not elsewhere as well. From a consideration of the combinations of specific subject-matter, situation-type, participant roles, mode and medium, may be predicted certain high-level semantic components which will at once display the points of similarity and dissimilarity amongst the various sub-types of a general register such as that of chemistry or politics. This observation is based upon the assumption that the social meanings of the different variable factors correlating with register provide an indication of the total range of what can possibly be meant – they determine what Halliday calls the 'meaning potential' (Halliday, 1971a) of a given variety. Under a specifiable circumstance we can only 'mean' from that set of meanings which the circumstance has set aside as potentially relevant.

To return to the main discussion, the gloss on the subject-matter of discourse may be defined as 'what is the language about?' This is what forms part of the contents of the discourse. The subject-matter controls the range of the lexicon from which selection may be made. This is so obvious that it does not need to be pointed out: in a discussion of the nature of volcanic eruptions, the lexicon referring to, say, the genres of musical composition is, as it were, irrelevant. The correlation between subject-matter and the range of the lexicon functioning as the field of effective choice is the most transparent of all relations – what is being talked about must be referred to, for in everyday life we do not function like the symbolist poet. If specific registers varied from each other only in this respect there would probably be no need to recognise the category of register.

The subject-matter is embedded in the situation-type. Situation-type is a cover term for the nature and purpose of the transaction in which language is being used and only refers to those parameters of the immediate situation (Ellis, 1966) which are encapsulated in the language of a text; that is to say, situation-type is an abstraction from the totality of material situational setting. When two situation-types are very different in nature, it is difficult to realise that the subject-matter constitutes only part of the contents of the text; the nature of the transaction as well as the purpose of the use of language function is just as important in determining the meanings of the text. Compare two texts regarding a piece of jewellery, one in a situation-type of expert evaluation and the other in sale, perhaps, in Petticoat Lane. The two are likely to run thus:

3   This chain is eight-carat rolled gold, 13 inches; the stone is semi-precious. Their total value is approximately £2.10p.

4   It's a beauty. Lovely stone and the chain is dainty. Want to try it on? It'll go beautifully with your dress – and very cheap for what it is. Lovely workmanship – new design in the market. Came in only yesterday.

In these two examples the difference in the situation-type obscures the fact that the language is in both cases about the same thing – i.e., a piece of jewellery. Such obscurity arises most often in cases where the subject-matter is what is not regarded as belonging to a technical discipline. Conversely, where the subject-matter belongs to a recognised discipline, the situation-type does not obscure the subject-matter – instead it may itself get obscured by this part of the content of the discourse. Criticism of works in recognised fields of discipline on the ground of their not doing what the speaker never set out to do in the first place are based on a misinterpretation of the situation-type. If the subject-matter functions as a control on the general relevant area of the lexicon, the situation-type functions as a modification of this area – excluding some part of what, on the basis of the subject-matter alone, would have been adequate, but what, in the combination of *that* subject-matter in *that* situation type, would not be. At the same time it may argue for the inclusion of some area(s) of lexicon which, on the ground of the subject-matter alone, could not have been predicted. If the situation-type in which the subject-matter of chemistry is embedded is pedagogical as opposed to exposition of hypotheses, this will inevitably modify the area of lexicon relevant to the two. Similarly, if the situation-type in which the subject matter of jewellery is embedded is ordering a piece of jewellery to be made, then certain areas of the lexicon referring to the weight and design particulars of the object in question would be relevant while they are not relevant *per se* to the situation-type of evaluation or sale. It is expected that the propositional relations holding the particular statements of the text together will vary with a variation in situation-types. Consider the implicit causal relation between the first and second sentences of text (3) above; in (4) the relationship between the sentences is what I have referred to as 'additive' elsewhere.

Participant roles within discourse may be glossed as 'who is using language to communicate with whom?' where *who* and *whom* do not refer to unique individuals but to some communally ascribed role, such as those of older, younger, male, female, mother, father, husband, wife, son, daughter, teacher, neighbour, stranger etc.; it will be readily seen that these are all socially defined positional roles. What may not be seen so readily is the fact that in any particular case a speaker may operate in the capacity of some particular role, the others being, as it were, irrelevant. This is why I have considered it necessary to add the qualification 'within discourse', which implies 'only that role which is relevant to the discourse, irrespective of others that the speaker is capable of assuming on other occasions of verbal interaction involving the self-same persons'. Thus when Mrs Jones, the teacher, interacts in the classroom with a student who happens to be also her daughter, the role-relations are likely to be those of teacher-taught, not of mother-daughter which may be assumed on some other occasions. Another attribute of the participants of a discourse which is subsumed in this head is what I have referred to as the 'personal distance'; this is the factor which underlies the distinctions made on the axis of formality-familiarity. It would seem that the roles of the participants are largely determined by the situation-type in which they interact with one another. Indeed, the more institutionalised the situation-type, the more likely it is that the role-constellation to be found would be totally predictable from the specific situation-type. In a situation of school pedagogy, the roles are institutionally also determined as those of teacher and taught. However, what cannot be predicted from the situation-type is the personal distance obtaining between the participants, even in institutionalised situations. It is interesting to note here that in some cases the factor of personal distance is built into the meaning of the items of a set; consider 'intruder, stranger, acquaintance, friend' in this light. In any given instance the personal distance factor may override the consequences of the publicly recognised roles. A father and son may in different situation-types interact with a different degree of personal distance, often depending upon the subject-matter of the discourse. Thus, the institutional role as such is not a sure indication of the degree of personal distance obtaining within an interaction, except in cases where the item referring to the ascribed role has this factor built into its meaning.

All things being equal, the participant roles and personal distance together act upon the lexicon and the syntax of a given register. The role and personal distance which allows:

5   His business has gone phut.

is different, however minimally, from that which allows:

6   His business has come to a sad end.

and the following is again different from the above example, its role relations as well as the distance obtaining between the roles:

7   The court have declared him bankrupt.

It may be of interest here to note that the exophorics, whose use has been cited above as one of the characteristics of language controlled by the restricted code, would most probably occur with a greater frequency in those registers where the personal distance is very reduced. The reasons in both cases are the same; the possibility of ambiguity arising is low where the distance between participants is reduced, just as it is low where the paradigm of known and possible behaviour is largely precategorised. Thus one and the same feature of language can arise from different sources depending on the context of the discussion; this is not a reason for ignoring these features of language – if anything it argues for an interpretation which takes the relevant factors into account, and therefore probes more deeply into the significance of these features. While it is easier to describe in general terms how the lexicon may vary according to the variation in role and distance, it is comparatively more difficult to make such general statements regarding their effect upon syntax. However, consider the following examples, in which it is assumed that only the personal difference is at variance:

8   I wondered if I might be allowed to leave earlier today. There are some personal matters I should like to settle this afternoon.

9   I've got this thing to do at home. Is it all right if I go off earlier today?

It is my tentative suggestion that the greater the stress on the institutionalised aspect of the role and the greater the personal distance, the more likely it is that the high-level semantic components of +/- *tentativeness* and +/- *uncertainty* would be relevant to the text, the plus and the minus signs distributing themselves in a coherent pattern for the dominated and the dominating role. Thus in example (8) the employee's language will have the semantic components +*tentative* and –*certain*, while the employer's is likely to possess –*tentative* and +*certain*. Some of the realisation of the component +*tentative*, for example, would be through the modification of whole statements, which may involve at the formal levels the selection of comment adjuncts, modality, modulation (Halliday, 1970) or of some subordinating circumstance. This mode of approach seems to be perhaps more helpful for stating characteristics of registers; it would certainly appear to be somewhat more productive than the counting of subordinate clauses or what-have-you.

Given the same situation-type and the same subject-matter as well as the same participant roles, registers may vary according to variation in the mode of discourse. Often the combination of the specific instances of the former three factors can effectively determine the mode to be employed. For example, in the situation of buying and selling, the mode would normally be 'persuasive'; it would be a-normal to find the 'imperative' mode used here. Non-technically, a salesman wheedles; he does not dictate. Again, in a situation of exposition of hypotheses, the mode is likely to be 'expository'/'explanatory' while it is not likely to be 'supplicatory' in the normal sense of the word. But in theory the mode of discourse *can* vary independently, even in the same given combination of situation-type, subject-matter and participant role. Thus we may have the following different statements from two different mothers:

10 If you climb up that wall you may hurt yourself.

11 You climb up that wall and I'll take a stick to you.

One might say that at one level what the mothers are saying is the same, namely *I don't want you to climb up that wall*, but the difference in the mode of discourse certainly changes some aspects of the meaning of the two statements, so much so that it is difficult to realise that they belong to the same situation-type basically, namely that of control. The mode of discourse is most effectively reflected in the mood choices of the clauses in the text. It is possible to make predictions regarding the structural characteristics associated with different types of mode. For instance, the persuasive mode is likely to produce texts in which the various statements are causally linked; the expository mode, those in which in addition to causal relations, relations of elaboration and exemplification will also be found, while in the imperative mode the causal relation between the propositions is likely to be of an arbitrary nature as in (11).

Medium of discourse has already been discussed in some respects earlier. Basically it refers to the channel of communication, which may be either oral (spoken) or graphic (written). Varieties differ according to whether they are spoken or written. It is perhaps important to emphasise that the actual nature of the manifestation is itself not crucial here. The transcript of a recorded conversation is not an instance of the written medium; equally the broadcast of news is not an instance of the spoken medium. Because individual bits of language have a tendency to occur in different media, a somewhat curious situation has emerged. It is possible to produce a text in writing which was never spoken but which is written-as-if-spoken; for example, consider some modern plays. Equally it is possible to speak out a text which was never written but which, as it unfolds itself, bears all the characteristics of written language, save the orthographic manifestation. It is therefore fair to assume that oral and graphic media as factors correlating with register variation, do not refer to the physical manifestations of the text in question, but rather to some properties of the text, which are normally associated with the two basic channels.

The medium of discourse is expected to affect the syntactic choices of a text. All things being equal, spoken texts display a greater complexity in syntax than the written ones, a point to which attention was drawn also by Halliday et al. (1964). In written discourse, exophoric cohesive devices have an almost negligible frequency, as compared with spoken discourse, where certain types of ellipses occur much more frequently than they do in the former type of discourse. These characteristic features – which do not exhaust all the peculiarities – of the spoken and written varieties stem from the fact that in spoken communication more information regarding the relevant immediate situation is available extra-linguistically to the participants of the discourse. It is therefore not necessary to encapsulate in language all the relevant components of the meaning of the message in an explicit manner. In written communication, on the other hand, extra-linguistically provided information is of a very limited kind and depends much upon the shared contexts between the participants. In order to be decoded appropriately, the relevant components of the meaning of the message must be encapsulated explicitly in language, since whatever is not so encapsulated may not be available to the decoder. The lower occurrences of exophoric cohesive devices and of certain types of ellipses in the written variety of discourse would appear to be governed by these conditions. In the spoken variety an elliptical clause such as *don't*, even when it occurs all by itself, can be interpreted as a request or order to desist from carrying out a particular action – the nature of which would be known to the decoder from extra-linguistic sources. In the written variety, the same elliptical clause cannot be assigned a specific interpretation – that is to say, the specific process under focus will not be known to the decoder – unless the elliptical clause functions anaphorically presupposing some item cohesively in the text.

Features referred to sometimes as cancellation, repetition and contradiction have been ignored in the above discussion. Although these features are normally associated with the spoken medium, they are not causally related to this factor alone. Rather, in general, they indicate the speaker's familiarity and control over the subject-matter in relation to his listener(s). To the extent that the language of a speaker, on some particular occasion, is more 'well-organised', it points to the fact that what is said and to whom it is said presents little or no problem to the speaker. Thus, these features are not a function of the medium of the discourse as such; they result from an interaction of the subject-matter, situation-type and participant relations relevant to a discourse.

Throughout the discussion of the category of register, the term 'tenor' of discourse has been avoided. It seems to me to be a particularly suitable term to refer to the 'tonal quality' of texts of various varieties. The tonal quality itself is the product of the interaction of the five factors listed and discussed above. In other words, the tonal quality of a text is not determined solely by the selection of any one factor, be it that of situation-type, of mode or personal distance or participant role. Instead, it would seem to be a result of the fact that x is being talked about, in y situation, with participant roles a and b, with reduced personal distance, in a particular mode and medium. It should be noted that the use of tenor to refer to the tonal quality of texts as a whole is a departure from both Halliday et al. (1964) and from Enkvist, Spencer and Gregory (1964). Halliday et al. use the term 'style', underlying which are the factors of role-type and personal distance, while Enkvist, Spencer and Gregory use the term 'tenor' for the same purpose, on the ground that the term 'style' is best used exclusively for literary texts.

Hopefully, the above discussion shows that the factors said to correlate with register variation stand in a causal relation to the formal patterns which are characteristic of a particular register. The details of these factors can therefore be used to predict the formal characteristics crucial to a given variety of register. By virtue of this attribute, register can be shown to be distinct from dialect: the correlation of extra-linguistic factors with formal patterns diagnostic of a given dialect variety is based upon what might be described as incidental co-occurrence. On the other hand, the particular type of causal relation described above is not specific to register alone. It may be recalled that in the discussion of code, some of the crucial formal patterns were shown to be predictable from the social factors underlying a particular variety of code (cf. pp 264-5). In this particular respect then code and register are alike; however, the terms are not synonymous. They refer to two distinct concepts, involving different levels of abstraction.

The difference between code and register can perhaps be indicated most economically by considering the extra-linguistic factors said to correlate with each category. The factors relevant to register have been discussed in some detail above (cf. pp. 272-81). Where code is concerned the key concept would appear to be that of 'role-system'. The term role has been mentioned as a factor correlating with register variation as well; to be more precise, variation in participant role in discourse is said to result in variation of register. It may be well to state the difference between participant role and role-system as used in the discussion of variation in register and code, respectively. The term role-system as used in the discussion of code variation is more abstract and general than the term participant role, as used in register. Any particular manifestation of participant role would be some instance of that type of role which may be labeled 'institutionalised'; thus the term covers only a fraction of what may be meant by the general term role-system. This is just another way of saying that the term role-system refers to a more general and abstract concept. At this level of abstraction, the role-system lies at the basis of all social relations: it acts upon social interactions available to members of a community. The type of social relations underlying the role-systems that is pertinent to code variation. The differences between specific ascribed roles in social hierarchies and institutions are, *per se*, not relevant to code variation; the differences between types of roles are. Thus, unlike register, code need not vary according to whether a speaker is operating in the ascribed capacity of father or that of son; it will, however, vary according to whether the role is communalised or individuated.

Role-system acts upon the more specific factors which correlate with code variation; in fact these factors may be seen as a function of role-system. I shall refer to these factors as 'mode of control', 'focus of interest' and 'focus of meaning'. The difference in role-type is expected to affect the nature of control-meaning and interest. In its turn this variation would be relevant to code variation. If we accept as our paradigm, the ideal types of restricted and elaborated code, then the relationship of the various factors discussed above to code variation may be presented as follows[3]:

General category	Specific sub-types of category	
role-system	communalised	individuated
mode of control }	strong boundaries	strong or weak boundaries
focus of interest }	on practice	on underlying principle
nature of meaning }	context dependent low situational contingency	context independent high situational contingency
	(idealised) restricted code	(idealised) elaborated code

It is important to emphasise that the schematic presentation above is highly simplified. Moreover, it presents that combination of factors which underlies the restricted and elaborated codes in their most idealised states, instances of which might not even occur in practice. The first column is labeled General category; it states general factors relevant to code variation. The second and third columns present the more specific sub-types of the latter general category. Thus, looking across the columns, communalised and individuated role-systems are more specific sub-types of the general category role-system. Looking downwards in columns 2 and 3, we find within braces those specific factors which stand in a causal relation to the specific sub-type of role-system: a two-way arrow is used to indicate the bi-directionality of this relationship. Thus, in the above representation, column 2 may be read out as follows: wherever role-systems are of the communalised type, there is a greater likelihood that the mode of control will utilise strong boundary maintenance, that the focus of interest would be on practice and that meanings would be context dependent with low situational contingency; conversely, wherever these particular factors combine, there is a greater expectancy that the role-systems would be of the communalised type. The arrow from the lower brace to the idealised code-type shows that in, say, column 2 the combination would correlate with a maximised restricted code. The labels for most of the factors within braces are self-explanatory, but a word must be added here regarding the sub-types of the factor 'nature of meaning', as this is probably most relevant to code differentiation where the concept is being considered as controlling certain varieties of language.

The term 'context dependent' when applied to language as used in any interaction may be paraphrased as follows: language that does not encapsulate explicitly all the features of the relevant immediate situation in which the verbal interaction is embedded. Crucial to this paraphrase is the distinction between 'material immediate situation' and 'relevant immediate situation'; the latter is that sub-set of the former to which reference is made implicitly or explicitly by the language of a message. The implicitness of the context dependent language implies that the correct decoding of the verbal message would be dependent upon an awareness of the relevant immediate situation, which awareness would be derived from sources other than the verbal message under focus. That is to say, in order to have access to the meanings of the verbal message, the decoder has to utilise other sources of information than just the language of the text under focus. As might be expected, 'context independent' has exactly the opposite meaning; context independent language is language that encapsulates explicitly all the relevant features of the immediate situation in which the verbal interaction is embedded. It follows that here the correct decoding of the message is a simple function of one's understanding of the language, requiring no extra-linguistic sources of knowledge.

The label 'low situational contingency' may be paraphrased as follows: the linguistic means of rendering entities unique are rarely employed. Where there is low situational contingency those details specific to particular persons, objects and situations are not treated linguistically which would set aside the entity under focus as unique. Rather, the attributes by reference to which an entity is characterised are likely to be such general ones as do not lead to an individuation of the entity. Conversely, 'high situational contingency' implies a greater explicit use of verbal means whereby some entity is rendered unique so that it is set aside as a particular case.

It may be of interest here to note that the two terms in each pair of contrasting factors cannot be treated as mutually totally exclusive. That is to say, it is not the case, for instance, that in language controlled by the elaborated code, every bit of the message would be explicitly encoded. The question regarding these factors then is not whether they occur or not; rather, it is to be formulated in relative terms. The degrees of, say, context dependence and situational contingency are variable and there is no absolute point which may be said to be diagnostic of one variety of code or of the other. This is one of the reasons why code variation is better studied in the background of the same social functional contexts, e.g. Bernstein's four socialising contexts. It is also to be noted that the relationship between the type of role-system and the factors (contained within braces) is not absolute; there is no total logical dependence between the two. In theory, at least, the possibility is allowed that social conditions may arise which would allow different re-alignments of the factors. It is therefore possible that we may have an array of the varieties of restricted and elaborated codes rather than just two highly idealised ones.

If we compare the factors which are said to correlate with code variation with those said to correlate with register variation, the difference between the two categories may be formulated. The code-correlating factors are derived directly from a coherent, albeit limited, theory of social structure and cultural transmission. Each factor here is relatable to the central concept of role-system; in its turn, role-system is basic to the theory of social structure and cultural transmission. There is thus a clear chain of causal relation, which traces the origin of the code to its very roots, offering hypotheses as to why certain forms of behaviour are the likely ones under certain specifiable social conditions. Underlying the register-correlating factors, there is no such theoretical coherence. Although largely social in nature, these factors are not relatable to any specific aspect of a social theory; indeed, in some cases the very basis of the distinction between two specific instances of factor is itself non-sociological. For example, the distinction between chemistry and biology as two distinct technical fields is not based upon sociological arguments, although this distinction may be regarded as a socially important one. As a concept, code points to something outside itself; register does not. Register does not presuppose a coherent sociological theory; the presupposition of certain observed social facts is sufficient for the discussion. In order for the concept of register to be viable, it is not necessary to establish any relation between the observed social facts which are built into the register-correlating factors.

It is an outcome of these attributes that whereas all code-correlating factors lie at the same level of abstraction, the question whether or not this is true also of register-correlating factors cannot even be raised meaningfully. Presupposing a coherent theory, the code-correlating factors can be placed *vis à vis* each other and within the theory. Register-correlating factors on the other hand cannot be so placed.

The code-correlating factors belong to a high level of abstraction. The theory of code is not only the theory of a linguistic variety; it includes a theory of both verbal and non-verbal behaviour in the sense that it offers some hypothesis regarding the effect of certain social phenomena upon the community's living of life. Code is thus a much more global concept than register.

The recognition of the concept of register has some interesting implications for the study of language in general. I have suggested earlier that registers may be better characterised by reference to some high-level semantic components, whose realisation would not be a function of individual items of any size or level but rather of a combination of such items throughout the text. It would follow that at least two types of meanings would have to be recognised – those which are localised and those which are text-wide. Thus any text may be seen to contain meanings whose pertinence is limited within some formal unit; at the same time it would contain meanings which are not unit-bound, these latter being realised across formal units and being pertinent to more than any one particular unit – no matter of what size or level – in the text. We may use two different labels for these two distinct types of meaning, referring to the former as 'localised semantic components' and to the latter as 'textual semantic components'. The need for a recognition of these two kinds of semantic components can be justified. Both the localised and the textual semantic components are equally relevant to an adequate decoding of a verbal message. *A priori* there appears to be no reason for suggesting that the study of only one kind – namely the localised semantic components – is the business of linguistics while the other kind of semantic components can be relegated to some vague area, such as that of 'stylistic variation' or 'performance', as if these meanings did not reside in language.

The category of register differentiates texts generally by reference to their textual semantic components. Registers are not set up to account for the semantic differences between the following:

12 If you climb up that wall you may hurt yourself.

13 If you climb up that wall you may ruin your nice new shirt.

This is one of the reasons for commenting that if registers varied simply by the variation in subject-matter and consequently showed distinctions only in the selection of lexical items, it would not be necessary to recognise the category of register. The two texts above do differ in meaning but this difference in meaning is not text-wide, as is the case with:

14 If you climb up that wall you may hurt yourself.

15 You climb up that wall and I'll take a stick to you.

Most current theories of semantics are inadequate for dealing with textual semantic components, whether or not they are capable of dealing with the localised ones. Moreover, it would seem that in order to move towards a semantic theory capable of adequately describing text-wide meanings, we may have to revise our linguistic models. A model that can accept and integrate the interaction of language with non-language as an important part of language study obviously stands a better chance of dealing with text-wide meanings. The autonomy of the verbal symbolic system appears to be restricted to the formal levels alone and it may be that an adequate semantic theory presupposes an adequate theory to account for the nature of contact between the formal linguistic and the extra-linguistic phenomena. The nature of this contact is not exhausted by such isolated notions as those of 'reference', 'representation' or 'naming'. The onomastic function is certainly basic to language; it is perhaps also necessary for other functions that language has. In view of our present state of knowledge, this particular type of relationship between language and non-language is perhaps also the easiest to handle. None the less, there is more to this rather neglected area of language study. Language is used to live, just as social structure is used to live. This introduces a complexity in the description of language and argues for a weakening of boundaries between various systems for communication. The exhaustive description of language is an ideal, which may perhaps never be achieved, but there will certainly be much *less* chance of its being achieved if language is separated from the living of life totally. The semantic structure of language is not absolutely unrelated to the total meaning structure available to a community. Hence, meanings in language cannot be described adequately by remaining enclosed within the formal symbolic system of language.

The adequate use of language must in some sense be a part of our linguistic competence. In actual practice the learning of language cannot be equated with the learning of formal relations obtaining amongst individual 'bits' of verbal symbolic system. Indeed, I have maintained earlier that such learning of language *as language* is impossible – language cannot be learnt in dissociation from how it is used. If 'competence' refers to a speaker's knowledge of his language rather than to just some particular aspect(s) of such knowledge, then it cannot be equated with grammar, unless 'grammar' equals total description – and such a use of the term grammar would be somewhat a-normal. The variation in the tonal quality of two texts is not a superficial matter, resulting form the randomness of performance; it has a meaning as basic to the message as the so-called 'cognitive' meaning. This is not to say that all variation is language is necessarily meaningful. However, when two items occur in a regular pattern, the pattern of their occurrence being generally definable by some such concept as that of code, register or dialect, it seems profitless to insist that they are free variants of each other simply because in some respects the meanings of the two may be similar. In the background of that clustering of register-correlating factors, where a mother may say:

16 If you climb up that wall you may ruin your nice new shirt.

She could not very well have said:

17 If that wall is climbed up by you, your nice new shirt might be ruined by you.

This is not because (16) is grammatical while (17) is not. It is because given the particular clustering of register-correlating factors, (17) would be highly inappropriate. The meaning components encoded in (16) are not identical with those encoded in (17) and it is only the former that are appropriate in the register of maternal control with reduced distance; the latter are not. This point is related to the definition of 'deviation' in linguistics. Language is an abstraction, and while it is not only justifiable but also necessary to describe the grammar of language disregarding those forms which are peculiar only to some specific variety, the limitations of such a grammar should not be forgotten. Consider the following:

18 She often buys in Switzerland.

19 They shivered their spears.

20 He hit many fours during the first Test match.

To say that the above are deviant or ungrammatical tells us little that is worth knowing about these sentences – what it does tell us about is the kind of limitations we have imposed upon the grammar which regards these as deviant – or worse, as ungrammatical. While the norms of the language, abstracted from its varieties, apply generally, the norms of specific varieties of language cannot be ignored, for in any confrontation with language, we do not encounter the abstraction 'language' itself – only an instance of some variety of it.

Concluding remarks

In the discussion of the three categories – code, register and social dialect – I have attempted to present what seems to me to be the essential difference in their nature. At the same time, I have tried to show the implications of the recognition of these categories to linguistics and to sociology. If sociolinguistics consisted only of the study of social dialects as characterised here, there would be no justification for its recognition as a separate field of study, since it would present little or no extension of either sociology or linguistics. This is not to say that dialect studies have no value; simply, that they can be adequately accommodated within the area of general linguistics known as institutional linguistics. It is a function of cross-disciplinary studies – or so it seems to me – that they pose a set of problems which could not be handled adequately remaining within one of the associated fields, thus providing further new insights important to both in different ways. It is true both of codes and registers that they provide an insight into language which could not be obtained simply by concentrating on the formal relations obtaining between the 'bits' of language.

In the discussion of both codes and registers one may find enough indications to suggest that Firth is correct in his assumption that a language text contains various levels of meaning. These meanings cannot be described simply by having recourse to the lexicon, no matter how complete it is – nor by working out a set or rules which tell us how to interpret sentences in isolation. It may be true that linguistics has not yet reached even this infant stage of describing such meanings explicitly. But this does not seems to be any reason for suggesting that explorations of the statements of meaning at various levels of analysis are either invalid in themselves or shorn of interest. Centuries of linguistic scholarship has allowed us to arrive at a stage where we can, perhaps with some justification, talk about the construction of explicit grammars – but the work of the preceding generations was certainly neither invalid within its own historical context nor a waste of time. The field of language study is wide and so full of legitimate inquiries into its varied aspects that it would be narrow-minded, indeed, to insist that every linguist should approach the study of language in the same manner. In the last resort, the aspects of language one chooses to study and the approach one follows would very much depend upon why one is interested in the study of language at all. The purpose of one's inquiry would seem to push one to emphasise one aspect over some other – as it may also determine the nature of the hypotheses regarding those aspects of language. Some hypotheses may have the substantiation of empirical work, but no hypothesis starts with such substantiation – all are equally suspect when they are first put forward and need recurrent reformulations in the light of better understanding. To this no discipline bears better witness than that of linguistics itself, even if considered just within the last decade. It is not too fanciful to suggest that a theory is like an artifact: it justifies itself if its different parts hang together coherently so that the inner logic of the structure is not disturbed and the total bears some viable relation to the 'reality' to which the artifact of theory stands in a symbolic relation. If a linguistic theory can achieve this, it will have made a positive contribution.

Acknowledgement

This paper draws heavily upon the writings of Basil Bernstein and Michael Halliday. Since explicit reference to their work has not been made at every relevant point, I take this opportunity to acknowledge my deep debt to both. My interpretation of Bernstein's concept of code is based not only upon his writings but also on several discussions with him. Although I have made every effort to present an interpretation of the concept code which is faithful to Bernstein's writings and comments in seminars and discussions, the responsibility for the views expressed here is strictly mine, without any implication of agreement on all points on Bernstein's part. To Halliday, I owe the basic framework for the discussion of the concept of register as well as the notion of 'semantic potential' and the relationship of semantics to social structure.

Notes

1 This paper is based upon a talk given at a seminar in the Language and Society series at London School of Economics in June 1969. I am grateful to the Nuffield Programme for the Sociolinguistics Study of Children's Stories for financing the work on this paper.
2 Although in Bernstein's earlier writings mention is often made of the kid of language patterns associated with the two codes at the levels of syntax, lexis and sometimes, phonology, I believe I am right in maintaining that the status of these statement is that of a means to an end – the end, in my view, has always been to characterise the varieties of code by reference to the differences at the level of meaning.
3 I owe this schematic presentation of the factors correlating with code variation to Basil Bernstein, since its present shape emerged during a discussion with him on the nature of codes.

7 Semiotic mediation and mental development in pluralistic societies: some implications for tomorrow's schooling

> That children's learning begins long before they attend school is the starting point of this discussion. Any learning a child encounters in school has a previous history. (Vygotsky, 1978: 84)

1 Introduction

The enormous reach of Vygotsky's theoretical approach to mental development derives from the very concept of semiotic mediation. What makes the concept so powerful is the fact that it establishes connections across some of the most important areas of human social existence. More specifically, it foregrounds a fundamental relationship between mental functions and discourse within the context of social/cultural activity. This, in turn, invites us to explore the relations between the disciplines of psychology, semiotics and sociology. Reflection on these interconnections suggests that if we wish to fully understand the implications of Vygotsky's claims about the sociogenesis of human mind, then, on the one hand, we must be willing to ignore the conventionally accepted boundaries erected in the name of specialisation across these and many other disciplines and, on the other hand, we must be prepared to probe deeper into the significance of the claims made by this powerful theory.

It is well recognised (Vygotsky, 1962; Wertsch, 1985a etc.) that in putting forward the concept of semiotic mediation, Vygotsky attached greater importance to language than he did to other modalities of meaning. We need, then, to ask why language has been granted this special status in Vygotsky's theory; what it is that language enables us to do which other semiotic modalities do not – or at least not to the same extent, or with the same facility. Similarly, in identifying social/cultural activity as the essential site for the operation of semiotic mediation, the theory opens up interesting questions, such as the relation between cultural activities and language, or whether different kinds of activities encourage different forms of semiotic mediation. Since the societies we know today are pluralistic, with multiple groupings whose boundaries are drawn by reference to interest, race, gender, occupation and socioeconomic status, it is important to ask whether the different social groups engage in the same range of activities; and if so, whether the performance of such activities takes the same form across the distinct social groups.

If there is an inherent relation between language, cultural activities and semiotic mediation and if we wish to understand the working of semiotic mediation, then we do need to focus on such questions. It seems to me that the extent to which we can benefit from the application of Vygotskian insights depends on how far we are able to engage successfully in enquiries of this kind. Nowhere does this appear truer than in the complex area of constructive thinking on education, both its theory and its practice. It is the aim of this chapter to begin an exploration of the concept of cultural activity in relation to semiotic mediation by using the modality of language. I hope that this exploration will reveal some important implications of accepting semiotic mediation as the essential means of making human minds and thus suggest avenues for conceptualising better programs for truly egalitarian education.

2 Semiotic mediation: one process, two manifestations

I shall use the term semiotic mediation throughout this chapter as a short form for *semiotic mediation by means of the modality of language*. The term 'semiotic' refers to all modalities for signing, not just language. In assigning this crucial place to language in the processes of semiotic mediation, I do not wish to prejudge the role of other semiotic modalities in the formation of higher mental functions, but simply to respect Vygotsky's own usage (Vygotsky, 1978; Wertsch, 1985a). The term 'mediation' on the other hand refers to a process that is inherently transitive: it requires at least two participants – *something/someone mediates something*. So for the purposes of this chapter the term semiotic mediation may be paraphrased as *mediation by someone of something to someone else by means of the modality of language*.

Using the term in this sense, I take it as axiomatic that semiotic mediation is a constant feature of human social life. The natural condition of language in use in the context of cultural activity is to mediate; the issue is not whether it mediates, but rather what it is that it mediates. In the writings of Vygotsky and his colleagues, as well as in its current discussions and applications, it has been customary to invoke the agency of this process with specific reference to concept formation and/or some form of problem solving. The concepts and problems cited belong typically to the specialised educational activities of officially recognised educational sites. To be sure, semiotic mediation is a powerful tool in these processes, but to emphasise its function only in such contexts is to encourage the questionable view that this constitutes the default function of semiotic mediation, that it represents its true essence and that semiotic mediation functions only intermittently, coming into play in cultural activities which call for explicit, deliberate teaching of specific concepts, knowledge structures and the like. I believe that such a view of semiotic mediation undersells the concept. In fact, to appreciate the full power of this notion, all we need do is to remember that semiotic mediation occurs wherever discourse occurs and that discourse is ubiquitous in the living of social life: semiotic mediation is what language naturally does in discourse. And the most important thing that language does in discourse is to enable the speaking subjects to internalise the world they experience in the living of their life. This includes but also goes beyond the formation of specific concepts, especially if by the term 'concept' we mean to refer only to technological or scientific concepts, the conscious inculcation of which is taken to be the main aim of formal education.

Seen from this perspective, the most basic and foundational achievement – but certainly not the only achievement – of semiotic mediation is the inculcation of mental disposition, 'the habits of mind, tendencies to respond to situations in certain ways' (see Carr and also Claxton, 2002), producing in social subjects a sense of what things are worth doing in their community and how they are to be done. The claim that this is the most fundamental aspect of the development of the human mind is in keeping with Vygotsky's framework, where concept formation is not a passive, receptive process; rather, it involves the active participation of the learners in their learning. By this logic, the learners' mental disposition, their readiness to engage in the appropriation of some concepts rather than others, as well as the mode of negotiation they habitually bring to the learning situation would constitute the foundation on which the edifice of the semiotic mediation of specific concepts and of specialised knowledge structures of one kind or another can be erected (however, see Section 6, concluding remarks, for certain important qualifications to this view). What this claim means is that the 'tendencies to respond to situations in certain ways' are as relevant in the context of educational learning as they are elsewhere in everyday life.

There are good reasons for attending to the differences between these two modes of the operation of semiotic mediation, one mode that creates the 'habits of the mind' – a sense of relevance which is active in the social subjects of actions and/or negotiations, furnishing motivations for engaging in them or not – and another that leads to the appropriation of the elements and structures of specialised knowledge. I will refer to these two manifestations of semiotic mediation as 'invisible' and 'visible' mediation, respectively. As the label suggests, visible mediation is deliberate and relatively more clearly focused on some specific concept or problem: interactants can actually 'see' what they are doing. Speaking cautiously, at least one of the interactants is aware that s/he is teaching or explaining something specific to someone; further, an essential requirement for success in learning is voluntary attention and active participation on the part of the learner. In this way both interactants have a fairly clear sense of the goal to be achieved. This is in contrast to invisible mediation where interactants are aware of neither the teaching nor the learning of any concept in particular, much less of any specific goal to be achieved – or, at least, the goal uppermost in the mind is not directly relevant to what language is mediating. The interactants do not 'see' what is being mediated; what they 'see' is some process of everyday living which furnishes the occasion for quite mundane discourse such as the following[1]:

Extract 1

1	Mother:	put it up on the stove and leave it there
2	Karen:	why?
3	Mother:	cause
4	Karen:	that's where it goes?
5	Mother:	yeah

The normal reaction to such discourse is that nothing is happening which could be considered significant from the point of view of mental activity. I will show later that this is not the case, that in fact important elements of mental disposition are being mediated. This is why I have chosen the term invisible for such mediation. Mediation of this kind is naturalised in the sense that at least one of the interactants, the one who is already well versed in the ways of her/his community, treats the sayings and their meanings as entirely natural, as if no other form of behaviour is possible. The important fact is that other forms of behaviour do exist within the same society: it is simply the habits of the mind that make one think otherwise.

Together these forms of semiotic mediation serve important purposes in the creation of culture on the one hand and in preparing social subjects to live with a lived sense of belonging to the culture in which they are located: the latter is of course a condition for the maintenance of culture. However, I would suggest that from the point of view of the development of an individual, invisible mediation is primary, both in terms of time and in terms of its pervasiveness, because it begins from very early infancy and it occurs across a large number of cultural activities. Because invisible mediation starts early in life, because it is instrumental in creating 'habits of the mind' and because habits of the mind are crucial to a subject's ways of engaging in visible semiotic mediation, it is reasonable to suggest that visible mediation is not entirely independent of invisible mediation. To appreciate these points, we need to examine language as it operates in the context of a variety of cultural activities. In the following sections I will discuss examples of natural, spontaneous discourse to support the claims I have been making. These examples are taken from naturally occurring dialogues between mothers and their young children, which formed the data base for a sociolinguistic research project I conducted with a view to examining the role of everyday talk between mothers and children in establishing ways of learning[2].

3 Semiotic mediation and cultural activities

The two modes of semiotic mediation identified above are typically associated with distinct contexts of cultural activities. The qualification 'typically' is important, because human activities vary along several dimensions and these dimensions cut across each other, thus creating a large number of activity types, each of which differs from the others in some respect. It is not so much some specific category of activity that is in question but rather some specific properties of the activities in question. Due to lack of space I will be concerned here only with two dimensions for activity classification. First, there is the dimension that I have referred to as the 'sphere of activity' (Hasan, 1999b)[3]. Cultural activities range from everyday, ordinary ones to those that are highly specialised. Everyday activities extend over a whole cultural community. Because of their ubiquity, they appear entirely ordinary and unremarkable; in fact most are so basic to the living of human life that we may think of them as universal. To cite a few examples, humans everywhere go about the business of preparing and eating food, minding their children, getting their cleaning, their washing and shopping done and equally importantly they take steps to indicate that they are members of their local 'village' (Lemke, 2002), though of course the details of how they do these things vary to different degrees across cultures and subcultures. What is however in common is the fact that everywhere the conducting of these activities becomes highly routinised, scarcely requiring concentrated attention. As members of a (sub)culture, we know how such activities are done; everyone around us is doing them and in our turn, we too just go ahead and do them effortlessly. Even if we happen to be individualists, devoted to the virtue of originality, it is just not cost effective to invest time and energy in rethinking from the ground up how we as unique individuals should go about such activities. It is in this absence of conscious reasoning about why and how one step in the activity should follow another, it is in this absence of the need for elaborate planning of how an everyday activity should be brought about that the power of these activities resides. Familiarity breeds invisibility: we fail to even notice that we are engaged in any activity.

By contrast, specialised activities do not extend over the whole community. One manifestation of the division of labour in society is precisely that certain specialised activities are typically performed by certain social groups and not by others. Activities of the professional type such as lecturing, welding, or banking are clear examples. And though in some cases, especially where the activity is physical – welding would be one example – the various actions in its performance can become routinised, typically specialised activities require reflection on how they are to be performed: for example, no amount of experience in lecturing ever means that we can lecture more or less on auto-pilot! And in all cases, the actants are aware of the end-point of the game they are engaged in.

Cutting across this dimension is the dimension of the 'form of action'. Here two major forms to note are acting by doing – material action – and acting by saying – verbal action. There are times when the interactants' action may be entirely material, ie it may be carried out physically such as mowing the lawn, or it may be entirely verbal, carried out purely linguistically such as talking on the phone, conducting a seminar, participating in a talk-back radio program etc. But very often both material and verbal actions co-occur spatio-temporally. This co-occurrence can be of different kinds and two are particularly relevant to the present discussion, since they have different significance from the point of view of cultural activity – one where the verbal action is ancillary to the material action: that is to say, language is used in aid of performing the material activity and the other where verbal and material action run side by side without either being relevant to the other, as in discussing linguistics while having a snack. In the first case a single cultural activity is at stake, while in the second, strictly speaking two activities are being performed in parallel, one material, the other verbal. It is important to recognise that in real life as opposed to academic analysis there is no readily obvious punctuation, no clearly demarcated division between one activity and the next: distinct activities weave in and out of one another and sometime there may be no indication of a shift from the context of one activity to that of the other, except that provided by the language of the text. Consider the following example taken from an interaction between mother and Helen (three years 11 months) as they wash and dry up dishes:

Extract 2

1 Mother: no, I'll wash 'em up darling, you can dry some little ones and put them [?here] for me, wait till I get a clean towel out.. there you go..

2	Helen:	thank you
3	Mother:	I'll put the little ones up here that you can dry up, OK?
4	Helen:	the dish.. The dish first..
5	Mother:	[COUGHS] pardon me.. hurry up because I've got a big dinner to get tonight
6	Helen:	what kind of dinner?
7	Mother:	we'll have a roast leg of ham
8	Helen:	goody!
9	Mother:	and roast vegies
10	Helen:	goody!
11	Mother:	I might ring up daddy and ask him to bring some peas home [?]
12	Helen:	goody!
13	Mother:	he'd like a nice feed of peas
14	Helen:	[?]
15	Mother:	I think you children can make some fruit salad, how about that?
16	Helen:	yeah, goody! I'll make it for you

In turns 1–4 of this extract, verbal action is assisting in the conduct of the on-going material activity of washing up: this is the ancillary use of language and at this point only one activity is being performed. However, at turn 5, a shift (Hasan, 2000b) occurs as the new topic of dinner is broached and this shift is con/textual: that is to say, it is a shift in the text as well as in the context of the text[4]. Turns 6–16 constitute a discussion of that evening's dinner. So at this point, side by side with the on-going material activity of washing up, we have the verbal activity of discussion running in parallel with the material activity of washing up. The activity of discussion is entirely constituted by language: the verbal action is not ancillary but constitutive of discussion. This suggests that the identity of cultural activities is not given by their spatio-temporal location, but by the mode of their realisation; if two persons are washing up, it does not follow that everything that is said during that time in that place pertains to the activity of washing up. Similarly, one may begin with an everyday activity such as getting lunch for one's child, but end up with two parallel activities, one of getting the lunch and the other the specialised activity of explaining about the food chain (see below). I shall return below to the significance of con/textual shift for semiotic mediation.

In the above extract, the discussion in 6–16 moves around in the general domain of things concerned with food, but it is not necessary for the two parallel activities to share the same domain. When a constitutive verbal activity runs parallel to some everyday material activity, the talk will quite often move to topics not at all related to the on-going material activity. Thus it was during one such activity of washing up that Helen and her mother had the following interaction. Helen was washing up a saucepan lid which apparently needed a good deal of scrubbing and the mother was guiding Helen's washing up of the lid:

Extract 3

1	Helen:	you have to do it hard, don't you/?
2	Mother:	mm, you do, don't you, yes...
3	Helen:	doesn't matter for you and me to do these
4	Mother:	no
5	Helen:	because we can do it the right way, God teaches us
6	Mother:	no, God doesn't teach you things like that, it's mummy's job to teach you things like that

The mother's comment in the last turn *it's mummy's job to teach you things like that* is very far removed from the business of washing up. As an adult well versed in the ways of her culture she is voicing one of the perceived ways of managing life in her community: she is telling her daughter explicitly about an expectation attached to being a mother. Casual conversation abounds in such explicit aphorisms. The fleeting appearance of an utterance of this kind which represents the distillation of some communal experience hardly reaches the point of conscious deliberate reflection, which would be typical of a sustained discussion on the same topic such as one might encounter in an educational setting. Had the interactants been asked what they were doing, they would have said they were just washing up, not that one was teaching the other about communal expectations attached to certain social locations. However, over time, talk of this kind occurring again and again constructs a design for ways of being, doing and saying that are viewed as legitimate within the speakers' community. In this sense, such discourse is a site for one kind of invisible semiotic mediation: what it mediates is elements of mental maps for living in the culture of one's immediate community. This kind of semiotic mediation typically occurs in the course of everyday physical activities precisely at the point where a con/textual shift turns the verbal action briefly from ancillary to constitutive.

Such explicit teaching, referred to by Bernstein (1990; 1996) as 'local pedagogy'[5], occurs frequently especially in the discourse of adults and children. It certainly has an important place in the child's mental development. But invisible mediation does not consist wholly or even largely in observations and aphorisms which explicitly present the distilled experiences of the community. The much more powerful instrument for the formation of mental habits is furnished by verbal action that cooccurs with everyday physical activities, whether this verbal action is ancillary as in turns 1–4 of Extract 2, or constitutive as in the rest of that extract. The difference between the discussion of dinner plan in 2 and the aphoristic saying in Extract 3, is simply that the latter explicitly invokes a cultural convention, whereas the other segments concern something purely local to the here and now of the specific speakers. What is most relevant to the production of mental habits are the ways of saying and meaning, where no cultural rules are being explicitly enunciated. This does not mean that culture is irrelevant to these encounters; it is simply that it goes underground. Sayings of all kind depend largely on taken-for-granted 'truths', truth whose basis is not contested; rather it is treated as self-evident. It is this experience of the 'facticity' (Berger and Luckman, 1971) of the world that underlies everyday discourse in which young children participate ordinarily and naturally every day of the week every waking hour of the day which in its turn produces in children an understanding of what their social universe is like and what ways of being, doing, saying and even thinking are favoured by those in their immediate social group. The appropriation of a certain set of mental habits is not so much the result of explicit injunctions; it is in fact nourished by sayings which scarcely seem to say anything significant, for example sayings of the kind presented in Extract 1. Everyday activities are the most hospitable environment for such sayings, because in the nature of things, everyday activities neither require nor allow the opportunity for deliberation. Their near automatisation, their unquestioned, almost unquestionable rationality for social subjects already initiated in the culture leads to an absence of reflection, to the certainty that what one is saying and/or doing is the most rational, the most normal thing to say and do. Mental dispositions come about in the primary experience of internalising the implications of meanings worded by speakers unselfconsciously in precisely such environments. To exemplify such talk, I quickly present a brief and partial account of the sort of things mothers say to their children while engaged in some everyday material activity.

4 Modes of questioning: the semantic features *prefaced* and *assumptive*

Take for example a mother who might ask her child *did you know that they are going to leave?* There is nothing extraordinary in someone uttering such a question: people ask such questions all the time, but consider what it is that the mother has actually done. She hasn't asked to be informed of some state of affairs that is unfolding in the world; nor whether something is the case in the world. Her concern is to find out the mental state of her child – what the child knows. I have referred to such questions as 'prefaced questions' (Hasan, 1989). There is a difference between *are they going to leave?* and *did you know that they are going to leave?* The latter which is a prefaced questions asks the addressee not about what is or is not going on in the world, but about the addressee's state of knowledge: did the addressee know something to be the case. The asking of such a question carries certain implications. First, it implies that knowledge about the child's mental state is not available to the mother unless the child explicitly tells her. To many of us, this is a self-evident fact; we believe it is entirely natural for us not to know other people's mental state unless they choose to inform us. However, below I will discuss other extracts which suggest that this belief is far from universal. Here I pursue the chain of implications following upon a prefaced question.

If you happen to believe that others' mental state is unknowable without the use of language, this in turn implies that language would be treated as the essential bridge spanning two individual minds. That being the case, one would expect such speakers to habitually use language so as to make the meaning of their message as precise as possible. In most languages, the way to do this is to qualify the state of affairs, specifying its manner, location, time, etc. Further, because language is seen as an important means of getting to know the other, it follows that others' questions must be attended to; comments and assertions must be heeded, answers should be provided that address the query point. In the analysis of some 2008 maternal questions and their answers, we found that the mothers who habitually asked prefaced questions were also the ones who asked highly qualified questions and provided highly developed answers. Consider the following example:

Extract 4

1	Mother:	did you know that they are going to leave?
2	Kristy:	no
3	Mother:	they've been building a house
4	Kristy:	mm
5	Mother:	oh they haven't been building it, somebody else has been building it for them and it's nearly finished and they're going to move to their house in May
6	Kristy:	why in May?
7	Mother:	they're going to wait until the end of the school term
8	Kristy:	mm
9	Mother:	because Cathy goes to school now and then she will change to her new school after **the holidays
10	Kristy:	**mm
11	Mother:	if they'd moved earlier she'd only go to the new school for a week or two and then they'd have holidays, you see, it would mess it up a bit for her

Note how the mother is careful to clarify the sense of her claim that *they've been building a house*, something that at three and a half years of age Kristy might well have misinterpreted. Note also how in response to Kristy's *why?*, she meticulously lays out the reasoning behind her friends' decision to move to their new house in May, not earlier. The mothers who ask prefaced and qualified questions, in their own turn hardly ignore the questions asked by their child and overwhelmingly offer relevant and developed answers, rather than minimal ones. There is significant statistical proof from my research as well as that of Williams' (1999) that the massive experience of engaging in discourse of this kind produces in the children a particular kind of orientation to meanings, a certain habit of mind, a tendency to respond to questions and to information in ways that are qualitatively different from those of children whose mental habits and whose experience of everyday discourse is different. To appreciate how different the experience of discourse is for this other group of children let us take a look at the following:

Extract 5

1 Karen: how did you get that?** you didn't get out of [?]
2 Mother: I walked over and got it, didn't you see me?
3 Karen: nup
4 Mother: you must be blind

Extract 6

1   Mother: d'you love daddy?... d'you love daddy
2   Julian: mm [AFFIRMATIVE]
3   Mother: d'you love Rosemary[6]
4   Julian: no
5   Mother: why don't you love Rosemary?
6   Julian: [LAUGHS]
7   Mother: why don't you love Rosemary?
8   Julian: [CONTINUES TO LAUGH]
9   Mother: you're a rat-bag [REALISES THAT JULIAN WAS TEASING]
10 Julian: I do
11 Mother: [?]
12 Julian: who else do you want me to love?

In these extracts the mothers ask what I have called an 'assumptive question'. Such questions are realised grammatically by a negative interrogative. I call these questions 'assumptive' (Hasan, 1989) because the person asking such a question, appears to have already made an assumption what the correct answer ought to be. In Extract 5, the mother's expectation is that the answer to *didn't you see me?* should be *yes I did*, otherwise *you must be blind* and we know that Karen is not blind: the mother assumes that had Karen been behaving according to normal expectations, she would have seen her mother go out to get the object. In Extract 6, the mother's question *why don't you love Rosemary?* assumes that as a normal brother Julian ought to love Rosemary. It does not seem far fetched to suggest that mothers asking such questions assume they know what their child's mental state is. Julian understands this as is clear from his message in turn 12, which we may paraphrase as: *it is clear to me by your ways of questioning that you think I should love Rosemary, this implies that you also have views on who else I should love; so who are those people that in your opinion I should love?*

It is perhaps obvious that assumptive questions are the converse of prefaced ones. If a mother habitually asks assumptive questions, she implies that she knows her child's mental state: she knows what her child knows, what s/he feels or senses. In an important sense the child's answer is irrelevant; the mother already knows without explicitly being told. This in turn implies that language has a less critical status in the establishment of the creation of intersubjective relations between them. Interestingly, mothers who very frequently ask assumptive questions, are also relatively less concerned about attending to their child's question; they also put in less effort into making their questions precise or their answers developed; in fact, minimal and what one might think of as inadequate answers are quite likely, as exemplified in Extracts 7 and 1:

Extract 7

1	Mother:	wait till Daniel comes home or daddy
2	Pete:	he won't come home
3	Mother:	yes he is
4	Pete:	when?
5	Mother:	he's coming home this afternoon
6	Pete:	when is it gonna be this afternoon?
7	Mother:	yeah, he'll get it this afternoon
8	Pete:	when is it gonna be this afternoon though?
9	Mother:	oh a long time

What I am suggesting is that sayings as trite as the exchange 'why?' 'Cause'. are not without importance in the formation of mental attitudes. It is a commonplace that questions are a way of finding out, but perhaps one's experience of discourse might discourage the formation of this attitude to questions.

This reading of the extracts might provoke the comment that what we have here is a case of over kill, that too much is being claimed on the basis of very little evidence. And the reaction would be justified if the case was built only on the strength of a few isolated examples. However this is not the case. First the extracts cited above are representative of a much larger corpus; further the main thrust of the finding has been validated by results achieved in other related researches carried out by other colleagues[7]. And second, the semantic features I have picked out above form part of larger clusters and their pattern of occurrence tends to differentiate significantly the speech of the two groups of mothers. The elements of these semantic clusters are logically/implicationally related to each other since a semantic feature, being purely relational, carries within itself some implication of what other semantic features may or may not 'reasonably' and 'rationally' keep company with it without jeopardising communication. This means that the children have a massive experience of certain specific ways of saying and meaning, which are characterised by a particular semantic direction. Participation in this discourse shapes the children's consciousness, orients them to taking certain ways of being, doing and saying as legitimate and reasonable; in short, it defines the contours of reality and provides a map for navigating that reality.

There is consistent and strong evidence that at this early stage of three and half to four years the children belonging to these two groups have established different ways of learning, different ways of solving problems and different forms of consciousness, or mental disposition. This evidence comes from an examination of these children's talk in three environments: (i) talk with their mothers in the same everyday environments, (ii) their negotiations with familiar neighbourhood peers during spontaneous play and (iii) their discourse in the classroom during the first few weeks after entry into the school at around the age of five. True that the patterns of language I have singled out are very ordinary. But this, in a way, vindicates the claim that the production of mental disposition is brought about by the invisible semiotic mediation of unselfconscious discourse which is embedded in everyday cultural activities. Such discourse *is* ordinary; and that is why it is so effective. As this process begins from early infancy, invisible mediation which occurs in the course of everyday activities as described above attains a primary status in the life of the individual. It becomes in effect the ruler of attention and interest, of motivation and relevance. The child's ways of participating in the negotiation and appropriation of technical concepts or specific knowledge structures etc. is coloured initially though not necessarily finally by the experience of this primary mediation.

Before leaving this section, it remains to point out one very important feature of this mode of semiotic mediation which is instrumental in producing primary mental disposition. The discourse that lends itself to this function is embedded in everyday cultural activities. These activities are overwhelmingly culture maintaining, since their efficient performance depends on routinisation, which means a suspension of reflection. This encourage the tendency towards preserving existing templates. Thus each group of mothers semiotically mediates precisely the ways of being, doing and saying that come natural to them, that are their way of coping with everyday reality. Through this mediation, the mother's culture becomes the growing child's map of reality, thus ensuring its own continuance. One way that this cycle of cultural reproduction can be given a different shape is through the working of visible semiotic mediation, to which I turn below. Although the sites *par excellence* for the operation of visible semiotic mediation are acknowledged to be schools and universities, for lack of space I will be concerned here only with visible semiotic mediation at home. This will allow us to see the different histories of semiotic engagement that children bring to the school.

5 Semiotic mediation, higher mental functions and specialised cultural activities

Consider the following extract that is taken from a very lengthy discussion between Kristy and her mother. The origins of this dialogue go back to an earlier scene where Kristy was having a meal. At that earlier point, a little moth had just died a soggy death by flying low over a steaming cup. Kristy was distressed by this death:

Extract 8

1	Kristy:	why did he die there?** why did he die there?** He wouldn't have wanted to die, do you know that?
2	Mother:	that's right, most things don't want to die
3	Kristy:	mm, a dog will get killed by something that wanted to eat a doggie
4	Mother:	yeah, sometimes people want to die, or animals want to die if they are very sick and it's hurting them
5	Kristy:	mm
6	Mother:	but yeah, usually animals and people don't want to die, so –
7	Kristy:	mm
8	Mother:	everyone has to die sometime and sometimes people or animals have accidents
9	Kristy:	mm
10	Mother:	or sometimes other things eat them, so other moths get eaten by birds
11	Kristy:	why do they?
12	Mother:	well, birds need to eat **and –
13	Kristy:	**yeah and –
14	Mother:	mm?
15	Kristy:	they [? should've] eat bigger things um mice
16	Mother:	you think birds should eat mice?
17	Kristy:	yeah
18	Mother:	well, you got upset the other day about the eagle at the museum eating the rabbit didn't you?
19	Kristy:	mm
20	Mother:	see, there's not much difference is there? I think you just don't want the moth to get eaten do you?
21	Kristy:	no
22	Mother:	well –
23	Kristy:	he didn't want to die?
24	Mother:	no..
25	Kristy:	that's [?broken]. Ruth teared it
26	Mother:	she what?
27	Kristy:	teared

208   *Language, Society and Consciousness*

28 Mother: oh it's OK
29 Kristy: why's it OK?
30 Mother: Peter just brought it home for me to have a look at, but he didn't need to keep it
31 Kristy: why didn't he?
32 Mother: oh! oh, I don't know [LAUGHS] I don't think he needed to keep it.. he'd probably read it already
33 Kristy: why he probably read it already?
34 Mother: um, I think if he had wanted to keep it and he needed it, he would have told me to put it somewhere safe, but he put it there which is the place where we put stuff we don't really care about, that's why I think that he didn't need it, either he had already read it or he didn't want it
35 Kristy: why did the eagle eat the rabbit?
36 Mother: because rabbits are the sort of animals that eagles eat, different animals eat different food, they they eat food that lives where they can catch it and food that's the right size for them to catch
37 Kristy: mm
38 Mother: an eagle couldn't eat a cow because a cow would be too big, but eagles can eat rabbits, they're a nice size for eagles, they give them plenty to eat and they're small enough for eagles to catch, but most animals eat other animals, even you eat chickens and every time you eat a chicken a little chicken has to die

There is much more of this discussion but we can stop at this stage of what is surely a model lesson on the grim rudiments of natural selection. I would like to use this extract to draw attention to some important points. First, compare this with Extract 3. In both cases the discussion runs parallel to some other everyday material activity and it goes without saying that the verbal action is constitutive. There are however some major differences between them: in Extract 3, the move into the constitutive is evanescent, hardly receiving conscious attention, whereas in Extract 8 the constitutive activity of discussion is much more developed. Had the mother been asked what she was doing, very likely she would have said that she was explaining to Kristy why every living thing has to die some time and how in order for one thing to live another thing might have to die. In 3, the aphoristic comment is a putative beginning of a specialised activity of explaining about maternal obligations, whereas in 8, the activity of explanation is full fledged. This too is a case of local pedagogy, but unlike 3 it displays a more deliberate and sustained effort at 'getting some point across' and at the same time it makes contact with a fragment of educational knowledge. In short, running parallel to an everyday cultural activity, we have an instance of a specialised one. This local pedagogic activity is not exactly like a lesson in a classroom, but it is as close to that activity as you can get at home, especially where one participant is relatively immature. This is thus a classic example of visible semiotic mediation, which occurs by means of discourse embedded in specialised cultural activities calling for sustained attention by participants.

As pointed out before, specialised cultural activities, unlike the everyday ones do not extend over the whole cultural community. There is an interesting paradox here: everyday activities are near universal, though the way they are carried out varies across different communities and in this sense, these near universal activities are essentially localistic in their manifestation. By contrast, specialised cultural activities are restricted in their distribution within a culture: not everyone engages in them, though wherever a category of such activity is found, the form of its manifestation is near universal. Specialised activities depend fundamentally upon verbal action; very often, they enlist other semiotic modalities in their performance, for example, figures, images, charts, scale models, logical and mathematical symbols, ritual representations of superhuman forces etc.: instances of non-verbal semiotic modalities pressed into service as abstract tools for the semiotic mediation of 'uncommonsense' concepts and knowledge structures.

For most of us today, by far the most common specialised activities are those experienced regularly in schooling. At least in the so-called advanced societies, for decades the school has been the major official site for the production and distribution of such knowledge. But it is really at home that the ontogenesis of what Claxton (2002) calls 'epistemic mentality' takes its first halting steps. Mercer (this volume) presents an example of such an interactive episode and my data too provides rich support for making this claim. However, with my colleagues, Cloran (1994; 1999) and Williams (1995; 1999), I find that the occurrence of such interactive episodes is selective: it is not children, as a general category, but *some* children belonging to a particular group, who typically experience discourse of this kind, as a comparison of Extract 8 with Extracts 9.1, 9.2 and 9.3 will confirm.

Let me turn now to another important point about Extract 8; this concerns the movement of the discourse. We note that at turn 25, Kristy's attention is diverted by some magazine page that Ruth, her baby sister, had torn up. She probably expects her mother to share her concern and as her mother disappoints this expectation, she wants to know the reason for the mother's lack of concern. This sets off a chain of explanations. When Kristy's need to know has been satisfied, she turns once again to the question of why one animal eats another. We note a con/textual shift at turn 25. Although the action in both cases is entirely verbal and although this verbal action in both cases is constitutive of the activity, they belong to different spheres: turns 25–34 represent an explanation of an everyday event, while the discourse surrounding it concerns themes of mortality, of survival, of life cycles of moths and of how the life and death of each organism in this world impinges on the life and death of the others: in short, it is the stuff of specialised discourse.

Extract 8 is representative of how discourse between mothers and children moves in one group. Time and time again in my data, the discourse of *qua-si* specialised knowledge occurs in the 'middle of' daily activities and by necessity it calls for a readiness on the mother's part to entertain contextual shifts, to be willing to reclassify the context of the on-going discourse (Cloran, 1999; Hasan, 1999b, 2000b). The tendency to move with the child's moving discourse, the readiness to re-classify context is a discourse characteristic of the same group of mothers who frequently ask prefaced questions made precise by qualification and who attend to their children's questions and provide them with well developed answers: this is evident not only from the examples provided in the section above but also from the last extract. By contrast the second group of mothers are significantly less willing to entertain contextual shift. Extracts 9.1–3, which form part of the same dialogue, present one such instance.

Extract 9.1

1	Mother:	come on, eat your tea please..
2	Karen:	could you put some more[8] in there?..
3	Mother:	[WARNINGLY] Karen!.. give me it, eat your tea
4	Karen:	[?]
5	Mother:	mm?
6	Karen:	[?put] lemon in it
7	Mother:	well, eat some tea, or you don't get nothing
8	Karen:	I see how many [?] there are [TALKS TO HERSELF AS MOTHER POURS DRINK]
9	Mother:	quick.. want the lid on it?
10	Karen:	no
11	Mother:	come on, eat your tea, less drink and more eat.. did you hear what I said Karen?
12	Karen:	mm
13	Mother:	well, do it

As Karen still persists in turning a tea-eating situation into one of imaginative play, of discussion of matters not directly dealing with the business of eating tea, the mother's unwillingness to make such a shift becomes more and more obvious. Within a matter of seconds this same interaction continues as follows:

Extract 9.2

1	Karen:	mummy that haven't got no sauce on it
2	Mother:	oh you've got plenty of sauce there now, now eat it
3	Karen:	on here
4	Mother:	oh there's plenty of sauce on your plate Karen, you don't need it on every single drop of tea

5	Karen:	eh?
6	Mother:	you don't need it on every little bit
7	Karen:	[? of tea]?
8	Mother:	mm
9	Karen:	is that [?tea]?
10	Mother:	that's sauce
11	Karen:	mm hot sauce
12	Mother:	no, mint sauce
13	Karen:	mince?.. why do you put mince sauce on here for?
14	Mother:	'mint' not 'mince'
15	Karen:	mint, this mint?
16	Mother:	use your spoon or your fork
17	Karen:	'Country Practice' is on now?
18	Mother:	no
19	Karen:	'Sons and Daughters'?
20	Mother:	no, the news
21	Karen:	oh..
22	Mother:	that's why I said use a spoon.. now sit up and use a spoon

Extracts 9.1–2 are fairly typical of this group of mothers, who appear to have a well-defined idea of the boundaries between contexts and are normally reluctant to permit the interpenetration of one context by another. If I understand Claxton (this volume) right, it would seem that the two groups of mothers belong to the two distinct cultures described by Edward Hall as monochronic and polychronic cultures. Karen's mother belongs to the group that, at least in this respect, may be said to have a monochronic culture. In this 20-minute recording of the meal time discourse, the mother produces 20 injunctions to the daughter to 'eat her tea'; she studiously ignores any opening of the discourse in directions other than those specifically pertaining to the meal time activity. In characteristic fashion questions are disposed of with an alacrity that misses their real query point (see for example the mint/mince discussion); and the mention of the TV soapies Country Practice and Sons and Daughters receives short shrift! But does this mean that in such cases, there is no con/textual shift, no reclassification of context at all? As Bernstein (1990) perceptively remarked the maintenance of the boundary between categories requires the exertion of power and control. Our example here is no exception. Elsewhere I have claimed (see Hasan, 2000b) that the context does shift, but the direction of its shift is quite predictable: in order to preserve what the mother considers to be the boundaries of this activity, Karen's mother's discourse moves resolutely into the regulative mode, as shown by Extract 9.3 which occurs some 3 seconds after Extract 9.2:

212   *Language, Society and Consciousness*

Extract 9.3:

1	Mother:	give me your spoon and I'll feed you, like a big baby, come on, baby! give me your spoon
2	Karen:	[SCANDALISED TONE] no
3	Mother:	well sit up properly and eat your tea.. Karen! [WARNING TONE]
4	Karen:	I'm falling down [i.e. OFF THE CHAIR]
5	Mother:	you're not falling down
6	Karen:	yes I am, I always fall down..**I am falling down
7	Mother:	**eat your tea
8	Karen:	I am falling down
9	Mother:	sit up, before I get a stick and smack you

If con/textual shift is an invariable condition for moving from the quotidian to the specialised discourse at this early stage in the child's life, clearly the reluctance to allow such shifts or to control their development is likely to have significant consequences for the ontogenesis of specialised discourse.

Turning to a related point, in my data, children's discursive style was not distinguished by the kind of questions they asked. Thus, quite often they will seek explanations, as did Kristy, but the response the second group of children receive is markedly different from the sort of reasoning favoured in specialised discourse. Consider the following, where the mother is putting Sam to bed (Valentine is Sam's pet budgerigar):

Extract 10

1	Mother:	he can hear you when you say 'Goodnight Valentine'
2	Sam:	where is he?
3	Mother:	in the kitchen
4	Sam:	what's he doing in there?
5	Mother:	he's going to sleep
6	Sam:	huh?
7	Mother:	and mummy's going to turn the lights out
8	Sam:	why?
9	Mother:	it's dark
10	Sam:	why?
11	Mother:	it's night time, it's ready for bed
12	Sam:	why?
13	Mother:	cause it is, when you wake up in the morning we'll have our breakfast

If the primary mental disposition is friendly to an unselfconscious preservation of the cultural templates as I argued above, one question is what are those templates like and where would their preservation take those practising subjects? The extracts I have presented suggest that the cultural templates for the two groups are significantly different and they are significantly different particularly from the point of view of what they imply in the context of schooling. The final section consists of a brief word on the implications of this situation and offers a suggestion for an approach to schooling that might go some way towards the ideal of equal opportunity.

6   Schooling for tomorrow: concluding remarks

In the preceding two sections I have attempted to show that 'any learning a child encounters in school has a previous history'. It seems to me beyond doubt that this history favours children differentially in today's industrialised pluralistic societies. The preschool learning history of the first group of children favours an easier engagement with the specialised discourses of the school; by contrast, for those of the second group, it favours easier adjustment to the regulatory aspect of the pedagogic discourse. To the extent that the real aim of education is to enable pupils not to reproduce knowledge, but to produce it, not simply to replicate but to create, this appears to place the first group in an advantageous position. Educational systems claim to provide equal opportunity for all to acquire the competence for engaging in specialised activities; but this remains an ideal goal, as yet never achieved in reality, anywhere. It would be a simplification of the complexities of the educational system to claim that the only reason it fails to achieve its ideal goal is the differential learning history of the pupils; but that this is one major reason for the schools' failure cannot be denied. To accept this is not to imply that the learning the child brings to the classroom is final, that the forms of consciousness, the mental dispositions are graven images which are no longer susceptible to the very instrument of semiotic mediation which has produced them in the first place. As complex self-organising systems, human brains learn by learning; there is as Wells (2002) points out, a spiral of learning. But an initial effort is required to create a situation in the classroom which recognises the nature of the challenge to draw all children into the activity of learning. The challenge is that those for whom the educational system is ostensibly designed bring many voices into the classroom, but even a cursory look at the classroom practices reveals that it privileges one single voice. This happens to be the voice of the more powerful segment of the society. Those who do not recognise this voice, cannot truly participate in the specialised discourse of knowledge production and must strive on their own to master this other epistemic dialect. In the continuation of my research where these children were followed into the first year of schooling, we found that across the spectrum of schools the teachers showed no significant variation in their ways of saying: the variation in the data was totally accounted for by the difference in how the children talked during lesson time. The challenge for tomorrow's education is to correct this situation. And one way of achieving this is to encourage pupils to question the taken-for-granted realities. By this I mean both the reality cherished by the mothers of the first group as well as that cherished by the second group. It is often pointed out that in the classroom it is the teacher who asks questions; I have no objection to this situation so long as the teacher knows how to respect answers – to respect them to the extent of actually involving the pupils in reflecting on the assumptions that underlie the answers and involving the child in articulating those assumptions, thus making them available for conscious reflection and questioning. This reflective mode has the potential of questioning all voices, listening to all voices and probing into all assumptions. A programme of this kind is what I described some time ago under the label of 'reflection literacy' (Hasan, 1996a). But to be able to encourage reflection literacy, those who educate teachers need to rethink the interconnections between the semiotic, the social and the cognitive.

Notes

1. The conventions for the transcription are as follows:
   (CAPITALS) = situational comment, based on analyst's listening to audio-recording
   [?go away] = segment not intelligible; best guess on the basis of context
   [?] = segment unintelligible; co-textual clues insufficient to allow guess <<3 abc >> = enclosed message(s), i.e. 3 interrupts the message surrounding << >>
   ?** = no time allowed for response after this question
   abc – = message abc left incomplete
   abc .. = a (longer than usual) pause at this point
   **abc **def = paired asterisks indicate turn overlap
   Note that the turns are numbered afresh for each extract.
2. This extensive research was funded by the Australian Research Council and by Macquarie University Research Grants. Details of the research design, subjects examined and mode of data collection and analysis can be found in Hasan (1989; 1992a; 1993) and Hasan and Cloran (1990).
3. For a more detailed classification and analysis of cultural activity, see Hasan (1999b) on which the present discussion is based.
4. For a detailed discussion of con/textual shift and its significance for the development of discourse, see Hasan (2000b). On how one category of verbal action may be embedded within another, see also Cloran (1994; 1995; 1999).
5. A good example of such pedagogy will be found in the conversational sequences in Mercer (2002) [in Wells and Claxton (eds), *Learning for Life in the 21st Century: socio-cultural perspectives on the future of education*].
6. Rosemary is Julian's sister.
7. For more detailed discussions see Hasan (1989; 1992a; 1993); Cloran (1994; 1999); Williams (1995; 1999).
8. On the basis of the preceding dialogue, it would appear that Karen is referring to some sauce.

8 Ways of meaning, ways of learning: code as an explanatory concept

> codes transform distributions of power and principles of control into pedagogic communication. Codes attempt to suppress contradictions, cleavages and dilemmas in the external order (classification) and set up psychic defences for intra-individual order through the insulation (boundaries) they produce. But code acquisition necessarily entails both the acquisition of order and the potential of its disturbance. (Bernstein, 2000: 203)

As members of the human species, we possess an almost unlimited potential for learning: in this sense the world is truly our oyster. However, what we actually learn in our life time is typically constrained by our social location, a problem that demands explanation: why and how does social location intervene in constraining what is learnt by whom? This question formed an important part of the research agenda in Bernstein's working life (Bernstein, 1971; 1975; 1990; 2000). Of course, one's social location is not inalterable as Bernstein took great pains to point out, but the conditions for such changes are fairly stringent, which may or may not be met. These conditions have little to do with our supposedly 'innate' mental capacities: in fact, recent research in the development of human brain reveals that at birth we have yet to acquire a 'mind' (Boncinelli, 2001; Greenfield, 2000b; Deacon, 1997). Our most precious biological assets – the plasticity of our brain and its potential for forming billions of connections – make us uniquely dependent on the social for turning that powerful brain into a usable mind. It thus transpires that the two basic supports of our existence, the biological and the social, are linked by a co-genetic logic; what forges this link between the two is our capacity for semiosis – for making meanings by the use of shared symbolic systems. Through centuries of evolutionary trial and error, the human brain is predisposed to make sense of symbols. Amongst the various symbolic systems, language, due to some of its defining characteristics (Deacon, 1997), proves crucial in the enterprise of linking the biological and the social. To gain consciousness, to become a usable mind, the human brain needs experience and language acts as a uniquely effective, immensely supple means of construing experience by acts of meaning (Halliday and Matthiessen, 1999). So, if we wish to answer our question – *why and how does social location intervene in constraining what is learnt by whom?* – we will need a theory that is sensitive to the complex interactions of language, culture and consciousness, for although learning is done by individual minds, the minds themselves are fashioned socially by means of semiotic mediation, which means largely through discursive interaction.

From this perspective Bernstein's code theory is exceptional. For a serious sociolinguist, it is perhaps the only sociological theory which takes the power of language seriously enough to give it a definite place in his theory; this theory has been deeply concerned with the relations of culture, communication and consciousness (see especially Bernstein, 1971; 1982; 1990; 2000). It thus represents a powerful resource for examining the complex interplay of the factors active in the formation of consciousness and the unequal distribution of knowledge. Developed and refined over decades, it describes on the one hand the dialectic of semiosis and consciousness and, on the other, it traces the relevant macro and micro social phenomena, identifying the attributes of the social system that enable social processes. This paper is not intended as a potted history of the development of Bernstein's code theory, as excellent and authentic accounts of this can be found in Bernstein, 1990; 1996 and 2000 which present particularly lucid accounts of how social class, social practice and forms of human consciousness are sociologically related. My aim in this paper is to show the power of the concept of code in explaining systematic variation in the meanings people habitually mean, an enquiry which was inspired by Bernstein's writings on the relations of coding orientation to knowledge distribution in modern societies (Bernstein, 1971; 1975).

I am aware of the various pejorative readings of the code theory, but again this is not the appropriate place to deconstruct them: to my mind, these mis/readings told us more about the standards of academic il/literacy than they did about the nature of the code theory. For, indeed, the potential of the theory was quite obvious from its early stages (Bernstein, 1965; Halliday, 1973b; Hasan, 1973). Certainly there were problems with the data – the data used in the SRU researches was collected via questionnaires and interviews (see for some details Bernstein, 1973) and so it did not represent naturally occurring language in the contexts of everyday life. The second major point of code criticism was that the linguistic evidence was not valid. And again it is true that much of the lexical and syntactic evidence which was cited (see Bernstein, 1971; 1973; 1975) could not be easily interpreted as decisive instantiation of code varieties. But a thoughtful reading would have conceded that the problem lay with the linguistic models, none of which offered any viable resources for the analysis of meaning in discourse. Bernstein's code theory is, above all, concerned with orientation to meaning and with the internalisation of orders of relevance (Bernstein, 1990). If one wished to cite evidence for how coding orientation may activate social subjects' selection and organisation of meaning, subjects' judgements of what is or is not legitimate social practice, then counting morphemes and words defined by their grammatical status was not going to be much help: what was needed was the ability to relate grammar and semantics in a non-ad hoc, systematic manner; linguists needed to offer Bernstein a theory of grammar as a resource for meaning. As systemic functional (SF) linguistics has shown, it is the nexus of grammar with meaning, as manifested in discourse in social life, that is crucial to the formation of consciousness; the latter is an essential element both in the reproduction of society and of social change. Meaning is, thus, critical to the very concept of Bernstein's code theory. But SF linguists as yet had no coherent theory of semantics, while formal semantics was largely unusable in the analysis of discourse.

To me this situation presented a dual challenge: a challenge to produce a linguistic tool capable of such an analysis of discourse in social life and a challenge to mount an investigation which would examine whether and to what extent the linguistic form of social interaction was instrumental in the formation of consciousness. In the rest of the paper I want to present briefly an account of this research[1]. My research project should not be seen as one that explores all the complex relations outlined by Bernstein in the explication of his code theory (Bernstein, 1971; 1982; 1987b etc.): this would be a daunting task for any single research effort (see Hasan, 1999a as a linguist's account of a relatively full architecture of Bernstein's theory). As a linguist my interest and my training prepared me to explore that element of the code theory which is concerned particularly with the relation between forms of linguistic communication and forms of consciousness. Accordingly, the major questions that the first phase of my research asked were:

Q1 Do mothers from different social groups / classes systematically vary in the meanings they habitually mean in talking to their three and a half year old children?

Q2 If the answer to Q1 is 'yes', then (a) does the experience of participation in different semantic varieties manifest itself in children's own ways of meaning; if so how; and (b) how can these patterns of variation be explained? What is/are the activating factor(s)?

By interrogating the results of the analysis of my data from these points of view I hoped to be able to show whether variation in forms of communication is particularly responsive to social positioning (Bernstein, 1990). By comparing the maternal sayings with those of the children, I hoped to find some indication whether the active experience of fashions of speaking has any bearing on forms of consciousness. If there is a significant correlation between the semantic styles of the mothers and the children, this could be taken as a confirmation of Bernstein's claims about codes, communication and consciousness (Bernstein, 1971; 1990; 1996).

Beginning in the mid 1980s, with Carmel Cloran's able assistance, I directed such a research project over a period of some six years. The title of the project was *The Role of Everyday Talk between Mothers and Children in Establishing Ways of Learning* (for details, see Hasan, 1989; 1992a; Hasan and Cloran, 1990). As for the tool for analysis, the main inspiration came from the systemic functional model, with its emphasis on meaning and its system oriented description. Although Bernstein had been working as early as the 1960s with the network representation of behavioural choices in specific contexts such as that of control (Bernstein and Cook-Gumperz, 1973), my own inspiration came from the seminal work of Halliday (1973c) and Turner (1973). The former in particular showed how the selection and organisation of meaning can be systematically related to lexicogrammatical resources. It thus served as the starting point for devising a semantic system network, which represents, up to a certain degree of detail, the meaning potential and the grammatical resources for its realisation, available to speakers of English in the environment of everyday discourse. Bernstein's early work in the area of socialisation and code varieties (1971) suggested that the principles governing systematic variation in the distribution of knowledge had to be inculcated at the early stages of life, where identities are formed, desires acquire legitimacy and orders of relevance get established. Accordingly, the children selected to participate in my research were quite young (3;6-4;0 yrs: mean age 3;8). The theory stipulated further that underlying the systematic variation in learning are relations of power and control in society: as Bernstein (1990: 1) put it:

> 'Class relations'... refer to inequalities in the distribution of power and in the principles of control between social groups, which are realised in the creation, distribution, reproduction and legitimation of physical and symbolic values, that have their source in the social division of labour.

Keeping this in mind, the 24 mothers participating in the research were selected from families which were evenly divided between dominating and dominated social groups. The specific parameter taken as indicator of domination was the degree of control on work place environment: the greater the possibility for making policy changes and for passing on executive decision to others as instruments for carrying them out, the more dominating the professional location. The dominating professions were referred to as Higher Autonomy Professions (HAP) and the dominated ones as Lower Autonomy Professions (LAP). To ensure the naturalness of the data, the mothers were requested to do the recording themselves. No contextual restrictions were placed; mothers were free to record at any time that suited them so long as they varied the time of recording and so long as they did the recording while carrying out their ordinary day to day household jobs. Some hundred hours of naturally occurring conversation was collected. When this data was examined from the point of view of what was going on at the time of these talks, three material situational settings were found to be in common to all mothers: (1) giving care to the subject child (such as bathing, providing food, putting the child to bed), (2) engaging in some cooperative activity with the child (such as tidying up a room, reading a book or playing a game together), or (3) carrying out some household jobs (such as cooking, cleaning, washing up) while the child simply hung about. Since the analysis was to be made in terms of a large number of semantic variables, say around 50, a representative sample was constructed taking just over 45 minutes per dyad divided as equally as possible across the three material situational settings described above. This sample consisted of just over 20,000 messages, each of which was analysed using the categories of the semantic network.

Rather than undertake here a step by step discussion of how the semantic analysis was carried out (for this see Hasan, 1989; 1992a), I want to present a brief semantic profile of my data, whereby I hope to show specifically what kind of information is distributed how and where during the mother-child interactions. I will initially identify two modes of meaning habitually displayed by the mothers: both are active in enabling the children to internalise experience and to make sense of their social world, but in different ways. I will refer to the two modes as (i) informative mode and (ii) formative mode. Neither of these corresponds exactly to any category suggested by Bernstein but the conceptualisation of both resonates with his views as my comments during the discussion of these two modes will show. Indeed, Bernstein's insights and predictions regarding code-governed selection and organisation of meaning are strongly supported by my research. Let me begin then with some actual extracts from the data.

Extract 1[2]

Mother: (1)... you were certainly very brave
Cameron: (2) (?I wasn't) very brave
Mother: (3) yeah you were brave (4) you mightn't think so you were brave (5) but I think you were
Cameron: (6) what for?
Mother: (7) because you acted in a very brave way
Cameron: (8) **no
Mother: (9) **you hurt yourself (10) and you cried (11) and that's good to cry (12) when you hurt yourself (13) but you only cried for a little while (14) and then you climbed back on your bike
Cameron: (15) **and didn't –
Mother: (16) **and when you were a little boy (17) you know what you would have done?
Cameron: (18) what?
Mother: (19) you would have run back to mummy (20) crying really loudly (21) shouting (22) and you didn't do that (23) you acted like a big boy
Cameron: (24) yes
Mother: (25) you got hurt (26) so you cried (27) because you were hurt

Cameron: (28) yeah
Mother: (29) and then after a little while you stopped crying
Cameron: (30) yes
Mother: (31) that's what big boys do
Mother: (32) yeah

Extract 2

Mother: (1)... when you plant seeds from mandarins or oranges (2) sometimes you get very strange fruit (3) or sometimes you don't get much fruit at all (4) so you have to plant a tree that's been grafted – that's been stuck on (5) they're special trees that they make (6) by sticking one tree to another tree
Stephen: (7) how do they stick it?
Mother: (8) well, I think they cut it in a special way (9) they cut them in a special way (10) and they put them together (11) and then they bind stuff around the outside (12) to hold them together (13) till they grow together.. (14) they eventually grow together the same way as when... (15) if you cut yourself (16) the skin grows back together again, doesn't it? (17) the two pieces of skin grow together again (18) well the tree – the two bits of the tree grow back too

Extract 3

Mother: (1) do you love daddy?
Julian: (2) mm
Mother: (3) do you love Rosemary?
Julian: (4) no
Mother: (5) why don't you love Rosemary? (JULIAN LAUGHS) (6) why don't you love Rosemary? (JULIAN CONTINUES TO LAUGH) (7) you're a (?ratbag) (MOTHER REALISES JULIAN WAS TEASING)
Julian: (8) I do
Mother: (9) (?)
Julian: (10) who else do you want me to love?
Mother: (11) you can love whoever you want to
Julian: (12) can I love Peter?... (13) can I?
Mother: (14) no (15) I think that's more like friendship
Julian: (16) pardon
Mother: (17) thought you'd say that (18) it's like friendship, isn't it?.. (19) you're friends with Peter, aren't you?
Julian: (20) yep... (21) mum!
Mother: (21) yes
Julian: (22) when I get as old as you (23) and (?Maree likes me) (24) could

	we marry each other?
Mother:	(25) no (26) because Maree is your cousin
Julian:	(27) oh
Mother:	(28) cause cousins aren't allowed to marry
Julian:	(29) why?
Mother:	(30) cause the law says they're not
Julian:	(31) who's that?
Mother:	(32) the law?
Julian:	(33) yeah
Mother:	(34) the policeman...

First, the informative mode, as it is illustrated by Extract 1: what the mother is doing here is informing the child about certain concepts, which happen to be descriptive and evaluative. She is telling Cameron what it means to be described as *a big boy*, or as *brave*. *The informative mode is an explicit mode of attempting to inculcate some concept, irrespective of the domain within which the concept is located.* This mode fits into Bernstein's category of elaborated code, especially if the explicit-implicit axis of differentiation is taken as crucial (Bernstein, 1971). In Extract 1 Cameron's mother explicitly identifies the child's behaviours to which the terms refer; the concepts she tells Cameron about pertain to the communal domain of life. In Extract 2, the same mode is used but here Stephen's mother explains the concept of *grafting* as used in the specialist field of horticulture, a domain regarding which the child has no practical experience. She recontextualises the information, so that it becomes immediately accessible to Stephen: *if you cut yourself, the skin grows back together again, doesn't it? the two pieces of skin grow together again, well the tree – the two bits of the tree grow back too.* In both extracts the discourse is about something, be it part of specialist knowledge or an everyday concept such as acting like a big boy. The informative mode as used by mothers in conversation with their children can also be seen as resonating with Bernstein's concept of local pedagogy (Bernstein, 1999) which may be interpreted for our purposes as the transmission of knowledge within the contexts of everyday life (but see comment below). One respect in which Extract 2 differs from Extract 1 is that the information transmission in 2 can hardly be distinguished from the instructional component of official pedagogic discourse for young children. Two issues are particularly relevant to the informative mode: what is the framing like and how extensive is the pedagogic segment. In my research the dominating group shows weaker framing and a greater readiness to continue with the informative mode (Cloran, 1999; Hasan, 2000b; 2001a). This finding is entirely in keeping with Bernstein's predictions (1975; 1990; 1996): weaker framing characterises dominating code modalities[3].

The mode I have called the formative is formative in the sense that, rather than instilling particular pieces of information, *it functions as a way of setting* up interpersonal relations *between the discursive dyads*. The two modes are not mutually exclusive: it is not that one mode characterises one group of speakers and the other, another group; in fact, the two modes can occur within the same discourse. Extract 3 illustrates the complexity of the simultaneous play of these two modes. Ignoring for the moment the Rosemary episode, turn to messages 12 through 34. Here, the mother is providing information on three issues: (i) whether Julian can love a male friend (ii) whether he can marry his cousin Maree and (iii) who in the community represents legal authority. I am not concerned here with evaluating the items of knowledge the mother provides: from some points of view, each is 'defective'. Some of us certainly believe that love is not restricted to members of opposite sex, marrying a cousin is not illegal and the police do not make the law, though they do have the reputation for maintaining it. The correctness or otherwise of information is an issue that is not relevant to my discussion here; nor does it matter that the three segments are less extensively developed than those in Extracts 1 and 2 though this is a significant parameter of variation between social groups (see Cloran, 1999): for a discursive mode to be informative, the information does not have to be extensively developed or to be factually correct, whatever the standards of correctness applied. That Julian's mother is explicitly telling him about the legal boundaries between love, friendship and marriage is all that matters for taking it as a case of the informative mode and from this point of view, messages (12) to (34) of Extract 3 are like Extracts 1 and 2: they all provide information in an explicit manner on specific topics.

To see the working of the formative mode, take the earlier part of Extract 3, especially the mother's repeated question *why don't you love Rosemary?* (messages 5 and 6). Here the mother is not giving information, but seeking it. Of particular interest is the form for seeking information: the question is framed in the negative. In my semantic network, negation in certain question types (yes/no or why/how questions) realises an important choice, referred to as 'assumptive'. A question with this feature does not simply seek information: it implies that the information sought is already known to the enquirer and that its nature is predetermined. So whenever an assumptive question is asked, there is an explicitly worded meaning, namely: this or that information is needed, as for example here: 'I am seeking an explanation for the fact that you don't love Rosemary'; but there is also an *implicational meaning*, which is not worded but simply implied. In our example, the mother's question implies: 'I believe you *should* love Rosemary'. One might think the distinction between explicitly worded and implied meaning is too subtle to make any practical difference especially to very young children, but note Julian's uptake on this assumptive question: he asks his mother *who else do you want me to love?* (message 10) This shows that, at some three and a half years, he had already got the covert message. The asking of an assumptive question implies that the enquirer presumes to know what the addressee's mental map is or should be like. The personal distance between them is greatly reduced: the mother is here behaving on the assumption that she and the child share the same experiences, expectations and mental maps.

The semantic feature 'assumptive' is not the only feature construed by implicational wording. Here is another example, again involving questions. Compare two questions (i) *are they leaving?* and (ii) *did you know they are leaving?* The first question seeks information about some state of affairs in the external world of our experience; the second seeks information about the addressee's mental state: did the addressee know something or not. In the semantic network this attribute of questions is referred to as 'prefaced': a preface such as *did you know, do you remember, did you see, would you like* implies that the enquirer does not presume to know what the addressee knows, remembers, sees or likes; the addressee's mental map is an unknown territory. The mother who asks *did you know they are leaving?* is not assuming a similarity of knowledge, feeling and expectations: it is as if there exists a personal distance between the two, which means that reliance must be placed on discourse as a means of bridging the distance. It is perhaps obvious from this account that the two semantic features of questions – 'assumptive' and 'prefaced' – are mutually incompatible so far as an individual's orientation to meanings is concerned: speakers who habitually use one feature are not likely to use the other. The features point to different expectations about one's relations to the other. In terms of the early code theory (Bernstein, 1971), these two features are indicative of two distinct codes: the theory would predict that the feature 'prefaced' which implies a greater sense of individuation would be an element of the elaborated code, while the feature 'assumptive' which implies a greater sense of reflexivity between speaker and addressee would be that of the restricted code.

Linguists have recognised the tendency of certain specific words to occur with certain other specific words: in fact, Firth's well known concept of 'collocation' (Firth, 1957b) is built on this tendency. I suggest that there is such prehension also between specific features at the semantic level. So the semantic feature 'prefaced' tends to co-occur with the feature 'related' and/or 'elaborated'. These features refer to aspects of information management. Specifically the feature related is realised by the linking of messages, so that details about the sequencing of the states of affairs become available as in: *you hurt yourself and you cried and that's good to cry* (Extract 1: messages 9-11). The feature elaborated is realised by messages which modify and/or develop the information concerning the state of affairs, as in: *when you were a little boy you know what you would have done? you would have run back to mummy, crying really loudly, shouting and you didn't do that, you acted like a big boy* (Extract 1: messages 16-23). This 'clustering' of the semantic features 'prefaced', 'related' and 'elaborated' makes sense: if the personal distance between the speaker and the addressee has to be bridged discursively, then the terms in that discourse need to be carefully displayed and information has to be detailed. Now, the semantic features 'related' and 'elaborated' are realised grammatically as 'modification' and 'subordination'; which means these patterns would be expected to occur more often. When in the 1960s Bernstein suggested that these features were relevant to the linguistic differentiation of code varieties, his claim was dismissed (Labov, 1972). With hindsight, it is obvious that Bernstein was right; my research shows that, given their meaning, certain categories of modification and subordination *are* relevant to code varieties. But there is more to the clusters.

In the environment of questions and answers, two additional semantic features co-occur: the addressee's message following a question is expected to be a 'response', which acknowledges that a question is on the floor. Responses are expected to be 'adequate': they will address the query point of the question. However, if two persons keep talking, this does not necessarily entail that questions are being responded to or that if they are, they address the question's query point. The significance of these semantic features is obvious from the following examples:

Extract 4

Mother: (1) oh hurry up… (2) quick… (3) sit down… (4) you're gonna have your hair washed now… (5) look –
Karen: (6) what? (7) what mummy?… (8) what?
Mother: (9) nothing
Karen: (10) why did you say 'look'?
Mother: (11) alright lay down (12) and I'll wash your hair

Here Karen repeats her question three times (6-8) before a response comes in message (9); and that response is not adequate: note, the child is not satisfied as message (10) shows. And although, following upon (10), the mother does produce a message, it bears no relevance to the question and so it can not seen as a response. Here is another example:

Extract 5

Pete: (1) can I play with (?)?
Mother: (2) no
Pete: (3) oh why not?
Mother: (4) no
Pete: (5) oh (PETE CRIES)

Here the mother's first response is adequate though it is minimal, without any further elaboration. Contrast this with Julian's mother (message 25-26, Extract 1) who immediately elaborates on her minimal response: *no because Maree is your cousin.* We have thus identified two clusters of semantic features, as shown in Table 8.1.

Cluster 1: centred on prefaced	Cluster 2: centred on assumptive
Questions are more often prefaced more often related more often elaborated	Questions are more often assumptive less often related less often elaborated
Answers are more often responsive more often adequate more often related more often elaborated	Answers are less often responsive less often adequate less often related less often elaborated

Table 8.1: Two significant clusters of semantic features

The semantic features in each cluster have a 'natural' affinity with each other. The nucleus of clusters 1 and 2 in Table 8.1 are the features 'prefaced' and 'assumptive' respectively: they form the basis for attracting or repelling the habitual occurrence of the other features. These clusters turn out to be statistically highly relevant in accounting for systematic variation in my data. The cluster in the left column is more likely to be found in the discourse of mothers from dominating families, while that in the right column is more likely to occur in the discourse of mothers from dominated families ($p<.0003$). Similar results were obtained by Williams (1999) in the context of joint book reading. Remarkably, when in my research young children's discourse is examined in terms of the same semantic features, an almost identical result is obtained ($p <.009$). Cluster 2 typical of the LAP dyads signifies that the mothers view the child as an extension of themselves, similar to them in essential ways so that there exists an *interpersonal trust* between them; their children too display reciprocal regard and a similar orientation toward their mother. Cluster 1 with its emphasis on individuation, on precision and explicitly conveyed information occurred more frequently in HAP mothers' discourse as well as in HAP children's (for details, Hasan, 1989). The expectations of discursive engagement that the two groups of children entertain, the principles for interactive practices that they internalise, are already being learnt at this early stage and the learning varies systematically, in keeping with the predictions of Bernstein's code theory (1971; 1973; 1975).

I have gone into some detail about what children learn through the formative mode of the maternal discourse: the point seems worth making that neither group of mothers consciously sets out to teach by the formative mode what the children appear to be learning. It is in this sense that the formative mode is not a variety of pedagogic discourse. Bernstein (2000: 199) points out:

it is necessary to distinguish between pedagogic consequences and a pedagogic relation. All experiencing carries a pedagogic potential but all experiences are not pedagogically generated.

Certainly in employing the formative mode, the mothers had no pedagogic intention: in fact even the word 'employ' overstates the case, for the mode is simply an expression of the mothers being themselves. What the mothers speak, their selection and organisation of meanings, is a realisation of their social positioning and 'the culturally determined device' for their social positioning is code, as Bernstein has pointed out (Bernstein, 1990: 13). It is true that experience of the formative mode of discourse carries a pedagogic potential; but every experience does that and all experience is utilised in the learning accomplished by the children. The relation between learning and teaching is not quite the same as that between buying and selling (Hasan, 1998): unlike buying and selling, learning and teaching are not necessarily the two sides of the same coin. But very often what we think of as learning is precisely that body of knowledge which is actively and consciously taught: the very word *knowledge* conjures up specialist domains where explicit concepts are the basic currency. Given this, one might wonder what if any significance can be attached to the learning by formative mode described above. I believe this learning is really the internalisation of the principles of the code that is the relevant code for the social subject. In closing this paper, I want to present my arguments for this view.

First, if we examine a child learning how to mean (Halliday, 1975; 1993) it becomes obvious that the edifice of all learning is founded on interpersonal relations: in fact, during the pre- and protolinguistic stages all functions in the 'child tongue' are relational functions. There is no concept of information and certainly the informative function – that of telling someone something that might be new to them – does not surface until the child has entered the threshold of his/her mother tongue. Learning how to relate to persons is thus an earlier and essential condition for all other kinds of learning. As Vygotsky (1978: 57) claimed 'all higher (*mental*) functions (*in the child*) originate as actual relations between human individuals'.

Secondly, the boundaries between the formative and the informative modes are not impermeable: in fact, the very same string of words carries both implicational meanings and explicitly worded meanings. Clusters of the kind presented in Table 1 show quite clearly that the informative and formative modes intersperse in discourse: most of the semantic features which are 'logically' entailed by the implicational meanings of 'assumptive' and 'prefaced' are essentially informative in nature. The information to be given is, as it were, cut to suit the image of the other: its nature is predicated by the perceived relation.

This has a third consequence: the readiness to receive information, the very perception of what constitutes appropriate information is fashioned through the specific experience of discourse and this means through how the formative and the informative modes are interspersed in the discourse children encounter everyday of their life. The school is where the business of learning is 'institutionalised': but again as Vygotsky (1978: 84) pointed out '... any learning the child encounters in school has a previous history'. Bernstein's message on this issue was more elaborated: he tried to show us what previous histories of discursive participation different groups of children bring to the school and how this history might impinge on learning in school given the nature of the official pedagogic systems. Part of the function of the child's previous history is precisely to help the child decide what is to be considered relevant by way of information and how information is to be framed. The semiotic mediation of specialist concepts and knowledge structures calls for a particular kind of discursive experience, a particular form of consciousness, which may or may not have been accessible to all who come to schools to learn. We might claim justifiably that in official pedagogic sites the informative mode, an aspect of Bernstein's elaborated code, is the privileged mode but in the experience of the growing child formation and information are integrated: the former gives a specific shape to the latter.

It seems appropriate to close this highly condensed paper on code varieties and their relevance to learning with the words of Bernstein himself (1971: 144):

> the particular form of a social relation regulates the options that speakers take up at both syntactic and lexical [and semantic] levels ... different forms of social relations can generate very different speech systems or linguistic codes ... the different speech systems or codes create for their speakers different orders of relevance and relation. The experience of the speaker may then be transformed by what is made significant or relevant by different speech systems

Notes

1 This research project consisting of several phases was funded by grants from the Australian Research Council and the Macquarie University Research Grants Scheme.
2 Conventions for the transcription of speech are as shown below:
(4) = The following wording is message number 4 in this extract
(?I wasn't) = segment unintelligible; enclosed is best guess on the basis of context & co-text
**no **you hurt ... = wording paired by message-initial double star indicates speech overlap
you didn't – = this message was left incomplete and/or interrupted by next speaker
(?   ) = this segment was unintelligible; no clues to help interpretation
(PETE CRIES) = situational information based on recorded information.
3 For discussion on classification and framing see, especially, Bernstein, 1990 and 1996.

9 Reading picture reading: a study in ideology and inference

Nigels's mother and I were planning a visit to the aquarium. Nigel (age 23 months) did not know what an aquarium was but he heard us discussing it.

'We're not going to see a rao ['lion'],' he said to himself. 'Vopa ['fishes']. There will be some water'.

(Halliday, 2003)

1 Introduction

Going beyond the information given is something we human beings do quite spontaneously and unconsciously. We engage in this activity with an ease that might persuade us to believe that making inferences on the basis of the information in hand inheres in the genetic make up of the human species. It may well be that the belief is justified to some extent: we may by nature be predisposed to reasoning of the type: *given that A is the case, then B must follow from it*: certainly, little Nigel, untutored in the art/science of reasoning is able to deduce that 'given there will be fish in the aquarium, it follows that there will be some water'. The value of such a genetic trait is obviously enormous for the survival of the species. But the actual act of inferential reasoning as a whole – which is what, after all, impinges on our life – involves much more than this formula suggests. Inferential reasoning is complex and like most complex processes it cannot be accounted for purely on the basis of our species specific endowments. This becomes clear on closer examination. From an analytical perspective, we need to recognise at least two parts in this process. First, the need to recognise the information for what it is: i.e., to understand what the significant elements of the scenario are that the given information is construing. I use the phrase 'given information' here for any object that requires interpretation, be it language, image, gesture or even a material situation. The only way we can go beyond a given instance of any of these phenomena is to interpret it, i.e., to understand its significance. Secondly, there is also the need to figure out what practice(s) the construed scenario implies – what steps are 'logically' necessary for the completion of the recognised scenario. Strictly speaking the word *inference* refers precisely to this latter activity, but it is obvious that the recognition of what is and the prediction of what follows from the recognised 'fact' are the two logically integrated parts of the same game, namely making sense. And it appears quite obvious that the requirements of neither of these stages in interpretation can be met automatically in a manner that has been, as it were, ordained by our biological make up; an equally crucial contribution is made by our social location – how we are positioned in society, as this is what would predicate how we perceive and interpret the situation. Our social positioning impinges on both stages of inferential reasoning. So far as 'taking in' given information is concerned, we know that it is seldom a neutral act. Information is typically processed from some specific point of view and to say that interpreter's point of view is crucial to the recognition and understanding of the given state of affairs is to grant that the process is ultimately ideologically informed. Then, again, the experience of living is crucial in guiding the prediction of what would follow from the information in hand. True that both memory and the ability to perceive similarities are important elements in inference, but memory needs something to remember and perception of similarity presupposes a (partial) acquaintance. It follows that the act of inference turns crucially upon the inferring subject's point of view, the ideology which s/he brings to bear on the recognition of that which *is*. So, whatever the biological basis for inferential reasoning, what the details of the *actual* act will ultimately turn on, is the social subject's ideology.

One might be tempted to reject the crucial role I have assigned here to point of view and ideology in inferential reasoning on the ground that there exist universal truths, which are understood in the same way by all human beings and which in all cases must lead to the same inference. Certainly the examples provided by logicians and philosophers appear to encourage this view. To take one of the very famous and recurrent examples: suppose the given information is that (1) *precious metals do not rust* and that (2) *gold is a precious metal*, then any one who perceives the logical relation between these two elements of the given information, would naturally complete the thought by inferring the implied conclusion, that (3) *gold does not rust*. At a cursory glance it seems reasonable to suggest that variation in ideology and point of view is not likely to affect our interpretation of the information given in the major and minor premises in (1) and (2) respectively and that the conclusion in (3) follows naturally and unavoidably from the acceptance of (1) and (2). In the literature on reasoning (see, for example, Evans, Newstead and Byrne, 1993), this kind of inference would be referred to as 'deductive' and it is assumed that all things being equal, such deductions are arrived at quite naturally.

A question we need to raise at this point is whether it is true that all human beings will reason this way? If it turns out that they do not then clearly there must be some significant elements in such reasoning that are not given by nature. We might argue of course that failure to reason thus simply indicates 'feeble intelligence' (Evans et al., 1993: 1), that all human beings, except those suffering from feeble intelligence, would arrive at a naturally given 'correct' inference. But granting this exception, on the one hand, raises questions about what we mean by feeble intelligence: how and why some might come to suffer from it and, on the other hand, it puts under threat the claim that the process of logical inference comes naturally to all members of the species *homo sapiens*. If what is called feeble intelligence is traced to the experience of living, then we might have to consider the possibility that given the 'same' point of departure, all human beings may not necessarily arrive at the same destination, for it may be that the point of departure itself does not bear an identical significance for all and so is, in truth, not the 'same' point of departure!

2 Thinking in society

It so happens that in 1930–31, the famous Russian scholar, Luria, conducted a research which is highly relevant to our debate. His subjects came from Uzbekistan and represented social groups with different experiences of daily life. Some were mature peasants with little or no formal education; others were younger and/or had received some formal instruction. Luria's research clearly demonstrated (Luria, 1976: 100ff) that the first group of subjects 'refused to resort to logical inference from the given premises' (Luria, 1976: 108) *especially if the premises were far removed from their personal experience*. Remarkably, Luria did not attribute this refusal to his subjects' 'feeble intelligence'; on the contrary he pointed out that 'These subjects can make excellent judgments about facts of direct concern to them and can draw conclusions, displaying no deviation from the 'rules' and revealing much worldly intelligence' (Luria, 1976: 114). In his opinion, three factors 'substantially limited their (i.e., the subjects') capabilities for theoretical, verbal-logical thinking' and these Luria listed as follows:

1: a mistrust of an initial premise that does not reproduce personal experience...

2: the unacceptability of the premise as universal...

3: ... [as] a consequence of the second, ... [a] ready disintegration of the syllogism into three independent and isolated particular propositions with no unified logic and thus no access for thought to be channelled within this system. (Luria, 1976: 114–5)

Reflecting on these three factors, it seems to me that the last two follow from the first and the first is rooted within the experience of life that Luria's subjects had encountered prior to engaging in this research: it is this factor that was relevant in Luria's subjects' interpretation and recognition of the nature of the given information. To us, who are in the business of dealing with the processing of this kind of 'disembedded information' (Donaldson, 1978; 1992), it is crystal clear that the major and minor premises of a syllogism constitute 'given information' and that if they represent generalisations, then in our culture they would be ascribed the status of universal truth, but the point of view that Luria's subjects brought to those premises negated their very status as information: to them the general assertions were neither relevant nor credible. It was this point of view, this way of engaging with the given information, that made a qualitative difference to the direction of their thinking. Were we to explain their response as arising from feeble intelligence, then in view of their social positioning, we would have to see feeble intelligence not as natural mental deficit but rather as a state of mind induced by the experience of their specific social positioning, which was instrumental in fashioning their ideas about what is worthy of attention, what is sayable, or even thinkable. And indeed Luria did go on to claim that this group of his subjects were those 'whose cognitive activity was formed by *experience and not by systematic instruction or more complex forms of communication*' (emphasis added).

I will return at a later point to the opposition Luria sets up between 'experience' on the one hand – by which he meant learning through everyday life and 'systematic instruction or more complex forms of communication', on the other. This latter term in Luria's opposition corresponds approximately to what Bernstein (e.g. 1990; 1996) used to call instructional discourse in official pedagogy. Inspired by Vygotsky's sociogenetic theory of cognitive development (see Vygotsky, 1978; Wertsch, 1985b; Mertz and Parmentier, 1985; Hickman, 1987; etc.) Luria claimed that the 'shaping of the foundations of theoretical thinking... can be regarded as one of the most important processes in the historical shaping of consciousness' (Luria, 1978: 115). He thus clearly dissociated himself from the view according to which the capacity for making a logical inference is taken as a gift of nature: what you need for logical inference is, according to Luria, schooled minds. Below is how he presented his position (Luria, 1976: 118):

> Only through school instruction and the concomitant creation of special 'theoretical' activity could the situation change markedly and the process of problem solving become an independent discursive activity, assuming forms similar to the familiar forms of verbal and logical and discursive thought that we see in school children.

The sociohistorical genesis of theoretical thinking – and this in Luria's terminology includes generalisation, abstraction, problem solving and logical inference etc. – is thus to be attributed, according to Luria, to 'systematic instruction and more complex forms of communication'. Far from being a natural mental activity, it is in fact learned in the experience of instructional discourse, which is characteristically associated with schooling, i.e. with official pedagogy. But how right was Luria in attributing this achievement to schools? In what follows I will examine some classroom discourse to see if there is any indication that the shaping of the foundation of theoretical thinking begins at school. But first a few words about the data to be used for this examination.

3   Classroom discourse: the data

The extracts from classroom discourse to be discussed here form part of a large body of data collected for the second phase of a multi-phase research project that I directed at Macquarie University[1]. In the first phase of this research, a substantial sample of naturally occurring everyday talk between 24 mother-child dyads was analysed semantically[2]. This analysis established a statistically robust pattern of semantic variation which was responsive to the subjects' social class position. In the second phase of the research, eight of the subject children were followed into the classroom in the first year of their schooling. In Australia, this stage is known as kindergarten; the word is often abbreviated in the usual Australian manner to 'kindy'. A recording of some kindy classroom sessions was made in the first and the last month of the year; the data presented here is from the first month of schooling. Twenty-four schools participated in the project; 11 of these were located in working-class areas and 13 in middle-class ones. The recording was done by the teachers themselves, all of whom were female. The reason for the recording was given as part of an attempt to find out what the children are able to say and do when they first enter school. The end of year recording was to be used as a measure for the distance the children had travelled intellectually in one year's schooling.

During the first batch of recording, the subject children were aged five to five and a half years old, which is normal for the start of official education in Australia. For the eight phase-one subjects followed up to the kindy class, we also had reliable information regarding their everyday life experience at home (see Hasan, 1989; 1992a; 1992b; Cloran, 1994; 1999; 2000). The data of classroom discourse from the first month of schooling would therefore appear to be particularly suitable for examining if and how the 'shaping of the foundations of theoretical thinking' might begin to take place through participation in 'systematic instruction or more complex forms of communication'. At this early stage the school would not have made any notable mark on the children's consciousness, but it is conceivable that it might be taking the initial steps in that direction. The teachers were advised to do the recording during whatever activity they thought would generate more participation in the talk by the children. It turns out that the majority of the data comes from 'number talk' and 'picture reading' sessions. Obviously at this early stage, no hard and fast lines are drawn between 'subject areas' or 'fields of discipline': in fact one might go so far as to say there are no recognisable subjects/disciplines with possibly the sole exception of mathematics. In any event, one would look in vain for any discourse concerned with the transmission of a systematic body of 'knowledge' which we tend to think of as a 'discipline'. However, to pass over the classroom discourse of these young kindy pupils and their teachers as trifling or irrelevant to the serious business of education would be a gross underestimate of its true significance. For, indeed, under the cover of quite mundane seeming discourse, some highly important things are going on, which do indicate the role of schooling in the *historical shaping of consciousness.*

4 Classroom discourse: the object of teaching

In the last few decades there has been a good deal of interest in classroom discourse and it has added to our understanding of its nature from different points of view (see for example Sinclair and Coulthard, 1975; Mehan, 1979; Edwards and Westgate, 1987; Lemke, 1990; Christie, 1996; and many others). To appreciate the schools' possible contribution to the shaping of the foundations of logical thinking, we need to focus on a more abstract issue, which is fundamental to education as such. We need to consider the nature of that which is taught, so the question I want to raise here is: what exactly is the object of teaching? Clearly, this is a large question. Schooling is far from homogeneous; there are different styles, different traditions and of course as you move up and down the various significant stages of education, the same tradition might have very different manifestations in pedagogic practices. I will ignore here that variety of educational practice associated with what became known as 'progressive education' (see, however, the close of the next section for some relevant comments on this pedagogic tradition). A fairly typical manifestation of the underlying assumptions of progressive education in the specific discipline of language education was 'process writing', which too is ignored here for lack of space.

One popular view, endorsed explicitly by most traditional teaching institutions is that the object of teaching is simply the transmission of some existing body of knowledge. In terms of the analysis of pedagogic discourse offered by Bernstein (1990; 1996 and elsewhere), this reduces the process simply to 'instructional discourse', ignoring the equally if not more important component that Bernstein called 'regulative discourse'. Oversimplifying somewhat, Bernstein (1990: 211) claimed that '... instructional discourse is concerned with the transmission/acquisition of specific competences and regulative discourse is concerned with the transmission of order, relation and identity'. Where the object of teaching is simply the transmission of specific competences, there knowledge is viewed as consisting of a reservoir of interrelated concepts that concern various aspects of our material and social environment, which for some reason or other have become foregrounded in the culture, becoming part of what must be learnt. Each such aspect comes to represent a 'field' or 'subject'. The knowledge in each field is recontextualised for use in schools and universities, having been packaged into the various curriculum genres such as those of physics, chemistry, biology, history, geography, politics and so on. The object of teaching is the mastery of these genres, whether this is recognised in as many words or not. In recent years, critical literacy scholars have been scathing about the value of focus on educational genres as the object of teaching (see for example Luke, 1996) so it needs to be pointed out that the reproduction of existing knowledge is a significant aspect of the maintenance of any culture. Cultures vary to the extent that they attach value to the management of their own continuity, but no living culture can afford to entirely ignore it. A culture that does not attend to its own maintenance – and such cultures are more the figments of our imagination than real historical facts – has no sense of history; where there is no sense of history there can be no sense of change. Cultural change and cultural maintenance are mutually defining phenomena: the one is unknowable without the other. So the reproduction of knowledge as the object of teaching has a definite value in the life of a community. Nonetheless, if it were to remain the sole object of teaching, this could give rise to some serious problems.

If the object of teaching were to be conceptualised *only* as reproduction of existing knowledge, this would lead to a kind of learning that Bateson (1972) described as 'zero level learning': you simply learn the categories and items – their labels and realisations – and perchance the relations of the categories to each other, but you do not learn the principles which underlie the production of these objects. Bateson suggests that a much more important form of learning is learning to learn: this he described as 'deutero learning'. Clearly, deutero learning would be enabling, as it would enhance the capacity to learn. And this is crucial in view of the nature of knowledge. We may certainly view already produced knowledge as an abstract semiotic product; but it is important to realise that the nature of knowledge is not static as the metaphor of knowledge as product might suggest. For human progress to continue, knowledge must always be on the move. Espousing this view in his discussion of the concept of World 3, Popper (1992) makes an observation that appears crucial at this point in our debate. Popper appears to think of knowledge as an existing reservoir of interrelated concepts: once produced it would go on to exist, as he put it, 'without a knowing subject'. As systems of interrelated concepts, a knowledge domain contains within itself the principle of its own development; the concepts and their relations within the field point to the direction of the field's future growth. There is no doubt that Popper is right to a certain extent: the developmental potential that inheres in knowledge is undeniable, but for this potential to become actual, some source of activation is needed. This activation, clearly, cannot come from within the systems of knowledge themselves. It is, therefore, equally undeniable that the activation of the developmental potential of knowledge systems calls for a knowing subject (i.e., not a *tabula rasa*, who is innocent of culture): to realise its potential, a knowledge system needs someone who can ask how and why questions at appropriate points in exploring existing concepts and their relations. It follows that for the continued evolution of knowledge, we need people who are capable of performing this function. And it is also not difficult to see that pupils who have only encountered teaching as the reproduction of knowledge will very probably lack this capacity to interrogate the existing knowledge systems: they would have engaged only in zero level learning.

So how does the production of knowledge continue in society? For continue it must, even in the most traditional societies. One possible answer is that at least so far as pedagogic institutions are concerned, knowledge production is always a late development: it occurs only at the advanced stages, when the student is, in terms of contemporary western cultures, working for a research degree. The attitude of enquiry coincides with the maturity of years and with the development of the intellect which has had to prove its excellence over the entire educational career. All this is perfectly true, but unless we maintain that producers of knowledge are born not culturally produced, the question still remains: when does the transformation of a person into a scholar actually begin? At what stage of schooling do our pedagogic institutions begin to lay the foundation of theoretical thinking? The data collected for our research has some surprising indications. It suggests that the business of shaping the intellect begins very early.

5 Classroom discourse and the production of the pedagogic subject

Consider Extracts 1a and 1b. Both form part of the same classroom interaction but they are separated from each other by intervening talk that is omitted here in order to save space. As the first message of 1a shows, this is not where the interaction begins; the messages in both extracts have been renumbered here for ease of presentation.

236   *Language, Society and Consciousness*

Extract 1a[3]

Teacher:	(1) well now, here is another picture (2) now, what do you think this is a picture about? (3) have a look at it
Pupils:	(4) a bus
Teacher:	(5) yes, its a picture of a bus (6) all right, well, who do you think is going to catch the bus? (7) who's catching that bus?
Pupils:	(8) kindies
Teacher:	(9) you think it might be Kindies (10) what about you Tony?
Tony:	(11) um... school[?bus]
Teacher:	(12) you think it could be a school bus (13) I think it could be too... (14) have a good look at it... (15) what do you think Kim?
Kim:	(16) I think it's pre-school
Teacher:	(17) you think it could be preschool (18) might be pre-school (19) what about you Verity?
Verity:	(20) first class
Teacher:	(21) first class (22) and what do you think about it, Jennie?
Jennie:	(23) [?I think it's preschool]
Teacher:	(24) you think it's preschool

Extract 1b

Teacher:	(1) do you think they are going to school? (2) or are they coming home from the school?
Pupils:	(3) home
Teacher:	(4) why do you think that? (5) why do you think that Verity?
Verity:	(6) because...
Teacher:	(7) why do you think they're going home?... (8) Kim?
Kim:	(9) um... cause its this afternoon
Teacher:	(10) yes it could be afternoon (11) the shadows are long (12) the shadows are long (13) it could be afternoon... (14) Steve?
Steve:	(15) [?because there's a high fence (16) and you don't usually have that kind of fence around houses]
Teacher:	(17) oh, isn't that a good answer! (18) (ADDRESSING WHOLE CLASS) did you hear that?
Pupils:	(19) **no
Pupils:	(20) **yes
Teacher:	(21) did you hear? (22) Steve said *because there's a high fence (23) and you don't usually have that kind of fence around your home* (emphasis added)

In Extract 1a, to use Sinclair and Coulthard's terminology (1975), there are five exchanges. Four of these have some version of the same question, viz., *who's catching the bus?* functioning as re/initiate. However, contrary to Sinclair and Coulthard's prediction, the teacher's persistence with the question is not indicative of her dissatisfaction with the previous responses. The teacher, in fact, appears to have a relaxed attitude, simply exploring what possible readings of this aspect of the picture can be entertained. This is not accidental behaviour, specific to this occasion or even to this teacher: our data indicates that it is by no means uncommon for teachers to, as it were, implicitly indicate the possibility of variant readings of the same picture. That variant readings are being entertained is shown by the fact that the teacher's feedback to the various pupils in Extract 1a simply acknowledges each reading: *you think it's an X, you think it's a Y*. There is no indication of a higher or lower valuation at any stage of these exchanges.

By contrast, in 1b, the issue centres round what substantiates a claim: what justification can the pupil offer in favour of his/her claim? And here it is quite clear that the teacher is not going to accept just any response. Variant readings will be offered and they might even be considered seriously but the pattern of differential evaluation will establish which response is the best. So when Kim justifies her claim that *they're going home* by saying *cause its this afternoon*, this is not seen as solving the problem. Rather, it is implicitly treated as giving rise to a new problem: how do we know it is afternoon? By her follow up messages (11)-(13) the teacher implicitly indicates that Kim's explanation raises a new problem. She models the possible move Kim might make to justify her assertion that its afternoon: *yes, it could be afternoon, the shadows are long, the shadows are long, it could be afternoon*. The suggestion hangs in the air tentatively until Steve offers his response: *(they're going home) because there's a high fence and you don't usually have that kind of fence around houses*. The teacher is delighted with Steve's response, which she holds up for the class to examine by repeating his words: *did you hear? Steve said 'because there's a high fence and you don't usually have that kind of fence around your home'*.

Why does the teacher prefer Steve's response to Kim's? We can paraphrase Kim's response as follows: *because I believe that it's afternoon, therefore I claim that the children are going home, not coming to school*. But what justification Kim might have for believing that it's afternoon is known only to her: she has not said anything to validate that claim. By contrast, Steve exploits objective evidence; he uses as justification for his claim something that is there in the picture for everyone to see; and as everyone knows, seeing is believing. The proceedings in the classroom leave no doubt that the teacher's real concern is with the viability of the evidence for the claim. The lesson continues with further discussion of what 'proof' there might be for claiming

238   *Language, Society and Consciousness*

that the kids are heading back home, not coming to school. The teacher adds her own observation to Steve's:

> *the children are coming **out** of the gate; if they were coming **to** school, they would be coming **in** in* [sic!] *the gate... so we see they're catching the bus going home **from** school* (emphasis in recorded data)

This complements Steve's response: the high fences he spoke about are **behind** the bus not in front. Together these comments clinch the argument; they validate the claim.

I am inclined to describe this early lesson, which occurred within the second or third week of the children's schooling, as an initial step in teaching the principles of argumentation. During this lesson which seems to completely absorb both the teacher and her pupils, at no point has the teacher explicitly enunciated her principles, which, if they had been worded, might have run as follows: *claims you make must be substantiated; and evidence you cite must be objective, which is to say, it should be accessible to others*. It is no part of my claim that the teacher is conscious of the significance of what she is doing. She may be or she may not; however, what does seem beyond doubt here, is that the importance of the principles of argumentation – such a central pillar of scholarly discourse – is being pressed upon these young children, who have, in the words of Wells (1980), just begun their apprenticeship to meanings – meanings that are specific to the educational trade. Here is another example:

Extract 2

Teacher: (1) do you think he's having fun?
Pupil$_1$: (2) yes
Pupil$_2$: (3) mummy's got some shells
Teacher: (4) (IGNORING PUPIL$_2$) what tells you? (5) what tells you he's having fun? (6) he's enjoying himself?
Pupil$_1$: (7) my brain
Teacher: (8) your brain tells you! (9) well, how can we tell ((10) by looking at the picture) that he's enjoying himself (11) having fun?
Pupils: (12) smile
Teacher: (13) good (14) he's got a smile on his face (15) do you think he'd be enjoying himself (16) if he didn't smile? (sic!)
Pupils: (17) no
Teacher: (18) I don't think so either

Pupil$_1$'s response in massage (6) that his brain tells him the boy in the picture is having fun receives short shrift from the teacher, who dismisses this category of evidence. A response of this kind is not of much interest, the teacher implies:

what is really at issue is *how can we tell **by looking at the picture** that he's having fun* (emphasis added). What we need is not subjective things like beliefs, feelings, but objective phenomena which others too can view. Note in passing also the fate of Pupil$_2$'s message: it remains 'unheard' as it goes against an important rule of classroom discourse: speak when you are spoken to and speak only of the matter in hand, which is to say, on the topic introduced by the teacher. One more example to round off the discussion of the principles of judicious reasoning:

Extract 3

Teacher: (1) why do you think this man is dressed up like this? (2) what do you think? (3) anyone like to help Paul?... (4) Ellen?
Ellen: (5) a scarecrow
Teacher: (6) can't hear you darling
Ellen: (7) a scarecrow
Teacher: (8) he's a scarecrow? (9) oh, he's not moving (10) he's just standing there, is he?
Ellen: (11) mm
Teacher: (12) do you all agree with that?
Pupils: (13) **mm yes
Pupils: (14) **no (MOST)
Teacher: (15) if you don't agree (16) you have to say why

In many such episodes, sometimes fleeting sometimes more elaborated, the rules of argumentation prevalent in our pedagogic ideology are being laid out for the children to imbibe: claims must be justified; justifications must be objectively validated; if an argument is rejected, the rejection must be justified. These are indeed the rules which govern, or at least should ideally govern, scholarly discourse and they are essential to the production of knowledge as we understand the term. Despite the fact that the teachers are dealing with perfectly mundane phenomena, such as children travelling in a bus, boys having fun and the conventions for dressing scarecrows, I would suggest that here we are witnessing the initial steps towards laying down the foundations for 'theoretical thinking'. The teachers are not (re-)producing official knowledge *per se*; they are not dealing with specific subject areas of serious concern such as physics; at least on the surface, their discourse does not represent 'complex forms of communication'. Strictly speaking in terms of Bernstein (1996) we are here witnessing not so much the functioning of instructional discourse as that of regulative discourse. And regulative discourse acts on the learning subject: it, first and foremost, regulates the mind. The teachers are engaged in the important business of beginning to shape the consciousness of the young children, transforming them into pedagogic subjects, subjects who might one day interrogate the existing body of knowledge (albeit within limits), who might one day actively participate in the production of knowledge (though the parameters of innovation might be invisibly controlled from above). It would seem then that Luria was right in putting his faith in the system of education: systematic instruction seems to be oriented towards laying the foundations for logical thinking. Whatever the consciously confirmed views about the object of teaching in traditional schools, extracts of the kind I have examined here show that from a very early stage of schooling a form of deutero learning is on the cards; children are expected to imbibe the rules of valid argumentation.

But can we say without reservation that all those who enter an official pedagogic site will necessarily learn the 'rules' for thinking 'logically'? In the last paragraph I deliberately used the word *imbibe* rather than *learn*. By doing this, I wanted to draw attention to the fact that this teaching of the fundamental conventions of scholarly discourse is not explicit; where the teaching is implicit, there any learning that could possibly occur is of that which struck the listener as relevant, which the learner could relate to and internalise due to his/her own interest. It is true that human beings are learning machines and the most effective dynamo for powering that learning is discourse, as Bateson (1972), Halliday (1975), Vygotsky (1978) and many others have suggested; but from this widely acknowledged maxim it does not follow that all learners learn the same thing from a discourse. A necessary but not sufficient condition for targeted learning is that the thing to be learned should be clearly foregrounded in the teacher's discourse, so that the prospective learner has a better chance of recognising what s/he is supposed to focus on, what they are to learn. The explicit foregrounding of information to be learned is a necessary step for counteracting at least to some extent the principle I stated in the introduction, namely that, given information is typically interpreted from the addressee's point of view. This principle applies everywhere and classroom discourse is no exception to it. So the fact that the teacher's discourse is materially available to all pupils alike, does not really mean that they all necessarily engage with the discourse in the same way. If the teaching is implicit, the hearing will be selective; and if the hearing is selective, the learning will be selective too: what the message will say to whom, what will or will not appear relevant to which student, will depend on the social identity of the hearer[4]. To return to Luria's optimistic prediction, there is no doubt that systematic instruction and complex forms of communication involving concepts and their relations have the potential of shaping a scholarly consciousness, but there is good reason to reject the easy assumption that they perform this function, in actual fact, for *every child* in the school. Some will learn, some will not; the distribution of knowledge in the school has been and still remains inequitable: as Bernstein puts it, education cannot compensate for society. Without trying to reduce a complex problem to a simple single parameter, the single most important reason for this failure appears to arise from the educational system's reluctance to hear the different voices in the classroom, to recognise multiple points of view that exist in every classroom in our pluralistic societies (Hasan, 1996a). These comments hark back to the introductory discussions: receiving information is not a neutral process. In the following section I present a segment of classroom discourse which brings this point home quite starkly.

6 Classroom discourse: symbol, interpretation and experience

The segment of classroom discourse I now want to examine is fairly lengthy, it will be broken up into appropriate extracts for discussion below. Note the consecutive numbering of the messages from Extract 4a through to 4d; this indicates the continuity of the discourse. However, the messages of Extract 4e are re-numbered afresh because a number of messages intervening 4d and 4e have been excluded in order to save space. Further, as it happens, Extract 4a is not where the reading of this picture begins, as can be seen from the first message presented below. The picture that the teacher and her class are reading constitutes a narrative tableau: a saucepan is on the stove, steam rising from it. A little girl who is so tiny that she can barely reach the stove is on the point of approaching the saucepan; she might be about to lift it. In the doorway of this kitchen stands another girl, older, watching the scene. In her discussion with the class, the teacher has just established that the little girl is about to lift the saucepan off the stove. This is where Extract 4a begins:

Extract 4a

Teacher: (1) you look at how tall the little girl is (sic!)… (2) she can only just reach that saucepan (3) what might happen to her?
Alan: (4) burn herself (5) burn herself
Teacher: (6) why do you think she might burn herself (7) how… how would she burn herself?
Alan: (8) [?if she be big]…
Teacher: (9) (ENCOURAGINGLY) you're right (10) just tell me again (11) I couldn't hear
Alan: (12) if she be big
Teacher: (13) (CORRECTING) if she was big…? (14) well, she's just a little bit tiny, isn't she? (15) she… what if… you know how sometimes you're just trying to reach something (16) and you can't quite reach it (17) and your hand slips (18) what do you think will happen (19) if her hand slips? (20) what will that saucepan do (20) if her hand slips? (21) Suzie?

Suzie: (22) burn herself
Teacher: (23) how will she burn herself? (24) what will the saucepan do?
Suzie: (25) tip down (26) and burn herself
Teacher: (27) right the saucepan will fall (28) and tip things all over her (29) and if the things in that saucepan are all hot (30) then she will –?... (31) Alan?
Alan: (32) tip it over her
Teacher: (33) tip it over her (34) and what will happen to her?
Alan: (35) [?it'll] burn her
Teacher: (36) and she'll get burnt (37) and she will burn herself

In this extract, the teacher seems to have two major concerns: one, the children must attend to the wording of their meanings and two, the steps in inferring what might happen must be spelt out. The appeal to children's own experience of a situation similar to that in the picture with the sequel half spelt out is particularly noteworthy: here the basis for the recognition of the situation and for the prediction of likely action is being sought in the experience of living. By the end of this interaction the teacher seems to have established in negotiation with her pupils that the little girl is in a situation where she could hurt herself. The teacher now shifts the pupils' attention to the big girl. What is going to be her role in this drama?

Extract 4b

Teacher: (38) what do you think this girl...? (39) who do you think this girl is? (40) who might she be? (41) Mandy?
Mandy: (42) um a girl that's gonna walk over (43) and smack her
Teacher: (44) do you think she might smack her?... (45) could be

As the teacher attempts to make her next move which is to identify the big girl in the picture, there comes the first surprise of the lesson. Mandy, as it were, hijacks the intended meaning of the teacher's question: *who might this girl be*? Mandy identifies the big girl by reference to a specific future action of hers. This is a rather unexpected response. Semantically speaking the question *who is this girl*? would typically receive a response that would identify the person in question by reference to some kind of identifying status, e.g., *she's her neighbour/ friend/ sister/ visitor* and so on. Lexicogrammatically, what we would have is an identifying clause with *she/the girl* as Identified and the identity indicating term as Identifier. It is of course possible to identify persons by their activity, but if so the activity is an occupational/habitual one and English has specific ways of managing this kind of situation: *she is the dancer/ receptionist/ cook/ teacher* etc. It would be rare indeed to come across a response that identifies the entity by reference to a specific one-time activity. Now, in face of this rather unexpected response, the teacher concedes the possibility that the big girl could be someone who might smack the little girl, but she does not welcome the response. She asks the question once again, throwing broad hints (see message 47; and 52–54) where to look for the answer:

Extract 4c

Teacher: (46) who do you think she is? (47) do you think she lives in this house with that little girl? (48) or do you think she's a friend? (49) who might she be? (50) Shirley?
Shirley: (51) ooh... live there
Teacher: (52) she might live there (53) so who would she be to this little girl? (54) she would be her what?
Shirley: (55) friend... sister
Teacher: (56) maybe her sister

As we shall see below, agreement on the identification of the big girl as a sister is critical to the direction in which the teacher wants the class to move. She expects this to clear the ground for her next move, but it will become obvious very soon, that there is no plain sailing. And here is the ensuing discourse:

Extract 4d

Teacher: (57) what do you think that big sister's thinking? (58) as she is looking at her little sister (59) and seeing her touching that hot saucepan? (60) Alan do you know?... (61) you don't know (62) does anybody know what she might be thinking? (63) Suzie?
Suzie: (64) getting mad (65) getting mad
Teacher: (66) getting mad? (67) who's getting mad?
Suzie: (68) the big sister
Teacher: (69) why do you think she's getting mad?

Since Orwell's great work, the descriptor 'big brother' has acquired a somewhat pejorative connotation in English. 'Big sister' is, however, different: in my understanding, it has no connotation of overbearing authority and still retains its meaning as in *loco matris*, thus expected to have the same tender loving, nurturing attitude as a mother. The teacher uses the expression 'big sister' in framing her question about the future intentions of the big girl. The children, however, do not appear to have any association of tenderness with the phrase 'big sister'. Alan is unable to provide any response and Suzie offers one that must be considerably different from the teacher's expectations. Suzie believes that the big sister is *getting mad*. Note the idiomatic expression which in the child's experience is very likely to have occurred in an everyday situation. What, the teacher wants to know now, is the justification for this prediction about the big sister's reaction to the situation? It takes a good deal of to-ing and fro-ing before she can get Rosa to come up with a reason why the big sister is getting mad: it's *because she's* [the little girl] *touching the thing* [hot saucepan on the stove]. Patiently and very carefully, through a series of questions and answers, the teacher re-establishes all the significant elements in her reading of the picture, finishing with the conclusion: ... *the big sister knows if she* [the little girl] *touches it* [the saucepan], *it might... slip... and pour everything over and burn her*. It is clear from this discourse that for the teacher the picture construes a context in which the little girl's well-being is threatened; being big, the big girl has a better understanding of the situation, so she has the power to avert this threat and of course we have now established that she is a big sister. So the question is: what would a big sister do in this kind of situation? The reading of the situation has been arrived at in negotiation with the children and the process has taken time – some two to three minutes – and, of course, a considerable amount of talk. This intervening talk which I have summarised above is excluded for lack of space (note that the messages are now renumbered). In Extract 4e the teacher once again puts her question. For her the answer to the question is quite clear: being a big sister the big girl will protect the little girl, but for the children this is not a transparently obvious solution:

Extract 4e

Teacher: (1) what could this big sister do (2) to help her little sister? (3) what could she do? (4) Derek?
Derek: (5) smack her...
Teacher: (6) maybe she could smack her (7) what else could she do (8) so she didn't burn herself? Shirley?
Shirley: (10) she could pick the saucepan up
Teacher: (11) and what could she do with it then?
Shirley: (12) put it (13) where she can't get it
T: (14) good girl! (15) that's very good thinking (16) she - the big sister – < (17) cause she's nice and tall (18) and she can reach that saucepan can't she?> she could pick that saucepan up < (19) and put it somewhere where the little girl cant reach it > couldn't she?

As we can see from message (2) the teacher is now making her question more precise: *what could the big sister do* **to help her little sister***?* (emphasis added). Even so Derek's response is: *smack her*. Conceding this possibility the teacher once again asks the question, spelling out the situated meaning of *to help her*: she asks: *what* **else** *could she do so she* [the little girl] **didn't burn herself***?*

(emphasis added). This does produce the response she has been trying to elicit from her pupils: with some help from the teacher, Shirley is able to provide this desirable response: *she* [big sister] *could pick the saucepan up and put it where she* [little girl] *can't get it*. For the first time since the beginning of this picture reading episode the teacher offers an unreservedly positive evaluation: *good girl! That's very good thinking*. And like the teacher of another lesson which was discussed above (see Extract 1b), she goes on to repeat this response, which in a very real sense is a response 'natural' to her, not to the children.

It is interesting to note the form of this repetition: an interpretation of its lexicogrammar reveals that by her choice of tag questions the teacher is attempting/expecting to get the children to subscribe to her view. She uses mood tags with reversed polarity (on grammatical terminology, used here, see Halliday, 1994a): *she can ... can't she*? (Message 18) and *she could ... couldn't she*? The semantic feature construed by reverse polarity negative tag has been referred to as 'reassure' (Hasan, 1989; Cloran, 1994; Williams, 1995), which can be paraphrased as the speaker takes something to be obviously the case and seeks reassurance from the addressee that s/he too does the same. This is why the choice of reversed polarity mood tags makes disagreement a less likely and therefore a marked response on the addressee's part. It is thus used in contexts where you do not entertain the possibility of dissent. Thus a question such as *you love your mum don't you* is unremarkable because there is a very high probability the answer would be *yes I do*, whereas *you tell lies, don't you* is definitely odd since very few people, if any, would be expected to ascribe this immoral action to themselves. In using the reversed polarity mood tags the teacher is, as it were pre-empting disagreement from her class. The form of the question that elicits the desirable response from Shirley is also noteworthy: *what **else** could she do so she* [the little girl] ***didn't burn herself***? (emphasis added). The question concedes that the children's initial response: *smack her* is a possibility. At the same time it suggests that there are **other** possibilities and, further, it unpacks the teacher's meaning of *help her little sister* (see message 2 in Extract 4e): ***what else could she*** [the big sister] ***do so she*** [the little girl] ***didn't burn herself***. This is reminiscent of an experiment conducted by Holland (1981) (see further discussion in Bernstein, 1990: 18–19) where children were asked to group coloured pictures of familiar food items whichever way they wished. Working-class children first grouped the items by reference to the items' direct relation to the specific local context of their own lives, e.g., *this is what my mum makes, this is what we have for breakfast* and so on. Middle-class children grouped the same items by reference to criteria that were relatively independent of local contexts e.g., *these come from the ground, all of these have butter in them* and so on. However, when the same children were asked to think of *some other way of grouping* the same items, the point of reference shifted notably: significantly more working-class children grouped the items by reference to criteria that were independent of local contexts, while the middle-class moved more toward the use of local contexts for their grouping of the items. By the end of the experiment almost one third of the working-class children had changed their 'principle' for the recognition and classification of the given food items (Bernstein, 1990: 19).

It would seem that in our picture reading lesson, the teacher has achieved success of a similar kind: it appears that she has managed to bring the class round to a view of the situation which does not come natural to them, but which they are willing to see as a possibility. The teacher achieved this result by making her question as precise and explicit as possible. But this success is short lived. This is not really surprising: although orientation to meanings can be changed, for this change to take root so that the alternative orientation becomes automatic, one would need many reiterations of alternative experience: a single lesson is not sufficient to shift the pupils from the position that seems natural to *them*. So in the case of the above discourse, despite Shirley's response and the teacher's careful re-play of it, the children do not now automatically believe that the big sister's role is to help the little girl. Thus during the struggle to establish what the big girl would do – and by now one begins to suspect that most probably it is not a question of what she *would* do, but one of what she *should* do – one of the children asserts: *the big girl could tell mummy... her sister was a naughty girl*. The teacher argues against this prediction, explaining that the little girl was not really naughty, she was just too small to realise the seriousness of her action, therefore she does not deserve to be punished. At the end of this exchange the teacher turns to Rob, presumably to check on what he has learned about reasonable behaviour in a similar situation: *Rob, what would you say to Jenny* [Jenny is Rob's little sister] *if she touched a hot saucepan?* Rob's response is both laconic and by now quite predictable: *smack her*. The basis of his prediction is not in what the teacher has been saying in this class, but what life has been teaching Rob and his peers day in and day out. It is clear then that the children's prediction of what the big girl would do is at odds with the teacher's prediction; this is because the point of view that the teacher and the children bring to the reading of this narrative picture are considerably different. The central problem is the incompatibility of their recognition of the situation in Bernstein's terms; their sense of what social practice is likely to flow from this understanding naturally depends on what they recognise the situation to be. The principle *if A then B* holds but the meaning of *A* and *B* does not. I summarise the position in Table 9.1, which shows that semantically the two parties are far apart: there is a considerable semantic distance between them.

Teacher's point of view	Pupil's point of view
context for protective action: the big sister will help avert danger from her little sister	context for control: the big sister will punish the little girl's naughty action
because	**because**
the little girl is too young to realise the consequence of her action and she is likely to burn herself	the little girl is being naughty in trying to lift a hot saucepan and she is likely to burn herself
therefore	**therefore**
since the big sister realises the little girl's danger, being older and wiser, she will remove the source of danger by moving the hot saucepan out of the little girl's reach	since the big girls can see that the little girl is being naughty, being bigger and stronger, she will smack her to stop her from touching the saucepan
and	**and**
she will explain to the little girl why she is doing this so that the little girl will be careful in the future.	she will tell mummy that the little girl is being naughty so that mummy can punish her to make her act properly in the future.

Table 9.1: Semantic distance: different points of view, different significance

In the data of picture reading interactions, we note a recurrent feature: teachers are very careful about establishing what it is that the children are physically 'seeing'. The picture reading lesson discussed above is no exception: here too the material attributes of the picture are identically present to both parties. The teacher and her pupils do not differ on what it is they see with their eyes. The real question is how they interpret what they see: what context does the material situation represent? What is the meaning of that particular physical arrangement of relevant objects and persons that they find in the pictorial tableau? The introduction of this paper claimed that the recognition of what the given information is construing depends on the receiver's social positioning, which is inalienably related to their experience of living. Let me add now that the picture reading lesson in Extract 4a-e comes from a school in the working-class area. Here, from phase one, are a few examples of working-class discourse in the context of control when the mean age of the children was three years eight months. In Extract 5 Pete is running around near his mother while holding a glass full of juice; the mother fears the juice will spill; she wants Pete to stop.

Extract 5

Mother: (1) don't do that... (MOTHER WAITS FOR PETE TO RESPOND. HE PAYS NO HEED) (2) now look you'll get it all over me
Pete: (PETE LAUGHS AND CONTINUES RUNNING)
Mother: (3) it's not funny (4) what's funny about that?** (5)[?] you do it gain (6) and I'll whack you

In Extract 6 Davie is hungry; he would like macaroni for lunch. His mother wants him to have sandwich. Davie rejects this suggestion somewhat rudely:

Extract 6

Mother: (1) go to your room
Davie: (2) no!
Mother: (3) I beg your pardon! (4) you do what I say (5) or I'll smack you (6) now do you want macaC do you want sandwich or not?
Davie: (7) yes (STAMPING ANGRILY) (8) Peanut butter... (9) peanut butter... please mummy! (CHASTENED VOICE? DID MOTHER SILENTLY THREATEN PHYSICAL PUNISHMENT)

In Extract 7 mother is trying to get Karen into her bed. In fact she has been trying for some time. She has reasoned, scolded, humoured and now she is really 'getting mad':

Extract 7

Mother: (1) Karen, do as you're – (SLAPS KAREN) (2) (IN ANGRY VOICE) put your legs down (3) or I'm going outside right this minute without a kiss (4) now put your legs down (ANGRY VOICE)
Karen: (5) mmhm (KAREN REFUSES TO OBEY)
Mother: (6) (ARRANGING KAREN'S LEGS UNDER THE BLANKET) now, give a kiss goodnight
Karen: (7) I'm not
Mother: (8) you're not gonna kiss me?** (9) why?
Karen: (10) 'cause
Mother: (11) 'cause why?
Karen: (12) 'cause I don't like you

It is not necessary to multiply these examples. Overwhelmingly, situations of control are situations of conflict in the working-class subjects' lives. It is the environment where the power of authority and the irrationality of power are brought home to the child. The meanings of the sayings make authority of power palpable: commands are direct, often unadorned by modification; reasons are terse, often upholding the power of hierarchy and/or conventions. With respect to these semantic features[5], the difference between middle-class and working-class mothers' discourse in the context of control is statistically highly significant (Hasan, 1992a; 1992b). The children's prediction about the big girl's behaviour is rooted in their personal experience. Like Luria's subjects, the children responding to the picture in Extracts 4a-e, are simply being 'natural', but their way of being natural is significantly different from the teacher's way of being 'natural'. The teacher's reaction is closer in its approach to the middle-class modes of control, where the power of authority is made invisible, commands are transformed into consultations about needs, desires, willingness and reasons typically celebrate the 'logic' of physical relations between things and events (Hasan, 1992a). It seems reasonable to conclude that in the picture reading lesson neither party is inherently more intelligent, more im/moral than the other: they are simply responding in the way that comes natural to them, that is to say, in keeping with their social positioning: their cognition is fashioned by their experience of living in society. This is not a fact simply about the working-class children; it is also a fact about the teacher and about middle-class pupils.

7 Experience and systematic instruction: social life, learning and discourse

The two sets of classroom discourse I have discussed appear to be quite dissimilar, but their juxtaposition here is deliberate. If the only discourses we knew about were of the type exemplified by Extracts 1–3, we would not hesitate to agree with Luria that anyone who has had the benefit of school instruction and concomitant creation of special 'theoretical activity' would achieve a particular kind of mental development. This would imply the belief that school instruction is equally efficacious for all children, which in its turn would imply that classroom discourses are heard in the same way by all pupils. It is this latter position that is thrown into doubt by lessons of the kind exemplified by 4a-e. A consideration of this classroom discourse tells us that what might be taken to be the 'same' in terms of its appearance is not necessarily the 'same' for everyone in terms of its meaning: what gets in the way of arriving at the same meaning is the difference in the experiences of persons who are socially differentially positioned, because meaning is refracted through the experience of one's social location. It follows that a given instance of systematic instruction may in fact not be the same for children coming from different social locations. In light of this finding, Luria's opposition of experience to systematic instruction (1976: 118ff) which suggested a clear boundary between the two appears rather questionable. Certainly, for purposes of analysis, this distinction has to be recognised, but it does not seem justifiable to believe that in the life of social subjects the two forms of consciousness created by the two ways of 'learning' remain forever compartmentalised, each having a separate existence from the other. Luria's own research and the data of phase two from my research demonstrate quite clearly that experience of everyday living will colour the meanings in systematic instruction. It is also possible, at least in theory, that systematic instruction might change our way of experiencing everyday life, though this latter position is less likely. To understand why this should be so, we need to understand the working of social positioning – what produces it and what it, in its turn, produces.

In the last decade or so positioning theory has gained a good deal of popularity, but in many of these discussions the term 'positioning' boils down to performative positioning of the interactive other or of the speaking self (see for example Harre and Langenhove, 1999); it is as if its genesis were independent of what else goes on in the social organisation of communal life. This approach to positioning is significantly different from Bernstein's use of the term, which locates it within the politico-economic structure of the society. For Bernstein, the production and distribution of capital is the fundamental social fact from which flow the distribution of power and the principles of control. The concept of social positioning is thus ultimately grounded in class relations: positioning can in fact be paraphrased as intersubjective class relations (Bernstein, 1990: 17). To quote Bernstein:

> class relations generate, distribute, reproduce and legitimate distinctive
> forms of communication, which transmit dominant and dominated codes...
> subjects are differentially positioned by these codes in the process of
> acquiring them... from this point of view, codes are culturally determined
> positioning devices... Ideology is constituted through and in such
> positioning. (Bernstein, 1990: 13)

In this view, ideology is not content. It is not that some ideas or attitudes are ideological, others are not; it is simply that through experience we develop a particular way of relating to whatever we encounter in life. The question is not whether someone has ideology or not; the question is simply what the ideology is actually like, how it is that one relates to one's experience of living.

For reasons that need not detain us here, Bernstein's concept of code has not been well understood. I very briefly present here my understanding of what Bernstein meant by codes. Codes are a device for positioning; to say this is to say also that codes are related realisationally[6] to positioning: it is through the coding orientation that our social positioning can be construed and it is our social positioning that activates for us the habitual choice of one code rather than another. But code itself is an abstract concept: it refers to orders of relevance, to what appears thinkable and sayable. What makes a person's coding orientation palpable is their actual ways of meaning, the way they manage their discourse with an other, the texts they are able to manage as producers and as receivers. Successful management of discourse with an other demands a certain degree of reflexivity. Linguists recognise this when they draw attention to the fact that the comprehension of an other's discourse presupposes a 'sharing of the same world' by the interactants: each must 'know' the other's world. This process of the internalisation of the world in which we live, act and speak begins very early in life and it is synonymous with learning the coding orientation of one's immediate group: the newly born infant is, as it were, automatically socially located at birth. This automatic assigning and assuming of social positioning is a condition for human survival. And a condition for the assuming of the social position is participation in the communication game. If we perceive a circularity in the relations of discourse, positioning and coding orientation, this is because underlying their relations is the fact of co-genesis (Hasan, 1998). A person's ways of saying and meaning are not independent of their social positioning and social positioning is itself construed by semiotic acts which enact the interpersonal relationships, without which the idea of social positioning is vacuous. Infants have to be drawn into this complex web from a very early stage (Halliday, 1975; 1980; Hasan, 2001), some might even suggest before birth (Greenfield, 2000a). As Firth put it perspicaciously '… the young human has to be progressively incorporated into a social organisation and the main condition of that incorporation is sharing the local magic – that is, the language' (Firth, 1957b: 185).

Firth went on to make a distinction between speech fellowship and language community. A speech fellowship sees itself and hears itself as different from those who do not belong:

> 'Within… [a] speech fellowship a speaker is *phonetically and verbally content* because when he speaks to one of his fellows he is also speaking to himself' (Firth, 1957b: 186; emphasis added).

One could go further; one could claim that within the immediate group, the child is content not only phonetically and verbally, but also 'semantically and ideologically'. It is in this experience of interaction that the child's social structure becomes a reality for him, as Bernstein pointed out some decades ago (Bernstein, 1971) and through his own and the other's acts of speech the child comes to internalise the world (s/he) experiences in the living of social life (Hasan, 2002). When young children first begin to learn how to talk, they are not simply learning language; they are also learning through language (Halliday, 1980) about the way their world is organised: the shape of reality is defined for them in and through these interactions. This internalisation provides criteria for both the recognition of the nature and identity of a context and the relevant rules for active participation in it. As Bernstein maintained, in providing the orders of relevance, the coding orientation logically sets aside as unnatural that which departs from the internalised orders of relevance, i.e., those which happen to be shared by one's own immediate community; alternative views of the world are thus suppressed (Bernstein, 1971; 1975a; 1990; 1996). Much of the innocence of childhood resides in the fact that for the child there is no other reality except that which the s/he knows through daily experience. Often the discourse of local pedagogy is seen as important simply from the point of view of educability. This is a trivialisation of the primary (early childhood) experience of social life. True, this experience does form the basis of our relations to official education; but far more importantly, at least initially, it makes us who we are. This is not to say that the ideological orientation is unchangeable, but nor can it be discarded easily like an old pair of socks. To divert the direction of this early orientation, concerted and informed help is needed.

The above is a simplified picture of what the positioning-positioned form of communication does in the very early years of a social subject's life. What this suggests is that the point of view, the ideology that I spoke of as being active in the processing of any information, becomes active fairly early. The analysis of phase one data in our research revealed significant semantic variation in the discourse of children from the two social classes (Hasan, 1989; 1992), suggesting that in some sense ideology begins to take hold early (recall that the mean age of the 24 children was three years eight months). It is not that these internalisations are engraved images destined to remain with the social subjects for ever and irrevocably, but it certainly seems to be the case that relatively more effort is needed to bring about this change in later years. Two considerations appear to support this claim. First, recent work in neurolinguistics shows (Deacon, 1997; Greenfield, 2000) that the early connections are also the longer lasting ones. Secondly and related to the first point is the fact that as we develop, the contribution of the mind will be to 'enhance each conscious moment by imbuing each snapshot of the outside world with meaning' (Greenfield, 2000: 164). This meaning is regulated by the developing coding orientation. If this is so, then it is very likely that simply because the world is already being refracted through an already established point of view, systematic instruction will need to make special effort to bring about the kind of change Luria spoke about, especially where it so happens that the learners' experience has not already paved the way to accepting the classroom discourse as legitimate. This is where the middle-class child coming to school finds herself in a crucially different situation: the discourse in the classroom is reminiscent of that at home (Cloran, 1999; Hasan, 2001a).

In this connection it is important to remember that as Bernstein pointed out, official education is 'essentially a moral activity which articulates the dominant ideology/ies of dominant groups' (Bernstein, 1990: 66). This is one reason for suggesting that the discourse in official educational sites may encounter a resistance from dominated groups or, at the least, it may not be heard in the way that the teacher takes it for granted it would be. This would not be surprising because, in a curious way classroom discourse presents the converse of the habitual orientations of meaning so far as the dominated group is concerned. For the dominating classes the discourse of control makes principles of power and authority invisible, while information is made explicit, its attributes made as visible, detailed and precise as possible. In this description, we can certainly recognise the classroom data that has been presented here: the semantic analysis and comparison of mothers and teachers in my research shows that teachers' talk presents itself as a somewhat exaggerated version of the semantic style characteristic of mothers from the dominating classes. So far as the dominated classes are concerned, our results reveal that the discourse of control makes the principles of power and authority highly visible, while information is left implicit, its attributes invisible, lacking precision and detail (Hasan, 1989; 1992a; 1992b; Cloran, 1994; 2000; Williams, 1995; 1999; 2001). Given these differences, it would be surprising if there did not exist an appreciable semantic distance between the children and the teacher in 4a-e.

If we are really serious about bringing social change through school instruction, then it is important that a form of communication be devised which bridges this distance, which breaks through the barrier without alienating the already dominated child. Currently there seems very little effort from this point of view. Official educational systems insist on retaining a 'univocal' discourse in the classroom, because either it is assumed that the dominating voice is the only voice that actually exists in the classroom or perhaps that it *should* be the only voice; that the alternative voices deserve to be suppressed. In any event, to my knowledge at least, no dialogue between the voices has ever been entertained. But, as I have suggested elsewhere (see Hasan, 1996a), this is the single most severe problem in official pedagogic systems. On the face of it, these systems appear to invest a good deal of vocal energy in attempts to devise strategies for overcoming the problem of failure in schools, but all these strategies are predicated on the assumption of univocality: it is as if we do not really wish to confront the real problem, or perhaps because the real problem is so difficult we shortsightedly try to solve other problems. When attention is drawn to this aspect as, for example, it was in the work of Bernstein and his colleagues some 40 years ago, instead of attempting to understand the problem, it appeared easier for many colleagues to simply attribute his comments to a deep class prejudice (for details of such critique and Bernstein's refutation of them, see Bernstein, 1990; 1996). There are certainly those who refuse to believe that in our pluralistic societies different ways of saying and meaning exist and that in the hierarchised organisation of our societies, the differences between ways of saying and ways of meaning are exploited by the dominating segments for their own benefit. Ironically, these same persons who pose as the saviours of the disadvantaged tend to see the meanings that characterise dominated coding orientations as unreal, generated by the distorted and distorting imagination of the researchers, as if they were meanings that could not possibly be meant by anyone. The twisted argument goes: the dominated classes are rational, therefore they must mean the same rational meanings that we the dominating classes do. This is the only interpretation that can be put on their claim that meanings regulated by dominated codes have been dreamt up maliciously by biased researchers who are bent upon creating divisive discourse, finding conflict where there is none!

There is an urgent need to problematise the question: what is the best way to encourage a dialogue between speakers whose discourse is regulated by different coding orientations. Linguists have written volumes on shared discourse axioms, conversational implicatures and shared worlds. It is time to ask: how can we talk across unshared worlds, across discursive axioms that are not in agreement and conversational implicatures that have distinctly different points of departure? How can a teacher capitalise on the presence of multiple voices in the classroom without creating in any of her speakers either a sense of superiority or a sense of being devalued? While I admire the patience of the teacher whose discourse I have examined in 4a-e, it is doubtful that by the end of the lesson the pupils had any idea what exactly was the issue and what difference it makes to punish or to protect. The central issue of the teacher-pupil talk during this session was the choice between punishment and avoidance as strategies for the prevention of something undesirable. The teacher at no point explicitly engaged with this central issue; she simply indicated, in an implicit manner, by her pattern of evaluations that she did not favour the children's spontaneous responses. What might have possibly helped at this point was the practice of reflection literacy (Hasan, 1996a): the teacher could have raised the why question. Why is punishment better than removing the source of the problem? Who would it benefit to punish the little girl? How soon do little children come to discriminate between good acts and bad ones that need to be punished? But to set up this kind of dialogue, the teacher herself needs to understand the history of the children's response. This understanding can only come if the conspiracy of silencing research of this kind under false pretences is abandoned. Those who examine classroom discourse have a responsibility to understand that discourse cannot be separated from social life. Speaking may appear effortless, always responding to the 'present' of the discourse to its 'now' and to its 'here', but every utterance has behind it the history of the speaking person, which is to say, the history of the speaker's speech fellowship; in the words of Bernstein between the system of language and the coding orientations, there lies the social structure of the speakers' society. Discourse analysis of classroom talk has, over the past quarter of a century, simply swept these deeper sociolinguistic issues under the carpet, focusing on the form of the discourse and/or its instructional content. We need an examination of classroom discourse which is able to highlight the unilateral design of this interaction and we need to ask why this design is preferred? Whom does it benefit? Whom does it disadvantage?

Notes

1. The project, titled *The Role of Everyday Talk between Mothers and Children in Establishing Ways of Learning* was conducted during 1984–1988. Funding was received from the Australian Research Council and Macquarie University Research grant Scheme, which is hereby gratefully acknowledged. For further details of this project see Butt (1989); Hasan (1989; 1992a; 1992b; 2000b); and Cloran (1994; 1999). My thanks are due to Carmel Cloran for her valuable contribution to every phase of this project.

2. The 24 dyads were evenly distributed by social class and the sex of the children. The children's mean age was three years eight months. The recording of the conversation was made by the mothers themselves during the course of going about their everyday household activities. The categories for semantic analysis were devised by me (Hasan, 1983). A partial account of these categories will be found in Hasan (1989; 1992b; 1996b); Cloran (1989; 1994; 2000); Williams (1995; 2000).

3. Transcription conventions are as shown below:
    (1) successive numbering of messages for the current presentation
    [?abc] unintelligible; interpreted by reference to context/cotext
    [?] unintelligible; could not be interpreted at all
    [(3) abc] message (3) is surrounded by message (2)
    (ABC) contextual commentary based on cotextual evidence
    abc – message is left incomplete
    ... a pause longer than would be normal at this point
    **abc matched pairs of double asterisks to the left of some segment indicate the start of overlapping talk
    abc?** double asterisk to the right of a question indicate speaker allowed no time for response to this question

4. This is precisely the criticism one might level at progressive pedagogy in schools, where the role of the teacher is said to be that of a facilitator. This is supposed to remove control on the child's learning, so that s/he can grow as his inner self dictates. There, however, remains the problem that when education becomes facilitation, the facilitator has no way of knowing what learning it is that is being facilitated – such knowledge comes to the teacher only in the moment of evaluation, and typically at the cost of the pupil.

5. For details of semantic analysis see Hasan (1989; 1992b; 1996b); Cloran (1994; 1999); Williams (1995; 1999).

6. On realisation see Halliday (1992; 1992/2003); Hasan (1995a); Halliday and Matthiessen (1999).

10 The ontogenesis of ideology: an interpretation of mother child talk

In their introduction to Karl Marx, Bottomore and Rubel comment that Marx used the term ideology in 'different senses'. In one of these senses, ideology for Marx is a 'deliberately misleading system of ideas' (1963: 21). The sense in which I wish to use this word will differ from the former, by expunging the modifiers 'deliberately misleading'. This is not to deny that the construction of ideology is non-accidental to the extent that it arises from sustained social practices; nor is it to deny that ideologies can be nurtured deliberately in the sense of receiving a coherent-seeming philosophico-logical rationale in the uncommonsense reflections of a community. Elshtain (1981) shows how the ideology of womanhood has been so nurtured in the Western traditions; Wearing's empirical study (1984) confirms the power of that ideology, which controls women's perceptions of their role(s) in society to this day. However, ideologies live through the common everyday actions – both verbal and non-verbal – of a host of social actors who are far from thinking consciously about it. In fact, if ideology is a misleading system, then conscious deliberation, once it becomes accessible, is likely to lead to exposure and could conceivably become instrumental in introducing change. Looked at from this perspective, the most important attribute for the maintenance of ideology appears to be its socially constructed inevitability. Again, a system of ideas can definitely be misleading even while it is being supported by an over-arching, most clear-sighted-seeming analysis of social phenomena. But the very description of some analysis as 'over-arching' or 'most clear-sighted' implies a point of view. One misleading system of ideas can be replaced by another ideology, which may in its turn be revealed as a misleading system of ideas. There is no intention to make a play on words here, but in one sense, at least, ideology cannot be misleading since it leads us to the essential principles governing the social structure in which the ideology is embedded and for which it provides support. Thus it becomes diagnostic of the values that (some section of) a community lives by. For these reasons, I prefer to think of ideology as a socially constructed system of ideas which appears as if inevitable.

I shall be concerned here with the ideology of woman's work – that is to say the system of ideas that surrounds the work women do in the privacy of their homes. Of course, the ideology of woman's work can be viewed from many angles; my own focus is limited – I am interested not in how the ideology came to be constructed – i.e. what is its historical genesis in the West – but in how the constructed ideology is transmitted. And my answer to even this limited question is not a complete one, since it is based on an interpretation of mother-child talk, which is neither supplemented by father-child talk nor a first-hand observation of patterns of daily living.

The conversations which form the basis of my answer were collected from 24 mother-child dyads in and around Sydney. All mothers were born and brought up in Australia; the average age of the children at the time of recording was approximately 3 years 8 months. The breakdown of the population is presented in Table 10.1.

	(A) Low education; manual occupation		(B) High education; specialised job	
	Cell 1	Cell 2	Cell 1	Cell 2
Child	3	3	3	3
Female	3	3	3	3
Male	6	6	6	6

Table 10.1: The apprentices to ideology

It does not appear necessary to explain the table further: for the present discussion the sub-classification of the population is not highly relevant. The data consists of natural conversation between the child and the mother and was collected for an ARGS project to examine the role of mother's talk in establishing ways of learning. Working on this project with me are Carmel Cloran and David Butt, though I alone am responsible for the views presented here. The recordings were made by the mothers themselves in their home environment. The mothers were requested to turn on the tape recorder whenever they felt that they were engaged in a chat with the child in question; no other requirements were made. On average each dyad took about six weeks to complete six hours of recording time, which, on average, yielded four hours of recorded tape.

I should like to draw attention to the suitability of such conversation as a means of understanding adult preconceptions. To a large extent, all casual conversation is revealing about the shared assumptions of a community, precisely because of its unselfconscious, casual nature which masks its deeper social purposes and gives it the air of an activity that is directed toward nothing but the achievement of talk itself. But casual conversation between a close adult and a very young child is especially revealing in that often the very basic assumptions necessary for the continuity of talk have to be spelt out. With such young children, the comfort of sharing the same language does not go so far as to produce the assurance that the other 'understands' the sayings as the adult speaker does. Garfinkle (1967) provides several examples of the breakdown of conversation in which an experimenting student deliberately displayed inability to understand another's 'perfectly ordinary utterances'. Example 1, is taken from his book to illustrate the point:

Example 1

(S) Hi, Ray. How is your girlfriend feeling?
(E) What do you mean, 'How is she feeling'?
Do you mean physical or mental?
(S) I mean how is she feeling? What's the matter with you?
(He looked peeved.)
(E) Nothing. Just explain a little clearer what do you mean?
(S) Skip it. How are your Med School applications coming?
(E) What do you mean, 'How are they'?
(S) You know what I mean.
(E) I really don't.
(S) What's the matter with you? Are you sick?
(Garfinkel 1967; p 42)

But this posture of 'you know what I mean' cannot always be adoped in regard to very young children's questions. In the following extract Kristy (3;7) is discussing with her mother the death of a moth whose wings had got steamed when it flew too low over a hot drink. The child is deeply concerned and on the verge of tears, because she believes ...*it wouldn't have wanted to die.* In the midst of this serious discussion, her attention is distracted by her younger sister's behaviour, who is busying herself with tearing some paper. This leads to the exchange below:

Example 2[1]

C: That's (? broken)...Rebecca teared it.
M: She want what?
C: Teared.

M: Oh. It's O.K.
C: Why's it O.K.?
M: Pete just brought it home for me to have a look but he didn't need to keep it.
C: Why didn't he?
M: Oh. Oh I don't know. (LAUGHING) I don't think he needed to keep it...
He'd probably read it already.
C: Why he probably read it already?
M: Um I think if he had wanted to keep it and he needed it he would have told me to put it somewhere safe. But he put it there which is the place where we put stuff we don't really care about. That's why I think that he didn't need it. Either he'd already read it or he didn't want it.[1]

It is only at this point, that presumably satisfied, Kristy returns to the question of life and death which had preoccupied her earlier. Probings by children, then, produce the near optimal environment for an explanation of those very phenomena which we consider most ordinary, most inevitable and most self-evident.

And there is an important difference between Garfinkle's experimenting students and young children; unlike the students, the children are not being metatextual: they are actually engaged in constructing the text of their immediate culture. So talk becomes a vehicle of learning the taken-for-granted aspects of lived reality. Of course this is not the only vehicle. The data shows the acuteness of children's observation. When Alison (3;5) helps mother make coffee, she observes her own actions, performed under the mother's close supervision; so much coffee per cup, so much sugar and then hot water and then milk. *Ah* says Alison, *milk after. Yeah* says the mother, *You gotta pour milk after.*

With so much listening and talking, so much confirming by observation, the picture of woman's work is constructed for the child through the innumerable small momenta of everyday life. I have chosen to talk about this aspect precisely because across the spectrum of my data, this picture emerges with a certain degree of homogeneity – a homogeneity that the data may very well not possess in some other respects. This explains my earlier comment that the sub-classification of the population is irrelevant, where the study of the ideology of woman's work from this data is concerned. It does not matter which section of the population the mothers belong to, they share similar views about woman's work. While not every dyad presents each of the features I discuss below, each displays some combination and none contradicts any of the features. So while the total picture is a synthesis, I believe it respects the mothers' views as displayed in their talk. Let me first spell out the four most outstanding kinds of things that these women with small children, with or without husbands, take in their stride every day of the week, every week of the year.

(i) First, every woman is an *instructor*. Quite irrespective of her place in the social hierarchy, every woman taking care of a small child is exposed to innumerable searching questions. These questions cover an enormous range: who looked after me when you were a baby, why is Johnny fatter than me, why are those clouds grey, why do you put parsley in water, don't birds talk like us, how does the lavatory chain work and do chickens have knees? Now there is no implication at all that the answers are always accurate, or that they are always provided. Sometimes questions get lost in the flow of conversation; sometimes they are answered tautologically, but it can be claimed with confidence that in every mother-child dyad there is evidence of effort to explain. I suspect that the differences will lie in kinds of explanation offered and the frequency with which they are offered.

(ii) Every woman is a *labourer*. As I remarked earlier, the setting for these conversations is everyday life. The conversations construct the picture of these women as busy around the house with cooking and washing, getting the kids to bed, getting them ready for school and ministering to their needs. Outside the house, there is the shopping and the garden.

(iii) Every woman provides *emotional support* to the child/children in the house; this can take the form of praise, concern over a physical hurt or the dispensation of justice if it is needed.

(iv) And finally every woman is a *companion* to her child. By companionship I mean that the mothers put time and effort into activities which are primarily for the diversion of the young child, participating in colouring pictures, playing with trains and car sets, joining in the football or the cricket game – whatever is going on.

The nature of my data does not permit me to make any systematic comments on the activities of these women in relation to other members – particularly, the adults of the household. No doubt mothers talk to other members of the family, both adults and other children; no doubt, they have friends and neighbours. And, no doubt, apart from these four aspects listed above, there is more to every woman's work. The reason I restrict myself to just these four aspects lies in the fact that proof of the mother's engaging in these four types of activities can be provided directly from my data and, for the present discussion, I am limiting myself entirely to what is in the data, ignoring other parameters whose relevance I would definitely accept.

Now, if the findings were limited to simply a construction of these four facets of every woman's work, there would be nothing remarkable. It is common knowledge that women do these things and we, perhaps, need no research project to show that this is how it is. Let me now shift my focus, by raising the question, how do these women present themselves and their work to the children, in the course of their talk?

Let us first look at the instructor role. There is not one instance in the entire data where a mother can be found to claim credit for having solved a problem, for having worked out, even cooperatively with the child, an explanation to some phenomenon. On the contrary, there is evidence that, at least some mothers, explicitly emphasise the picture of 'silly mummy'. Here is Helen's mother in Example 3. She is a remarkably capable woman and the evidence of her ability to think on her toes can be found across her conversations with Helen. Here she is finding out what Helen did at preschool that day.

Example 3

C: Play with the playdough.
M: And what else?
C: And you forgot my painting!
M: Did you do a painting? ... You didn't tell me ...
C: Well you should've looked at the [?] on those cupboards.
M: Oh I know but I'm such a forgetful mother you should know by now you have to tell my you have to remind me a about these things because I – my brain doesn't work too well sometimes.
C: Mum.
M: Mm?
C: All you have to do is tell the teachers if you forget.
M: Trouble is I forget to tell the teachers.

This is not an isolated instance; nor is the 'silly mummy' picture limited to one class. Of course, a simple rationale for such behaviour is easy to find: it makes the child feel superior and, after all, should it not be regarded as simply a 'game', a 'pretence' whose aim is to boost the child's ego? I have no clear-cut answer to this question, but I cannot help wondering if such behaviour is totally unrelated to the popular picture of woman as somewhat lacking in intellect. In reviewing the *Fontana Biographical Companion to Modern Thought* (Bullock and Woodings) for *The Sunday Times* (2 October 1983), John Vincent pointed out how thinking as an intellectual enterprise is seen by the authors to be the preserve of the white male:

> Thinking, it appears, is what white males do. The most numerous people, the Indians and Chinese, do not figure. The Japs seem to get along splendidly without thinkers. All three lag behind speakers of Portuguese.

> As for women, they are dragged in, as it were, by the hair, Iris Murdock and Bessie Smith, Queen of the Blues, for instance. Less than one per cent of modern thought is female. Women are good at writing novels and being entertainers, but then they always were, back to Scheherzade.

Of course, we could shrug off this publication as an example of the authors' unthinking bias, but two points appear relevant. First, there is very close relationship between unthinking biases and the maintenance of ideology and secondly, centuries and decades of unthinking biases, codified in scholarly tomes do represent that which by and large becomes 'fact'. 'Truth', we have the saying 'will out'. But, whose truth? And seen from what point of view? I do not think that it is fanciful to claim that it is codified 'fact' generated by unthinking biases that speaks every day out of the mouths of the mothers. In my view, this 'fact' does not fall on fallow ground. If language plays any role in the development of consciousness – and I believe it does – then, it must shape the consciousness of the apprentices to ideology, the mothers' children.

Equally important is the question, is there anyone else in the house we might say to the child, 'clever mummy'? My data of course provides answer here. But it does have Julian's mother saying to him, *I don't know ... you must be clever... Maybe you got it from your Dad,* where it refers to the child's cleverness. Across the data, irrespective of the family's socioeconomic location, with the exception of single-parent families, mothers do build an image of the fathers as the one who should know, as the one who is resourceful in finding practical solutions, as the one who is the locus of intellectual authority. Isn't it quite obvious that organising 14 meals a week, for every week of the year, for a family of three or more requires no practical organisation? And whoever heard of the need for 'rational thinking' in answering children's questions? Would you believe that knowing the names of all the herbs and spices is an accomplishment of the same order as knowing the name of all the tools in a carpentry set? Adrian's mother knows about the herbs anyway, but she also reels off the name and function of all but two items from a carpentry tool set. So she tell Adrian, *Daddy'll know the names of them,* which is more or less echoed by the child, *Yes, he'll know all the names. Daddy'll know.* I would like to draw attention particularly to the near-certainty of the mother's prediction. It may be that Adrian's father, a banker by trade, is also an accomplished handyman and the near-certainty of her prediction through the use of the auxiliary *will* (in reduced form) is justified. However, the interesting fact remains that in talking thus of their husbands, the mothers do not make use of the modals of lower orders of probability; we find *Daddy'll/will* but, in such environment, we do not find *Dad might/may/could/perhaps be able to.* Let me hasten to add that there is no implication that excellence cannot be shared by both partners; I simply do not have the data to confirm or refute this view. It is, however, remarkable that through thousands of transcribed messages these women's assessment of their own accomplishment is meager in their own wordings, while, in many cases, their handling of the children's questions is relatively a contradiction of this assessment.

If the mother's presentation of her instructor role is muted, that of her role as labourer carries certain ambiguities which, at the least, are interesting to note. There are various strands to this. First, there is the view that the exertion and toil in the house are not work. Example 4 is a dialogue between Alison and her mother.

Example 4

C: Is Pop home?
M: No... They're all out. They're all at work.
C: Bob and Mark are working.
M: Yes, Bob's at work. Mark's at work. Everybody's at work.
C: I not at work.
M: No, you're only little.
C: Youse at works?
M: I don't work. I look after you...
C: Who's playing with Pammie?
M: Nobody. Who'd look after you if Mummy went to work...eh?

Not all mothers are as explicit about the non-work nature of their work at home; the view ranges from this to the mother in group B who comments that the child's grandmother does not babysit her anymore because the mother is no longer working. Small wonder, that in the *Macquarie Dictionary*, there is not one sense of worker that fits woman as a worker in her house. This definition is reproduced as Example 5 below:

Example 5

WORKER (2003)
1. one who or that which works: *he's a good steady worker*.
2. one employed in manual industrial labour.
3. an employee, esp. as contrasted with a capitalist or a manager.
4. one who works in a specified occupation: *office workers, research workers*.
5. (in the U.S.S.R.) a citizen, excluding the peasants and members of the army or navy.
6. Entomol. the sterile or infertile female of bees, wasps, ants, or termites, which does the work of the colony.
7. Also working girl. colloq. a prostitute.

The nearest a woman engaged in woman's work comes to is sense 5, but we are not in the USSR; or to 6, but women with offspring are obviously not sterile or infertile, even though they may be busy as bees! There is then the paradox that when, like David's mother, one employs someone to look after the children, then that person is worker, but the person whom she replaces is not a worker! It would be a mistake to take Example 5 as an attack on the *Macquarie Dictionary*. It is no part of a dictionary to moralise; its business is to record the usage of the community. For the community, in general, woman's work is just not work, as the definition of 'work' in the same dictionary will show. By these 'fashions of speaking' (Whorf, 1956) whose motivation ultimately traces itself to the principles of the community's economic organisation, a woman working in the privacy of her home is consigned to the grey space between the 'dole-bludger' and the 'honest worker', who brings home a 'decent pay', for his/her physical exertion. She is not even 'self-employed'; she is 'house-wife'. The assumption is not lagging far behind that what a woman works at in her house is her private business, without any more consequence for the life of the community than you or me polishing our shoes, or weeding our own private patch of the garden.

The second strand to which I would draw attention is the presentation of the work as uninteresting. In Example 6 Cameron's mother is decidedly trying to get him off her hands; Cameron is interested in staying back to watch the cartoons, but note how much more is passing between the two interactants:

Example 6

M: [? You'll probably] have to get changed into your work clothes later, because Daddy's going to the tip.
C: What for?
M: Daddy needs a helper.
C: Oh.
M: When he goes to the tip.
C: What?
M: Daddy needs a helper when he goes to the tip.
C: Oh I want to play on my bike. I don't want to go to the tip.
M: You do?
C: I want to stay here [?] ...
M: You haven't been to the tip [? With your Daddy] for a long time.
C: No
M: It'd be much more interesting going to the tip than helping Mummy do the Vacuuming.
C: Mm.
M: Because that's a boring job isn't it?
C: I have to stay home to watch my cartoon.

Now it is true that Cameron's mother wants him out of her way; but this is definitely not the whole of the story. For lack of space I have not included the remaining part of this dialogue covering about a page and a half, in which the mother points out to Cameron that he is behaving like Piggie Won't, whose brothers were adventurous, went out into the world and had fun while Piggie Won't, staying at home, missed out on everything worth doing. The same fate, she suggests, awaits Cameron unless he gets out to help Daddy at the tip instead of helping Mum clean the house. Kristy's mother who shows exemplary patience and a sensitive understanding of her own children's needs, tells Kristy:

> *I think that you probably don't play with little kids because they're not very interesting most of the time*

Cameron's mother discusses with him the various professions that he might take up when he's big. The fire brigade, the police force and the construction and building trades are discussed in some detail. Cameron appears to work with a paradigm: if I can't be this, what can I be? As the possibilities of those professions which presently engage his attention are exhausted, he asks at least twice, *mum, what could I be in the home, in the house*? Is it at all significant that Cameron's mother does not even 'hear' this question?

The household labour is a fact that impinges upon people in the house all the time – but it impinges upon them as a necessity, not as something that could ever be enjoyed. And this is the third strand.

Pete's mother says:

> *I have to take in laundry*

Daniel's mother echoes:

> *I just have to go and get the washing in now, I'm afraid*

Sam's mother explains her tired yawn:

> *I had to get up twice last night because Johnny kept crying*

And, of course, many of the mothers say at one time or another,

> *I have to fix the tea/dinner now*

The modals of necessity and obligation come into full play. This is definitely not the only environment in which they appear, but this is one environment in which they are used with a high frequency.

Finally, woman's work is presented as hard work, but in an oblique manner. It is an interesting aspect of this presentation that such comments on the part of the mother occur unexpectedly and fleetingly in the middle of some other activity, the course of which is hardly disturbed by such admissions. In Example 7 Julie's mother has been bathing her, playing with her daughter's toes and letting the daughter play with her own fingers. Julie is trying to get her mother's fingers soaped and washed, she requests the mother to lay them down flat in the bath.

Example 7

C: 'Cause the water's [? Low] now... you've got strong glue that one.
M: Yes, I have rather, Haven't I? Oh, they're beautiful. Thank you.
C: Up.
M: Oh, Mummy's fingers are so tired tonight.
C: You can put them down.
M: They've been very busy fingers, haven't they?

Child and mother continue playfully as if the tired fingers had never been mentioned. There is no point in multiplying such examples, but of the 24 mothers nearly three quarters mention the fact of tiredness at some time. Significantly, the mother's tiredness never appears to affect the flow of activity. Whether it is 'work' in the 'true' sense or not, it still 'has to be done'.

Moving now to the third aspect of woman's work in the home – that of providing emotional support, I come to a finding that was completely unexpected. Many of the mothers express the need for such support from their children – it is as if, the actual roles were being reversed through these sayings. In Example 8 it is Karen's mother who seeks this support:

Example 8

M: Oh I've got a bad cold.
C: Oh.
M: Are you going to look after me ... eh?
C: Oh.
M: Oh ah, sorry. (COUGHING AGAIN)
C: I can't when I have to go to school.
M: But you don't have to go to school for a few days.
C: I know.
M: You going to look after me?
C: Yeah.
M: O.K.

In Example 9, it is Nathan's mother who seeks such support and the child's bewilderment appears quite obvious:

Example 9

M: I have to lie down and put my leg in the air. Will you look after me?
C: No.
M: You won't! (SURPRISED)
C: Why?
M: You won't look after me?
C: Where are you – where are you gonna do it?
M: in the loungeroom [I think]
C: No, do it here

On the question of companionship, the data presents nothing significant, apart from the fact that mothers are lavish in the expression of appreciation whenever the child helps in the house – this happens more often with girls than with boys. So what conclusions can we draw about the ways that mothers present themselves and their work to their children?

I feel that there is a tension here. The child's active experience of happenings in the house must, in some sense, create the idea that mothers are busy; that their 'non-work' is in some sense 'work'. But the evaluation of that which claims that mother's physical efforts and attention is a different matter. With but a few possible exceptions, most human action is neither inherently good nor bad; it neither inherently merits prestige nor stigma, as Durkheim (1964) suggested; nor is that evaluation rationally commensurate with the benefit that might accrue from human action to (some sections of) the community. There is, thus, an essential arbitrariness about values attached to human actions. I shall comment briefly on this point below. Here let me say simply that while language is not the only means for (re)producing the values attached to human action, it is, nonetheless, one of the most powerful instruments for the purpose. If this premise is accepted, then, from the example of mothers' sayings presented here, it would appear inevitable that the very young child, whose primary domain of experience is the home, would imbibe a view of woman's work in which it has the status of a toil imposed by necessity, a physical exertion which is not work, a tiresome enterprise which is inherently uninteresting and definitely lacking in demands on the higher functions of human intellect. As the young children walk out of their homes, where the foundations of their social being are laid, they are more than passively prepared to acquiesce in a confirmation of this early, perhaps not yet well articulated view, which will be strengthened to a clear certainty, by experiences outside the house. The evidence from my data suggests, then, that the ontogenesis of ideology occurs early, if the ideology is to take hold. And the mechanisms for this ontogenesis are the habitual forms of communication, wherein the taken-for-granted nature of the social world is transmitted. A dominant ideology has to receive support at every level of human experience to survive, otherwise the fabric of inevitability is torn and glimpses of an alter-ideology are afforded which have the potential of undermining the credibility of the dominant ideology. Whatever one's reservations against or enthusiasms for the 'feminist' discourse, it certainly has performed the function of rupturing the credibility of one of the most dominant, most universally shared ideologies.

Seen from this point of view, the distinction between deep and surface phenomena, so fashionable in today's academic discussions appears entirely unconvincing. There is no essential discontinuity between what human beings do, which includes what they say (Halliday, 1973; 1978) and the social structure is which they have a locus. The social structure comes into being and is continuously enacted through what human beings are doing, have done and will do. It would, however, be naïve to suppose that the ideology of woman's work can be changed simply by changing the habitual forms of maternal communication. Such an implication is nowhere intended in this paper. Habitual forms of communication spring from a perception of what appears socially relevant. There is thus a logical contradiction in entertaining the belief that the habitual forms of communication can be consistently and successfully changed without other accompanying changes; it is my understanding that this is one of the arguments Bernstein (1971) developed some time ago. Clearly this argument holds not because forms of communication, as many other human acts, display only "the regularities and complexity perceived on the surface of the social world" (Sharp, 1981); rather, it is because ideologies, like other social facts, are orchestrated simultaneously at multiple levels of human existence. For example, the ideology of woman's work reaches out beyond the house into the market place where labour is sold for wages and thus turned into 'work'. And no doubt that behaviour, in its turn, reaches out to other areas of socioeconomic organisation. The values attached to the actions of women in the privacy of their homes appear arbitrary – i.e. unmotivated – only so long as the wider context is ignored: within the four walls of the house, it appears extraordinary to think of woman's work as non-work, but as it makes contact with a wage-based economy, which operates in most societies today, its non-work nature is legitimised. One important reason why woman's work is not work lies in the fact that, of itself, it does not create the kind of economic independence granted to most wage-earners. At this stage of the analysis, the standard dictionaries are not 'misleading', they are simply recording what we actually do. It seems to me that none of these levels of analysis is just a 'surface' behind which hides the 'ultimate truth'. The examination of ideology – and of social phenomena in general – requires a spiral model, rather than a box model in which the lid – the surface – is lifted to reveal the content, or the ultimate truth. Subscribing to the age-old division of the ultimate cause existing independent of the effect, we tend to be looking for the "underlying determinants of surface manifestation" (Sharp: 1981). I would suggest that Barthes' generalisation regarding the relation between 'content' and 'form' in literature can be usefully extended to the study of the social as well, so that a social phenomenon would be like "an onion, a construction of layers (or levels, or systems) whose body contains finally no heart, no kernel, no secret, no irreducible principle, nothing except the infinity of its own envelopes – which envelop nothing other than the unity of its own surfaces." (Barthes, 1971)

Rejecting, then, this dichotomy between the surface and deep, we can turn to language as a form of human action (Malinowski, 1923; 1935), which contributes, along with other semiotic systems, to the construction of the social world. A special focus on language is clearly required in the study of the onset of forms of social consciousness. This is because the location of very young children in society is ambiguous. They are not active participants in many of its processes and, at least in the early years of their life, they may be said to enter society, as it were, secondarily through their contacts with adults. In this contact many of the social systems do not impinge upon them directly, but are refracted through the adult's systems of communication, amongst which language undoubtedly has an important place, if only due to the child's early developed ability to enter into linguistic processes. In talking about the role of maternal linguistic communication in the ontogenesis of a particular ideology, I have borrowed the expression "fashions of speaking" from Whorf (1956), while the phrase 'habitual forms of communication' is derived from my reading of both Whorf and Bernstein. I believe the full import of these expressions needs to be understood to grasp their relevance to the role of language in the creation and maintenance of ideology.

Even to imply that ideology, through however many layers of the 'onion' of culture can finally be seen as language is at once claiming too much and saying too little. It is claiming too much, because of the simple fact of omission, it ignores the many nonverbal semiotic systems, whose existence side by side with language is not immarerial to the examination of ideology. The claim of a bi-unique connection between ideology and language – even though many-layer-mediated – could be valid only on the assumption that there exists a complete translatability between language and other semiotic systems. I would suggest that this assumption is questionable. To quote Foucault (1970):

> It is not that words are imperfect, or that, when confronted by the visible, they prove insuperably inadequate. Neither can be reduced to the other's terms: it is in vain that we say what we see; what we see never resides in what we say. And it is in vain that we attempt to show, by the use of metaphors, or similes, what we are saying; the space where they achieve

their splendour is not deployed by our eyes but that defined by the sequential elements of the syntax.

Vološinov (1973) voices the same position:

> None of the fundamental, specific ideological signs is replacable wholly by words. It is ultimately impossible to convey a musical composition or pictorial image adequately in words. Words cannot wholly substitute for a religious ritual; nor is there any really adequate verbal substitute for even the simplest gesture in human behaviour. To deny this would lead to the most banal rationalism and simplisticism.

Complete translatability is a myth not only across two languages, but also across the verbal and non-verbal semiotics within the same culture. To the extent that this claim is true, it would be misleading to create the impression that the examination of ideology boils down to an examination of language. Language may presuppose ideology, but, both for its genesis and its sustenance, ideology needs more than language. The semiotic potential of a culture is not equal to the semantic potential of the languages of a culture (Halliday, 1973). It appears, then, that a linguist who would aspire to throw light on the construction and maintenance of ideology, must be prepared, first, to place the verbal semiotic side by side with other semiotic systems and, secondly, to examine the ways in which the various sign systems operative within a culture, do not 'remain in isolation' from each other: but mutual support is not tantamount to mutual identity.

On the other hand, the claim that language can be shown to be entirely a purveyor of ideology does not say enough; it provides no explicit indication of how the same language can be used in the construction and maintenance of qualitatively distinct ideologies. Granted that the notion of 'same language' is theoretically problematic, still, I believe, we would wish to say that both Halliday and Chomsky use the same language for the exposition of their ideologies about language, which are miles apart from each other. It is true that if two texts by these authors are placed side by side, the lexicogrammatical analysis of the two will show them to be different; but it is equally true that any two texts by any one of these authors will show lexicogrammatical differences. So naturally there arises the question: which differences are significant for their ideologies and which are not? I believe that this question cannot be answered without some such concept(s) as 'orientation to coding' (Bernstein, 1971) or 'configurative rapport' and 'fashions or speaking' (Whorf, 1956) or 'consistency of foregrounding' (Hasan, 1984b) or 'semantic style' (Hasan, 1984c) or 'semantic drift' (Butt, 1983), without implying that each of these concepts is entirely identical. A brief discussion of at least the Whorfian notions appears necessary.

The belief is widely accepted that 'language is independent of any specific purpose' (Hjelmslev, 1961) More explicitly, by virtue of its internal design, every language has the potential of meeting any of the needs of its speakers. This is not because language is an impartial mirror of an immanent reality; rather it is because the speakers' reality is a reality largely created by language (Hasan, 1984a). This position implicit in Saussure's work (1966) is made explicit in Hjelmslev (1961) and better elaborated in Whorf's studies, who maintained that:

> the world is presented in a kaleidoscopic flux of impressions which has to be organised by our minds – and this means largely by the linguistic systems in our mind. We cut nature up – organise it into concepts and ascribe significances as we do, largely because we are parties to an agreement to organise it this way – an agreement that holds throughout our speech community and is codified in the patterns of our language. The agreement is, of course, an implicit and unstated one, *but its terms are absolutely obligatory*; we cannot talk at all except by subscribing to the organisation and classification of data which the agreement decrees.

I would draw attention to the latter half of this extract, according to which (i) the codified patterns of a language are universal to all its speakers and (ii) the flouting of these patterns is tantamount to the impossibility of talk. Had Whorf stopped at this point, he could have been accused more justifiably of a simplistic hypothesis about 'mind in the grip of language' (Bolinger, 1975). But Whorf also made an important and systematic distinction between commonsense and uncommonsense knowledge, showing how the vicissitudes of the evolution of the latter are related to commonsense knowledge constructed by everyday fashions of speaking wherein the lexicogrammatical patterns of a language assume a background status, making certain concepts of reality appear inevitably real. There is thus a qualitative difference between habitual forms of communication and communications in which one is attempting to be, as it were, metasemantic, though the latter is still not completely freed from the exigencies of the former (Halliday, 1984b). The possibility of the evolution of uncommonsense knowledge to the point where in some specific respect it runs counter to everyday reality constructed by language – e.g. the Einsteinian hypothesis – is important to Whorf's argument: it points to the tenuousness of the relationship between 'codified patterns of language' and our pro-tem 'dissections of nature'. Such tenuousness would not exist if language were a mirror of reality. At the same time the relationship between the form of language and concepts of reality accounts for the persistence of commonsense knowledge, according to which the speakers of English, for example still subscribe to a concept of time as independent of space and as an aggregate of discrete, individual moments. For example, this concept of time is validated each time we say 'each time'. Whorf argues that the concepts of reality constructed by everyday habitual forms of communication are accepted at some level of consciousness by all speakers of a language; that this tacit acceptance is essential to the possibility of talk.

If we argue that the reality constructed by the background phenomena of a language – its automatised formal patterns – is a reality specific to that language and not necessarily an account of 'how things really are', then all speakers of a language may be said to subscribe to the same ideology at some level of consciousness, in the specific sense of seeing something as inevitably so. I would suggest that this kind of general 'agreement' represents an infrastructure whose presence is a *sine qua non* for the construction of more specific ideologies, e.g. that of woman's work. But Whorf showed quite clearly that even at the most general level of analysis the characterisation of the ideology cannot be achieved by the examination of isolated lexicogrammatical patterns. He suggested that for such an examination we need the concept of configurative rapport. I believe by this expression Whorf meant the bringing together of those patterns of language which, in toto, construct a consistent semantic frame, leading to the 'deep persuasion of a principle behind phenomena'. One outstanding example of configurative rapport provided by Whorf is that which articulates the principle of objectification. Articulating this principle in SAE languages are phenomena – i.e. patterns of language – which from the point of view of lexicogrammar could only be considered heterogeneous. According to Whorf they include the number system, the tense system, the binomial pattern and the weakening of grammatical distinctions between abstract and concrete nouns. No single category here is by itself sufficient for the articulation of objectification, which can be glossed as the treatment of abstracts as if they were concrete objects with spatial extension and clear boundaries. Together they all point in the same direction. Using similar techniques, I have attempted to show (Hasan, 1984c) that in Urdu there exists a configurative rapport between patterns of reference, ellipsis and a bundle of patterns normally known as 'honorifics'. One principle this configurative rapport articulates is that of the sanctity of boundaries between hierarchies of social roles.

In my view it is this kind of analysis which is capable of indicating which linguistic patterns are relevant to the construction of which ideology and, by so doing, such an analysis can provide a basis for understanding the meaning of lexicogrammatical differences between two or more texts – i.e. whether the differences are ideologically significant or not. I do not think that we can argue that modality or suppressed negation (Kress and Hodge, 1979) or subordination (Martin and Peters, 1984) are inherently significant ideologically. Nor can we argue that all differences between texts are necessarily constitutive of different ideologies. Each one of the extracts from my data presented above differs from the others in some lexicogramatical respect(s). But if by presenting this data I have been able to construct a picture of (at least some aspects of) the ideology of woman's work, then this is because there are linguistic patterns present whose constellation articulates a consistent semantic frame. Some of theses patterns are:

(i) a contrast in attributes ascribed to male and female parent, whereby the latter carries the less desirable attribute(s);

(ii) the presence of modals of obligation in the environment of material actions e.g. *cook, wash-up, make, clean*, if the role of actor is realised by an item referring to mother;

(iii) the textually ambiguous status of the ascription of physical exhaustion to mother, which ambiguity arises from the lack of cohesive support for such items as *tired, exhausted* etc.;

(iv) the juxtaposition of work and behavioural processes e.g. *look after, take care of*, so that their equation is negated, whether explicitly or implicitly. Although a more meticulous analysis might reveal other relevant patterns, perhaps the above list is sufficient to support the claim that to the articulation of an ideology what is criterial is the constellation of a set of linguistic patterns – a configuration of patterns in rapport with each other.

But wherein does the origin of such constellation lie? If we consider language as a paradigmatic, then the system permits, certainly not all, but many combinations – which is one of the reasons why language can be independent of any specific purpose. For example, the selection of almost any modal feature is possible with material action – not only *have to wash up*, but also *can/might wash up*; contrasting with the attribute *silly* for *mummy*, is also the possibility of the attributes *clever/bright* and so on. The selection of a specific constellation of patterns cannot, then, be seen as dictated by the system of language. If a specific set of options is selected it is there because it is capable of constructing the meanings the occasion is perceived to require. This implies that the patterns in a constellation – the patterns possessing a configurative rapport – display a semantic consistency. If in the context of control, it would be odd to find an utterance such as, *I'd rather you didn't make so much noise, otherwise I'll hit you*, this is because the meanings of the two messages are not consistent with each other; threats are not consistent with the granting of personal discretion. Using Bernstein's terminology we may say the production of texts – language operating in the context of situation – requires 'coding orientation'. It is probably true that our ideas about the study of meanings have not reached the stage where the kind of semantic consistencies I have drawn attention to can be described in an explicit way. But if linguists are interested in the examination of ideologies and other important matters concerning the relationship between language and society, then such advances in the study of language as a meaning potential will have to be made. And it is my belief that when progress in this area begins, we shall need to bridge the gulf between Saussure's *langue* and *parole*, probably very much along the lines suggested by Hjelmslev (1961), Firth (1957b) and Halliday (1977b). If a specific configurative rapport – a constellation of linguistic patterns – is perceived as criterial in the context of some ideology, it is not because the system of language has forced these patterns together; its contribution lies in providing the resources. The configurative rapport comes into existence and acquires a life because of our fashions of speaking as our fashions of speaking are the bearers of our ideology. It is through these fashions of speaking that the prehension between the patterns of a configurative rapport becomes established and we come to recognise that the deployment of such and such lexicogrammatical patterns constructs such and such a grouping of meanings, which finds support through such and such of our doings and thus perpetuates an ideology which we ourselves have created through our sayings and doings. Helen's mother is far from having attempted an analysis of these phenomena, but she appears to subscribe to some such view in the following extract. Helen is helping mother wash up a saucepan lid which appears to need a lot of scrubbing:

C: You have to do it hard, don't you?
M: Mm you do, don't you, yes ...
C: Doesn't matter for you or me to do these.
M: No.
C: Because we can do it the right way, God teaches us.
M: No God doesn't teach you things like that, it's mummy's job to teach you things like that.

Notes

1 Transcription conventions:
 M = mother
 C = child
 [?] = unintelligible
 [? + item(s)] = item(s) not clearly intelligible, best guess in view of contextual, co-textual and phonological clues
 ( ) = encloses contextual comment, not evident from wording alone
 large square bracket left open covers overlapping speech by the dyad.

Section 3

Language and society: conflict or co-genesis?

Editor's Introduction

In the two chapters in this section, Professor Hasan discusses Pierre Bourdieu's view of language. Chapter 11 is *The Disempowerment Game: Bourdieu on language* (1998). Chapter 12 is the response to those commenting on that critique, *Bourdieu on Linguistics and Language: a response to my commentators* (2000).

Drawing mainly but not exclusively on Bourdieu's *The Production and Reproduction of Legitimate Language* (1992: 43-65), Professor Hasan organises her discussion around the following four interrelated arguments (Chapter 11):

that Bourdieu's view of linguistics and his reading of Saussure's text are, both, 'monocular'. To the extent that these limited readings are presented as definitive, they are misleading;

that Bourdieu's view of language as a semiotic is akin to that of a formal linguist's, such as, say, Chomsky; it fails to appreciate crucial features of language as a semiotic system;

that his 'spontaneous socio/linguistics' is largely equal to what Saussure called 'external linguistics'; since external linguistics, like internal linguistics, is only half the story, it fails to present a convincing model of the relations of language and society;

that if Bourdieu's view of language is accepted as the point of departure for pedagogic action, its deficiencies will inevitably result in a less than satisfactory programme for literacy education, denying pedagogic action any role as a liberating force.

Bourdieu dismisses the discipline of linguistics as a whole on the basis of the formalist caricature of language as 'an entirely homogeneous invariant object,' which in Bourdieu's view, 'simply entails equating it with dominant and 'legitimate' language at the cost of ignoring the conditions of linguistic domination' (Chapter 11). As Professor Hasan explains, her critique of Bourdieu is prompted less by his slighting of those working outside of formalist framework than by the ensuing trivialisation of the role of literacy in education:

> A critique of this kind is urgently required as an essential step in clearing the ground in the 'great literacy debate'. I believe that some of the most pressing problems in the examination of literacy as significant pedagogic action are rendered invisible if the formalist conception of language is treated as the only possible one. These problems do not concern simply the domain thought of as language education *per se*, i.e., curricula and classroom practices; they implicate, in the first instance, ideas about the relations of language and society, and beyond that, to views on whether pedagogic action could function as a *liberating force*. (cf. Bourdieu and Passeron, 1977)

A comparison can be drawn between Bourdieu and Bernstein, both eminent sociologists, both of whom recognised 'the pathology of the pedagogic system'. However, unlike Bernstein, whose 'interest in language rests on a clearly enunciated conception of a dialectic between the social and the semiotic,' Bourdieu 'downplays the role of the linguistic semiotic in the evolution of the social' (Chapter 12). Lacking 'the clear enunciation of a theory which grants legitimacy to the introduction of the semiotic – and therefore the linguistic – perspective into the social and of the social into the semiotic/linguistic,' Bourdieu's sociology is hindered from contributing to a better understanding of the goals or processes of language education (Chapter 12).

The processes of teaching and learning entail the exchange of meaning, which serves as 'a specific kind of abstract tool for the development of the consciousness of those involved in the processes'. Viewing the processes of education and literacy as equal is tantamount to accepting the centrality of language across the curriculum, prompting Professor Hasan to call for a view of language which highlights its 'meaning making character' (Chapter 11).

11 The disempowerment game: Bourdieu on language

it should be possible to point to a specific event and say: it was at such and such a point that everything went wrong. But I have not found such a moment or such a cause although I have sought hard and long for it.

(Achebe's *Ikem* quoted in Gordimer, 1995: 76)

1 Introduction

It would be a fascinating academic exercise to trace the motivations underlying the vicissitudes of the 'new' discourse on literacy which began somewhere around the middle of the 20th century as a concern with the teaching and learning of reading/writing in schools[1], but which has now in the 1990s transformed itself into a discourse on literacy in a sense that goes far beyond those initial concerns. While reading/writing in the conventional sense of the terms are generally taken as central to the meaning of the term, the notion of 'literacy' has long surpassed the simpler issues of the calibration of the two distinct modalities – the vocal-aural and the graphic-visual – for access to linguistic forms[2]. It is probably true to say that for many educators today the term has become almost synonymous with the processes of education itself, forming a significant element of what Bourdieu and Passeron (1977) refer to as 'pedagogic action'.

This elasticity of the term creates something of a dilemma. On the one hand, the contested nature of the concept calls for an identification of one's position in this debate. On the other, the many ambiguities, myths and controversies that surround claims about its 'true' meaning make such an identification problematic[3]. To identify my own position I propose to side-step this troubled terrain by simply referring to my own interpretation of the term (Hasan, 1996a) according to which literacy is the practice of using the resources of language for making sense – for exchanging meanings. It is an ongoing process of semiotic development whose culmination consists in enabling the activity of reflection on the discourses prevalent in one's society, including reflection on the social and semiotic conditions for the occurrence of these discourses; on the social bases of their legitimation; on the structuring of their content, both ideational and interpersonal; and on the differentially valued possibilities of textual forms as variant realisation of some specific material-semiotic action. In short, this view of literacy integrates reflection on literacy as an essential part of the process of becoming literate. As reflection, it would differ from folk perceptions of discursive prowess (such as are reported in anthropological accounts; see for example Frake, 1964; 1972) by being self-conscious and analytic rather than simply intuitive and subjective, with the implication that 'reflection literacy' as proposed in Hasan (1996a) assumes the development of writing as indispensable[4].

This view of literacy suggests a Vygotskian understanding of the relations between language use and human consciousness. It is also in agreement with the current tendency to see the term as largely synonymous with education. To equate the processes of literacy with those of education is to affirm not only the centrality of language across the curriculum, but also to think of the processes of teaching/learning as essentially the exchange of meanings and to think of this exchange of meanings as a specific kind of abstract tool for the development of the consciousness[5] of those involved in such processes. It seems to me that the acceptance of this set of equations calls for a view of language which would highlight its meaning-making character. Surprisingly, though, this meaningful view of language is often absent from the literacy debate, where the conception of language tends to be based on the sort of theory described once by Firth[6] (1950/1957: 181) as one which 'leads to static structural formalism, to mechanical structures, to mechanical materialism in linguistics'. The tacit acceptance of an idea of language as nothing but (meaningless) form is all the more remarkable when it comes to us from educational sociology, whose discourse on language often begins as, for example, in the case of Bourdieu (1990; 1991), with trenchant critiques of 'the' linguist's myopic view of language.

This paper is intended as a critique of that conception of language which a certain variety of educational sociology buys – perhaps, unwittingly – from formal linguistics. A critique of this kind is urgently required as an essential step in clearing the ground in the 'great literacy debate'. I believe that some of the most pressing problems in the examination of literacy as significant pedagogic action are rendered invisible if the formalist conception of language is treated as the only possible one. These problems do not concern simply the domain thought of as language education *per se*, i.e., curricula and classroom practices; they implicate, in the first instance, ideas about the relations of language and society and beyond that, to views on whether pedagogic action could function as a *liberating force* (cf. Bourdieu and Passeron, 1977). This wide reach of the problems justifies a close reading of authorities on educational sociology.

There are obviously different conceptions of language even within the field of educational sociology. This necessitates a more precise identification of the object of my critique. I could, of course, talk simply about 'the' educational sociologist; this would be in keeping with the tradition set by Bourdieu (1990; 1991) who in his critique of current ideas about language typically refers to 'the' linguist and to 'linguistics' as a whole. But perhaps Bourdieu would be the first to point out that this has the disadvantage of *totalising* the object of investigation; it ascribes to the field a mythical unity by effacing all evidence of conflict, with the result that the less privileged paradigms become doubly invisible. Unfortunately, this is what Bourdieu's account of 'linguistics' does for that discipline: the linguistics that his reader ever hears about from Bourdieu is infected by a multitude of malaise – and how could it not be since this is precisely the reason for its being chosen? Anyone reasonably familiar with the field named 'linguistics' knows that, contrary to the impression Bourdieu's discourse conveys, there is not and there never has been, any such thing as 'the linguist' or even 'structural linguistics', much less 'the' field of linguistics as an undifferentiated unified whole. Ironically, this disregard of conflict and contestation in Bourdieu's discourse on linguistics runs parallel precisely to what Bourdieu finds most objectionable in linguistics: 'the' linguist's error lies in his idea of what constitutes the object of his enquiry; he totalises language, treating it as an entirely homogeneous invariant object and this in Bourdieu's view simply entails equating it with dominant and 'legitimate' language at the cost of ignoring the conditions of linguistic domination. I will try to avoid such pitfalls in my own discourse by providing a more precise identification of the object of my critique. My focus will be on the view of language presented and/or implied in the sociology of Pierre Bourdieu: more precisely, I draw mainly on 'the production and reproduction of legitimate language' (Bourdieu, 1991: 43–65), though I shall occasionally refer to other sources as well.

There are good reasons for choosing to comment on Bourdieu's conception of language. At some point or other, language is mentioned in the writings of most sociologists, but sustained engagement with language is quite rare. Bourdieu's discourse is exceptional both in its incisive sociological analysis and in the extent to which it has concerned itself with language. Certainly, as is well recognised, language is a crucial element in Bernstein's sociological theory as well. His interest in language rests on a clearly-enunciated conception of a dialectic between the social and the semiotic: he certainly does not conceive of language as a meaningless formalism, into which somehow social realities/nuances are poured[7]. The main attraction of this theoretical framework has been its clarification of the details of the part language plays in the production and reproduction of society. And to the best of my knowledge, Bernstein has never professed to tell 'the' linguist how to do a sociopolitically correct linguistics. Bourdieu by contrast does precisely that; and to his credit, his penetrating sociological gaze combined with his rhetoric achieves effects of a kind which numerous volumes of sociolinguistics put together might fail to do. For this, 'the' linguist must be grateful – even if the grateful linguist is not very likely to be the one whom Bourdieu so relentlessly castigates for his defective view of language. That linguist, I suggest, rests secure in the certainty of his unassailably correct position.

There is, of course, a flip side to Bourdieu's phenomenal success in the field of sociology. For the past so many years post-modernism has been telling us that the author is dead and meanings are not constrained by such unnecessary and mundane things as forms of locution[8] (Rosenau, 1991). This may be so, particularly where one expert's reading of another expert's locutions is concerned[9]. But experience of academia provides no evidence at all to support the view that authorial authority is altogether extinct: the authority of selected authors remains powerful and it can hardly be denied that Bourdieu is just such an authority. So when he sets out to expose the counterfeit sovereignty of linguistics (cf. Bourdieu, 1991: 32) so as to free sociology from its domination (Bourdieu, 1991: 37), it is not surprising[10] that the authority of his voice as a sociologist-critic lends credibility to his pronouncements on language and linguistics: given the conventions of academic discourse, his authority in one field certifies his views as legitimate on any intellectual enterprise. Even if Bourdieu presents a picture of 'the' linguist which is something like a caricature, or an account of 'linguistics' which is far removed from the practices of many linguists, it is quite likely to be heralded as a masterly revelation. This places an immense burden on anyone wishing to point out that Bourdieu's own conception of language is in many crucial respects less than viable; that his own judgment of some linguistic model or some linguist is open to question – in short, that there exist alternative readings of an author or a field, which are perhaps more justifiable than his. However, by the same token the critique of Bourdieu is an enterprise worth undertaking on the principle that the greater the authority of the author, the greater the obligation on the reader to question the views.

My decision to examine Bourdieu's view of language is not actuated by a desire to salvage 'the sovereign discipline' of linguistics (Bourdieu, 1991: 32), or to shore up its 'intellectual imperialism whereby a particular model of language could assume a paradigmatic status in the social sciences as a whole' (Thompson, 1991: 3). I accept without hesitation that linguistic models lack perfection: they have never been perfect in the past nor are they ever likely to be – what business have models with perfection, anyway? But even granting the imperfection of linguistic models, it has to be said that the use of a linguistic model by social scientists has often been based on less than sound understanding. This is not something any thoughtful linguist would welcome: the propagation of a linguistic model on the basis of only a partial understanding – Levi Strauss being one example of the phenomenon – is, in the long run, more likely to bring 'the' linguist's empire into disrepute than enhance its grandeur. Then, again, the perception of the usefulness of the concepts and/or methodology of some discipline – to use a less loaded expression than 'intellectual imperialism' or 'domination' – depends less on that discipline's unilateral declaration of imperialistic presumptions than on what Langer has described as a 'productive' concept – not in the sense of a *panacea*, but a concept that happens to meet some need that is felt rightly or wrongly by some scholars at some given moment in the history of some enterprise. If at any time linguistics has been found to be in the position of having acquired control over a substantial part of the academic market, this probably happened less because of its active efforts at imperial encroachments than because others, impelled by their own desires, led by their own visions, were attracted into investing in its shares![11] With these introductory comments I turn to the task in hand. The four issues I would like to discuss in this paper may be restated as follows:

(i) that Bourdieu's view of linguistics and his reading of Saussure's text are, both, 'monocular'. To the extent that these limited readings are presented as definitive, they are misleading;

(ii) that Bourdieu's view of language as a semiotic is akin to that of a formal linguist's, such as, say, Chomsky; it fails to appreciate crucial features of language as a semiotic system;

(iii) that his 'spontaneous socio/linguistics' is largely equal to what Saussure called 'external linguistics'; since external linguistics, like internal linguistics, is only half the story, it fails to present a convincing model of the relations of language and society;

(iv) that if Bourdieu's view of language is accepted as the point of departure for pedagogic action, its deficiencies will inevitably result in a less than satisfactory programme for literacy education, denying pedagogic action any role as a liberating force.

From a narrow perspective only the last of these points might appear relevant to the literacy debate. However, it is no secret that the disempowerment game played in non-egalitarian societies – which is to say in any society we have ever known – receives considerable support from the practices of the educational system. The ease with which language education in particular can be conscripted in the production and reproduction of patterns of disempowerment in a society makes both the modelling of language and the details of language education programmes highly sensitive areas. Underlying every language education programme is some view of language. That very often this view of language is a taken for granted view, seemingly never in need of being explicitly debated or discussed, suggests that it is a dominant view of language, which voices official ideology. This, as Bourdieu himself points out (see Section 3 below), is essentially what gives the imprimatur of legitimacy to the language education programmes[12]. There is no reason to suppose that those who are keen to preserve official ideology would wish to foreground the manner in which language acts as a means of semiotic mediation in the development of human consciousness. While it is true that the impetus for social change cannot be located in any one single factor, which is another way of saying that *each factor has some part to play*, the less visible the role of language in the development of consciousness and the less clear the relation of this to change in societies, the easier it is to maintain the *status quo*. This line of reasoning suggests that all four claims should receive attention and I shall address all four claims beginning with Bourdieu's view of 'the' linguist and 'linguistics'.

2 Bourdieu's idea of 'the' linguist's idea of language

The most economical way of presenting my reading of Bourdieu's view of language seems to be to recapitulate his criticisms of 'the' linguist. These point eloquently to what is wrong with the conception of language in linguistics, thereby implying how the field might be redeemed. As a linguist I am interested in making clear to the reader Bourdieu's ideas on how language works – what are its elements and what part they play in the production of a message. Here his comments on Saussure, his critique of the practices of 'the' discipline of linguistics, as well as his characterisations of 'official' language will be important because they reveal directly or indirectly his image of language.

2.1 The misleading map of linguistics: the diminishing contours of *parole*

If one were forced to identify one single basic reason for Bourdieu's discontent with linguistics, the pride of place would go to the steps linguistics took to achieve what Bourdieu has described as an 'appearance of scientificity' (1991: 33)[13], an ambition to act as a 'social physics'. From this flowed the principles whereby *langue*, to the exclusion of *parole*, became the object of study in linguistics while *parole* was to be set aside or at best to be studied as peripheral/external to core linguistics. But did Saussure model himself in the image of the physicist? Here is what one linguist, Firth (1950/1957: 179), had to say about the inspiration behind Saussure's 'scientific pretensions' which led to the elevation of *langue*:

> De Saussure's general linguistics is closely linked with the sociology of Durkheim. His theoretical approach may fairly be described as Durkheimian structuralism... De Saussure, thinking in Durkheimian terms, regarded social facts as *sui generis* and external to and on a different plane from individual phenomena. The 'collective conscience'... is not arrived at by studying the psychology of the individual. The social fact is on a different plane of reality. The group constrains the individual and the group culture determines a great deal of his humanity.

Consequently de Saussure in terms of his linguistics could only refer to my personal linguistic activity, writing or reading this paper, as emanating from *un sujet parlant*. And individually each one of you as a listener or reader would be a *sujet parlant*. After bearing with me to the end, he might even express the opinion that I was *mauvais sujet*.[14]

So much for Saussure leading the unsuspecting, innocent social scientist into the wilderness of apparent scientificity! The historical stages in the achievement of intellectual imperialisms are not so clearly laid out as to permit the unequivocal tracing of the origins of the ills of sociology/anthropology to Saussurean linguistics! It is interesting to note that so far as linguistics was concerned, while the Saussurean proposal became popular with many linguists – 'Nowadays professional linguists,' said Firth (ibid.), 'can almost be classified by using the name of de Saussure' – still, the rigid dichotomisation of *langue* and *parole* always had its opponents and the 'various possible groupings' that Firth (ibid.) mentions include 'Saussureans, anti-Saussureans, post-Saussureans, or non-Saussureans'. Firth himself was, of course, firmly opposed to what in Bernstein's (1975a) terminology would be a 'strong classification' of *langue* and *parole* and even more to the exclusion of *parole* from that linguistics which is sometimes improperly called linguistics proper! There is not much in the current critique of Saussure – including Bourdieu's – that is new, except the rhetoric.

It seems important to point out that there are at least two separate issues in the *langue-parole* debate: first, their mutual relation and secondly their place *vis à vis* internal linguistics. To say that Saussure failed to recognise the close relation between *parole* and *langue* is at the least a problematic reading of the Course[15]: it is certainly one that is contradicted at several points within the body of that variegatedly stitched text. Even more important is the fact that if the description of language is not to consist in the 'universalisation of subjective experience' (cf. Bourdieu, 1990: 46), if language is to be studied as a 'structured structuring structure', then a conceptual distinction between *langue* and *parole* is necessary. It seems to me that in trying to define *langue*, Saussure was in fact attempting to achieve, some 80 years prior to Bourdieu, Bourdieu's (1993: 272) own ideal of 'grasping the *invariant*, the structure, behind each of the variations observed' (emphasis original). Saussure might have elaborated the 'invariant' not as 'the structure' but as *the system*, in which too he would not have been far from Bourdieu's notion (cf. class habitus) of 'so many linguistic habitus which are *at least partially orchestrated*' (p. 46; emphasis added). Grasping the invariant behind the variant, the system behind the process (Hjelmslev, 1961) is essential to the formation of a theory, whether it is Saussure's theory of language or Bourdieu's theory of class habitus. To say that one is attempting to arrive at the orchestration of the many linguistic habitus, is to say by implication that one is no longer attempting to account for each attribute of each 'oral production' of each specific linguistic habitus, i.e., of each act of *parole*. The opposite claim would be a theoretical absurdity and this was one of the points that Saussure was anxious to establish. Such orchestration of so many linguistic habitus (each in the last resort with its own unique voice) involves a theoretical process which calls for some distancing from the actual: one pays for the power of generalisation by giving up the power of description over at least some unique attributes of an actual performance (Hasan, 1995a), call it a unique 'oral production' of linguistic habitus, or a unique act of *parole*. It is never in doubt that the analysis of the actual will be incomplete: the issue is the grounds for treating something as non/unique. It is for this reason that one needs a theory that allows focus both on the potential and the actual, the system and the instance – in fact that very synthesis of the objective and the subjective perspective, which I understand Bourdieu (1977; 1990) to have argued for so as to rid the social sciences from the shortcomings of the Saussurean approach.

The problems in Saussure's linguistics do not arise from the fact that he unjustifiably and capriciously postulated the notion of *langue*: that notion is essential to the study of language as I have just argued. The contradictions in his discourse arise from how he saw *langue* and *parole* in relation to linguistics (Hasan, 1987a; 1993). Granting the historical dependence of *langue* on *parole* (not simply of *parole* on *langue* as Bourdieu implies through his repetition of the metaphors of the 'execution' of a 'score'), Saussure still recommended – in fact quite illogically – that internal linguistics, which formed the core of the study of language, should focus only on *langue*, on what is invariant in the variations observed in the *paroles* of a community. He thus privileged the system over instance and blocked that descriptive activity which Firth (1957a: 29) referred to as 'the renewal of connection with experience'. Contradiction there certainly is in Saussure, but it is open to doubt that he was fashioning a theory of competence inherently independent of performance. That doubtful distinction belongs to Chomsky!

Saussure's declared aim was, then, to exclude consideration of *parole* from internal linguistics. But what harm does Bourdieu suggest this does to practices in linguistics? Bourdieu (1991: 34) remarks in his inimitable style:

> bracketing out the social.. allows language or any other symbolic object
> to be treated like an end in itself, [which] contributed considerably to the
> success of structuralist linguistics, for it endowed the 'pure' exercises that
> characterise a purely internal and formal analysis with the charm of a game
> devoid of consequences.

That is to say, linguistic analysis becomes a pointless formal game. Students of language who have *ad infinitum* 'segmented' the string s into NP+VP and the like would sympathise with Bourdieu's view, while the inanity of a mindless binarism as employed in a good deal of the analysis of anthropological material in the name of Saussure is proof that others found the 'charm' irresistible. But as a description of linguistic analysis as a whole, Bourdieu's account is something of a misrepresentation to at least those who have reflected on Saussure's analysis of the 'associative bonds', whose network defines the semantic space claimed by the word *enseignement*. Is it the analysis of the form of language as such that should be castigated, or should one be critical of a formal analysis that fails to link linguistic forms to meanings by which speakers live? Bourdieu, of course, does not ask, but goes on to draw attention to other dangers inherent in the exclusion of *parole* from linguistics (1991: 33), which:

> excludes from it all the investigations which establish a relationship between language and anthropology, the political history of those who speak it, or even the geography of the domain where it is spoken, because all of these things add nothing to a knowledge of language taken in itself.

I think I am right in claiming that this criticism – which, incidentally, ignores much of the Saussurean discourse on diachrony – is representative of Bourdieu's disquiet at the exclusion of *parole* from linguistics: at one level one may interpret this as a disquiet over the possibility of a linguistics that makes the sociology of language insignificant by comparison with the study of the form of language. Linguists such as Firth (1957b: 177ff) and Halliday (1992/2003; 1996a), while deploring this aspect, have given more cogent reasons for disagreeing with Saussure. I consider these reasons more cogent because they are fundamental to the study of language itself. To quote Halliday (1996a: 30):

> Saussure problematised the nature of the linguistic fact; but he confused the issue of instantiation by setting up langue and parole as if they had been two distinct classes of phenomena. But they are not. There is only one set of phenomena here, not two; language (the linguistic system) differs from parole (the linguistic instance) only in the position taken up by the observer. Langue is parole seen from a distance and hence on the way to being theorised about.

According to this view, if *parole* is truly banished from the study of language, then logically there can be no *langue* – the very object of study disappears and the activity of linguistics becomes 'undo-able'. Halliday (1992/2003: 8) points to the harm done to the study of language by the false dichotomisation of *langue* and *parole*:

> This failure to construe the link, in semiotic system-and-process, between the INSTANCE – the act of meaning... – and the SYSTEM (prototypically, a language) has haunted our late twentieth century linguistics, which has oscillated wildly between system and instance, creating a massive disjunction between the two. In the 1960s, if you dared to mention the text [i.e. socially situated *parole*], you were dismissed as 'data-oriented'; while in the 1980s

if you ventured to refer to the system, you were attacked for 'totalising'. But combining being data-oriented with being totalising is a useful recipe for understanding things; we sometimes call it scientific method.

In fact the course Halliday recommends is what Bourdieu calls a 'theory of practice' when he presents, at least by implication, a similar relation of mutual dependence between the system and the instance – between the 'variant' and the 'invariant' (cf. Bourdieu, 1993: 272) – as a desirable condition for doing social science. But his critique of the strong classification of *langue* and *parole* fails to highlight the centrality of this same relation for doing linguistic science. This too is fairly typical of Bourdieu's reflections on language. Anticipating a little, it is as if for Bourdieu there is nothing to be said about the meaning making potential of language 'taken in itself'; linguistics 'has' no facts that are not given by social institutions; language is simply 'a secondary flow of verbal equivalents' as Malinowski (1935: 5) derisively commented, which just corresponds to a social reality that is always already there. More will be said in Sections 3 and 4 about this aspect of Bourdieu's conception of language which runs curiously parallel to the formalist's approach.

2.2 The misleading map of linguistics: the elevation of *langue*

If the exclusion of *parole* from internal linguistics has appeared problematic to scholars, the idea of *langue* itself is no less contentious. Bourdieu unquestioningly accepts the view common amongst dominant linguists that 'Chomskyan 'competence' is another name for Saussure's *langue*' (p. 44); in fact, the discussion moves between Saussure and Chomsky as if their theories were identical, which, in very important respects, they are not. Thus the tendency to equate *langue* and competence, for all its currency, is problematic on several counts. The issues are too involved to permit a full discussion here, but I mention four interrelated differences between the two concepts.

(i) Competence is innate – a biological attribute of all normal humans; *langue* '*is a social product* of the faculty of speech and a *collection of necessary conventions* that have been adopted by a social body' (Saussure, 1966: 9; emphasis added); 'language never exists apart from the social fact... Its social nature is one of its inner characteristics' (ibid. 77). It is noteworthy that Saussure's *faculté de langage*, unlike competence, subsumes both *langue* and *parole*.

(ii) Since competence is innate it is logically independent of the community and, so, intraorganic; *langue*, a social product, is interorganic (cf. Halliday, 1974). It 'is not complete in any speaker; it exists perfectly only within a collectivity' (Saussure, 1966: 14); competence is complete in each native speaker; it exists perfectly in each individual, except in cases of brain pathology.

(iii) Competence at its most abstract is the innate knowledge of the universal rules of human language; as opposed to the Chomskyan concept of 'human language', Saussure's *langue* is strictly language specific: the *langue* of one language is never the same as the *langue* of some other. In fact where one is engaged in the description of a (sub-standard/dominated) dialect, it could be maintained strictly within the terms of Saussurean definition that one is studying the *langue* (i.e. 'system') of that dialect (comparable to the linguistic habitus of say a class), not its *parole*, not the oral/graphic productions.

(iv) Finally, the homogeneity of competence is simply a logical concomitant of its universality – at its deepest level competence consists in a genetically endowed knowledge of the rules common to natural languages; by contrast the homogeneity of a *langue* arises from the fact that it is a system representing what is treated as invariant in the *parole* of a community; it consists of only what is considered to be in common to all members of the speech community (however defined) because the theory (rightly or wrongly) requires such an abstraction.

This comparison highlights the consistently social nature of *langue* as opposed to the consistently biological nature of competence. *Langue* is not a theory about the structure of the human brain; competence is[16]. *Langue* was a concept designed to account for the possibility of semiotic exchange in a community; ironically, one reason why Bourdieu is so critical of the notion of *langue* is that it fails to achieve this aim. Bourdieu's critique pertains to two distinct levels – that of language description and that of theory. I report first on the problems for the descriptive level.

2.2.1 *Langue*: the illusion of linguistic communism

According to Bourdieu, Saussure's concept of *langue* as homogeneous has created an 'illusion of linguistic communism which haunts all linguistic theory'[17]; it leaves unresolved 'the question of the social and economic conditions of the appropriation of language' (p. 43). It might not be unreasonable to suppose that had Bourdieu considered linguists other than those legitimised as 'the linguist' by their domination of the field, he would have quite possibly agreed with Firth, always a thoughtful and outspoken opponent of dominant linguistic theories whose roots lay in formal structuralism. Here is a comment by Firth on homogeneity in language (1935/1957: 29):

> Unity is the last concept that should be applied to language. Unity of language is the most fugitive of all unities, whether it be historical, geographical, national, or personal. There is no such thing as *une langue une* and there never has been.

As for the relation of the community to language, Firth (1950/1957: 187) believed that language takes form in the living of life and that 'Such language systems can... be regarded as actively and consistently maintained by persons in the social process'. It followed from this that linguistics was the study of language as a social process and the character of the language that persons 'appropriated', or to use Firth's words, learned and used for the living of their life, is described as follows (1950/1957: 184):

> There is the element of habit, custom, tradition, the element of the past and the element of innovation, of the moment, in which the future is being born. When you speak you fuse these elements in verbal creation, the outcome of your language and your personality.

And while Firth did not discourse in detail on 'the social and economic conditions of the appropriation of language', he introduced the concepts of 'language community' and 'speech fellowship' (1950/1957: 185–6) to show how with the complicity of language itself, the lines of inclusion and exclusion into social categories are drawn along the lines of linguistic variation. Bourdieu's concern with what according to him follows from the acceptance of *langue* as homogeneous, is elaborated in remarks such as the following (1991: 45):

> To speak of *the* language, without further specification, as linguists do, is tacitly to accept the *official* definition of the *official* language of a political unit.. Produced by authors who have the authority to write, fixed and codified by grammarians and teachers who are also charged with the task of inculcating its mastery, the language is a *code*, in the sense of a cipher enabling equivalences to be established between sounds and meanings, but also in the sense of a system of norms regulating linguistic practices.

It is certainly true that the object of linguists' descriptions has typically been the *langue* of a language, be it English, French, German, Pushto, Pitjantjatjara, Weri or Gooniyandi. The juxtaposition of *langues* whose social status differs so remarkably from each other perhaps serves to throw doubt on the easy equation of the concept of *langue* with that of official/legitimate language[18]. But Bourdieu is not thinking of languages such as Gooniyandi. So far as languages such as English, French and German are concerned, it has to be granted that the standard variety, however unfairly, is also the socially salient variety. Which is another way of saying that its market is wider than that of any other variety, which gives it relatively higher visibility. Linguists are no exception to the general tendency of paying attention to what is socially salient and easily visible. It is indeed fascinating to ask: when scholars bend their minds to the study of some phenomenon, why do they typically choose to focus on the most socially salient, the most visible of its instances, be it language as in the case of the linguist or theoretical frameworks as in the case of a theoretician such as Bourdieu?

On the other hand, to be fair to linguists, at least some of them have engaged in the description of dominated languages/lects as well. I have often quoted Firth above, but he is not the only linguist who was critical of Saussure's internal linguistics or who recognised the social nature of language. Naming single names – Gumperz, Firth, Halliday, Haugen, Hymes, Labov, Mathesius, Mukaovský, Vološinov, Weinreich and the list could continue for some time – gives the wrong impression in this context. The field of 'linguistics' has been no less fragmented than other intellectual fields and alongside the formalist traditions, there has also flourished some linguistics of language as social process. Bourdieu criticises the dominant, the institutionally accepted variety of linguistics for conceptualising the system of language as homogeneous, for ignoring the politico-economic bases of linguistic behaviour. However, beginning with Malinowski (1923; 1935a) and Firth (1935/1957) – not to mention earlier scholars – there has been continued interest in the study of the relevance of 'social context' to language use; there have been socioeconomically sensitive concepts e.g. Gumperz's (1971) 'code switching' and 'register repertoire', Halliday's 'register' theory (1964), his sociosemiotic theory of language development (1975) and his concept of 'anti-languages' (1976), as well as Hymes' writings on 'speech variety' (1962; 1967). Apart from these, one could hardly miss the fervour with which some have adopted the position of defending the 'dominated/non-standard varieties' (for example see Labov, 1972). Bourdieu is not much impressed by this evidence of interest in the social conditions of speaking; he draws attention, instead, to its negative side (1990: 53):

> The bringing to light of the presuppositions inherent in objectivist construction has paradoxically been delayed by the efforts of all those who, in linguistics as in anthropology, have sought to 'correct' the structuralist model by appealing to 'context'' or 'situation' to account for variations, exceptions and accidents... They have thus avoided a radical questioning of the objectivist mode of thought.

In other words, what linguists do by way of describing dialects/languages other than the official one, by way of relating language varieties to social hierarchies, to different markets, to different fields, is of less consequence than the fact that they have an objectivist point of view, introduced into the field most successfully by Saussure. Their descriptions reveal an '*intellectualist philosophy* which treats language as an object of contemplation rather than as an instrument of action and power' (1990: 37) – a fault, which one is tempted to conclude, can be avoided only if one embraces Bourdieu's notion of 'habitus'. This brings us to Bourdieu's objections to *langue* from a theoretical standpoint.

2.2.2 *Langue*: the dangers of objectification

In Bourdieu's view the greatest damage done by Saussure's theory was its harmful influence in orienting theories to the limiting and limited objectivist stance. In his *Logic of Practice* Bourdieu presents a masterly analysis of current approaches to theory-making in the social sciences, suggesting that if the aim of the social sciences is to describe social practice in an illuminating way, then neither objectivism nor subjectivism by itself will prove adequate. The professional practices of 'the' linguist amply manifest the problems that characterise the objectivist approach.

Saussurean semiology – or more precisely, Saussurean 'internal linguistics'– is in Bourdieu's view, an example *par excellence* of objectivism. The basis of this objectivism lies initially in the 'fundamental division between the language and its realisation in speech, that is, in practice and also in history and from the inability to understand the relationship between these two entities as other than the model and its execution...[19]' (1990: 32–3). Distancing himself from the practical concerns that social agents have with language, 'the' linguist adopts (1990: 31):

> the viewpoint of an 'impartial spectator' who seeks to understand for the sake of understanding... taking it [i.e. language] as an object of analysis instead of using [sic!] it to think and speak.

In seeking to understand language just for the sake of understanding it, 'the' linguist comes to bear a 'purely theoretical relation to language' and fails to understand 'the practical relation to language of someone who seeks to understand it in order to act and who uses language for practical purposes' (1990). The failure to understand the nature of the social agents' practical concern with language inclines the linguist 'to treat language as an autonomous, self-sufficient object' (1990) meant for interpretation alone. He thus bestows a spurious reality on it as if it existed independently of speakers. Thus, 'sliding from the model of reality to the reality of the model' (Bourdieu, 1990: 39), the linguist fails to 'call into question the presuppositions inherent in the position of the 'objective' observer who seeking to interpret practices, tends to bring into the object the principles of his relation to the object' (1990: 27). Bourdieu argues that neither the question of the genesis of an 'immanent' structure such as *langue* nor the social agent's relation to it can be resolved either by appealing to 'the participationist option' or by postulating universal categories, themselves explained by appeal to 'the unconscious activity of the mind'. He claims (1990: 52; emphasis added):

> Objectivism constitutes the social world as a spectacle offered to an observer who takes up a 'point of view' on the action and who, putting into the object the principles of his relation to the object, proceeds as if it were solely for knowledge... The theory of practice as practice insists, contrary to positivist materialism, that the objects of knowledge are constructed, not passively

recorded and, contrary to intellectualist idealism, that the principle of this construction is the system of structured, structuring dispositions, the *habitus*, which is constituted in practice and is always oriented towards practical functions... *One has to escape from the realizm of the structure, to which objectivism... necessarily leads... without falling back into subjectivism, which is quite incapable of giving an account of the necessity of the social world.*

For this elegantly expressed cogent critique, those linguists should be grateful who have always opposed the principle of the exclusion of *parole* from linguistics, who have studied language as part of the social process and who have insisted on the logical necessity of maintaining the dual perspective of system and instance – a description that fits rather well a group of linguists who have worked with the systemic functional model of language. It seems appropriate to draw attention here once again to some views of Firth's (1948/1957: 143) that maintain a position essentially similar to that of Bourdieu's though without the same elegance or the wide sweep of his discourse (emphasis added):

Linguists and sociologists have to deal with systems, but systems very different from physical systems. Personal systems and social systems are actively maintained (with adaptation and change) in the bodily behaviour of men. Most of the older definitions (and de Saussure's must fall in this category) need overhauling. Language and personality are built into the body, which is constantly taking part in activities directed to the conservation of the pattern of life. We must expect therefore that linguistic science will also find it necessary to postulate the maintenance of linguistic patterns and systems [including adaptation and change] within which there is order, structure and function. Such systems are maintained by activity and in activity they are to be studied. It is on these grounds that linguistics must be systemic.

One need abandon neither the system nor the instance so long as the historical relation between the system(s) and the various instances – between the invariant and the many variations observed – can be studied under some principle which combines the two perspectives. The explanatory principle Bourdieu (1990: 53) offers us is that of 'habitus':

The conditions associated with a particular class of conditions of existence [sic!] produce *habitus*, systems of durable, transposable dispositions, structured structures predisposed to function as structuring structures, that is, as principles which generate and organise practices and representations that can be objectively adapted to their outcomes without presupposing a conscious aiming at ends or an express mastery of the operations necessary to attain them.

Important as the concept of habitus is, many issues in relation to it cannot be addressed within the scope of this paper, such as the details of how linguistic habitus is produced, how it responds to conditions other than those it was produced in and how one might describe, *beyond generalities*, the details of the physiognomy of some category of linguistic habitus, such as, say, that of the working class. Bourdieu's writing on habitus is certainly inspirational, but I have not found such details in it, which when it comes to the actual analysis of a linguistic problem is a distinct disadvantage. Let me now close this discussion of the error and failure of linguistics in Bourdieu's own words (1990: 37–8; emphasis added):

> On the one hand, there are the socially constructed dispositions of the linguistic habitus, which imply a certain propensity to speak and to say determinate things… and a certain capacity to speak, which involves both the linguistic capacity to generate an infinite number of grammatically correct discourses and the social capacity to use this competence adequately in a determinate situation. On the other hand, there are the structures of the linguistic market, which impose themselves as a system of specific sanctions and censorships.
>
> This simple model of the linguistic production and circulation as the relation between linguistic habitus and the markets on which they offer their products enable(s) us to understand the error and failure to which linguistics succumbs when, *relying on only one of the factors involved* – a strictly linguistic competence, abstractly defined, *ignoring everything that it owes to the social condition* of its production – it tries to give an adequate account of discourse. In fact, as long as they [i.e. linguists] are unaware of the limits that constitute their science, linguists have no choice but to search desperately in language for something that is actually inscribed in the social relations within which it [i.e. language] functions, or to engage in a sociology without knowing it, that is, with the risk of discovering, in grammar itself, something that their spontaneous sociology has unwittingly imported into it.

The discussion so far has been concerned with what Bourdieu finds problematic in the way 'the' linguist does his linguistics. This issue is far from simple, as I have tried to show by importing alternative views from the field of linguistics. If 'the' linguist of Bourdieu's critique is real, then side by side there also exist linguists whose position has not been remarkably different from that of Bourdieu's, especially in their criticism of 'static structural formalism' (Firth, 1950/1957: 181) which *ignores everything that language owes to the social condition*. From the perspective of such linguists, Bourdieu's critique of a homogenised, totalised linguistics is obviously an act of disinformation about the field, which obliterates all forms of linguistics that do not contribute to his not-so-hidden agenda of discrediting 'the sovereign discipline' (Bourdieu, 1991: 32). Most systemic functional linguists would agree with Bourdieu's critique of Saussurean linguistics, at least as that theory got interpreted and used by simply formal linguists. Most systemic functional linguists would share Bourdieu's disquiet at the strong classification of *langue* and *parole* and at the exclusion of the latter from 'internal linguistics'; in fact they would be opposed to the very idea of the divided house of internal and external linguistics, again for a reason that is not very different from what Bourdieu has to say about a viable theory of practice. Where I believe the systemic functional linguist will part company with Bourdieu is on his ideas about language itself. This is the issue to which I turn in the following section.

3 Bourdieu on language

Since to the best of my knowledge Bourdieu has not provided any account of what, by virtue of the multitudinous acts of languaging as part of the social process of living, 'language taken in itself' becomes/is *as a semiotic system*, it will be necessary to begin by examining his account of official language. It is in the course of commenting on the genesis and nature of this variety of language that Bourdieu reveals his views on such phenomena as linguistic variation, the concept of style, the working of a semiotic system, the nature of grammar and of lexicon and the like.

We are already familiar with Bourdieu's view (1991: 45) that 'To speak of *the* language, without further specification, as linguists do, is to tacitly accept the *official* definition of the *official* language of a political unit'. (See extract Section 2.2.1). Given the social structure of human communities, a 'pan-communal' language, equally appropriated by all, is no more than a theoretical myth, as Firth had pointed out; what 'the' linguist typically ends up describing is what appears the most salient – what is known in the trade as 'the standard dialect'; but according to Bourdieu the salience of the standard dialect is simply the measure of its domination. Bourdieu uses the terms 'official language', 'legitimate language', 'standard language' and 'authorised language' more or less interchangeably to refer to that variety of language which is 'a product of the political domination that is endlessly reproduced by institutions capable of imposing universal recognition of dominant languages' (1991: 46); and it is this language that 'the' linguist describes, thus contributing to the invidious devaluation of common language. What is the origin of this 'official language'? What are its characteristics? How does it differ from other varieties of the same language? In the following sub-sections, I will present some of Bourdieu's ideas on these questions, before presenting his views on language as a formal system.

3.1 The production and reproduction of official language

Let me begin with one of Bourdieu's remarks (1991: 48) on the genesis of official language:

only when the making of the 'nation'', an entirely abstract group based on law, creates new usages and functions does it become indispensable to forge a *standard* language, impersonal and anonymous like the official uses it has to serve and by the same token to undertake the work of normalizing the products of the linguistic habitus.

The educational system 'plays a decisive role' in 'the construction, legitimation and imposition of an official language' (1991: 48), which is crucial to the reproduction and the differential valuation of the different dialects. The educational system is able to exercise this power especially by virtue of its 'unification' with the 'labour market' as Bourdieu points out (1991: 49; emphasis added):

> The educational system.. no doubt directly helped to devalue popular *modes of expression*, dismissing them as 'slang' and 'gibberish'... and to impose recognition of the legitimate language. But... doubtless the dialectical relation between the school system and the labour market –... between the unification of the educational (and linguistic) market ... and the unification of the labour market... –... played the most decisive role in devaluing dialects and establishing the new hierarchy of linguistic practices. To induce the holders of dominated linguistic competences to collaborate in the destruction of their *instrument of expression* ... it was necessary for the school system to be perceived as the principal (indeed, the only) means of access to administrative positions, which were all the more attractive where industrialization was least developed.

In the devaluation of popular language – which, be it noted, is simply 'an instrument of expression', a 'mode' of stringing together the signifiers, the signified perhaps being no part of language, but simply a gift of the social – the educational system finds willing collaborators among its female apprentices (1991: 50: emphasis added):

> women are more disposed to adopt *the legitimate language (or the legitimate pronunciation)*: since they are inclined toward docility with regard to the dominant usages both by the sexual division of labour, which makes them specialise in the sphere of consumption and by the logic of marriage, which is their main if not the only avenue of social advancement and through which they circulate upwards, women are predisposed to accept, from school onwards, the new demands of the market in symbolic goods.

Although the concepts of 'markets' and 'fields' are relevant to Bourdieu's account of the production and reproduction of the official language, he does not develop them sufficiently from the point of view of language; for example, how does one linguistic market differ from another, or what if anything has language to do with the specificity of one field as opposed to another. I will touch briefly on some of these issues in Section 4.

3.2 On the distinction of an official language

The production and reproduction of official language can thus be explained entirely in terms of external factors: 'the political will to unification', which must ultimately underly 'the unification of the market in symbolic goods which accompanies the unification of the economy' (1991: 50). And the same is true of the valuation of the different linguistic varieties: 'All linguistic practices are measured against legitimate practices, i.e. the practices of those who are dominant' (1991: 53). In Bourdieu's narrative, the nakedness of the emperor is never visible. Indeed, so convinced is Bourdieu of the critical role of the purely external factors in the production, reproduction and evaluation of social dialects that he warns us against attempting to find the secret of their constitution elsewhere. To do this is to court trouble (1991: 52–3):

> one inevitably falls into one or other of two opposing errors. Either one unconsciously absolutises.. the dominant usage, failing to look beyond the properties of language itself, such as the complexity of its syntactic structure, in order to identify the basis of the value which is accorded to it [i.e. official language], particularly in the educational market; or one escapes this.. fetishism only to fall into the naïvety *par excellence* of the scholarly relativism which forgets that the naïve gaze is not relativist and ignores the fact of legitimacy, through a.. relativisation[20] of the dominant usage, which is socially recognised as legitimate and not only by those who are dominant.

So in trying to decide what factors distinguish the dialects of a community's linguistic repertoire, we are advised by Bourdieu not to make the error of assuming that the official language is valued because it has any linguistic properties *per se*: to do this would be to succumb to linguistic fetishism, a *malaise* that, we are told, infects Bernstein's discourse on educational sociology. Nor should one fall into the error of assuming, *a là* Labov, that all dialects are equal 'in themselves': to do this is to ignore the community's (intersubjectively) objective perception of the official dialect as indeed 'better' being the privileged variety.

But if official language has no specific properties in respect of which it might be differentiated from the other varieties in the community's linguistic repertoire and if all speakers in the community still have 'virtually the same recognition of authorised usage' (1991:. 62), are we not faced with a puzzle: what is it on the basis of which the speakers recognise whatever it is that they do recognise? Not so, says Bourdieu. To understand the reason, we must consider the nature and role of habitus, which is 'constituted outside the spheres of consciousness and constraint'. Here is a more detailed description of how the dispositions of the habitus are formed (1991: p. 51)[21]:

> There is every reason to think that the factors which are most influential in the formation of the habitus *are transmitted without passing through language* and consciousness, but through suggestions inscribed in the most apparently insignificant aspects of the things, situations and practices of everyday life. Thus the modalities of practices, the ways of looking, sitting, standing, keeping silent, or *even of speaking* ('reproachful looks' or '*tones*', 'disapproving glances' and so on) are full of injunctions that are powerful and hard to resist precisely because they are *silent* and insidious, insistent and insinuating.

Ignoring the implicit contradictions in this extract, note an important consequence that follows from the diffuse condition for the formation of the habitus: it is not the so-called linguistic properties that are crucial in the production and reception of messages; rather, what is crucial is 'the whole body which responds by its posture... by its inner reactions or more specifically the articulatory ones, to the tension of the market' (1991: 86). Giraud's notion of 'articulatory style' is presented as particularly relevant in this respect (1991: 86):

> The most frequent articulatory position is an element in an *overall way of using the mouth* (in talking but also in eating, drinking, laughing, etc.) and therefore a component of the bodily hexis, which implies a *systematic informing* of the whole phonological aspect of speech... (such) bodily hexis characteristic of a social class determines the system of phonological features which characterises a class pronunciation.

It is not surprising then that in the recognition of the privileged variety, the official, authorised language, the 'synthetic unity of the bodily hexis' (1991: 88) creates a complex syndrome of differentiating features, which inextricably mixes the linguistic and the non-linguistic (1991: 89):

> Not only are linguistic features never clearly separated from the speaker's whole set of social properties (bodily hexis, physiognomy, cosmetics, clothing), but phonological (or lexical, or any other) features are never clearly separated from other levels of language; and the judgement which classifies a speech form as 'popular' or a person as 'vulgar' is based,.. on sets of indices which never impinge on consciousness in that form, even if those which are designated by stereotypes (such as the 'peasant' 'r' or the southern *ceusse*) have greater weight.

The habitus permits the speaker, who naturally has a practical relation to language, to deploy successfully, albeit quite unconsciously, this complex identificatory syndrome. This facility is not available to 'the' linguist who applies the tools of his trade to the same problem, treating it as an intellectual exercise. We have already seen (Section 2.2.2) that lacking the viewpoint of a practical user, the linguist treats language as an object of analysis; since his focus is on oppositions of features internal to language (such as 'voiced' vs. 'devoiced'), not surprisingly his analytic categories prove totally inconsequential (1991:):

> The linguist, who has developed an abnormally acute perception (particularly at the phonological level), may notice differences where ordinary speakers hear none.

It would seem that it is the spontaneous sociolinguistics of the sociologist – to turn Bourdieu's phrase around – that in fact manages to tap into the 'deep-rooted dispositions of the habitus' (1991: 88), an example of which is to be found in Bourdieu's discussion of the 'opposition between the bourgeois relation and the popular relation to language in the sexually overdetermined opposition between... *la bouche*... and *la gueule*', the former 'closed, pinched, i.e. tense and censored and therefore feminine' and the latter 'unashamedly wide open,.. i.e. relaxed and free and therefore masculine' (1991: 86). As opposed to this amazingly archaic insight into the reliable heuristics of linguistic variation, we have the linguist, who with his objectivist preoccupations, can obviously not be expected to notice these subtle phenomena; his categories are irrelevant for explaining the 'objective' differences between language varieties (1991:. 54; original emphasis):

> the differences which emerge from the confrontation of speech varieties are not reducible to those the linguist constructs in terms of his own criterion of pertinence... there exists, in the area of pronunciation, diction and even grammar, a whole set of differences which, though negligible in the eyes of the linguist, are pertinent from the sociologist's standpoint because they belong to a system of linguistic oppositions which is the *re-translation* of a system of social differences.

Note the uselessness of the linguist: on the one hand, the differences his acute perception notices are unhelpful and on the other, he has the misfortune of missing out precisely those clues which turn out to be actually relevant to the differentiation of linguistic varieties. I do not question Bourdieu's thesis that the whole comportment is relevant in 'placing' a social agent, nor do I doubt that the linguist within the confines of his discipline is unable to describe the whole comportment. What gives me pause is the total dismissal of 'the' linguist's ability to show anything worthy of attention. This dismissal fails to impress, particularly in view of the thesis of the sexual over-determination, which – the only instance of spontaneous linguistic analysis of a dialect feature by Bourdieu – is itself so easily falsified. The suggestion that the essence of social-class dialects can be described by such fanciful phenomena as *la danse buccale*, must be rejected as a claim without basis, if for no other reason than that there are only two sex determined articulatory positions: feminine and masculine, but there are a large number of social class accents. Further, the 'unashamedly open' therefore 'masculine' articulatory posture does describe rather well the phonological features of some of the best known genteel varieties of English.

Granted that language typically operates in cooperation with other semiotic modalities as at least some linguists had not failed to notice, it is still valid to ask what is the optimal environment for this cooperation? What is the domain where non-linguistic semiotic modalities, sometimes referred to as 'extra-linguistic' indices – indices that Bourdieu has described as 'the speaker's whole set of social properties (bodily hexis, physiognomy, cosmetics, clothing)' (1991: 89) – can actually be employed effectively? Clearly such social indices enjoy the most play only in the context of 'spoken mode' and, more specifically, in 'face to face' interaction. In the 'written mode' the indices of bodily hexis, physiognomy, cosmetics, clothing and suchlike can obviously have no impact. Of course given our natural facility for producing semiotic systems (Hasan, 1996a), we can create other extra-linguistic signs suitable even for this 'distance mode', such as the type of note paper (a question of 'good taste'), the nature of orthographic representation (calligraphic 'excellence'), the layout of the message (meaning by images, on the reading of which see Kress and van Leeuwen, 1990; van Leeuwen and Humphrey, 1996). Even so, with the homogeneity of appearance imposed increasingly by the publishing trade on its products, at least in the domain of published writing, the contribution of the extra-linguistic modalities to the meanings of the message must be greatly reduced. We know also that there has long been an interest amongst linguists in dialects other than the official/standard – witness publications such as *Transactions of the Yorkshire Dialect Society*, now in its 100th year; more crucially, we quite often find mixed use of the non-official and official dialects within the same work of fiction. If speakers have a recognition of official and non-official language even in the written medium within the same œuvre e.g. a Hardy novel, which it is not unreasonable to claim that they do, what do they base their judgement on when it comes to printed matter? It is obvious that at least in published writing, the 'phonological, lexical and any other features' must become 'separated from the speaker's whole set of social properties' and certainly from those of bodily hexis etc. If the varieties are still differentiated unerringly, as we know that they are, this must be largely on the basis of phenomena that pertain to 'the lexical and other features of language' as a semiotic system. What are these? And how are they to be described?

Bourdieu does not address these issues as such, but in talking about the literary field he points out (1991: 57–61) that what is 'needed to produce a written discourse worthy of being published... made official' is the appropriation of the 'instruments of production such as rhetorical devices, genres, legitimate styles and manners and, more generally, all the formulations destined to be 'authoritative' and to be cited as examples of 'good usage'' (1991: 57–8). This is what confers power over language and power over ordinary users of language, augmenting the author's linguistic capital. Style and diction is what matters.

'The properties which characterise linguistic excellence [in official legitimate language] may be summed up in two words: distinction and excellence' (1991: 60) of style. In keeping with the view made fashionable by the Chomskyan tradition, style is said to be deviation from the norm; and, since the norm in authorised language is set by 'excelling' in deviation, albeit with 'taste', the stakes in the game are raised with each successful, officially recognised innovative/deviational foray into the production of an authorised authorising style. Throughout Bourdieu's discussion, style is presented, to turn Bourdieu's expression around, as a charming game devoid of semantic consequences, meaningless mannerisms, which arbitrarily attract value. This has the effect of emphasising the arbitrary nature of the privilege accorded to authorised, official language, the very production of which has the social consequence of devaluing popular language. In Bourdieu's account we do not find any heuristic criteria which can actually be used in the identification of genres, varieties, styles of whatever kind; certainly the idea that style may construe any meaning other than that of signalling hierarchisation is entirely foreign to Bourdieu's discourse. So the age-old dichotomy between style and content, between the 'how' and the 'what' is ratified in Bourdieu's analysis of authorial style as it is in all formalist discourse and as I propose to show language emerges – not surprisingly – in its traditional guise as but an onomastic system.

3.3 Language as a formal mechanism

It would be wrong to give the impression that Bourdieu does not recognise any 'elements' intrinsic to language. As is obvious from the extracts quoted above, there are certainly frequent references in his writing to the three conventionally accepted components of language: phonology/pronunciation, lexicon/words, syntax/grammar. In fact, as we have seen, he goes beyond these to styles/diction and genres which some have regarded as linguistically *construed*. Notably, in each of these cases, Bourdieu's starting point is the formalist's position. This may be simply because the formalist perspective is most friendly to his interests, lending itself to attack because it is 'inward looking'. For what Bourdieu strains to establish in the discussion of each of these components of language, is their lack of autonomy, their dependence on the social, implying that their very specificities are to be found in the social rather than in the 'substance of speech'. We have seen in Section 3.2 that pronunciation/phonology is systematically informed by bodily hexis. 'Language is a body technique and specifically linguistic, especially phonetic, competence is a dimension of bodily hexis' (1991: 86). But the fact that phonology is also a network of relations internal to a language variety and that it makes a substantial contribution in the expression of meaning is a theme remarkably invisible from Bourdieu's discourse.

The situation is not very different when it comes to words/lexicon: true to the formalist notion, Bourdieu's words have denotation and connotation. But denotation 'the stable part, common to all speakers' and 'enshrined in the dictionary' is a poor sort of thing. People speak the 'same language' only in the sense that they share the same signifiers whose meanings are often antagonistic. Connotation based on personal life experiences of individuals is the socially real thing (1991: 39; emphasis added):

> Connotation refers to the *singularity of the individual experiences,* this is *because it is constituted in a socially characterised relation to which the recipients bring the diversity of their instruments of symbolic appropriation...* The all-purpose word in the dictionary, a product of the neutralisation of the practical relations within which it functions, *has no social existence*; in practice it [i.e., a word] is always immersed in situations, to such an extent that the core meanings which remain relatively invariant through the diversity of the markets *may pass unnoticed.*

Since speakers do not really function with the denotation of words, it is a figment of the linguist's imagination; what speakers act with symbolically is of a social origin, namely, connotation. 'In fact, there are no neutral words.. Communication between classes... always represents a critical situation for the language that is used' as the social connotations of the word tend to take over. For example, we cannot be sure how the word *peasant* will be taken by someone who has just left the country. This means there can be no regularity of word meaning. Bourdieu congratulates himself on the excellence of his analysis: 'This objective effect of unveiling destroys the apparent unity of ordinary language' (1991: 40).

Words are also said to have the power of naming, a typically formalist formulation[22] and it is by virtue of this naming power of the words that human languages come to possess the symbolic efficacy to structure their speakers' perception of the world and to construct social reality (1991: 105):

> By structuring the perception which social agents have of the social world, the act of naming helps to establish the structure of this world and does so all the more significantly the more widely it is recognised, i.e. authorised.

Moving along the powerful flow of Bourdieu's style we may fail to notice that this gives rise to a contradiction: when it comes to the naming power of words, there is an exception to the dysfunctionality of denotative meaning – 'the stable part, common to all speakers' – since clearly the authorised, so widely recognised, structure of the social world must be based on commonly shared 'denotative' meanings of words; or, more precisely, both denotation and connotation must operate at one and the same time, displaying once again that interaction of the invariant and the variant which is typical of every aspect of language and of society.

Somewhat reminiscent of Katz and Fodor (1964), who declared that 'grammar minus syntax equals semantics', words seem to be the heart of meaning by language for Bourdieu as well: it is the words of a language that name the categories of the world. The notion of word itself slides between words as dictionary entries, as lexical categories such as common and qualifying noun and dicta, proverbs and all the stereotypes or ritual forms of expression, all of which are 'programmes of perception' and help to impose 'a more or less authorised way of seeing the social world' (1991: 106). This I take to be Bourdieu's view of semantics.

When Frege's theory of reference is read as a version of naming theory, there comes an uncomfortable moment when one cannot ignore the concept of sense, which defies the concept of naming. However, philosophers and formal linguists have found a way around that: they attempt to contain the problem by invoking the concept of truth, a route that Bourdieu too follows (1991:. 41):

> We have known since Frege that words can have meaning without referring to anything. In other words, formal rigour can mask *semantic freewheeling*... the generative capacities of language can surpass the limits of intuition or empirical verification and produce statements that are *formally* impeccable but semantically empty.

On the basis of such assertions I conclude that for Bourdieu only that is semantic – so has *legitimate meaning* – which is verifiable, a logical concomitant of the naming theory of meaning. As distinct from these verifiable semantic categories, legitimised by nature itself, there is 'semantic freewheeling', 'semantic emptiness', deceit and untruthfulness, which many philosophers (e.g. Austin, 1979: 181–2) have found in language. It is this semantic emptiness, deceit and untruthfulness that underly 'the autonomy of language, its specific logic and its particular rules of operation' and thanks to this semantic freewheeling (1991: 41–2):

> language is the exemplary formal mechanism whose generative capacities are without limits. There is nothing that cannot be said and it is possible to say nothing... One should never forget that language, by virtue of its infinite generative but also *originative* capacity – ... – which it derives from its power to produce existence by producing the collectively recognised and thus realised, representation of existence, is no doubt the principal support of the dream of absolute power.

This generative, originative, semantic freewheeling power of language must, in Bourdieu's framework, derive from the naming power of words, for, so far as grammar is concerned, Bourdieu believes that 'it defines meaning only very partially (sic!): it is in relation to a market that the complete determination of the signification of discourse occurs' (1991: 39). Systemic functional linguists would agree that linguistic meaning is context-sensitive. But this view of grammar does not represent Bourdieu's typical position. In the first place, it represents an advance on the real formalist's position so often shared by Bourdieu, which holds that grammar is altogether semantically innocent and is of course context free. At the same time, the extract does not represent Bourdieu's typical view of grammar. In Bourdieu, reference to grammar and grammarians is overwhelmingly associated with the idea of rules of correct usage, prescription of official forms, which is the traditional, conservative notion of what grammars and grammarians are like – an approach that 'the' linguist (at least in most English speaking countries) had explicitly decried even a generation earlier than the Chomskyan revolution. Ignoring these developments, Bourdieu tells us that it is due to the collusion between the state and the grammarians that 'the state language becomes the theoretical norm against which all linguistic practices are objectively measured' (1991: 45):

> Ignorance is no excuse; this linguistic law has its body of jurists – the grammarians – and its agents of regulation – the teachers – who are empowered *universally* to subject the linguistic performance of speaking subjects to examination and to the legal sanction of academic qualification.

By describing the way a certain category of social agents speak, the grammarian plays a discreditable part in 'the objective dispossession of the dominated classes', since his standard of correctness is set by reference to the official language and the authorised style. Inevitably, even if unintentionally, this devalues popular languages (p. 58–9):

> grammarians... hold the monopoly of the consecration and canonisation of legitimate writers and writing. They play their part in constructing the legitimate language by selecting, from among the products on offer, those which seem to them worthy of being consecrated and incorporated into the legitimate competence through educational inculcation... (they) take upon themselves the power to set up and impose norms, (and) tend to consecrate and codify a particular use of language by rationalising it and 'giving reason' to it. In so doing they help to determine the value which the linguistic products of the different users of language will receive in the different markets – particularly those most directly subject to their control such as the educational market – by delimiting the universe of acceptable pronunciations, words or expressions and fixing a language censored and purged of all popular usages, particularly the most recent ones.

Finally on the nature of grammar itself, what it is and where it originates from (1991: 61):

the paradox of all institutionalised pedagogy is that it aims to implant, as schemes that function in a practical state, rules which grammarians have laboured to extract from the practice of the profession of the professionals of written expression (from the past), by a process of retrospective formulation and codification. 'Correct usage' is the product of a competence which is an *incorporated grammar*, the word grammar being used explicitly (and not tacitly, as it is by the linguists) in its true sense of a system of scholarly rules, derived *ex post facto* from expressed discourse and set up as imperative norms for discourse yet to be expressed.

A modern linguist/grammarian, who fails to recognise herself and her activities in these descriptions, is clearly suffering from a delusion, engendered by her self-interest.

Style, a deviation from the norm of the normalised legitimate language, is purely indexical, with no semantic function.

> 'To speak is to appropriate one or the other of the expressive styles already constituted in and through usage and objectively marked by their position in a hierarchy of styles which expresses the hierarchy of corresponding social groups' (Bourdieu, 1991: 54).

The form of language, apart from the choice of the 'choice' words, phrases etc., seems to have no role in the identification of a style. Whatever patterns of the form of language are utilised in the creation of one or the other style may be safely ignored: they are no more than table manners, since anything said anyhow by those in authority would be regarded as a realisation of the legitimate, authoritative style. I read this as implying that in the *production* of authority, as opposed to its *re*production, language plays no part: authority must, therefore, be manufactured wordlessly!

This leaves us with notions such as genre/discourse. Bourdieu is silent when it comes to the relation of genres/discourse to the three components of language – its phonology, lexicon and grammar – except in the context of the discussion of performatives where he deplores the error that linguists make in thinking that they might find 'in discourse itself – in the specifically linguistic substance of speech, as it were – the key to the efficacy of speech'. So far as objective reality is concerned, it is clear that 'authority comes to language from outside' (1991: 109). The following extract I take as fairly typical of Bourdieu's position (1991: 113):

> In order to gauge the magnitude of the error in Austin's and all other strictly formalist analyses of symbolic systems [sic!], it suffices to show that the language of authority is only the limiting case of the legitimate language, whose authority does not reside, as the racism of social class would have it,

in the set of prosodic and articulatory variations which define distinguished pronunciation, or in the complexity of the syntax or the richness of the vocabulary, in other words in the intrinsic properties of discourse itself, but rather in the social conditions of production and reproduction of the distribution between the classes of the knowledge and recognition of the legitimate language.

If the last two lines here remind one of the mythical seven veils of Salome, so be it: the complexity of the embedding in Bourdieu's expression, viz., *in the social conditions of production and reproduction of the distribution between the classes of the knowledge and recognition of the legitimate language,* is iconic of the complexity of social relations; one must peel layer after layer of qualifiers before one's intelligence can grasp the concept that Bourdieu's grammar is construing here. But if we have read Bourdieu at all carefully, we know that social relations are complex things, quite unlike language which, if we have again read Bourdieu carefully, is simply an epiphenomenon. This is a conclusion that, on reflection, should cause no surprise: after all, Bourdieu does buy the formalist view of language, at the same time castigating it. Whatever the origin of his views on the nature of language, its consequences for modelling society and for reflections on the role of language in pedagogy appear less than desirable: the former suffers by internal contradictions, the latter by an exaggerated sense of futility, as I will attempt to show in the concluding sections. But first, the grounds for my disagreement with Bourdieu's spontaneous linguistics.

4 Modelling language, modelling social world

Why do I find Bourdieu's discourse on language at once fascinating and disquieting? Is it because, as Wacquant (1993: 247) suggests, through this discourse my social self is 'stripped bare' and I am revealed to myself as one amongst the other 'wielders of a dominated form of domination that scarcely wants to recognise itself as such'? I do not think so.[23] Never having doubted that my existence is insidiously implicated in the condition of other fellow beings around me, I have not found this aspect of his analysis a revelation, though of course I have been fascinated by the unrelenting quality of his critical gaze which so remorselessly identifies the details of the many ways in which we collude with the processes of domination. But this remark applies to Bourdieu's sociological discourse as a whole, while what I am referring to here is more specifically my reaction to his discourse on language. I rather believe my fascination and disquiet have to do with an unevenness that I sense in his views on the topic: on the one hand, presented remarkably powerfully are his acute critical observations on language use, on the other hand, side by side or rather inhering in them, are certain internal contradictions almost in danger of being missed under the dazzlement of this powerful style. It takes some effort to see that Bourdieu's discourse on language presents as one-sided a picture of language as Saussure's, if not more so. If Saussure privileged 'internal linguistics' – the study of language as a network of relations internal to language in terms of which alone was the linguist allowed to study the categories of language – Bourdieu simply reverses the situation: his spontaneous (socio)linguistics is a celebration of 'external linguistics'. As the extensive extracts presented above demonstrate, Bourdieu (1991) implies overwhelmingly that everything one needs to know about language can be known by reading sociological tracts. In short, to Saussure's linguistics as ideally the study of an idealised language taken entirely in itself, Bourdieu poses a study of language in which language taken in itself is nothing but a stream of noise arbitrarily linked to certain social percepts through the accident of being associated with certain social conditions; everything comes to language from outside, from the external conditions of speaking; the conditions themselves owe nothing to language.

While agreeing with much of his criticism of dominant linguistic practices, the objective reality of language seen as a social semiotic process forces me to reject his monologic stance. In creating a model of the production, reproduction and circulation of language in society we cannot make the error of *relying on only one of the factors involved*, that of the social conditions of *parole*; *ignoring everything* that 'the circulation of discourses in the linguistic markets' owes to the semo-logical component of language (with apologies to Bourdieu, 1991: 37–8; see Section 2.2.2 of this paper). To be viable, the theory of linguistic practice must reject a monologic stance whether it originates in Saussure's texts or in Bourdieu's. Instead of the polarised one sided vignettes, we need the concept Markova (1990) calls 'co-genetic logic' which, as is obvious from a language's use and its history, governs the simultaneous evolution of both language and society. There can be no *either/or*, no *first language/society, then later society/language*. As Halliday (1992/2003: 11) says:

> Language neither drives culture nor is driven by it; the old question about which drives which can be set aside as irrelevant, because the relation is not one of cause and effect but rather... one of realisation[24]: that is, culture and language co-evolve in the same relationship in which, within language, meaning and expression co-evolve.

We do need to emphasise that language is, in a very important respect, sociogenetic, just as we need to insist that society is in an equally important respect semo-genetic: the human world as we know it may or may not go round with love, but it certainly could not go round without talk. Much of the complexity of describing language lies in maintaining both the social and the semiotic perspectives simultaneously, something that the systemic functional linguists ideally attempt to do.

4.1 Naming reality: formal semantics

But to view language from this dual perspective means that language as *social semiotic praxis* – which is the only true condition of its active existence – should be seen unequivocally as a *construer* of reality, not just as its *representer*, not as a mirror that reflects the categories of nature, that simply names them, transgressing from the authority of the really real world in such acts of aberration as might be called *semantic freewheeling*. One must make a distinction between a representational and a constructivist view of language, just as one must acknowledge the significance of the difference between *what there is* and *what some speech community collectively believes there to be*. This difference is the measure of the power of language as a semiotic system active in social practices (Hasan, 1984a; Thibault, 1991). Acknowledging the existence of this power implies that we cannot in the same breath talk, as Bourdieu does, both of linguistic meanings as the naming of reality and of language as a means of 'structuring the perception which social agents have of the social world' (p. 105). For without doubt human languages 'structure' distinct schemes for the perception of the material world: between the really real and our perception of the real lies our language, which is to say language is not a surrogate of some absolute, real, reality: it does not *represent* reality; it simply *construes a model* of reality.

Bourdieu's external linguistics looks at language as a side-effect of social practices, effacing everything internal to the semiotic system of language. His external linguistics never asks what makes it possible for language to participate in social practice; or rather, it pre-empts any discussion of this question by assuming that all that comes to language, not authority alone, comes from outside, without pausing to elucidate the complexity of the expression 'comes to language'. This perspective on language is in keeping with Bourdieu's conceptualisation of the 'formal mechanism' of language, which as I have pointed out before (see Section 3.3) is as close to the formalist position as makes no difference. In the context of the present debate, I would single out two interrelated elements of this position. First, the formalist view of semantics, which despite a variety of respectable sounding labels such as for example 'correspondence theory', remains locked in what Butt (1985/1989) has called the 'mirrorite' approach; and, secondly, the belief that the lexicon – the word – is the stuff of which the semantics of human language is made; grammar itself is innocent of meaning. While Bourdieu does grant 'partial' meaning making capacities to grammar, for him too linguistic meaning is lexical, largely word based; words have meaning by naming (denotation) and come to accrue personal nuances (connotation) in use. This view is hospitable to Bourdieu's ideas about arbitrariness (on which see, LiPuma, 1993): there can be no logical connection between a name and the object the name names. And, while the term 'signifier' is generally used freely to refer to any physically perceptible object, that acts as the 'expression' of something other than itself, in the formalist theory of meaning, the signifier is typically treated as another name for 'word'. Thus it tends to be assumed that if there *is* a formal mechanism of language, it must consist of just those relations of opposition and combination which give the signifier/word its specific identity. So far as the 'signified' is concerned, it is something out there in the world to which the signifier/word corresponds.

I am claiming that these perspectives typical of correspondence and truth functional theories of meaning are quite close to Bourdieu's expressed view of semantics and that they contradict many of the claims he makes *en passant*, such as the role of 'the dialectic of the meaning of the language and 'sayings of the tribe" (1990: 57) in the formation of the habitus or the nature of the relation between social class and habitus (1990: 58–60) or the conscription of female subjects by the pedagogic system in the devaluation of the common language or the genesis of official language and the nature of society. Much of the contradiction and suppression in Bourdieu's discourse on language arises from his view of how language comes to mean. As all instances of contradiction I have just named cannot be examined within the scope of this paper, let me support my claim by a brief consideration of the last problem – how official languages are produced and reproduced.

To pursue this, let me refer to the extract quoted in Section 3.1 from Bourdieu (1991: 48). Throughout this account, a sequencing of moments in history is implied which appears[25] quite problematic. If a nation is 'an abstract group based on law', this would suggest that the law was already around in some form or other, on which this transformation of the group into a nation is based; this in turn poses the problem of the variety of language in which that law was formulated. Is it an official, legitimate variety? If so, what is the genesis of *that* official variety? A similar sequencing of moments – *only when ab happens, does yz come about* – is again evident in his claim that 'only when *the making of a nation...* creates new *usages and functions* does it become necessary *to forge a standard language*'. By contrast as I see it, there is a dialectic of the social and the semiotic processes. The fact that certain persons in a group experience the need to use language in bringing about certain new social processes and that they proceed to actually do so thereby putting the meaning-making resources of their language under pressure, is one important element in the group becoming a nation. The standard variety is not 'forged' *ex post facto* after the nation has already come about; rather, given the logic of the role of language in the life of human groups, the transformation of a vernacular into a standard and of a group of people into a nation are concurrent phenomena. As the SF linguists would put it, a variety of language becomes the/a standard language in the course of being used by its speakers for bringing about an increasing range of social processes. This experience does not simply change the social life of the speakers in question and of others in relation to them, *it also changes their language*.

Bourdieu would have us believe that the change that comes to the popular language is limited just to the level of phonology (cf. his discourse on pronunciation and articulation which cannot be extricated from bodily hexis), or to phenomena that make up what he calls style (using latinate vocabulary, rhetorical strategies and the like, all semantically empty but socially so fraught). In fact, much more significantly *what changes also is the meaning making resources of that language*, as well as its *register repertoire*. It is in the combined operation of human social action and locution that what Bourdieu calls 'linguistic markets' are created; there is no linguistic market unless there is language to identify its specificity and this specificity could not consist in semantically empty vocalisations. It follows that if you typically do not find dadaist discourse in the cabinet, as Bourdieu (1991) points out, this is not because its pronunciation is not legitimate; rather, it is because, until developed further by use, its meaning making resources are incommensurate with what (some section of) the community has come to believe as meanings appropriate to a cabinet meeting and, in this social context, dadaism would not do even with the most legitimate pronunciation in the world *unless and until its meaning making resources are stretched*. Which is not to say that the meanings specific to the cabinet meetings are in themselves superior – that may or may not be so, depending on what your standards for the assessment of superiority are; it is simply to say that these meanings have the property of being seen as the ones pertaining to a specific register, a specific field. It is not the racism of social class which prompts the observation, *objectively real*, that the register repertoire of dominated varieties is always narrower than that of the dominating one(s); rather, the observation is based on the principle that the wider the range of social processes one engages in the greater one's social power. Further, a variety of language that is specific to a field evolves in and through practice changing in all its aspects, i.e. in its meanings, its syntax and its lexicon not just phonology and articulation[26]. It could hardly be otherwise if *parole* is to constitute *langue* and if social institutions, units, processes whatever have to be thought of as ongoing processes, not as self-enclosed sequentially ordered 'moments' – first the nation, then the standard language, first the market then the linguistic capital suited to that market, first domination then dominating discourse. I believe this static model of the social, inscribed in a particular view of language, is entirely at variance with Bourdieu's modelling of society – in fact he it is who has done most to develop the dynamic perspective in the social sciences. So his theory of language sits uneasily with his theory of society. Perhaps spontaneous linguistics is as undesirable as spontaneous sociology!

In my view, the appropriation of power is – importantly – also the appropriation of new *meaning making resources*, the addition of new elements in their register repertoire, of those who are in a position to experience the ever growing new needs for the use of language as they engage in the always (infinitesimally) changing social processes. There is a spiralling effect in the mutually supportive relation of the elements of this trajectory, where the holding of a social position is tantamount to engagement in a larger range of social processes, which is tantamount to holding a wider register repertoire, which is tantamount to the capacity to recognise the opportunities that call for new social processes, which in turn underlies the users' struggle to use their existing resources to stretch out to meet these needs, which further enhances their power to hold on to their social position. This complex relation in which one element feeds into the next is a powerful secret of the power such speakers typically own. Granted that by virtue of the social logic of the present moment, the commander's command to the soldier is more likely to be efficacious than the soldier's to the commander, let us however not make the error of assuming – or by our silences, even leaving room for such assumptions to be made – that armies come about in silence, that commanders' positions get created without language, that in fact the entire social logic develops without the complicity of the meaning making resources of language. I would reject the claim asserted or implied repeatedly by Bourdieu that this complicity can be reduced to features that relate only to *accent variation*, that they do not implicate any other kind of linguistic variation with semantic significance. I would also view with scepticism what appears to me an absurd claim by Bourdieu, implied logically by his discourse (e.g., p. 51), that in the formation of, say, the commander's habitus, language might play no important role, that the fact of social authority is in some sense prior, more basic, than human speech. One need not repeat the truism that authority in human communities today has become dramatically different from the higher ape's breast beating. This specifically human mode of behaviour co-evolved[27] with the evolution of speech, the most flexible instrument in the fashioning of the instruments of symbolic violence and symbolic violence, as Bourdieu has shown, is the most powerful weapon in the struggle for domination. Contra Marx, language is not a superstructure, not an epiphenomenon: it is right there on the ground, participating with other, material forces, in the creation and maintenance, in the production and reproduction, of social structure, which is to say in the fashioning of social distinctions (Bernstein, 1965; 1990; 1996; Halliday, 1971c; 1974; 1976; 1990 etc; Hasan, 1973; 1984a; 1995a; Lemke, 1995).

I believe we do need a theory of language that avoids the sorts of inadequacies which Bourdieu's external linguistics suffers from. If I am right in thinking that the source of the problem for Bourdieu lies in his ideas on language – in particular, how he theorises linguistic meaning – then we need a qualitatively different semantic theory.

4.2 Construing reality: functional semantics

There is a fairly well established tradition of attributing the formalist views on meaning to Saussure, though I believe the view is mistaken (Hasan, 1985b; 1987a). Without going into the various senses in which Saussure employed his term 'arbitrary' (Hasan, 1985b, for discussion), for him to describe the relation between the signified and the signifier as arbitrary, was to say that the *value* and *identity* of the signified is not defined by the signifier; all that the signifier does is to signal that a signified has been *called up*. Because their association is arbitrary, based purely on conventional pairing, the essential nature of the signified is in no way determined by the nature of the signifier associated with it.

Saussure's text provided only rather programmatic statements on how the value and identity of the signified is construed. It was Hjelmslev (1961) who developed these programmatic statements. He argued that the signified, which he called 'content', is a complex entity, constituted in the solidary relation between 'content-substance' and 'content-form'. Ignoring the details of his arguments, his 'content-substance' is what we may paraphrase as 'linguistic meaning', i.e., the semantic level of language, while his 'content-form' is the formal level of language. This formal level subsumes both syntax and lexicon, not as two separate language components as in formalist accounts[28], but as the endpoints of the same continuum (Halliday, 1961; Hasan, 1987b). Hjelmslev's interpretation of the Saussurean term 'signified' has been adopted in SFL with certain modifications (for detail, Hasan, 1995a), where his content-form is referred to as the level of 'lexicogrammar' (informally, 'wordings'), while his content-substance is known as 'semantics' (informally, 'meanings'). SF linguists claim that the semantics of a language is construed by its lexicogrammar, i.e. by both its grammar and its lexicon working together, not simply by its words naming bits of reality. As Wittgenstein (1958: 92e, 257) points out: 'when we speak of someone's having given a name to pain, what is presupposed is the existence of the grammar of the word 'pain'; it shews the post where the... word is stationed'. If linguistic meaning is lexicogrammatically construed, it follows that the relation between the two levels of meaning and wording is not arbitrary, but logical. If choices in linguistic meaning are construed systemically by choices in lexicogrammar, a change in the possibilities of choices in wordings will be tantamount to a change in the language's meaning potential. In using language, the details of which are predetermined by the dispositions of the speaker's linguistic habitus, his coding orientation, the speaker is first and foremost engaged in acts of meaning. His choice of wordings is activated by his view of meanings suited to what he perceives as the context of his discourse. This solidary relation of 'realisation', a dialectic of wordings and meanings is an important element in the (semo-)logic of language.

Note also that in this interpretation, Saussure's signified is not the object out there in the material or social world. It is a composite structure which inheres in the union of lexicogrammar and semantics. The lexicogrammatical choices, which underlie such units of a language as sentence, clause, group/phrase, word and morpheme, are the 'formal mechanism' which construe the language's semantic potential. The semantic potential is itself not *what there is* by way of extra-linguistic reality; rather, it acts as a grid on that reality. The grid thus created by the signified – by the dialectic of meanings and wordings – is, on the one hand, arbitrary from the standpoint of the potentiality of the human species which is capable of construing many different models of reality (Whorf, 1956) and, on the other hand, it is entirely non-arbitrary, in the sense that it is (socio)logical in the context of that community's social practices and (semo) logical in the context of the internal systemics of that language. This grid, at once arbitrary *and* (semo- / socio-)logical, structures 'the perception that social agents have of the social world' (p. 105). It does not name reality; what it does is to help make sense of it: the concept of meaning as naming simply elides the distance between the model of reality and the reality that the model models.

But what of the *signifier*, which Hjelmslev called 'expression'? The entities at this level are 'acoustic images', phonological patterns, which are conventionally associated – arbitrarily paired – with the complex construct called 'signified'. In theory, any acoustic shape would have done just as well without disturbing the essential nature of the signified. As the signifier plays no part in the *definition* of the signified, changes at the level of expression do not entail changes at the level of lexicogrammar. Contrast this with the situation described above with regard to meaning and lexicogrammar. When in the interest of symmetry we claim that the phonological relations (of the signifier) realise lexicogrammatical relations (of words etc), while the latter realise semantic relations (of meanings), the use of the same term, viz., 'realisation', may be misleading by implying that the relation of realisation is the same in both these cases; in fact, they are crucially different. The relation between phonology and lexicogrammar is simply one of expression, whereas the realisation relation of lexicogrammar and semantics is complex. The phonological signifier simply *signals* some wording say, a specific word; it does not *constitute* it. By contrast, the lexicogrammatical signifier *constitutes* a meaning within the semo-logic of that language. It follows that far from naming any element of the real world, the phonological signifier does not even have a direct 'connection' with linguistic meaning, for between the levels of semantics and phonology lies lexicogrammar as an interface between linguistic meaning and phonological expression. Nor do lexicogrammatical units such as word relate directly to any element of the world; between the sensuously apprehended universe and the level of lexicogrammar lies semantics, acting as an interface. It follows that the signifier can name neither a meaning nor a thing in the world. The acoustic image as signifier has no direct relation to the material/semantic world of our experience;

it labels no part of it. If it labels anything, then that thing is some configuration of lexicogrammatical relations that constitute the identity of a word.

Since linguistic meaning has no physical reality, it is in the words of Russell (1940), not a *sens-ible* phenomenon but an *intelligible* one. Presented to the speakers' intelligence[29] by the *sens-ible* phonological signifier's 'naming' of the *intelligible* lexicogrammatical signifier, linguistic meaning is so automatised through the daily practices of living by language and possesses such efficacy in summoning up elements of the already construed reality[30], that it is misrecognised as the real thing, what there actually is. This misrecognition – treating the realities construed by the linguistic meanings of his language as really real – is part of the practical relation of the practical user to his language. If 'wherever a sign is present, ideology is present' (Vološinov, 1986: 10), this is in no small measure due to the speaker's misplaced faith in the faithfulness of his own language to the really real world, whether material or social. And this illusion is maintained crucially by the cooperation between the social and the semiotic: the formal resource for the creation of linguistic meaning resides in the semo-logical relations of opposition and combination – paradigmatic and syntagmatic relations – at the levels of meaning and wording. The choice of what meanings will be created as refracted through these relations, resides largely in the social agent's practical relation to his material and social conditions of existence. It is the speaker's living of life in social contexts that, in Butt's term (1987), places 'semantic pressure' on the 'formal mechanism'; and it is the formal mechanism of the language – its semo-logical component – that takes cognisance of this semantic pressure – to create the means of meaning the as-yet un-meanable in language[31].

This solidary bond between meanings and wordings does not imply, as is often wrongly supposed, that the lexicogrammar of a language delivers identical copies of meanings to every speaker of that language. The referential potential of linguistic meanings – what in the world of our practical experience they might relate to – develops in speakers through the functioning of their language in the contexts of the living of life (Malinowski, 1923; Firth, 1957b; Halliday, 1975; Painter, 1984; 1989; 1996; Hasan, 1989; 1992b), a view that also underlies Bourdieu's concept of habitus as I understand it (see especially, 1990: 56ff). Language operative in the contexts of the living of life is *parole*; it takes the form of discourse. In this obvious fact lies an important aspect of the speakers' un-self-conscious relation to his language: it is in the materials of discourse that speakers find the grounds for perceiving, for internalising if you will, the formal relations of opposition and of combination, actualised as the relations between the wordings, which constitute the specific content of the semo-logic of their language and it is in the social context of the discourse that they find the frame for the perception of the referential potential of the lexicogrammatically constituted meanings.

The above provides a highly condensed outline of 'functional semantics', itself part of the theory of linguistic practice widely known as systemic functional linguistics[32]. One may ask: what practical purpose is served by such an abstract theory of linguistic meaning? How does it relate to speakers' linguistic practices? What relevance does it bear to Bourdieu's discourse on language in relation to society? A few words then on the implications of this view of language.

4.3 Implications of functional semantics: modelling language

Perhaps, for our purposes, the most important element of functional semantics is in its re-thinking of the relation between meaning and lexicogrammar as *constitutive* and *not arbitrary*[33]. It follows from the acceptance of this principle that linguistic meanings cannot come about without the internal logic of language. If, following this logic, some wording is worded[34], there is no avoiding meaningfulness; conversely, if there is no wording, there can be no linguistic meaning: 'it is only in a language that I can mean something by something' (Wittgenstein, 1958: 18e, 38). It is in this sense that contra Bourdieu (1991: 41), there are no *'formally impeccable but semantically empty'* statements: historical truth is not a necessary condition of meaningfulness and 'situationally false' is not synonymous with 'semantically empty'. In fact, the principle of linguistic logic implies that there are no 'true synonyms' in a language; much less is it possible to find 'the same meaning' across languages. It is also in this sense that language goes beyond the individual: its meaning making efficacy is not constrained by speaker intention, otherwise slips of the tongue would be always meaningless. As Vološinov (1986: 33) put it: 'Intention is always a lesser thing than creation' and what the semo-logic does is to create meanings that for the receiver of the message are not constrained by the speaker's intentions. Nor is this meaning making potential subservient to context: to say of some specific meanings that they are contextually infelicitous, lacking legitimacy etc. is to admit that they have a meaning independent of the context in relation to which they are being judged as lacking.

These elementary facts are widely accepted. I repeat them here because they shed light on the troubled notion of the *autonomy* of language. To claim that the semo-logic of language is inherently independent of both speaker intention and of social context is not to deny that, typically, a speaker words those meanings that s/he means to mean and, typically, these meanings tend to be responsive to the speaker's perception of the social context and what that context is a context for. Nor is it to deny even that the specific content of a language is fashioned by the social history of its speakers. But it is simply to affirm that to turn the elements of the speaker's social history into content-substance, into linguistic meanings, what is needed is semo-logic. And this semo-logic creates a vast network of relations; it does the 'stage-setting' that is 'presupposed' in any act of linguistic meaning. As Wittgenstein pointed out, to the extent that one *can* 'intend the construction of a sentence in advance, that is made possible by the fact that.. (one) speak(s) the language' (1958: 108, 337); and to the extent that one responds with sensitivity to the customary semiotic 'needs of a situation', this is possible only because one is accustomed to customs.

All this is true but it is equally important to remember that customs can be challenged and they are; they can change and they do; new meanings can be created and they are. This is so largely because the semo-logic of a language is not constrained by individual intention or social situation. To Bourdieu, for whom 'authority comes to language from outside... Language at most *represents* this authority, manifests and symbolises it' (1991: 109), 'it is clear that not anyone can assert anything, or else does so at his peril' (1991: 74). There is more than a hint in Bourdieu that the former half of this principle (that 'not anyone can assert anything') is somehow more important, has greater force, than the possibilities inhering in the latter (namely that 'speaking at one's peril' no matter how devastating, is still an option that one may choose to exercise). To me it seems that in the history of humanity both observations are important; but speaking out of turn, without the authority to speak and so at one's peril, as Steve Biko did, or Wei Jingsheng is doing, is the more remarkable for it is an important element in changing the course of human history by creating in one's fellow beings a sense of the *real* possibility of mounting a challenge to power and authority. If one continues the practice, even from an initial position of weakness, one might contribute to wresting power as Gandhi did or Mandela. The historically actual is not isomorphic with the human potential. No one convinces us better than Bourdieu of the need, in describing social life, to avoid on the one hand the mechanical necessity of the historical and on the other, the mechanical necessity of the universal. Naturally, it would be silly to suggest that for engaging in such acts of meaning all one needs is language. But irrespective of what else is necessary for such acts of meaning, one thing that is certainly necessary is language, not simply because it is in language that you can mean something by something, but also because, as Vygotsky argued (1962; 1978) it is in languaging that your mental functions evolve, functions which are the necessary foundation for perceiving that authority can/must be challenged. It is surprising how often in the social sciences the expression 'not only language' is taken to mean 'without language': as I see it, the expression means: 'language in cooperation with other social forces'.

We return once again then to the dialogical logic of the semiotic and the social in describing the social practices of being doing and saying. To claim autonomy for the semo-logical component is not to deny that in *parole* the choice of meaning – and so of wording – is determined by the speaker's perception of social context and the practices of being, saying and doing that a context permits/provokes. The fact that the semantic potential of a language evolves under such circumstances as these, has a consequence for the linguistic level of lexicogrammar: the wordings of a language too evolve in and through the speakers' efforts to exchange meanings. The social context within which acts of meaning are embedded is an occasion for carrying out some *social action*, by co-actants in some *social relation*, placed in some *semiotic contact*. The meaning potential of language and its lexicogrammatical resources must be such as to enable its speakers to construe these important aspects of their social experience. In other words, language has to be functional, for social contexts are first and foremost semiotically construed; they cannot be known simply by their material attributes. For this reason, the principle of linguistic functionality resonates through the elements of social contexts to meanings and wordings. In SFL these functions are known as 'ideational' (construing social action), 'interpersonal' (enacting social relation) and 'textual' (creating semiotic contact). Meaning and wording are socially saturated just as the social world is linguistically created. Bourdieu (1991: 38) has warned his unsuspecting reader that (emphasis added):

> as long as they [i.e. linguists] are unaware of the limits that constitute their science, linguists *have no choice but to search desperately in language for something that is actually inscribed in the social relations* within which it functions, or to engage in a sociology without knowing it, that is, with *the risk of discovering, in grammar itself, something that their spontaneous sociology has unwittingly imported into it.*

If linguists are tempted to engage in spontaneous sociology, this is because sociologists of even Bourdieu's calibre have ended up practising, no matter what they preach, a monologic logic in which even social relations are treated as if, like rivers and mountains, they could come into being without semiotic interaction. How does authority 'come into language'? What is the mode of its entry? What are the means of its conservation in language? With his one-sided views on language, it is not surprising that Bourdieu does not raise these questions. What exactly are 'the limits that constitute' my linguistics? It depends on how I conceptualise what language is. If I subscribe to functional semantics, then as a linguist my job is to describe how language works in its speakers' living of life and this, in my view would reveal that there is no market in a society that is not a linguistic market, nor is there a field in society that is not at least partially construed by language. Which would in turn mean that, for me, Bourdieu's external linguistics is as inadequate as Saussure's internal linguistics. To describe language as a meaning potential active in the social processes of a society, SF linguists must import, *wittingly* and *deliberately*, not professional sociology, but an understanding of social life into the grammar and the semantics of language, for combined with the semo-logic component of language, this is what will enable them to explain how language never fails its speakers, how it is able to meet all their needs (Hasan, 1984a). For the systemic functional linguist, a socially informed grammar is not a risk; it is a requirement.

It follows that so far as the SF linguist is concerned, the grammarian's task is rather different from that which Bourdieu assigns him. If the lexicogrammar is a resource for meaning, this task is to show how the resource works in the various fields of discourse, how lines are drawn across the various social strata and how in this drawing of line some meanings get seen as *privileged* and *privileging*, in the words of Bernstein. The SF linguist would not be doing justice to the study of language if s/he did not ask: how can the privileged and privileging meanings of the dominant group be characterised semo-logically? Certainly a linguist subscribing to functional semantics would never be misled into thinking that all variation in language flows along the phonic stream, if for the simple reason that domination requires a control of many fields and many markets, the doing of which calls for different ways of meaning. And surely the functional description of the lexicogrammar of a language will be based on what the community of speakers have created in their *paroles*. I say 'surely', for this is the condition of practising the science of social practice, whether what is being described is the exchange of gifts in the Kabyle society or the exchange of meanings. The slippages in Bourdieu's discourse are misleading: description *per se* does not equal prescription; the origin of prescription is in social discrimination and control.

4.4 Implications of functional semantics: linguistic practices

When the question of linguistic variation is re-examined with this insight into the internal logic of language, the picture looks somewhat different from that presented either by the 'official', i.e. Labovian, sociolinguistics or by Bourdieu's external linguistics. We are forced to recognise that given the semo-logic of language, linguistic practice was destined to become the instrument for linguistic variation, which would have occurred whether or not social hierarchisation existed. In fact the sort of linguistic variation that Labov's work made famous rests on the manifestation of what might be called phonological serendipity: for what varies across varieties is a syndrome of phonological features whose *origin* lies in chance and which, without any logical connection to social hierarchy, gets conscripted as a signal of status in the social processes of discrimination. This kind of linguistic variation, known as 'accent' (Abercrombie, 1951/1965) is now called 'social dialect'. Manifested typically at the level of the phonological signifier, the domain of such dialect/accent variation at most includes isolated lexical variation (e.g. *pip* vs. *pit* vs. *stone*). Bourdieu's official language – a standard dialect/accent – is a variety of this kind. It is hardly surprising that this kind of variation, which Labov (1972) has described as different ways of saying the same thing, is arbitrary, since it is a variation that implicates only the phonological signifier, whose relation to context, meaning and wording is never constitutive but simply one of expression. For linguists subscribing to the formal paradigm, linguistic variation logically cannot implicate the level of semantics and since in this approach form has no function – meaning is not constituted by lexicogrammar – variation in wording too would have to be arbitrary (Weiner and Labov, 1983). Logically then variation can only have a socially imported meaning; this is Labov's 'social meaning', which must come to language 'from outside', as Bourdieu, again in conformity with the formal approach, observes. The formalist approach is incapable of ever finding a form of linguistic variation whose relation to the socially lived life is other than arbitrary. The reason for this lies in how the formalist conceptualises language: while this limitation is attributed to the nature of language, it is in fact an artefact of the nature of a formalist theory (for some discussion, see Hasan, 1989; 1992b; 1993).

Our everyday experience of variation in language contradicts this formalist view of language and linguistic practice. For example, we know that irrespective of whether we are speakers of a standard dialect or a non-standard one, we engage in a range of social processes, with differing fields/domains, differing social relations between agents and differing modes of semiotic contact. And we know also that the language we use in one kind of social process as opposed to another systematically differs in its meanings and wordings – without necessarily differing in its accent. Given the dialectic of context, meanings and wordings, it can hardly be otherwise. A specific structure of a class of social process will legitimise only a certain class of meanings for a specific class of social agents: this is *the sociological imperative*. But, just as important is the fact that those meanings can only be meant in certain linguistic ways: this is *the semo-logical imperative*. In other words, one cannot write *The Logic of Practice* as one would a letter to a friend and it would be enormously misleading to pretend that the relation between the wordings and meanings of that book is simply arbitrary and accidental, or that, given the socio- / semologic, any other class of meanings would have been perceived as constitutive of the field of sociology. Here we see that the systematic variation in meaning and wording is *not* arbitrary: it has an inner logic. This kind of variation in language which correlates with variation in social processes – what social practice in which field you are engaged in with whom and how – is generally known in SFL as 'register variation'[35], a category close to what Hymes called 'speech variety'. In the final analysis the basis for this correlation is the dialectic relation of language and society, which accounts for the co-genetic logic that governs their co-evolution. I have claimed that the register repertoire of a standard dialect is wider than that of the non-standard dialects. The justification for the claim lies in the fact that speakers of the standard dialect, typically the dominant groups, engage also in a larger variety of social processes: in fact, it is socio- / semologically impossible to have a dominant status in any society, whether primitive or post-capitalist, without the potential and practice of such engagements. Those who can speak a propos most things most fundamental to their society have power indeed. Language does not need to dream of power; the power it has, it actually controls by insidiously infiltrating every aspect of social practice. Thus, typically your accent/dialect, i.e. Bourdieu's official language, *signals* who you are – where you come from geographically/socially; by contrast, at least partly, your register repertoire *constitutes* and is itself *constituted by* who you are socially. This process wherein the self is fashioned begins early.

4.5   Implications of functional semantics: language and consciousness

In the mundane line of language development (Hasan, 1996a), which following Bourdieu and Passeron (1977) may be viewed as an aspect of *unofficial pedagogy* devoted to the pedagogy of language, when children learn their mother tongue they are, in the words of Halliday (1975), learning how to mean. But unofficial pedagogy is altogether *the* most effective instrument of social reproduction: what children learn is how to mean within the specific range of social processes placed in their reach by virtue of their place in their social world. The inculcation of the details of this social space and of the relations within it begins very early in life (Hasan, 1986; 1989; 1992b; Cloran, 1994; Williams, 1995).

However, the specialisation of social process by subjects' place in the social system is not absolute: that is to say, in most societies, at least some social processes – especially in respect of field of discourse, in terms of register theory – such as giving care to children, shopping, talking to neighbours and so on are in common to members of all social groups. This does not mean, however, that in such social processes, the same meanings are perceived as legitimate by members of every social group. Rather, in the words of Bernstein (1981), the criteria for the recognition of a context as also for the practices 'suited to' a context differ across social strata. What appears relevant to the carrying out of that social process is not the same across all social groups: in fact the way the consciousness of subjects from different social strata engages with the situation they find themselves in is so remarkably different as to encourage the belief that their consciousness is not the same, that their perception of and their action in, the situation is conditioned by their 'habitus' formed 'within the limits of a class of conditions of existence' (Bourdieu, 1990: 58). Thus, within the frame of the 'same' social process, ways of meaning and wording differ across groups differentially positioned in society. It is important to emphasise that the difference I am drawing attention to here is not restricted to linguistic practices alone, but subsumes ways of being, saying, doing, thinking and feeling[36]. My interest is from the standpoint of linguistic variation and in this sphere empirical research (Hasan, 1989; 1992b; Cloran, 1994; Williams, 1995) has shown that within the context of the 'same' social process, a systematic variation in ways of meaning exists across differentially positioned social groups. This kind of variation I have referred to as 'semantic variation': semantic variation correlates with variation in coding orientation, in (specifically linguistic aspects of) habitus. Neither semantic variation nor register variation can be described as 'different ways of saying the same thing', since the variation in these cases implicates the semantic level itself. Neither is therefore 'arbitrary' in the sense in which phonological variation can be: just as in the construal of a social process meanings play a constitutive role so also in the construal of subjects' coding orientation, their habitus, their predisposition to certain meanings is crucial. Speakers' ideological affiliations are constituted for them through their acts of meaning embedded in their social material existence and to the extent that the social and the semiotic are in a dialectical relation it must follow that social subjects' ways of meaning co-evolve with their social and material existence.

It is possible that the view just presented departs from what is currently considered 'politically correct': the notion of semantic variation does claim that different social classes habitually display orientation to different orders of meaning. So is this a case of *linguistic fetishism* – an instance of 'the racism of social class'? I do not think so and I will defend this claim by referring to Bourdieu himself. First, I believe that Bourdieu is right in claiming that 'All symbolic domination presupposes, on the part of those who submit to it, a form of complicity' (p. 50) the principles of which are 'inscribed in a practical state, in dispositions [of the habitus] which are impalpably inculcated, through a long and slow process of acquisition' (ibid.). Once this principle is granted, we need to show the details of this complicity. How does the complicity work and what is it that is inculcated, what is acquired? Based on the findings of my research and that of my colleagues, I am suggesting that variant semantic orientation in the dominating and dominated classes is one form of the 'dispositions impalpably incluated'; that this is one important element of 'the systems of durable, transposable dispositions, structured structures predisposed to function as structuring structures' (Bourdieu, 1990: 53) that is 'acquired' by way of classed linguistic habitus, that it is complicit in maintaining the structures of domination: the characteristics specific to the semantic orientation of the dominating group equip them, within the social logic of the historical moment, to dominate without premeditation, while those of the dominated group expose them to domination. Further, our research suggests that the 'long and slow process of (the) acquisition' of these dispositions, these structured structuring structures takes the form of everyday discourse in the child's everyday life.

Secondly, if it is accepted that 'class (or group) habitus' exists, as it is by Bourdieu, then it seems reasonable to suppose that there must be class specific *linguistic* habitus as well. We cannot on the one hand insist on the malleability of language in the hands of hierarchisation and on the other maintain that the very principles of practice – the habitus – is innocent of language: while there are passages in Bourdieu's writing where the role of language in the formation of habitus is rendered close to insignificant (see extract from p. 51 quoted in Section 2.2.2) on the whole, Bourdieu's texts do not permit such a reading. Thus if class habitus is 'a subjective but non-individual system of internalised structures, *common schemes of perception, conception and action, which are the precondition of all objectification and apperception*' (Bourdieu, 1990: 60; emphasis added), it appears highly improbable that a habitus so characterised could be formed without the complicity of language, or even that its basis could lie purely in the phonological signifier, having nothing to do with wordings and meanings, or that in extending to wordings, the basis of such a habitus would only lie in the table manners of the sorts of stylistic features that Bourdieu discusses in connection with official language. The linguistic practices of agents enjoying a 'community of consciousness' (Bourdieu, 1990: 58) must involve meanings and to the extent that class habitus is a principle and this principle is not identical across classes, it has to be assumed that ways of meaning across classes will be distinct. In a functional conception of language, semantic variation logically implicates the level of wordings. Once the concept of class habitus has been postulated, it is incoherent to describe descriptions of the lexicogrammatical and semantic features associated with specific class-based coding orientations as inspired by 'the racism of social class', unless it were to be maintained that in the fashioning of class habitus language plays no part, which would be absurd.

Reflection on the nature of semantic variation shows the ultimate power of language working in cahoots with society. If, as Whorf (1956) said, 'Talk is the best show man puts on', this is because of what talk *does*: the essence of talk – its meanings – are not evanescent unlike the noise stream of a language. The latter as the sens-ible, physical phenomenon disappears; the meaning, on the other hand, is integrated as the intelligible into the consciousness of speakers. Through the sociosemiotic experience of living, the human mind acquires certain 'structured structuring structures', certain modes of systemising the world: the world looks different depending on your social positioning. This is why the idea of absolute facts or of absolute logic is problematic. As Whorf pointed out (1956: 235) 'Facts are unlike to speakers whose language background provides for unlike formulations of them'; this is true not only with reference to the grand cosmology of the physical universe with which Whorf dealt but also with reference to the microcosm of one's social world with which Bourdieu deals. In the last analysis there are only two kinds of logic – sociologic and semologic – and it is precisely these logics which underly the privileging and privileged meanings. To describe them as arbitrary is to suggest the possibility of the existence of some absolute logic which is independent of human history.

5 Modes of disempowerment in literacy pedagogy

My debate has gone on and very little room is left to talk about the relevance of all these issues to literacy education. The decision to foreground the debate about the nature of language was not taken lightly, for it is my thesis that one mode of disempowering the learning subject is by disempowering language. When language is disempowered, what many learners learn by way of language education itself becomes an instrument for inducing disability: literacy education designed on the basis of a diminshed model of language – either internal or external – will result in specifiable cases, in reproach that is born of the sense of failure and futility over many hours a day, many days a week, many weeks a month, many months a year and years and years of the learner's life. This is not to claim that by changing language education we could change the face of society or the fate of an individual altogether and/or all at once, but it is to say that whatever little contribution language education could make to this process is definitely barred by the pathetic programs known traditionally as language education and by the unintended conspiracy of keeping teachers as innocent of knowledge about language as possible. It is my view that just as Bourdieu allies himself with the regressive views of formal linguistics on the nature of language, so also aspects of his discourse regarding what part language education might play in any change, contribute to the perpetuation of traditional language education, which he so eloquently decries. In other words the contradictions in Bourdieu's writings pervade his discourse of language education as much as they do his discourse of language in relation to society. This is the thesis I will develop in this section.

5.1 Disempowering the pedagogic subject: pedagogic field

It is very possible that some readers are asking 'what has one's view of language to do with issues of literacy?'. If so, this wonderment is itself a measure of the poverty of literacy education. One of the most notable features of literacy education is the fundamental inability or unwillingness of policy makers, curriculum producers and educational experts to problematise the very notion of language: what it is as social practice and what it is taken in itself, i.e. as a semiotic. Language is disempowered when it is severed from social practice as in Saussure's internal linguistics, leaving us by implication with a literacy education that basically derives from an 'intellectualist' engagement with formal categories which bear no relation to the practical living of life. But language is equally disempowered when it is severed from its semologic base as in Bourdieu's polarised one-sided celebration of external linguistics, which places all emphasis on social institutions suggesting that everything sociosemantically significant comes to language from outside, thus leaving the study of language stranded once more with the same formal categories without practical function. In both cases language is severed from precisely all those connections which reveal its awesome claims to power – a power whose source is *neither* just sociologic *nor* just semologic. It is not surprising that in either case language education is, in fact *has to be*, reduced to the inanity of learning to 'speak proper', learning (meaning-less[37]) sentence structures, correct usage, 'vocab' and such like. This keeps everyone busily occupied, allowing the ministers of education to moralise on the virtues of 'correct' usage[38], permitting the journalists to pompously present their unanalysed subjective experiences as definitive facts about language[39] and leaving the pedagogic subject after years of schooling so disempowered as to be incapable of using his language to reflect on how the world goes round largely by linguistic acts of meaning, or what, if anything, actuates the minister of education's view of language, why journalism must pander to popular views, or what difference it would make to the science of sociology if one rewrote Bourdieu in 'plain English' – in fact, could one actually do so in any real sense? With this as the background against which programs for literacy education are fashioned, why should we be surprised that forms of 'recognition literacy' (Hasan, 1996a) thrive in the majority of schools, or that literacy education as purveyed in schools encourages a feeling of general antipathy towards learning about language? Why should it not be suggested that the optimal function for a language education class is the discussion of issues such as sexuality? Isn't language taken in itself nothing but a stream of noise and patterns of syntax and lexicon to which meaning comes from outside? What can there be to teach about language that is not sociology? The protest against the privileged status of language in education is truly based on a misrecognition of the case: even in literacy education, language is seriously disempowered in the sense that it is truly trivialised.

5.2 Disempowering the pedagogic subject: social agents

The trivialisation of the pedagogic subject occurs in both senses – subject as a field of knowledge and subject as social subjects, the learners. 'The' learning subject is, like 'the' linguist, homogenised and sanitised to meet the needs of some interested party: the fact that across our social universe we have multiple classes of consciousness, that facts are filtered through different points of view, that social subjects bring different orders of relevance into the classroom is very easily forgotten – IF it was ever allowed to be recognised which is itself open to doubt. The existence of semantic variation in a society which is implied in 'classed' habitus, in turn implies that 'the same' will not be perceived or received as the same. But as Halliday (1990) points out, ironically these perspectives cannot be brought to the consciousness of teachers, because, of course, to talk about variation in meaning and wording as related to social class is anathema: dubbed subversive in the late 1960s and 1970s in debates against Bernstein, now it is to display 'the racism of social class', or to indulge in an immoral 'linguistic fetishism'. An understanding of language based on the dialogic logic of the social and the semiotic (as briefly presented in Section 4.2ff) being thus barred from entering the classroom, what is left is a void. No, it is in fact much worse: given the conventions of educational practice, voids cannot be tolerated. The void is thus filled with the same age-old trivia about language, the dangers of which Bourdieu reveals to his reader with such masterly perspicuity. Literacy education remains an environment for subjecting the pedagogic subject to learning about formal categories that are semantically innocent, for affirming one particular view of linguistic practices, for condemning the 'divergent' practices and practitioners as deficient. This is not a frame where the learning intellect might encounter and reflect on different points of view. However far the roots of the etiology of this condition penetrate, however much the faceless dominating classes have to do with this situation, some of the responsibility for it must rest also with those who make pronouncements on the nature of language and who bring 'into the object [of analysis] the principles of their own relation to the object' (Bourdieu, 1990: 52) proceeding as if there was nothing to an understanding of language except how *they* from their standpoint perceive it.

5.3   Habitus, change and literacy pedagogy

A little reflection will show that, for all the reasons which Bourdieu so excellently presents in his accounts of the habitus, the mundane, i.e. everyday social line of literacy development cannot be anything other than reproductive. The linguistic habitus that children bring to the class is, therefore, bound to be a 'classed' habitus, a coding orientation specific to specific social classes as Bernstein has suggested, to the continuing chagrin of the self-appointed champions of the dominated classes, since the early 60s. That it is different categories of classed habitus that confront the pedagogic practices in the classroom has a palpable consequence, a brief account of which is presented below in the words of Bourdieu, Passeron and St Martin (1994: 40):

> Of all the cultural obstacles, those which arise from the language spoken within the setting of the family are unquestionably the most serious and the most insidious. For, especially during the first years of school, comprehension and manipulation of language are the first points of teacher judgement. But the influence of a child's original language setting never ceases to operate.

It is a commonplace of discourse on pedagogy that in some specific cases a gulf exists between what the educational system presents as knowledge of language and what the social agents bring to the school as knowledge of language. The exact nature of this gulf is an important issue, but for the moment I am interested in the last statement of the above extract. Is there a logical reason behind the fact that 'the influence of a child's original language setting never ceases to operate'? The answer may be found in what used to be known in the 1960s in Bernstein's sociology as 'primary socialisation'. Everyday learning in early years plays a crucial role in defining the child's identity and the 'lessons' of this learning are integrated as the principles of social practice at the deepest levels of the social subject's consciousness. Bourdieu comments on the significance of early habitus as follows (Bourdieu, 1990: 60–1):

> Early experiences have a particular weight because the *habitus* tends to ensure its own constancy and its defence against change through the selection it makes within new information by rejecting information capable of calling into question its accumulated information, if exposed to it accidentally or by force and especially by avoiding exposure to such information.

We know, however, that society changes and to suggest that it could change all by itself, or even only in reacting to physical events would be just about as absurd as Saussure's view (if indeed Saussure ever held that view, which is itself open to doubt) that changes in an *état de langue* are independent of the speaking subjects. We then have to grant that in some sense, somehow the habitus as the 'structured structuring structures', flexible enough to cope with all eventualities (see Bourdieu, 1990: 52–65), must also engage actively in the processes that bring about social change. The simpler hypothesis would be that change in society at least *accompanies* change in habitus. In other words early habitus is not entirely immune to change and not necessarily reactive even though change in habitus may be a rare phenomenon since the conditions for its success are not easily met as Bourdieu points out (p. 82):

> We know, in general terms, that the effects that a new experience can have on the habitus depend on the relation of practical 'compatibility' between this experience and the experiences that have already been assimilated by the habitus, in the form of schemes of production and evaluation and that in the process of selective re-interpretation which results from this dialectic, the informative efficacy of all new experiences tends to diminish continuously.

These observations might be taken as a reason, particularly in early pedagogic action, for a planning that is more sensitive to variation in habitus. But I am not aware that in the great literacy debate there has been any serious effort to problematise the question of how information to do with language could be negotiated in a language classroom in ways that would not arouse resistance, that would be compatible with experiences already assimilated by the classes of habitus represented in the classroom. Instead there is, in fact, a firm conviction that attempts to create the conditions where new information might not arouse resistance are tantamount to the inculcation of middle class ideology in working class children. The unspoken axiom that multiple voices have no place in the pedagogic site is never questioned; and it gets assumed that there will be one single voice. Thereafter the sociological imperative pronounces on the inevitability of the official voice as that single voice.

I am not denying the difficulties in creating a pedagogic program which would succeed in presenting information and experience of language so that it has better chances of being assimilated by that class of habitus furthest removed from the discourses of educational knowledge: all I am claiming is that we do not really know how difficult it is, what problems it might give rise to, because we have never seriously tried. Faced with the possibility of being accused of the racism of social class, we have played it safe by agreeing with our intellectual leaders in denying the existence of any real differences in the linguistic habitus of different classes. The absurdity of the idea that we can have classed habitus, but that this classed habitus should show no linguistic difference is never questioned (Hasan, 1989).

5.4 Habitus, discourse and literacy pedagogy

What Bourdieu calls the 'comprehension and manipulation of language' is very much what traditional literacy development programs think of as language education when it comes to teaching *self-expression*, which is the linguistically un-informed variety of 'action literacy' (Hasan, 1996a). But seen in the practical contexts of everyday life, these linguistic processes are properly described as the ability to participate in the discourses of one's society, 'for what circulates on the linguistic market is not 'language' as such, but rather discourses' (p. 39). The importance of discursive ability in real life contexts can, therefore, be hardly exaggerated. Here is how Bourdieu describes the situation (p. 55):

> Speakers lacking the legitimate competence [specific to a discourse type] are *de facto* excluded from the social domains in which this competence is needed, or are condemned to silence. What is rare is.. the competence necessary in order to speak the legitimate language [of the various social domains] which, depending on social inheritance, re-translates social distinctions into the specifically symbolic logic of differential deviations, or, in short distinction.

It is no secret that discursive abilities do not belong to children by birth. It is the reproductive unofficial pedagogy of everyday life which schools them in these matters in their early life (Halliday, 1979b; Painter, 1989). Bourdieu, of course emphasises the accent and idiolectal features, though he does add, for example, that producers and recipients of the message bring to its production and reception 'everything that makes up (their) singular and collective experience' (see p. 39). Clearly, there can be no justification for assuming that all that matters for the circulation of discourses on the linguistic markets is the phonic stream, minus the meaning and the wording. My discussion of the interaction between register variation and semantic variation as inevitable aspects of sociosemiotic practices (see section 4.4–5) implies unevenness in degrees of familiarity with varieties of register amongst the pupils: the discursive abilities children bring to the classroom are also 'classed' and they are classed in respect of phenomena that are logically related to markets and fields. The fact that the dominating classes have wider register repertoires is relevant in at least two ways. First, the experience of a wider register repertoire prepares one to assimilate the principles of other, unfamiliar registers with greater ease; children with such experience can 'comprehend and manipulate language' more adroitly. Secondly, in the everyday register repertoire of the dominating classes, there are some discourse types which are much closer to the social domains introduced in the pedagogic system. This prepares children from the dominating classes to receive the discourses of educational knowledge with much greater readiness. In addition to this, the semantic orientation of the dominant classes is congruent with the required semantic orientation for the (re-)production of 'exotic', uncommonsense knowledge. The discourses of education, thus, present little or no threat to the habitual ways of meaning and saying which children from the dominant classes bring to the school (Hasan, 1989; 1992b; Cloran, 1994; Williams, 1995; Painter, 1996). By contrast, the social domains introduced in the pedagogic system and the principles implicit in the discourses of educational knowledge, not to speak of the classification and framing of discourses in the classroom (Bernstein, 1975a; 1990; 1996; Williams, 1999), are unfamiliar more often to learners from the dominated classes. It follows that lacking 'the legitimate competence' for these social domains such learners will be '*de facto* excluded from the social domains in which this competence is needed or condemned to silence', whether or not they possess other competencies. If of all the cultural obstacles, the linguistic ones are 'unquestionably the most serious and the most insidious', it is because the language education classroom is not the only place where language matters: the pedagogic field is, in a true sense, also a linguistic field for the simple reason that all forms of knowledge, whether everyday commonsense ones or the exotic uncommonsense one, are unproduceable without the ability to use language in certain specific ways (Vygotsky, 1962; 1978; Halliday, 1994b). Lack of legitimate competence translates readily into educational failure.

If the veracity of these comments is accepted, it would suggest that pedagogic action in literacy development might have a better chance of success if, together with sensitivity to variation in classed habitus, it paid specific attention to the development of discursive abilities. Genre-based literacy pedagogy, which grew out of research conducted by Martin and colleagues in Australia (for some accounts, see Martin, 1985b; 1986; Painter and Martin, 1986; Christie,

1990; Rothery, 1996; Macken-Horarik, 1996; Veel and Coffin, 1996) claims to be a literacy program designed to develop discursive abilities with specific reference to 'educational genres'. This program has been criticised (e.g., Luke, 1996) because it is reproductive of educational knowledge and because it makes the false assumption that change in register repertoire or educational success can be converted into material capital. Ignoring the desirability or otherwise of the genre-based literacy pedagogy as such, let me raise some questions on these critiques themselves.

Consider first the issue of reproduction. It is certainly true that the pedagogic system is reproductive of social relations; and to focus exclusively on educational genres is to reproduce educational knowledge. But is this a feature of official pedagogy alone? In fact it is hard to name any social practices and the discourses associated with them that are not largely reproductive. It is thanks to this trait that children from the dominant section of the community come to the pedagogic system better equipped to succeed in education. Why should it be less acceptable to attempt to help children from the dominated groups to succeed, simply on the ground that the pedagogic system is reproductive? Does the higher probability of the educational failure of children of this category lessen that evil? Why would it be reprehensible to attempt to take official pedagogic action of the kind which might conceivably change the linguistic habitus of the dominated? To say in response that genre-based pedagogy is incapable of achieving these goals would be to shift the terms of the debate. My question is: why are these goals not worth striving for in view of the reproductive nature of much that we do by way of social practice? What else are we proposing to boycott in order to defeat the reproductive tendencies of human societies?

Turn now to the advantages of educational success. It does not take a great deal of sociological sophistication to realise that educational success does not necessarily spell material success. However, it is still worth asking whether *without* educational success, persons from the dominated groups are more likely to succeed in the job market? The situation is not so clear-cut as to permit an unequivocal claim here either way. As against this uncertainty, there might still be other uses of educational success not to be shrugged off as irrelevant. For example, success of any kind is commonly held to contribute to self-esteem: if so, how do we rate the value of such self-esteem against the possibility of failure in the job market? In the context of this debate, it is best to remember Bourdieu's perceptive remark (1984; 1991) that the criteria for hierarchising distinctions are always on the move. One may be guilty of naivety in believing that by taking definite pedagogic actions to facilitate the development of discursive abilities in pupils from the dominated group, one would contribute to their educational success and thereby to their self-esteem, since the nature of the game is such that the rules will always shift to the disadvantage of the already materially disadvantaged. In this logic, all moves to significant action are blocked in advance and with specific reference to language we are warned (1991: 64):

> Since the very motor of change is nothing less than the whole linguistic field or, more precisely, the whole set of actions and reactions which are continuously generated in the universe of competitive relations constituting the field, the centre of this perpetual motion is everywhere and nowhere. Those who remain trapped in a philosophy of cultural diffusion based on a hydraulic imagery of 'two-step flow' or 'trickle-down' and who persist in locating the principle of change in a determinate site in the linguistic field, will always be greatly disappointed.

I admit that I find this mode of reasoning less than convincing on more than one count. It seems to me, the conclusion that no action towards change is likely to be useful does not follow necessarily from the acceptance of the fact that the forces of change are complex and have no clear boundary or identity. We can use these same facts as the ground for arguing that therefore well-considered actions should be taken in every conceivable direction: this too is a possibility. I believe Bernstein is right when he claims 'education cannot compensate for society'. But there is a significant difference between this position and the claim that education cannot *contribute to change* in society. It would be difficult to argue in light of the modes of material existence in the third world that the contribution of education to change is negligible. Even if we were to attribute the material advancement of the first world, which is no utopia, to the growth of technology, there is no way we could gainsay the fact that advancement in a science-driven technology cannot come about without massive changes in the discursive abilities of large segments of the society. Besides, in the context of language education, social change does not have to be thought of as 'cultural diffusion', especially if by this phrase Bourdieu means to refer pejoratively to the elegance and distinction of pronunciation, diction, syntactic devices and such other phenomena he singles out in relation to official language. It is open to us to strive towards a language education which is not simply a purveyor of lessons in elocution and correct punctuation but which aims to develop in the pupils a discursive ability which can turn back to reflect on discourse itself – i.e., the inculcation of an ability to question what the pupils encounter in the discourses of the society they live in. This is what I mean by 'reflection literacy' (Hasan, 1996a).

I take reflection literacy as an indispensable condition for the production of knowledge, as opposed to its replication. A language education program whose aim it is to encourage the pupils to question the very discourses to which it exposes them is not necessarily translatable into material benefits, but I believe it would yield a benefit without parallel, as it would enable one to decipher the world, to read closely the propositions one is confronted with. I want to clarify two points here with regard to reflection literacy: the first has to do with the sort of language development which is the aim of reflection literacy and the second has to do with the feasibility of achieving this aim, which some might think elitist. To turn to the first point first, it is often thought that reflection, like thinking and reasoning, is a logical process quite independent of language; in this view, language simply represents thought, reflection and reasoning, which operate independent of one's linguistic experiences. This is a serious mis-recognition of the nature of language in use. For if it is true that languaging, i.e., participation in discourse, plays an important part in the development of human consciousness – and there does not seem to be an alternative way of accounting for this development – then ways of thinking cannot be independent of one's languaging experience. A deep understanding of language as a meaning potential which functions on the dual principles of semo-logic and sociologic prepares one to enquire on what basis one might claim that something means something and on what basis one evaluates those acts of meaning. Reflection literacy is thus a logical culmination of the development of discursive abilities. As to the possibility of achieving the goals of reflection literacy, I do not discount the force of Marx's famous claim in his *Preface* to the *Critique of Political Economy* (quoted in McLellan, 1975: 40) that:

> The mode of production of material life conditions the social, political and intellectual life process in general. It is not the consciousness of men that determines their being, but on the contrary, their social being that determines their consciousness.

I do certainly agree that 'men [and women!] make their own history, but they do not make it.. under circumstances chosen by themselves, but under circumstances directly encountered, given and transmitted from the past' (Marx quoted in McLellan, 1975: 43), a point of view so eloquently presented also by Bourdieu. I am simply suggesting that even though the past is a powerful presence, the present may not be as devoid of possibilities as it is commonly made out to be. In fact, today the pedagogic process is part of the condition of social existence, an important element in the production of the material life itself and it is important that those who deconstruct the pedagogic system should not simply look at what that system does; they should also consider what, given the advance in our ability to understand the world around us, it may be possible for it to do. We cannot reconcile ourselves to the idea that the possibility of reflection is, as a matter of course, closed to the majority of social agents. As Achebe's Emmanuel declared (quoted in Gordimer, 1995: 92):

> I don't accept that. The ideas is one lecture by Ikem changed my entire life from a parrot to a man.. And the lives of some of my friends. It wasn't Ikem the man who changed me. I hardly knew him. It was his ideas set down on paper. One idea in particular: that we may accept a limitation on our actions but never, under no circumstance, must we accept restrictions on our thinking.

I would, on the one hand, not wish to dispute that the social positioning of social agents is a powerful determinant of much in their life, on the other hand I would be reluctant to deny agents the possibility of departure from the predicted trajectory for two reasons: first we know that habitus is not static; it is subject to change. And secondly, we know that hardly any serious attempt has been made to design a series of pedagogic actions with sensitivity to the different classes of habitus represented in the classrooms. Pedagogic action has thus been condemned ineffective or regressive without proper trial. But this condemnation itself draws attention to certain problems.

6 Conclusion

Sociological analysis has successfully argued that the pedagogic system is dominated by the dominating group: this, in the last resort, is what underlies its massively reproductive nature. All elements of the pedagogic process, including the selection of what will count as educational knowledge, aspects of the management of its presentation to the pedagogic subjects and the modes of evaluation, are controlled by the logic of social domination. It follows that the dominating group will always attempt to raise the stakes in the competitive struggle for power; the dominated will always be positioned as lacking in competencies. And on these bases, it is suggested that pedagogic action can never be a liberating force. The reproductive nature of the pedagogic system thus becomes an excuse for inaction. Despite my agreement with the analysis of the situation as it is, I suggest that claims about pedagogic action need to be scrutinised seriously from the standpoint of the practical participants in the social processes under discussion.

In the first place given the complexity of human social systems, the issue of what will count as a liberating force is not all that easy to decide. How is a liberating force expected to operate? How to reveal itself? And could it be that human struggle continues in infinitely small steps, that these steps make a firmer mark on social time than do cataclysmic events as the prototypic manifestation of political struggle? With this view of the liberating force, we might look carefully at the range of pedagogic actions around us. Unless I have missed the point entirely, it could be said that the production of texts such as *The Logic of Practice* is a kind of pedagogic action. I think it would be a complete misrepresentation of facts to pretend that this particular pedagogic action is without any effect. Certainly it has not toppled the hegemony of the dominating group and it is not a liberating force in the cataclysmic sense. But to the extent that it has managed to arouse reflection in its readers, to the extent that it has affected the pedagogic actions of pedagogues, to the extent that it has freed theory makers, to that extent it has been far from futile. It is fair then to ask: why where Bourdieu has succeeded might it not be possible for lesser humans to achieve perhaps lesser successes of a similar kind? Which would be considerably removed from the kind of futility that haunts the pedagogic system in this sociology of education.

Then again in citing the litany of the woes of the pedagogic system, it would be best not to do the great injustice of writing off teachers as simply unquestioning dupes of 'the' system, worse still as 'agents of regulation' (p. 45) aided and abetted by the caricature of a linguist as 'the jurist': a large number of teachers and linguists consciously dissociate themselves from affiliation to the dominant group and would wish to inculcate the ability in their pupils to analyse, to understand and to act in ways that challenge social reality. We have no right to question their 'good faith' any more than we have the right to question the good faith of sociologists analysing society. However, teaching successfully is not simply a matter of good intentions: at the least, teachers need to feel confident of their own understanding of what they are teaching. With specific reference to language education, they need to be able to reflect on how language works both in society and taken in itself. In this context Bourdieu's denigration of 'the' linguist and of linguistics as a whole, is guilty of disinformation, for given the authority of his authorised discourse, his readers are likely to believe that what *all* linguists and grammarians do is trivial, not worthy of attention. This would not be so bad if what he put in place of linguistics were more viable. But as I have argued above, the efforts of Bourdieu's sociology, however successful they may be in trouncing the sovereign discipline of linguistics, contribute almost nothing to a better understanding of the goals or processes of language education, because a clear understanding of the relations of language and society is lacking. I reject the validity of pursuing a struggle between the academic disciplines of sociology and linguistics in a world where struggle against bonded labour is still a real and pressing need, even though issues such as bonded labour may not affect the post-capitalist first world directly. Where levels of elementary literacy are so low, as say in certain remote areas of Pakistan, that one literally signs one's life away unknowingly simply because one cannot read, to speak there of the uselessness of language education is a gesture that can have no credibility at least for those who are actually affected. By writing off the role of literacy in change, the attitude colludes wondorously in the continuation of the exploitation of the already exploited!

Bourdieu's sociology of education presents to us the pathology of the pedagogic system. No matter however much we agree with the analysis we have the right to ask: what, if anything, will change this state of affairs? How can we hope to emerge from the grip of 'the system'? As the logic of the arguments stands, it seems that to change the pedagogic system, we must change society. But who or what will change society? These questions press ever more urgently particularly in view of the fate of revolutions led by the Lenins and Maos of this world. To repeat the words of Gordimer (1995: 86):

> A question for us to ask ourselves in this time of the forced retirement of political gods? What structure for 'meaningful actions' do we have to house personal conscience; according to what plan that will translate the general good into action shall we re-form?

In attempting to re-form pedagogic actions in the domain of language education, we cannot pretend to be undertaking a 'revolutionary' activity, which would suddenly usher in the dawn of freedom from dominations, from exploitations. All, it seems to me, we can do is simply to attempt, in a restricted and local sense, to do well what needs to be done in the teaching of any knowledge: namely, try to reveal the nature of that knowledge to those who are responsible for pedagogic action, so as to enable them to take an informed approach to their own pedagogic practices. Together with Achebe's *Ikem* (quoted Gordimer, 1995: 81) we need perhaps to search for a new radicalism which would be 'clear-eyed enough to see beyond the present claptrap that will heap all our problems on the doorstep of capitalism and imperialism'.

Notes

1 Concern with reading/writing has of course been endemic to education. However, this period is of particular interest since it was around this time that concern with literacy became a specialist issue, attracting a spate of psycholinguistic and linguistic researches designed to reveal the 'true' nature of the processes, though sociology, despite Hoggart (1957), had yet to make its mark on the scene.

2 This is certainly the case at least so far as the academic discourse of theory makers on literacy pedagogy is concerned though the story may be different, where classroom practices are at issue. I have argued elsewhere (Hasan 1996a) that, in much of today's language education, the atomistic focus on isolated linguistic patterns – what I call recognition literacy – forms an extension of the simplistic 'coding-decoding' approach. See also Collins (1989) for the discussion of a classroom interaction where concern with the calibration of orthography and pronunciation dominates while social meaning of accent variation is ignored.

3 See Graff (1987), Halliday (1996b), Luke (1996) for some perspectives on literacy.

4 Brubaker (1993: 215ff) argues that the 'intentionless invention' of habitus needs to be 'complemented, controlled, and corrected by other regulative techniques .. This control occurs in and through writing. As an objectified product of the habitus, written (or otherwise recorded) work is amenable to modes of inspection and control that the habitus itself and its non-objectified products necessarily escape.' He goes on to add: 'Writing thus permits the social and logical control of the sociological work.' However, it should be emphasised that what makes writing significant for 'inspection and control' is not simply its material, 'recorded' i.e. graphic, nature; rather it is what is implied in the recording: namely, the physi-

cal absence of the other, the situational disjunction that inheres in the distance between 'saying' and 'hearing', making necessary a remarkably distinct variety of semiotic management. Even though writing is initially presented to the senses of the reader as a material object, i.e. Brubaker's recorded message, it is in fact a specific kind of semiotic process. It is the underlying characteristics of writing which contributes to what Vygotsky called conscious realisation and voluntariness, permitting the development of a 'deliberate semantics – deliberate structuring of the web of meaning.' (Vygotsky, 1962: 90ff). For further discussion of writing, see Halliday (1985; 1996a); Halliday and Martin (1993); Goody (1987).

5 I am aware that, from certain points of view, this conceptualisation of the possible role of language and education could be criticised as 'romantic', 'idealistic' or 'elitist'. However, for the moment I present this perspective as if it were non-contentious. In Section 5, I shall return, though briefly, to the complex relations of language, education and the mind in non-egalitarian societies where education is 'in the hands of' some power group.

6 All page references to Firth are to Firth (1957b).

7 This is not the appropriate place for attempting a substantiation of my claims about the nature of Bernstein's engagement with language. For an indication of some details of the dialectic between language and society in Bernstein's theory, see Hasan (1995b), and (1999a).

8 And I believe Bourdieu is not unsympathetic to this view. See Bourdieu (1991), for example Authorized language (esp. p. 113), Symbolic power and the political field (esp. p. 170).

9 The art of the reading of a master by another master appears to demand 'misreading'. See for example Hasan (1987) on Derrida's reading of Saussure. To appreciate how Derrida does it, see Martin (1993) who demystifies the power of that style through his linguistic analysis. See also Labov's (1972) reading of Bernstein, challenged in Hasan (1989; 1992b; 1993).

10 On second thoughts, I should say that the phenomenon is surprising. It is at any rate a remarkable example of the internal contradictions of academia: on the one hand we place faith in specialist expertise, whereby sociologists are the authority on society, linguists on language. On the other hand, we also appear to subscribe to the belief that great minds think great thoughts without exception about everything under the sun! The question of expert knowledge seems not to arise.

11 I believe Bourdieu's account of why the social sciences were seduced by linguistics does concede this point, though it seems to me that he blames Saussure more for having thought those thoughts than he does the social scientists for unthinkingly embracing those thoughts! On the other hand, there seems good reason to believe that one of the main sources of Saussure's inspiration was, in fact, sociology (see Section 2.1 below).

12 Consider for example the struggle for control over language education in NSW schools and the intervention of the state government so as to 'safeguard' the honoured 'basic' linguistic skills of 'correct' punctuation, spelling, and monolithic standards of meaning-less categories of grammar. See also Carter 1996 on similar experiences in the UK. Against neither of these interventions, have any of the respected formal linguists raised a voice. This is all the more remarkable in the Australian context since these same linguists had keenly

expressed their dismay at the introduction of a language education program which without doubt was socially, discursively and semantically far more advanced than the time-honoured 'basic' linguistic skills programmes. For an account of the programme which dismayed some of the formal linguists of Australia, see Martin, 1985b; Rothery, 1996; Macken-Horarik, 1996.

13 All unidentified page references are to Bourdieu (1992) unless otherwise indicated.

14 Note as a matter of interest that this paper, called Personality and Language in Society, first appeared in 1950 in *The Sociological Review*, Journal of the Institute of Sociology, Vol. xlii, section Two. Of course, less than a decade later, with the rising influence of Chomsky's linguistics, Firth was given the status of mauvais sujet as by Lyons (1966) and Langendoen (1968).

15 Saussure's Course has of course been 'synchronised' (I use the term as in Bourdieu, 1993: 264): one can hardly protest against this synchronisation, since it became the condition of its existence. But it has also been mercilessly 'post-modernised' (to borrow a term again from Bourdieu, op. cit.) even though this was not a necessary condition of its reading. I do not doubt for a moment that the Course contradicts itself on its initially strong classification of *langue* and *parole* (Hasan, 1987a; 1993). However, it is equally obvious that scholars have chosen to focus solely on those parts of the Course that are friendly to their interests, ignoring to comment on the 'return of the repressed' (cf. Bourdieu) even within the pages of that one slim volume. This is not said as a defence of Saussure, but simply to correct the mistaken perception of Saussure which partial readings of his work encourage. Saussure's theory of how *langue* is actively created, changed and maintained ('produced and reproduced' in Bourdieu's sociological terminology) by the workings of *parole* brings back into his theory of language a concept of linguistic variation whose sophistication is yet to be acknowledged, though one should hasten to add that Saussure does not undertake any detailed sociological analysis of the genesis of either linguistic variation or standardisation.

16 My pointing out of these differences does not imply agreement with Saussure's formulation of his concept of *langue* or its privileged relation to linguistics. It seems, however, important not to lay at Saussure's door the sins of others. For further discussion see Hasan (1987a; 1993); and Thibault (1997).

17 It is important to add here that Bourdieu's point of departure for this critique (p. 43) is an extract not from Saussure but from Comte which cannot be said to have a voice identical to Saussure's on the relation of language and society, as a careful reading of the chapters on diachronic linguistics in the Course will no doubt show.

18 The notion of 'standard/legitimate' variety is very much more complex than Bourdieu's account suggests. Consider for example the linguistic scene in the colonised Indo-Pakistani region early this century. There was not simply one language of public or political administration: English and some indigenous language(s) acted side by side. There was not simply one standard language within even one (geo-political) region: for example, in what is now Uttar Pradesh two varieties of Urdu, a Delhi-Urdu and a Lucknow-Urdu, both had the status of official/legitimate/standard, not to speak of the other standard languages e.g. Hindi recognised within the same region as equally official etc. Naturally the historical processes that Bourdieu considers important in the production of official language are specific to the west, within that to Europe, and

within that more specifically to France, which has been singularly authoritarian in linguistic/cultural imposition. See for example five pages of *Grammatical Reforms authorised by the French Minister of Instruction* which are inserted without comment by the authors between the table of contents and the Introductory chapter of *The Tutorial French Grammar* by Weekly and Wyatt (1907). Parallels to this degree of meticulous and efficient control on language by the state will seldom if ever be found in other countries of Europe, which is not to say that the state does not intervene (cf. Carter's experiences; see note 13).

19 I have already argued in Section 2.1 that the Course offers more than one single reading on these points; the role of *parole* in the maintenance and change of *langue* is a constant Saussurean theme, albeit he does not consider this aspect of the study of language as part of internal linguistics. Given this ambivalence in the Saussurean text, an interesting question is why a majority of social scientists have chosen to pursue only one interpretation as 'the' interpretation, ignoring the contradictions.

20 I have elided Bourdieu's use of the word 'arbitrary' (and forms related to it). Although it proceeds from the Saussurean signifier arbitrary, it has a (cluster of) signified(s) whose character is not always in keeping with that of the Saussurean term, which itself has several senses (Hasan, 1985b). As through silence a congruence is assumed in the uses of the term between and within the writings of the two scholars (see, however, Li Puma, 1993: 17), there obviously exists a complex situation to unravel which would have called for a much longer chapter. For some comments see Section 4 here.

21 Emphases throughout this extract are mine to alert the reader to what I at least perceive as problematic, especially when applied to the formation of linguistic habitus.

22 On some thoughtful critiques of the 'meaning as naming' metaphor, see Wittgenstein (1958); Whorf (1956); de Saussure (1966); Hjelmslev (1961) etc.

23 Though it could be that my state of delusion is so advanced as to prevent me from seeing that I do not see. But attributing hidden motives to other minds gives rise to an interesting conundrum: how do I ever establish that the other party accusing me of self-delusion is not equally self-deluded?

24 For an understanding of Halliday's term realisation, which is not a simple relation of expression, see Lemke (1984); Halliday (1992); Hasan (1984a; 1995a) and the discussion of the signified below (Section 4.2).

25 It might be argued that I am 'mis-reading' Bourdieu, something that he fears greatly (Bourdieu, 1993). But, ironically, if Bourdieu's view on language is accepted, it robs the term 'mis-reading' of any meaning; the concept of mis-reading presupposes the objective reality of meaning as construed by the forms of language, in short a linguistic communism of some sort. No theory of field or market can account for the approximation between the writer's meaning and the reader's interpretation, the distance between which is what we mean by mis-reading.

26 On types of linguistic variation and the levels of language that are implicated in them, see Hasan (1973; 1989); a brief discussion follows in Section 4.4-5 below.

27 For an imaginary account of this evolution, see William Golding's *The Inheritors*, and for a revealing linguistic ananlysis of 'meaningful' differences between the early stages of this evolution, see Halliday (1973).

28 Interestingly the undesirable artificiality of separating grammar and lexicology in the study of the form of language is discussed, though very briefly, in Saussure's text (p 135), a fact, hardly acknowledged in linguistic literature.

29 I use the words intelligence here to refer to the human capacity for non-sensuous apprehension.

30 Bourdieu's comment (1990: 58) on intention and habitus describes the situation in excellent terms: 'Automatic and impersonal, significant without a signifying intention, ordinary practices [of meaning by language rh] lend themselves to an understanding that is no less automatic and impersonal.'

31 For lack of space this account is highly simplified. More accurately it is not single elements of meaning, but rather 'fashions of speaking' (Whorf, 1956), 'coding orientations' (Bernstein, 1965), 'ways of meaning' (Hasan, 1984a; 1989; 1992b), the semantic design of the habitus in Bourdieu's theory (1990), each of which can be shown to be responsive to the material and social conditions of human existence.

32 See for further details Fawcett (1987); Fawcett and Young (1987); Halliday (1973; 1975; 1974; 1976; 1992; 1994a; 1996a); Hasan (1973; 1978a; 1984a; 1984c; 1985b; 1987b; 1989; 1993; 1995a; 1996a); Martin (1985b; 1992); Matthiessen (1995) etc.

33 The use of the term arbitrary in relation to the sign has more often misled us into intellectual culdesacs than not, reminding one of Wittgenstein's (1958: 108e, 339) comment that 'An unsuitable type of expression is a sure means of remaining in a state of confusion. It as it were bars the way out.'

34 It is irrelevant to this argument that different listeners might hear different meanings from the 'same' wordings: that they are the same wordings is itself a misrecognition of the facts of language, for what sensuously impinges is not sentences, words etc but their phonological or graphic expression.

35 For an alternative view see Martin (1992). For a commentary on that view see Hasan (1995a).

36 Whether we refer to these as a difference in consciousness (Marx & Engels, 1985) or in worldview (Whorf, 1956) or in mental function (Vygotsky, 1962; 1978) or in coding orientation (Bernstein, 1965) or in ideology (Vološinov, 1986) or in habitus (Bourdieu, 1990), or in orientation to meaning (Hasan, 1989; 1992b) is immaterial. This is not to say that the terms are synonymous but to claim that there is a large degree of overlap among them.

37 Meaningless both in the sense that they constitute a meaningless activity for the learner and in the sense that they are not related to any meaning making capacities of language, except spuriously as in 'noun is the name of a thing' presumably as 'mountain' in 'mountain spring'.

38 Labov's important work in attempting to show the 'in principle' equal status of all social dialects made very little impression on literacy education. And one reason for this is precisely the lack of interest in understanding about language which is so typical of those who manage the field of literacy education.

39 I refer here to a comment by a famous Australian media personality that the learning of traditional grammar did him no harm; he could not see why it was necessary to make any changes in the teaching of grammar in schools.

12 Bourdieu on linguistics and language: a response to my commentators

1 Introduction

I must begin by thanking my commentators who engaged in a task that, judging by their comments, was at best a mixed blessing and at worst an intellectual *faux pas*. It is difficult to do justice within one piece of writing such as this to all the comments they make though I shall try my best to address at least the major ones. In turning to this business, it would be pertinent to briefly identify the main thrust of my carefully documented critique of Bourdieu's views on linguistics and language. It has seemed to me that the commentaries vary in the extent to which they reveal an understanding of my concerns; that none in fact comes to grips with the serious contradictions to be found in Bourdieu's views on society and language. I rather suspect that this situation arises largely because none appreciates the full implications of the notion of co-genetic logic which governs the evolution of the social and the semiotic. Co-genetic logic simply confirms the existence of an inherent relation between the social and the semiotic, not between all varieties of sociology and linguistics. And while the co-genetic principle implies the participation of both social and semiotic processes in the development of an individual, it in no way suggests that individuals as theorists must therefore be necessarily aware of or subscribe to the principle of co-genetic logic, much less that their theory must/will integrate this dialogical principle within itself. Nor does the co-genesis of the social and the semiotic imply that any instance of specialist discourse on the social or the semiotic must allow equal space to the discussion of sociology and semiotics in each discourse concerning either: it simply requires that discourse must not create frames that bar the entry of the other (Hasan, 1999a), or view the two disciplines as engaged in a struggle for priority as if what they attempt to explain is less important than the *intellectual capital* the authorship of the discourse might generate. From this point of view, all that matters is the clear enunciation of a theory which grants legitimacy to the introduction of the semiotic – and therefore the linguistic – perspective into the social and of the social into the semiotic/linguistic. Bourdieu, I suggested, grants the latter, but through his contradictions casts doubt on the desirability of the former: in keeping with the spirit of his sociological theory, he does point to the role of language in the formation of consciousness, but he downplays the role of the linguistic semiotic in the evolution of the social. Understandably, this has, to say the least, rather undesirable consequences preventing the mutual prehension of theoretical concepts.

2 Language, linguistics and Bourdieu

In *The Disempowerment Game: Bourdieu and language in literacy* (henceforth referred to as 'my paper'), I was scrupulously careful to limit my discussion to Bourdieu's pronouncements on linguists, linguistics and language. I am no expert on Bourdieu's, or on anyone else's, sociology; and I am in sympathy with Bourdieu when he rejects 'spontaneous sociology' as an undesirable activity[1]. In fact, so thoroughly do I agree with this proposition that in my paper I have extended the same principle to 'spontaneous linguistics' as well: one of my complaints against Bourdieu is precisely that he himself indulges in spontaneous linguistics, but is less than complimentary to the linguist for engaging in spontaneous sociology: Bourdieu's linguistics is as borrowed and as fragmentary as the sociolinguist's sociology is, which he rightly criticises for this lack. While my credentials for commenting on sociology are not much greater than those of many sociolinguists, I flatter myself that the situation is different when it comes to assessing views on language and linguistics. And it was in my capacity as a practitioner of systemic functional linguistics that I reviewed that particular element of Bourdieu's writing which bears most directly on my professional practices. The clarification of my paper's point of departure is relevant on two counts, one general and one specific. The general point has to do with the explicit or implicit assertion by all commentators on my limited reading[2] of Bourdieu; the specific point relates to a comment made in passing by Robbins. I will say a word about the latter here, leaving the general issue of the quality of my reading of Bourdieu to a later point (See Section 5, *On misrepresenting Bourdieu*).

To imply, as Robbins does, that my paper is motivated by a 'slight resentment' against Bourdieu's treatment of linguists and linguistics is to reduce my concerns to a personal and private matter: in terms of Bernstein (1999) it is to treat my critique as an instance of horizontal discourse, which cannot be taken seriously in the world of the sociologist's serious knowledge structure. But the attribution of personal resentment is, in my opinion, quite unjustified. Certainly the tone of my paper is harsh, but to borrow freely from Jane Austin's *Pride and Prejudice*, in my choice of style Bourdieu's own style of presentation 'spared me the concern which I might have felt' had Bourdieu himself spoken in a less pejorative tone. Apart from the interpersonal move of matching his less than polite style, so far as I am aware, in the substance of my critique of Bourdieu there is nothing at all personal: my comments on Bourdieu's linguistics are not excited by resentment but rather by amazement that his views have so far never been seriously examined. Far from it, for some their truth is above question. However, to me it seems that if, for whatever reason – strategic or otherwise – Bourdieu has taken it upon himself to tell the world what is wrong with 'the' linguist's professional practices and what is the sociologically, even morally, correct way of doing linguistics, then as a practising linguist, I owe it to myself to draw attention to what strike me as partial or questionable interpretations of the field and its founding scholars. I certainly need to look critically into the alternatives which Bourdieu has to offer as better tools for my trade than those I use currently. If the alternatives he would have me accept appear problematic and self-contradictory then in my understanding the only sensible course of action is to question them. I take it as self-evident that if I invested so much time and effort in attempting to spell out what I find unacceptable in Bourdieu's so-called theory of language, this is because I find his work worth the effort: as Jenkins remarks (1992: 176) Bourdieu is 'good to think with'. This admiration of his scholarship and his originality is, to my mind, not a reason for suspending critical judgement when I look at his writing. On the contrary, precisely because Bourdieu's voice carries considerable weight in the social sciences, it is important to ensure that it does not condemn without cause and simply because someone or something appears to him strategically dispensable (cf. Robbins on Bourdieu on Saussure).

In my paper (p. 29)[3], I had outlined the four interrelated arguments around which my discourse was organised. These concerned (i) Bourdieu's reading of Saussure; (ii) his conception of language; (iii) his insistence on the primacy of language-external explanations for the efficacy of semiosis; and (iv) a brief comment on the implications of the last two for language in literacy. I will briefly review what the commentators had to say on my elaborations of the first three arguments. In doing this I will point out why some strategies in the defence of Bourdieu do not strike me as legitimate, while others appear quite beside the point. On the last topic I will not say much because I agree with Robbins that my conception of reflection literacy is not really very different from what Bourdieu might himself view favourably. The point I made in my critique was that this goal is not achievable with the conception of language that Bourdieu's work presents. The commentaries despite much valuable discourse fail to argue in any sustainable way that my reading of Bourdieu's dicta on language are incorrect.

3 On reading Saussure: strategic position-taking

Neither Collins nor Chouliaraki and Fairclough comment specifically on my claims on Bourdieu's reading of Saussure. However Robbins briefly concedes that there is

> a strong sense that Bourdieu had not re-read Saussure in detail since his first early studies and consequently rather facilely reproduces the 'line' on Saussure that functioned strategically for him in the 1960s. (Robbins, p. 12)[4]

The significance of this concession is immediately negated by Robbins' claim that although the 'texts considered by Hasan are vulnerable to criticism', nevertheless 'Hasan is guilty of misrepresenting the "spirit" of Bourdieu's work – a spirit that I [i.e., Robbins] have been seeking to retrieve' (Robbins, p. 12).

Leaving aside the question of my misrepresentations of Bourdieu, to which I shall turn later, I read this as suggesting that despite Bourdieu's misrepresentation of the views of the founder of modern linguistics, on the basis of which he proceeds to reject much of modern linguistics not excluding sociolinguistic work, Bourdieu's 'heart is in the right place'; and it is this which should have been regarded as the important fact, not the facile reproduction of a strategically functional – functional, presumably for Bourdieu's purposes only – (mis)interpretation of Saussure. It is hard to believe that the dubious claims Bourdieu makes about Saussure, about linguistics, about the form of language and about linguistic variation are, as Robbins suggests, simply 'elements of his [i.e., Bourdieu's] strategic position-taking'. But even if they are, one wonders why one is obliged to adopt this attitude of unquestioning reverence towards them. It seems as if in reading Bourdieu, one is required to follow certain rules which by some strange dispensation do not bind the author of *Language and Symbolic Power* as he bends his rhetoric against Saussure, or for that matter against any other scholar. These rules demand that the reader must respect the spirit of Bourdieu's discourse, never mind what Bourdieu actually says in so many words. And yet, one might argue successfully that the spirit of Saussure's work is indeed not simply misrepresented but fairly badly mauled in Bourdieu's own work. The second rule for reading Bourdieu is presented as 'Bourdieu asks that his texts should be read contextually' (Robbins, p. 1). And again I am bemused by this requirement. Obviously to be read in context is the right of every speaker, since that is what permits the possibility of true dialogue between disciplines as opposed to verbal power play. But by that same token, doesn't Saussure ask to be read in context? And also Bernstein, whom Bourdieu quite unfairly attacked for making explicit what he, Bourdieu, leaves ambiguous in his own work, namely the nature of classed linguistic habitus? Why is it legitimate to read Saussure largely through the work of Levi Strauss[5]? Why is it legitimate to ignore the spirit of Bernstein's writings? The third rule that the reader of Bourdieu must observe is to place all Bourdieu's sayings in the context of his intellectual development; not only that, but also in the context of his biography, so that the views are not seen as 'static', so that they reverberate with all that has been said and done by him in the living of life over decades. It does not need to be pointed out that the relevance of one's biography to how one comes to see the world is not unique to Bourdieu. As a woman born and brought up in an Asian Moslem family and transplanted in the West from a colonial background, engaged in academic practice where even the recognition of masculine hegemony is a recent phenomenon, I too happen to know at the most intimate levels of my being, what it feels like to experience inclusion/exclusion, to be treated as insider/outsider; I too have become familiar with the many ways there are of putting down, ignoring, or praising with condescension. In my view, this does not mean that any work I do on the semantics of tense and aspect or even on the relations of language and social positioning must be read in the light of this history. How do Bourdieu's Béarnaise origins influence his view of denotation and connotation? Of grammars and grammarians? Of *langue* and *parole*? Of the ways in which language variation is realised? I have to say that this line of the defence of Bourdieu reminds me of an Urdu saying: *neither will there be nine mounds of oil, nor will Radha dance*. Neither will any reader meet such strict conditions for '*the* true' reading of Bourdieu, nor will there ever be a *legitimate* critique of any aspect of Bourdieu's work: whenever you criticise Bourdieu, it will be from a position of ignorance or inadequacy! To raise these absurd requirements is to create a zone of protection, which hardly befits Bourdieu's stature and reputation as a scholar and an original thinker.

In passing I must point out that Robbins' utilisation of some of the terms in my paper leaves me rather puzzled – for example, it is not clear to me what he means when he talks of indicating 'the "co-genetic" character of [Bourdieu's/anyone's?] intellectual production' (Robbins, p. 1). Granted the point that the evolution of consciousness is sociosemiotically mediated: the thoughts one thinks, the abstract theoretical structures one postulates have their roots in being, doing and saying within one's community. This, however, does not say anything of serious substance about Bourdieu's scholarly position on the relations of language and society. If one were to take the sociosemiotically mediated nature of intellectual work as proof of belief in co-genetic logic, then on this principle even Chomsky would turn out to be a staunch defender of the principle, since in his intellectual productions too the external and the internal, the social and the semiotic would have been active! Nor am I able to understand what one might mean by referring to 'biogenetically transmitted culture of the home embodied in the habitus' which apparently stands in contrast to 'the socially constructed culture by possession of which it becomes possible, through judicious capital investment, to maximise social power and position'. (Robbins, p. 2). Culture transmitted biogenetically? This is indeed strange! I fear I cannot subscribe to this position; rather I find myself in complete agreement with Bourdieu's view, which is after all widely accepted, that culture is not a biologically transmitted phenomenon, hence the importance of the notion of habitus. So what can Robbins mean by his biogenetically transmitted culture? Perhaps he is making an effort to address the concerns of my paper by borrowing certain key terms from it, but the way he recontextualises these terms has not been helpful so far as I am concerned. Or things may be more serious and need the sort of explanation Bernstein (1999: 163) offers:

> In the case of horizontal knowledge structures [such as those of linguistics, sociology, literary criticism etc.]… the set of languages which constitute any one horizontal knowledge structure are not translatable, since they make different and often opposing assumptions, with each language having its own criteria for legitimate texts, what counts as evidence and what counts as legitimate questions or a legitimate problematic. Indeed, the speakers of each language become as specialised and as excluding as the language.

4 Bourdieu on language

There is more to my critique of Bourdieu's linguistic framework than the issue of what Robbins translates as the reciprocities of internality and externality. My paper examined (1) Bourdieu's account of the formal structure of language – what the 'code' is like, (2) his view of linguistic varieties and (3) his perspective on the relations of the semiotic and the social. The issue of external/internal linguistics arose in the course of the discussion of themes (2) and (3). Robbins largely concerns himself with this latter dichotomy, without however actually appreciating the sequence of theoretical propositions which tie the issue of external/internal linguistics to the dialectic of the social and the semiotic. In a somewhat strange move the logic of which I regret I am unable to follow, he declares:

> She fails to realise, in other words, that Bourdieu asks that his texts should be read contextually and that *therefore they enact the reciprocity of the internal and the external which she theoretically favours*. (Robbins, p. 1; emphasis mine)

It is not clear to me how this demand of Bourdieu's to be read contextually disproves my claim that so far as Bourdieu's modelling of the relations of language and society is concerned, he consistently underplays the contribution of language, a point which is accepted not only by Chouliaraki and Fairclough but also by Collins. Throughout my paper I deliberately refrained from developing my understandings of Bourdieu's theory of the social: this was a deliberate decision. My aim was not to produce a critique of his sociology; it was to review his views on language. And in the course of doing this in my paper I pointed out more than once that his view of the social sits uneasily with his conceptualisation of the semiotic and specifically the linguistic. Bourdieu considerably under-rates the contribution of language both in terms of its systemic potential and in terms of its actual practice: that is to say, neither does his account do justice to the kind of resource that language is, nor does it present a well-argued set of propositions on what the use of this resource can achieve in interaction. The fact that I chose to focus on Bourdieu's linguistics, does not mean that I fail to appreciate the efforts Bourdieu has made to create a dynamic and comprehensive theory of the social, or that he has been the most persuasive writer on the need for the social science to adopt a theoretical perspective that respects the reciprocities of the objective and the subjective. As I see it, the main difference between myself and Robbins as the reader of Bourdieu's work is that I do not attempt to find reasons for ignoring those locations in his framework where the theory does not 'jell', where the ambitious synthesis fails. Like Alexander (1995) and Jenkins (1992), I believe that the synthesis does fail – which in no way detracts from the grandeur of the original vision. A claim in my paper, at least implied if not explicitly asserted, was that one element in the failure of this synthesis is Bourdieu's weak theory of language and his somewhat overblown extension of the principle of arbitrariness to all aspects of language without due regard to Saussure's further comments on the value and identity of the linguistic sign.

In general terms both Collins and Chouliaraki and Fairclough agree that Bourdieu's views on language leave something to be desired. They have however chosen not to say much on the specifics of my reading of Bourdieu's conception of the internal nature of language or its lexicogrammar, though commenting on my claim that Bourdieu's discourse contains many tensions and contradictions, Chouliaraki and Fairclough make a somewhat ambivalent statement to the effect that they would read Bourdieu:

> with a rather different objective from Hasan's – not to prove that Bourdieu is, contrary to his own claims, a formalist (*though his view of language suffers from formalist sins*). (Chouliaraki and Fairclough, p. 1; emphasis mine)

They further go on to comment:

> We agree with Hasan that in systematically subordinating discourse to social structures Bourdieu is *guilty of some sort of external linguistics*, but at the same time we believe that this does not necessarily entail *a 'wholesale' formalist view of language*. We believe, in fact, that his epistemology allows for more than one reading. (Chouliaraki and Fairclough, p. 3; emphasis mine)

In the first place I would like to dissociate myself from the somewhat uncomfortable religious metaphors of *sin* and *guilt*: after all one is not in the business of judging the morality or otherwise of Bourdieu's writing on the structure of language. No, I have to say that mine is an entirely practical stance. I ask myself: where can a conception of language such as Bourdieu's take us, in the sense of what will it allow us to explain about language and about society in terms of its own language of description (Bernstein, 1996)? It was from this point of view that I found a good deal to dissatisfy me as a linguist. It is a pity that the commentators do not elaborate on their views quoted above. For example, what does it mean to say that Bourdieu is not a 'wholesale formalist'? In what aspect of the description of the form of language is he not a formalist? And is there any implication that being a little bit of a formalist is not a hindrance to his theory of the social? How do we quantify/identify the innocuous variety of formalism from that which is to be viewed with alarm in a social constructivist theory? On the basis of extracts from Bourdieu's writings, I put together an over all picture of Bourdieu's view of the internal form of language and I must admit that despite flashes of brilliance not much in it appeared to offer a viable basis for the kind of understanding of language that a sociology such as Bourdieu's demands. It would have been educative to have Chouliaraki and Fairclough develop their claim with citations from Bourdieu to show the details of grounds that might support their 'different reading' that his epistemology permits and that Bourdieu's actual words on language and linguistics support. I find their assertion less than satisfactory that:

> In constructivist structuralism language is not seen as a *'mirror... (of) the categories of nature'* nor is there a world that is *'really real'*; what Hasan names *'categories of nature'* are *'principles of classification'*, whereas the *'real world'* is a particular construction of the social world in terms of field relations. (Chouliaraki and Fairclough, p. 3; emphasis original)

Two comments appear pertinent to me *a propos* this passage: if my paper is read attentively, it will be seen that *I* do not term anything 'categories of nature'; rather, I attribute this view to Bourdieu, precisely because this is what would be implied if his view on the lexicogrammar of languages and on linguistically construed meanings, i.e. semantics, is to be accepted. And secondly I agree with Chouliaraki and Fairclough that one fair description of Bourdieu's theoretical framework is to refer to it as 'constructivist structuralism'[6]. However, they seem to be saying that because Bourdieu holds this view, therefore what he actually says in so many words about the internal form of language should be interpreted as in keeping with this view, even though the conventional meaning of those claims about the nature of lexical meaning, about the a-semantic nature of grammar etc. flatly contradicts any such supposition. Essentially, then, they are in agreement with Robbins: attach priority to the favoured and favourable reading; ignore what the words actually say. One consequence of this admirable generosity is that by definition Bourdieu's work would never display any disjunction; and if we were so generous as to extend this principle to all accounts of the structure of human knowledge then the need for debate and clarification would disappear altogether. In the absence of more cogent arguments and evidence that Bourdieu's claims about grammar, lexicon and meaning can be read as conforming to the social constructivist perspective, I am inclined to maintain the point that disjunctions do exist in Bourdieu and that those disjunctions are dysfunctional for his sociological theory. If this is the case, then surely it is legitimate to ask for clarification. My paper claimed further that the disjunction exists because of his 'spontaneous linguistics', which does not sit well with his general theory of the social. When in my paper I commented that:

> I believe that this static model of the social inscribed in a particular view of language is entirely at variance with Bourdieu's modelling of society – in fact he it is who has done most to develop the dynamic perspective in the social sciences. (Hasan, 1999c: 55)

I was in effect saying: if we were to take his sociology seriously, then we could not logically expect him to be making these sorts of statements about language. There are plenty of linguists who subscribe to the views expressed in Bourdieu. If these views appear preposterous in his discourse, this is because of what Bourdieu professes the wish to achieve. Any theoretical framework that relies on *structured structuring structures* as the main principle for the production and reproduction of society must recognise the centrality of semiotic mediation. To coherently argue in favour of semiotic mediation with a formalist model does pose problems and here I am in disagreement with Collins, who believes that talk of 'making meanings' is somehow detrimental to understanding the true nature of language[7]. Witness the need Vygotsky (1962) felt to break from the formalist models in his account of children's development of higher mental function; note also Vološinov's (1986) stringent critique and rejection of both the objective and subjective schools of linguistics, as he attempted to clarify the part language plays in the formation of human consciousness and ideology. Without the explicit recognition of the centrality of semiotic mediation and the consequent view of language along the lines developed in my paper, the theoretical framework will remain open to criticism, no matter how much it professes to be inspired by constructivist structuralism. The view is not original that the recognition of the meaning making power of language is essential to any claim of its role in the formation of consciousness: the idea had been around for some time before Bourdieu began his reflections on society; it had surfaced in various guises, for example in the work of Vygotsky, in the work of Mead, Bateson, Whorf and, amongst our contemporaries, in the work of Bernstein. The fact that Bourdieu's theory of the social can be interpreted the way that Chouliaraki and Fairclough point out – and that I hint at in my paper – does not make his view of language appear less open to criticism. Quite the contrary: it puts both under serious question.

I would take issue with Chouliaraki and Fairclough on their valiant effort to render meaningful within Bourdieu's epistemology, expressions such as 'semantic freewheeling' and 'semantically empty'. To say that because a particular word or expression might 'fail to construe or internalise the social experience of particular groups' (Chouliaraki and Fairclough, p. 5) it is therefore legitimate to describe it as semantically empty seems questionable. Certainly, as a specific claim with reference to that particular section of the community, the expression would be applied sensically to some unit of form. But there are important issues involved here. First, Bourdieu, if I recall right, was talking in general terms, not with reference to any specific subset of a community. And from that perspective, the fact that for one particular group the expression construes nothing is no more and no less significant than that for another group it does do so. Much more serious, nothing that is semantically empty is actually perceivable as a signifier; contrary to the popular conception of the term signifier, the identity of the signifier cannot be separated from some signified (Thibault, 1997; Hasan, 1984a): we cannot know anything as a signifier to which the possibility of attaching some sense is absent. Thus the whole question of something being a word or an expression is itself inextricably linked with the construal of some sense. And finally, language, like many sociosemiotic creations of humanity, acquires what Berger and Luckman (1971) refer to as 'facticity': once created language IS, just as mountains and trees are, whether any one group of individuals manage to see them or not. In fact this principle works across ages as the language represented by Linear B demonstrates quite effectively. The language stayed as language, though for centuries it construed no meaning for any one; it would be questionable to say that the language was semantically empty and it is the readers who put meaning into it, as if it is socially efficacious for speakers to mean anything by anything! The granting of this possibility amounts to a solipsistic view of semiotic behaviour which is indeed completely irreconcilable with any constructivist theory of the social.

It would take too much time to respond in any detail to Chouliaraki and Fairclough's suggestion regarding the recognition in systemic functional linguistics of 'an aspect of the social structuring of the semiotic that centres upon *the dialectic of structure and event*' (ibid., p. 6; emphasis in original). Their discussion is of necessity highly condensed and in principle I am sympathetic to their account of the 'dialectic between structure and event in situated practices' (ibid.). However, my initial reaction is that in SFL, this aspect is already described through the notion of the permeability of contexts and discourses (Hasan, 1995a; 1999b). When we say that register variation is in dialectic with variation in social process, we use the term social process as a complex concept which may be paraphrased as the contextual configuration of social action, social relation and social modes of contact. Which is to say that I think of social process or event as a multifaceted phenomenon, that is as much a creation of the speaker's subjective relation to her/his situation of speaking as it is a set of conditions objectively present. At the same time, what is said becomes an integral element in the definition of the specific ongoing social process. The significance of all this is as follows: the theory recognises that the interactants' subjective relation defines the nature of the social process for them and that their verbal and nonverbal actions contribute to construing, maintaining, or changing the character of that ongoing social process; it seems to me that the theory is therefore able to capture the dialectic of structure and event. Where it seems to me SFL needs to grow is the incorporation of Bernstein's account of the conditions of speaking as discussed for example in his *Codes, modalities and the process of cultural reproduction* (Bernstein, 1990a), specifically the relations of *positioning* to the *recognition* and *realisation rules* for performance in some situation. The incorporation of this would enrich the model so that the structured structuring principle can be made explicit.

On one issue I sense myself in some disagreement with Chouliaraki and Fairclough. They seem to imagine that because the evolution of the semiotic and the social is governed by a co-genetic principle, this entails giving, as it were, equal time and attention to both aspects in any act of analysis or description (cf. their comment about Hasan's prioritising of the semiotic). I do not share this view: the linguist is not King Solomon dispensing just justice to the two disciplines! What one does and how by way of analysis and description, depends on what it is that one is most interested in explaining: one engages with a problem because the problem itself engages one in the first place. While granting this subjective bias in the selection of the focus of one's own enquiry, I do want to emphasise that, objectively speaking, the descriptions pertaining to the phonetics and phonology of a language are as much a concern of the linguist, as the analysis of the lexicogrammar of a piece of text is, even though phonological patterning (notwithstanding Bourdieu's accounts) by itself plays a much less important role in the construal of the social. The fact that phonology is relatively more distanced from the social than are semantics and lexicogrammar does not mean that it is not worthy of our attention, or even that it is irrelevant to our understanding of how language works. It would be odd to chide a phonologist, who maybe works in the area of instrumental phonetics, for not saying anything about markets, fields and umpteen kinds of capitals, leave aside the power and the ideology in all of that! As a person what I would aspire to be able to do in my capacity as a linguist – and I hasten to add that this is an entirely individual inclination, not morally, politically or intellectually binding on all practitioners of the trade – is to show how and by what devices the various meanings get construed in discourse so as to enable it to exercise the power that it does on our consciousness, our emotions, our relations to others and our place in social life. The expertise for revealing this is part (but only part) of what it means to be a linguist. And in this connection, it seems to me important that claims of interpretation be reasoned, not simply asserted. Certainly the subjective is present in every analysis but analysis is revealing precisely because/if its ground rules are explicitly displayed and consistently followed. What I would most wish to avoid as a linguist is engaging in half-way analysis of both the social and the semiotic, so that the nature of neither is illuminated and so that the categories of description are not moored in my overall conceptualisation of the potentiality of linguistic phenomena, to borrow a phrase from Mathesius. What comes across with such analyses is a sense of the analyst's involvement, without necessarily any sense of how the revealed was revealed, what the ground rules for such an analysis are.

I close this section fully aware that I have not responded to much that has been interesting reading for me in the commentaries of Collins, of Chouliaraki and Fairclough and of Robbins, all of whom I thank for their thought provoking contribution. The materials in their commentaries that I have not mentioned here were definitely interesting for further dialogue; however, the scope of a paper such as this forced me to be selective. But before I leave this section to talk about the question of my misreading of Bourdieu, I must say a few words regarding my fourth commentator who apparently found my critique of Bourdieu most distasteful. I refer to Corson, who, whether modestly or truthfully, conceded in his opening paragraph that he lacked 'the breadth of scholarship necessary to respond to many of the discourses that she [i.e. Hasan] brings together'. Professing to lack this breadth of scholarship, he proceeded to appoint himself the diagnostician of mortality in theories. Since I am not blessed with prescience in such matters, I have felt quite content to leave him engaged in what appears to strike him as a gratifying exercise – that of contemplating the death of systemic functional linguistics in the near future. But this move on his part did seem to obviate the necessity of my responding to the many non sequiturs in his commentary. What I wish to do here *a propos* his contribution is to make but a very simple comment on the nature of writing, reading and discussion which is relevant to the tenor and content of his comments.

As I have already suggested, it is a condition of speaking that a speaker must expect some mis-reading and be willing to accept some responsibility for such misreading. While it is true that much substantive criticism can be brushed aside as merely based on misreading, it is also the case that the claim of misreading can be used as a basis for dialogue, as my response to the remaining three commentaries on my paper demonstrates. By contrast, when a series of assertions is produced on the basis of no reading at all, as seems to be the case when Corson directs his critical acumen towards my work, this closes all openings for productive discussion. The implied innuendoes by which the veiled denigration of the object of one's criticism is achieved, no matter how amusing its style, cannot equal in weight the careful substantiation of the critical assertions one makes – that is, of course, assuming that one is really interested in dialogue not in an intellectual bun-fight! It is not as if Corson did not know where to find my views on, say, 'reflection literacy' which he is content to equate with genre based pedagogy despite the fact that my article in question presents an explicit critique of the latter approach to literacy. As the reader will note I had supplied a fairly detailed bibliography of systemic functional linguistics (and of my own work, since I can hold myself responsible for my own words!); but this he dismissed as activated by 'insularity', not a source of information. Thus instead of finding out what I have actually said, he has preferred to rely on his own imagination to supply him with a view of what he thinks I *might* mean by that term. He has then gone on to castigate his own invented conception; not surprisingly his comments have nothing much to do with my work in general or with anything I said in my critique of Bourdieu. It is possible that his fear of the inaccessibility of SFL ideas, which he claims to find intricate, deterred him from attempting any reading. But this would seem somewhat surprising in any one who is even reasonably fluent in the theoretical discourses of Pierre Bourdieu, as surely Corson must be to defend him so spiritedly! After all, Bourdieu is not exactly famous for either the simplicity of his ideas or the lucidity of his prose. The upshot of Corson's strategy for commenting on my paper is that there is hardly any ground for dialogue: the interested reader might compare my careful documentation of Bourdieu's views on language, linguists and linguistics with Corson's less than careful treatment of my own work. This will be a good indicator of what it means to adopt a doxic position.

5 On misrepresenting Bourdieu

As I have already pointed out, my reading of Bourdieu was deliberately limited to his reading of Saussure and his views on language and linguistics. These are concentrated to the best of my knowledge in *Language and Symbolic Power*, to which I have referred most frequently, even if the references and extracts are not limited to the single paper which I, perhaps mistakenly, identified as my main focus. Apart from this, in my paper there is certainly evidence of much wider reading. But the commentators have felt that the reading was limited in the sense of ignoring important aspects, not to mention the fact that it fell far short of the mastery of the entire Bourdieu œuvre. For example, it is pointed out that I refer to limited segments of the Bourdieu *œuvre*. Surely, I cannot claim to have read everything produced by Bourdieu and surely I focused on those texts which were most relevant to his views on language. The discerning reader will note scattered throughout my paper Bourdieu's own words and vocables which do not come simply from the chapter from *Language and Symbolic Power* that my paper particularly mentions: these informal 'quotes' range over a good deal of Bourdieu's writing. The important question to my mind is whether there is any writing of Bourdieu's that I have ignored which in as many words presents a critically different conception of language, a criterially better reading of Saussure, a more objective attitude to the work of 'the linguist' and the sociolinguist. I feel satisfied that this is not the case. Collins suggests that unawareness of Bourdieu's theory of markets and fields has vitiated my interpretation. I fail to see how this can be true. As my paper claimed: there can be no market, no field in the delineation of which language has not been complicit and this to me means that language has the power to make meanings, to create abstract structures, to reinforce structures assisted by practical action. Language must, therefore, be able to do more than function as a surrogate of the formally postulated pre-existing realities, whether they exist in the brain from birth or in the physical universe. That in turn calls for a conception of language remarkably different from that implicit in Bourdieu's sayings[8]. Besides comments such as those made by Collins or Couliaraki and Fairclough hardly take note of the details I presented regarding Bourdieu's views of grammars, grammarians, lexicon and semantics, not to speak of language variation. I am gratified to note that the commentators by their silence on these aspects of my critique appear to concede the points I make, except Robbins of course who it seems to me rather misses the point of that discussion (see paragraphs below).

As I pointed out earlier, no one can meet the unrealistic conditions for reading laid down by commentators such as Robbins. But then those conditions are really meant to silence, not to encourage enquiry or understanding. My decision not to comment on Bourdieu's theory of the social has been, I fear, misinterpreted as either ignorance, or lack of understanding. Of course ignorance is a matter of degree and moreover ignorance is an unavoidable condition of being human. I may be forgiven for saying that my ignorance of Bourdieu's work is certainly not anywhere near the degree of ignorance displayed by many who profess to understand the kind of linguistics I do. To the best of my ability and more carefully than most critiques do, I have cited the actual words of the author; taking the (inter)textual context of their occurrence, I have discussed them in reasonable detail. It would have been gratifying if in commenting on my paper someone had taken half the trouble to demonstrate how the claim of my misrepresentation of Bourdieu can be justified by confronting my Bourdieu citations with those of his sayings that oppose and nullify the views I have attributed to him on the basis of his own locutions. But such engagement with my text is largely absent. In this connection, there is one notable exception where Robbins actually cites a passage from my paper (see my paper pp. 39-40), with the comment that 'Hasan is even guilty of seeking to reinforce her point by imprecise quotation from Bourdieu' (Robbins: 12-13). The passage in question occurs on pp. 37-8 of Bourdieu, 1991. In the second paragraph of this Bourdieu citation I elided the italicised portion below:

> This simple model of the linguistic production and circulation as the relation between linguistic habitus and the market on which they offer their products *does not seek either to challenge or to replace a strictly linguistic analysis of the code. But it* does enable us to understand the error and failure to which linguistics succumbs when relying on only one of the factors involved – a strictly linguistic competence, abstractly defined, ignoring everything that it owes to the social conditions of its production – it tries to give an adequate account of discourse in all its conjunctural singularity…

Robbins suggests that the elision is deliberately deceptive (even though I have exercised other elisions as well for purposes of economising on space: my dishonesty is apparent however only in this particular case!), presumably because it shows that Bourdieu does not actually require that 'a strictly linguistic analysis of the code' by linguists be discontinued, but is simply making 'a plea for internalist analysis to be produced in the service of practice rather than an end in itself' (Robbins, p. 13). In the first place, I would not have described the tenor of Bourdieu's prose as making 'a plea' of any kind. Secondly, so far as my critique of Bourdieu's views was concerned, I was not claiming that Bourdieu forbade linguists from doing any linguistic analysis (what would give him that right anyway?): rather Bourdieu's point was to make his readership aware of what he, Bourdieu, thought of the poor quality of the linguists' analysis; it was to offer pejorative descriptions of what 'they' typically do, the error of their ways, the lacunae in their work. This I take to be the burden of Bourdieu's message. In the midst of the extensive citing of extracts from his work to substantiate this point, it did not seem to me at all misleading to elide this insignificant concession which magnanimously allows the linguist to continue with internal (though useless) analyses of the code. This was simply because my focus was on suggesting that so far as Bourdieu is concerned whatever analysis the linguist does is hardly worth the paper on which it is produced! Linguists could go on doing their analyses till kingdom come; so far as Bourdieu's scholarly assessment of these is concerned the analysis is of little consequence since it reveals nothing worth revealing. Robbins is mistaken if he thinks that the concession by Bourdieu, which I apparently deceitfully elided, overcomes my criticisms of his conception of language. The entire paragraph in Robbins where he professes to find similarities between my critique of Bourdieu and that of Willis'[9] is completely unrecognisable to me as a rendering of anything I have said. My worry is not that:

> Bourdieu's denial of any intrinsic meaning to language prevents the language acquisition of the disempowered *from being anything other than the language of the dominant...* (ibid.; emphasis mine)

Rather, I was suggesting that the disempowered never get anywhere close to any language education, as they are completely alienated by the kind of instruction offered in the classroom. Teaching about language is not at a premium where everything that is potent in language is simply identifiable as having its origin somewhere else and where the analysis of language as a resource for meaning is reduced to analysing the 'code'. Robbins closes his commentary with the innuendo that it is the threat of the marginalisation of the scientific linguist from the scene of literacy education that prompts such critiques of Bourdieu as mine: this seems to me to imply that in the end, my critique does not arise from a spirit of enquiry but from something personal and petty. All I can say is: Robbins is not the first, especially amongst critical theorists, to attribute 'bad faith' to a critic; Bourdieu himself is not above hurling such accusations. I suppose this disdain against critique on the part of the defenders of critical sociology is understandable on a certain assumption. To spell it out, so long as one can go on believing that all critiques of one's favoured framework are motivated by nothing but ignorance, or by inability to comprehend, or by recidivist tendencies, or by personal resentment or by self interest on the part of the critic, or by the anguish of the approaching death of their own theories, one need not contemplate any serious re-thinking of that framework. But what makes Bourdieu and his followers so confident that the principle of self interest applies only to others, not to them? What makes them believe that they are the best judge of what social progress means? Or what morality consists in? What makes Robbins believe that if Bourdieu were to be read 'rightly' then, like the word of God, his dicta would be found perfect, free of any flaws that ordinary mortals are prone to? These attitudes are fine only on one assumption on the holder's part: '*the truth* as revealed to me shall for ever remain *the truth*'.

Notes

1. Cf. his remarks (1991: 37-8) quoted in my paper on p. 40.
2. I am deliberately using the expression 'limited reading' ambiguously to refer to both limitations in the extent of reading as well as limitations in comprehending Bourdieu's point of view.
3. All page references to my paper are as they appear in the published version.
4. All page references to the commentaries are as they appear in the manuscript form.
5. In this respect, it is completely irrelevant to an outside reader what careful critique of Saussure Bourdieu might or might not have done much earlier than attacking Saussure became fashionable (cf. comment by Robbins)! The academics' cabinet always contains such treasures, but the reader must read on the basis of what s/he has access to.
6. For other descriptions, see Alexander, 1995.
7. It is unfortunate that one cannot address all the issues that have been raised. Collins also queries my reading of competence. Competence as the word is used in Chomsky, 1965, is indeed a multiply ambiguous word as a reading of the first few pages would reveal.
8. Collins suggests that formal linguistics has been misrepresented in my paper. Obviously I have not referred to either West Coast functionalism or to Cognitive Linguistics or even to the latest incarnations of Chomskian models: these in the context of Bourdieu's reflections on language appear quite irrelevant for I have a very clear sense that Bourdieu's linguistics is closest to the dominant model of the early 1960s.
9. Which I have to admit with regrets that I have never yet seen.

References

Abercrombie, D. (1951/1965) RP and local accent. *The Listener*, 6 September 1951 (as *The way people speak*). Reprinted in D. Abercrombie, *Studies in Phonetics and Linguisitcs*. London: Oxford University Press.
Achebe, C. (1988) *Anthills of the Savannah*. Garden City, NY: Doubleday/Anchor.
Alexander, J. C. (1995) The reality of reduction: the failed synthesis of Pierre Bourdieu. *Fin de Siècle Theory: relativism, reduction and the problem of reason*. London: Verso.
Atkinson, P. (1985) *Language, Structure and Reproduction: an introduction to the sociology of Basil Bernstein*. London: Methuen.
Austin, J. L. (1962) *How to Do Things with Words*. Cambridge: Cambridge University Press.
Austin, J. L. (1979) A plea for excuses. In J. O. Urmson and G. J. Warnock (eds) *Philosophical Papers*. 3rd edition. Oxford: Oxford University Press.
Axel, E.(1999) One developmental line in European activity theories. In M. Cole, Y. Engeström and O. Vasquez (eds) *Mind, Culture and Activity: seminal papers from the Laboratory of Comparative Human Cognition*. Cambridge: Cambridge University Press.
Bakhtin, M. (1984) *Problems of Dostoevsky's Poetics* (translated and edited by C. Emerson). Manchester: Manchester University Press.
Bakhtin, M. (1986) *Speech Genres and Other Late Essays* (edited by C. Emerson and M. Holquist). Austin: University of Texas Press.
Barthes, R. (1971) Style and its image. In S. Chatman (ed.) *Literary Style*: a *symposium*. New York: OUP.
Bateson, G. (1972) *Steps to an Ecology of Mind: a revolutionary approach to man's understanding of himself*. New York: Ballantine Books.
Berger, P. and Luckman, T. (1966) *The Social Construction of Reality: a treatise on the sociology of knowledge*. New York: Doubleday.
Berger, P. L. and Luckman, T. (1971) *The Social Construction of Reality*. Harmondsworth: Penguin.
Bernstein, B. (1958) Some sociological determinants of perception. *British Journal of Sociology* IX, 159–74. Reprinted in B. Bernstein, *Class, Codes and Control, Volume 1: theoretical studies towards a sociology of language*. London: Routledge & Kegan Paul, 1971.
Bernstein, B. (1965) A sociolinguistic approach to social learning. In J. Gold (ed.) *Penguin Survey of the Social Sciences*. Harmondsworth: Penguin. Reprinted in Bernstein 1971.
Bernstein, B. (1967) Open schools, open societies? *New Society*, September.
Bernstein, B. (1969) A sociolinguistics approach to socialization: with some reference to educability, I. *The Human Context*, Volume I. London: Chaucer Publishing Company.
Bernstein, B. (1970a) Education cannot compensate for society. *New Society*, February.

Bernstein, B. (1970b) A sociolinguistics approach to socialization: with some reference to educability, II, *The Human Context*, Volume II, No 2. London: Chaucer Publishing Company.

Bernstein, B. (1971) *Class, Codes and Control, Volume I: Theoretical Studies toward a Sociology of Language*. London: Routledge & Kegan Paul.

Bernstein, B. (1971a) Social class, language and socialization. In A. S. Abramson (ed.) *Current Trends in Linguistics*, Volume 12. The Hague: Mouton.

Bernstein, B. (1971b) On the classification and framing of educational knowledge. In M. Young (ed.) *Knowledge and Control*. London: Collier-Macmillan.

Bernstein, B. (1972) A sociolinguistic approach to socialization: with some reference to educability. In J. J. Gumperz and D. Hymes (eds) *Directions in Sociolinguistics: the ethnography of communication*. London: Blackwell.

Bernstein, B. (1973) *Class, Codes and Control, Volume 2: applied studies towards a sociology of language*. London: Routledge.

Bernstein, B. (1975) *Class, Codes and Control, Volume 3: towards a theory of educational transmission*. London: Routledge & Kegan Paul.

Bernstein, B. (1975a) Classification and framing of educational knowledge. *Class, Codes and Control, Volume 3: towards a theory of educational transmissions*. 2nd revised edition (1977). London: Routledge & Kegan Paul.

Bernstein, B. (1977) *Class, Codes and Control Volume 3: towards a theory of educational transmission*. 2nd revised edition. London: Routledge & Kegan Paul.

Bernstein, B. (1981) Codes, modalities and the processes of cultural reproduction: a model. *Language and Society*, 10: 327–63.

Bernstein, B. (1982) Codes, modalities and the process of cultural reproduction. In M. W. Apple (ed.) *Cultural and Economic Reproduction in Education: essays on class, ideology and the state* 304–55. London: Routledge & Kegan Paul.

Bernstein, B. (1987a) Elaborated and restricted codes: an overview 1958–85. In U. Ammon, N. Dittmar and K. J. Mattheier (eds) *Sociolinguistics/Soziolinguistik: an international handbook, Volume 1*. Berlin: Walter de Gruyter.

Bernstein, B. (1987b) Social class, codes and communication. In U. Ammon, N. Dittmar and K. J. Mattheier (eds) *Sociolinguistics/Soziolinguistik: an international handbook of the Science of Society, Volume 1* 563–79. Berlin: Walter de Gruyter.

Bernstein, B. (1990) *Class, Codes and Control Volume 4: the structuring of pedagogic discourse*. London: Routledge.

Bernstein, B. (1990a) Code, modalities and the process of cultural reproduction: a model. *Class Codes and Control Volume 4: the structuring of pedagogic discourse*. London: Routledge.

Bernstein, B. (1996) *Pedagogy, Symbolic Control and Identity: theory research critique*. London: Taylor & Francis.

Bernstein, B. (1999) Vertical and horizontal discourse: an essay. *British Journal of Sociology of Education* 20(2): 157–73.

Bernstein, B. (2000) *Pedagogy, Symbolic Control and Identity: theory, research, critique*. 2nd edition. Revised. Lanham, Maryland: Rowman and Littlefield.

Bernstein, B. and Cook-Gumperz, J. (1973) *The Coding Grid in Socialisation and Social Control: a study of class differences in the language of maternal control*. London: Routledge & Kegan Paul.

Bernstein, B. and Henderson, D. (1969) Social class differences in the relevance of language to socialization. *Society* 3(1).
Bolinger, D. (1975) *Aspects of Language* (2nd edition). New York: Harcourt Brace & Javanovich.
Boncinelli, E. (2001) Erasmus Lecture: brain and mind. *European Review* 9(4) 389–98.
Bottomore, T. B. and Rubel, M. (eds) (1963) *Karl Marx: selected writings in sociology and social philosophy*. Harmondsworth. Penguin.
Bootomore, T. B. and Rubel, M. (eds) (1976) *Karl Marx: on sociology and social philosophy*. Harmondsworth: Penguin.
Bourdieu, P. (1977) *Outline of a Theory of Practice*. Translated by R. Nice. Cambridge: Cambridge University Press.
Bourdieu, P. (1984) *Distinction: a social critique of the judgment of taste* (translated by R. Nice). Cambridge, MA: Harvard University Press.
Bourdieu, P. (1990) *The Logic of Practice*. Translated by R. Nice. London: Polity Press.
Bourdieu, P. (1991) *Language and Symbolic Power* Translated by G. Raymond and M. Adamson, edited by J. B. Thompson. First paper back edition. Cambridge: Polity Press.
Bourdieu, P. (1993) Concluding remarks: for a sociogenetic understanding of intellectual works. In C. Calhoun, E. LiPuma and M. Postone (eds) *Bourdieu: critical perspectives*. Oxford: Polity.
Bourdieu, P. and Passeron, J. (1977) *Reproduction in Education, Society and Culture*. London: Sage.
Bourdieu, P., Passeron, J. and de Saint Martin, M. (1994) *Academic Discourse: linguistic misunderstanding and professorial power* (translated by R. Teese). London: Polity Press.
Bourdieu, P. and Wacquant, L. (1992) *An Invitation to Reflexive Sociology*. Chicago: The University of Chicago Press.
Brandis, W. and Henderson, D. (1970) *Social Class, Language and Communication*. London: Routledge & Kegan Paul.
Brubaker, R. (1993) Social theory as habitus. In C. Calhoun, E. LiPuma and M. Postone (eds) *Bourdieu: critical perspectives*. Oxford: Polity.
Bühler, K. (1990) *Theory of Language: the representational function of language*. Translated by D. F. Goodwin. Amsterdam: Benjamins. First published in 1934, Jena: Gustav Fischer Verlag.
Bullowa, M. (1979) Prelinguistic communication: a field for scientific research. Introduction in M. Bullowa (ed.) *Before Speech: the beginnings of interpersonal communication*. Cambridge: Cambridge University Press.
Butt, D. G. (1983) Semantic drift in verbal art. In *Australian Review of Applied Linguistics* 6.
Butt, D. G. (1985/1989) *Talking and Thinking: the patterns of behaviour*. Geelong, Vic: Deakin University Press. Reprinted in Oxford: Oxford University Press, 1989.
Butt, D. (1987) Randomness, order and the latent patterning of text. In D. Birch and M. O'Toole (eds) *Functions of Style*. London: Francis Pinter.
Butt, D. G. (1989) The object of language. In R. Hasan and J. R. Martin (ed.) *Language Development: learning language, learning culture* (Meaning and Choice in Language: studies for Michael Halliday) 66–110. Norwood, NJ: Ablex.

Butt, D. G. (2001) Firth, Halliday and the development of systemic functional theory. In S. Auroux, E. F. K. Koerner, H. Niederehe and K. Versteegh (eds) *History of the Language Sciences: an International handbook on the evolution of the study of language from the beginning to the present*. Berlin: Walter de Gruyter.

Calhoun, C., LiPuma, E. and Postone, M. (1993) *Bourdieu: critical perspectives*. Oxford: Polity.

Carr, M. (2002) Developing learning dispositions: a perspective from early childhood education. In G. Wells and G. Claxton (eds) *Learning for Life in the 21st Century: sociocultural perspectives on the future of education*. Oxford: Blackwell.

Carter, R. (1996) Politics and knowledge about language: the LINC project. In R. Hasan and G. Williams (eds) *Literacy in Society*. London: Longman.

Chomsky, N. (1965) *Aspects of the Theory of Syntax*. Cambridge, MA: MIT Press.

Christie, F. (1990) *Literacy for a Changing World*. Radford House, Hawthorne, Vic: Australian Council for Educational Research.

Christie, F. (1996) *The Pedagogic Discourse of Secondary School Social Sciences: geography*. Melbourne: University of Melbourne Press.

Christie, F. (1999) *Pedagogy and the Shaping of Consciousness: linguistic and social processes*. London: Cassell.

Claxton, G. (2002) Education for the learning age: a sociocultural approach to learning to learn. In G. Wells and G. Claxton (eds) *Learning for Life in the Twenty-first Century: sociocultural perspectives on the future of education*. Oxford: Blackwell.

Cloran, C. (1989) Learning through Language: the social construction of gender. In R. Hasan and J. R. Martin (eds) *Language development: learning language, learning culture* (Meaning and choice in language: studies for Michael Halliday). Norwood, NJ: Ablex.

Cloran, C. (1994) *Rhetorical Units and Decontextualisation: an enquiry into some relations of context, meaning and grammar*. Nottingham: Nottingham University. [Monographs in Systemic Linguistics No 6]

Cloran, C. (1995) Defining and relating text segments: subject and theme in discourse. In R. Hasan and P. H. Fries (eds) *On Subject and Theme: a discourse functional perspective*. Amsterdam: John Benjamins.

Cloran, C. (1999) Contexts for learning. In F. Christie (ed.) *Pedagogy and the Shaping of Consciousness: linguistic and social processes* 31–65. London: Cassell.

Cloran, C. (2000) Socio-semantic variation: different wordings, different meanings. In L. Unsworth (ed.) *Researching Language in Schools and Communities: functional linguistic perspectives* 152–83. London: Cassell.

Cloran, C., Butt, D. and Williams, G. (eds) (1996) *Ways of Saying, Ways of Meaning: Selected Papers of Ruqaiya Hasan*. London: Cassell.

Cole, M., Engeström, Y. and Vasquez, O. (eds) (1997) *Mind, Culture and Activity: seminal papers from the Laboratory of Comparative Human Cognition*. Cambridge: Cambridge University Press.

Collins, J. (1989) Hegemonic practice: literacy and standard language in public education. *Journal of Education* 171(2): 9–34.

Cook, G. (1990) Transcribing infinity: problems of context presentation. *Journal of Pragmatics* 14(1): 1-24.
Cook, J. (1972) *Social Control and Socialization*. London: Routledge & Kegan Paul.
Cook, J. (1973) Language and socialization: a critical review. In B. Bernstein (ed.) *Class, Codes and Control Vol. 2. Applied Studies towards a Sociology of Language*. London: Routledge & Kegan Paul.
Dawkins, R. (1982) *The Extended Phenotype*. New York: Oxford University Press.
Davies, A. (1969) The notion of register. *Educational Review* 22(1).
de Saussure, F. (1966) *Course in General Linguistics*. Translated and annotated by W. Baskin, edited by C. Bally and A. Sechehaye with A. Reidlinger. New York: McGraw-Hill.
Deacon, T. (1997) *The Symbolic Species: the co-evolution of language and the human brain*. New York: W. W. Norton & Co; London: Penguin Books.
Dennett, D. (1991) *Consciousness Explained*. London: Penguin.
Donaldson, M. (1978) *Children's Minds*. Glasgow: Collins; London: Fontana.
Donaldson, M. (1992) *Human Minds: an exploration*. London: Penguin Books.
Douglas, M. (1972) Speech, class and Basil Bernstein. *The Listener,* 2241, 9 March. London.
Dumont, R.V. Jr. (1972) Learning English and how to be silent: studies in Sioux and Cherokee classrooms. In C. B. Cazden, V. P. John and D. Hymes (eds) *Functions of Language in the Classroom*. New York: Teachers College Press.
Durkheim, E. (1964) *The Division of Labour in Society* (Translated by G. Simpson.) New York. The Free Press.
Edelman, Gerald M. (1992) *Bright Air, Brilliant Fire: on the matter of the mind*. New York: Basic Books.
Edwards, A. D. and Westgate, D. P. G. (1987) *Investigating Classroom Talk*. London: Falmer Press.
Ellis, J. (1966) On contextual meaning. In C. E. Bazell, J. Catford, M. A. K. Halliday, R. H. Robins (eds) *In memory of J. R. Firth*. London: Longmans.
Ellis, J. and Ure, J. N. (1969) Language varieties: register. *Encyclopaedia of Linguistics, Communication and Control*. London: Pergamon Press.
Elshtain, J. B. (1981) *Public Man, Private Woman*. Oxford: Martin Robertson.
Engeström, Y., Miettinen, R. and Punamäki, R. (eds) (1999) *Perspectives on Activity Theory*. Cambridge: Cambridge University Press.
Enkvist, N. E, Spencer, J. and Gregory, M. (1964) *Linguistics and Style*. London: Oxford University Press.
Evans J. St. B. T., Newstead, St. E. and Byrne, R. M. J. (1993) *Human Reasoning: the psychology of deduction*. Hillsdale: Lawrence Erlbaum.
Fawcett, R. P. (1987) The semantics of clause and verb for relational processes in English. In M. A. K. Halliday and R. P. Fawcett (eds) *New Developments in Systemic Linguistics: Volume 1: theory and description*. London: Pinter.
Fawcett, R. P. and Young, D. J. (eds) (1987) *New Developments in Systemic Linguistics Volume 2: theory and application*. London: Pinter.
Firth, J. R. (1935/1957) The technique of semantics. *Transactions of the Philological Society*. Reprinted in *Papers in Linguistics 1934–1951*. London: Oxford University Press.
Firth, J. R. (1948/1957) The semantics of linguistic science. *Lingua*, i.4. Reprinted in *Papers in Linguistics 1934–1951*. London: Oxford University Press.

Firth, J. R. (1950/1957) Personality and language in society. *The Sociological Review: Journal of the Institute of Sociology*, xlii. section two. Reprinted in *Papers in Linguistics 1934–1951*. London: Oxford University Press.

Firth, J. R. (1957a) A synopsis of linguistic theory 1930–1955. *Studies in Linguistic Analysis* (Special Volume of the Philological Society) 1–32. Oxford: Blackwell.

Firth, J. R. (1957b) *Papers in Linguistics 1934–1951*. London: Oxford University Press.

Firth, J. R. (1957c) Ethnographic analysis and language with reference to Malinowski's views. In R. Firth (ed.) *Man and Culture: an evaluation of the work of Bronislaw Malinowski*. London: Routledge & Kegan Paul.

Fishman, J. A. (1970) *Sociolinguistics*. Rowley, Mass.

Foucault, M. (1970) *The Order of Things*. London: Tavistock Publications.

Frake, C. O. (1964) How to ask for a drink in Subanun. *American Anthropologist*, 66.6, part 2. 127–32.

Frake, C. O. (1972) Struck by speech: the Yakan concept of litigation. In J. J. Gumperz and D. H. Hymes (eds) *Directions in Sociolinguistics: the ethnography of communication*. New York: Holt Rinehart & Winston.

Gahagan, D. M. and G. A. (1970) Talk Reform: *Explorations in Language for Infant School Children*. London: Routledge & Kegan Paul.

Garfinkle, H. (1967) *Studies in Ethnomethodology*. Englewood Cliffs. Prentice-Hall.

Gazzaniga, M. S. (1993) *Nature's Mind*. London: Penguin.

Goody, Jack (1987) *The Interface between the Written and the Oral*. Cambridge: Cambridge University Press.

Gordimer, N. (1995) *Writing and Being*. Cambridge, MA: Harvard University Press.

Graff, Harvey J. (1987) *The Labyrinths of Literacy: reflections on literacy past and present*. London: The Falmer Press.

Greenfield, S. (1997) *The Human Brain: a guided tour*. London: Phoenix.

Greenfield, S. (2000a) *The Private Life of the Brain*. London: Penguin Books.

Greenfield, S. (2000b) *The Human Brain: a guided tour*. London: Phoenix Paperback.

Gregory, M. (1967) Aspects of varieties differentiation. *Journal of Linguistics* 3.

Gregory, M. (1988) Generic situation and register: a functional view of communication. In J. D. Benson, M. J. Cummings and W. S. Greaves (eds) *Linguistics in a Systemic Perspective*. Amsterdam: Benjamins.

Grice, H. P. (1975) Logic and conversation. In P. Cole and J. L. Morgan (eds) *Syntax and Semantics, Volume 3: speech acts*. New York: Academic Press.

Gumperz, J. J. (1971) *Language in Social Groups* (edited by A. S. Dil). Stanford: Stanford University Press.

Halliday, M. A. K. (1961) Categories of the theory of grammar. *Word*, 17)(3): 242–92.

Halliday, M. A. K. (1964) The users and uses of language. In M. A. K. Halliday, A. McIntosh and P. Strevens (eds) *Linguistic Sciences and Language Teaching*. London: Longman.

Halliday, M. A. K. (1970) Functional diversity in language. *Foundations of Language* 6.

Halliday, M. A. K. (1971a) Language in a social perspective. *Educational Review* 23(3).

Halliday, M. A. K. (1971b) Semantics and syntax in a functional grammar: [towards a sociological semantics]. paper to be read at international Symposium on Semantics, Urbino.
Halliday, M. A. K. (1971c) Linguistic function and literary style: an enquiry into the language of William Golding's The Inheritors. In S. Chatman (ed.) *Literary Style: a symposium.* NY: Oxford University Press.
Halliday, M. A. K. (1973) *Explorations in the Functions of Language.* London: Edward Arnold.
Halliday, M. A. K. (1973a) Relevant models of language. *Explorations in the Functions of Language.* London: Arnold.
Halliday, M. A. K. (1973b) Foreword. In Bernstein, Basil (ed.) *Class, Codes and Control Volume 2: applied studies towards a sociology of language.* London: Routledgte & Kegan Paul.
Halliday, M. A. K. (1973c) Towards a sociological semantics. *Explorations in the Functions of Language.* London: Edward Arnold.
Halliday, M. A. K. (1974) *Language and Social Man.* London: Longman (Schools Council Programme in Linguistics and English Teaching: Papers Series II, Volume 3).
Halliday, M. A. K. (1975) *Learning How to Mean: explorations in the development of language.* London: Edward Arnold.
Halliday, M. A. K. (1976) Anti-languages. *American Anthropologist.* 78(3): 570–84.
Halliday, M. A. K. (1977a) Text as semantic choice in social context. In T. A. van Dijk and J. S. Petöfi (eds) *Grammars and Descriptions.* Berlin: Walter de Gruyter.
Halliday, M. A. K. (1977b) *Aims and Perspectives in Linguistics.* Applied Linguistics Association of Australia (Occasional Paper No. 1).
Halliday, M. A. K. (1977c) Language as social semiotic: towards a general sociolinguistic theory. In A. Makkai, V. B. Makkai and L. Heilmann (eds) *Linguistics at the Crossroads.* Illinois: Jupiter Press.
Halliday, M. A. K. (1978) *Language as Social Semiotic: the social interpretation of language and meaning.* London: Arnold.
Halliday, M. A. K. (1979a) Modes of meaning and modes of expression: types of grammatical structure and their determination by different semantic functions. In D. J. Allerton, E. Carney and D. Holdcroft (eds) *Function and Context in Linguistic Analysis.* Cambridge: Cambridge University Press.
Halliday, M. A. K. (1979b) The ontogenesis of dialogue. In W. U. Dressler (ed.) *Proceedings of the Twelfth International Congress of Linguistics.* Special volume by Innsbrucker Beiträge zur Sprachwissenschaft.
Halliday, M. A. K. (1980) Three aspects of children's language development: learning language, learning through language, learning about language. In Y. Goodman, M. M. Hausler and D. M. Strickland (eds) *Oral and Written Language: impact on schools.* International Reading Association & National Council of Teachers of English. (IRA & NCTE). A. fuller version has appeared in Collected Works of M. A. K. Halliday Volume 4: *The Language of Early Childhood,* edited by J. Webster. London: Continuum, December 2002.
Halliday, M. A. K. (1984a) Language as code and language as behaviour: a systemic functional interpretation of the nature and ontogenesis of dialogue. In R. P. Fawcett, M. A. K. Halliday, S. M. Lamb and A. Makkai (eds) *The Semiotics of Culture and Language,* Volume 1. London: Frances Pinter.

Halliday, M. A. K. (1984b) On the ineffability of grammatical categories. *The Tenth LACUS Forum*. Columbia. Hornbeam Press.

Halliday, M. A. K. (1985a) *An Introduction to Functional Grammar*. London: Edward Arnold.

Halliday, M. A. K. (1985b) *Spoken and Written Language*. Geelong, Vic: Deakin University Press.

Halliday, M. A. K. (1988) On the ineffability of grammatical categories. in J. D. Benson, M. J. Cummings and W. S. Greaves (eds) *Linguistics in a Systemic Perspective*. Amsterdam: Benjamins. First published in A. Manning, P. Martin and K. McCalla (eds) *The Tenth LACUS Forum 1983*. Columbia, SC : Hornbeam, 1984.

Halliday, M. A. K. (1990) New ways of meaning: a challenge to applied linguistics. *Journal of Applied Linguistics 6 (Ninth World Congress of Applied Linguistics: Special Issue)*. Greek Applied Linguistics Association. pp 7–36. Reprinted in M. A. K. Halliday, *Language in a Changing World*, Canberra, ACT: Applied Linguistics Association of Australia 1993.

Halliday, M. A. K. (1991) The notion of 'context' in language education. In T. Lê and M. McCausland (eds) *Language Education: interaction and development*: Proceedings of the International Conference, Ho Chi Minh City, Vietnam 30 March – 1 April 1991 1–26. Launceston: University of Tasmania.

Halliday, M. A. K. (1992) How do you mean? In M. Davies and L. Ravelli (eds) *Advances in Systemic Linguistics: recent theory and practice* 20–35. London: Printer.

Halliday, M. A. K. (1992/2003) The act of meaning. In J. E. Alatis (ed.) *Language Communication and Social Meaning: Georgetown University Round Table on Language and Linguistics 1992*. Washington, DC: Georgetown University Press. 7–21. Reprinted in Halliday, *Language in a Changing World, Occasional Papers* 13. Applied Linguistics Association of Australia; and Collected Works of M. A. K. Halliday, Volume 3, 2003.

Halliday, M. A. K. (1990/2003) New ways of meaning: a challenge to applied linguistics. *Language in a Changing World, Occasional Paper* 13: 1–41. Applied Linguistics Association of Australia. First published in *Journal of Applied Linguistics 6*, 1990, 7–36 (Ninth World Congress of Applied Linguistics Special Issue: Greek Applied Linguistics Association). Reprinted in Collected Works of M. A. K. Halliday, Volume 3, 2003.

Halliday, M. A. K. (1993) Towards a language based theory of learning. *Linguistics and Education* 5(2) 93–116.

Halliday, M. A. K. (1994a) *An Introduction to Functional Grammar*. 2nd edition. London: Edward Arnold.

Halliday, M. A. K. (1994b) The place of dialogue in children's construction of meaning. In R. B. Ruddell, M. Rapp Ruddell and H. Singer (eds) *Theoretical Models and Processes of Reading*. Newark, Delaware: International Reading Association.

Halliday, M. A. K. (1995a) On language in relation to the evolution of human consciousness. In S. Allén (ed.) *Of Thoughts and Words: the relation between language and mind*, Proceedings of Nobel Symposium 92. London: Imperial College Press.

Halliday, M. A. K. (1995b) Language and the theory of codes. In A. Sadovnik (ed.) *Knowledge and Pedagogy: a commentary on the sociology of Basil Bernstein*. Norwood NJ: Ablex.

Halliday, M. A. K. (1996a) On grammar and grammatics. In R. Hasan, C. Cloran and D. Butt (eds) *Functional Descriptions: theory into practice*. Amsterdam: Benjamins.

Halliday, M. A. K. (1996b) Literacy and linguistics: a functional perspective. In R. Hasan and G. Williams (eds) *Literacy in Society*. London: Longman.

Halliday, M. A. K. (1998) Things and relations: regrammaticizing experience as technical knowledge. In J. R. Martin and R. Veel (eds) *Reading Science: critical and functional perspectives*. London: Routledge.

Halliday, M. A. K. (2002a) *On Grammar: collected works of M. A. K. Halliday Vol 1* (edited by J. J. Webster). London: Continuum.

Halliday, M. A. K. (2002b) *Linguistic Studies of Text and Discourse: collected works of M. A. K. Halliday Vol 2* (edited by J. J. Webster). London: Continuum.

Halliday, MA K. (2003) *On Language and Linguistics: collected works of M. A. K. Halliday Vol 3* (edited by J. J. Webster). London: Continuum.

Halliday, M. A. K. (2004a) *The Language of Early Childhood: collected works of M. A. K. Halliday Vol 4* (edited by J. J. Webster). London: Continuum.

Halliday, M. A. K. (2004b) *The Language of Science: collected works of M. A. K. Halliday Vol 5* (edited by J. J. Webster). London: Continuum.

Halliday, M. A. K. and Hasan, R. (1985/1989) *Language, Context and Text: a social semiotic perspective*. Geelong, Vic: Deakin University Press. Revised edition, Oxford: Oxford University Press 1989.

Halliday, M. A. K. and Martin, J. R. (1993) *Writing Science: literacy and discursive power*. London: The Falmer Press.

Halliday, M. A. K. and Matthiessen, C. M. I. M. (1999) *Construing Experience through Meaning: a language based approach to cognition*. London: Cassell.

Halliday, M. A. K., McIntosh, A. and Strevens, P. (1964) *Linguistic Sciences and Language Teaching*. London: Longman.

Harré, R. and Langenhove, L. van (eds) (1999) *Positioning Theory*. Oxford: Blackwell.

Hasan, R. (1964) *A Linguistic Study of Contrasting Features in the Style of Two Contemporary English Prose Writers*. Unpublished PhD dissertation. Edinburgh: The University of Edinburgh.

Hasan, R. (1968) *Grammatical Cohesion in Spoken and Written English*, part I, Nuffield Programme in Linguistics and English Teaching, Paper No 7, series 1. London: Longmans.

Hasan, R. (1971) Syntax and semantics. In J. Morton (ed.) *Biological and Social Factors in Psycholinguistics*. London: Logos Press.

Hasan, R. (1973) Code, register and social dialect. In Basil Bernstein (ed.) *Class, Codes and Control, Volume 2: applied studies towards a sociology of language*. London: Routledge & Kegan Paul.

Hasan, R. (1978) Text in the systemic functional model. In W. U. Dressler (ed.) *Current Trends in Textlinguistics*. Berlin: Walter de Gruyter.

Hasan, R. (1980) What's going on: a dynamic view of context in language. In J. E. Copeland and P. W. Davies (eds) *The Seventh LACUS Forum* 106–21. Columbia: Hornbeam Press.

Hasan, R. (1983) *A Semantic Network for the Analysis of Messages in Everyday Talk between Mothers and Their Children* (Mimeo).
Hasan, R. (1984a) What kind of resource is language? *Australian Review of Applied Linguistics* 7(1): 57–85. Reprinted in C. Cloran, D. Butt and G.Williams (ed.) *Ways of Saying, Ways of Meaning: selected papers of R. Hasan.* London: Cassell 1996.
Hasan, R. (1984b) The nursery tale as a genre. *Nottingham Linguistic Circular* 13: 71–102.
Hasan, R. (1984c) Ways of saying, ways of meaning. In R. P. Fawcett, M. A. K. Halliday, S. M. Lamb and A. Makkai (eds) *The Semiotics of Culture and Language, Volume 1: language as social semiotic.* London: Francis Pinter.
Hasan, R. (1985a) *Linguistics, Language and Verbal Art.* Geelong, Vic.: Deakin University Press.
Hasan, R. (1985b) Meaning, context and text: fifty years after Malinowski. In J. D. Benson and W. S. Greaves (eds) *Systemic Perspectives on Discourse, Volume 1: selected theoretical papers from the 9th International Systemic Workshop* 16–50. Norwood, NJ: Ablex.
Hasan, R. (1986a) The ontogenesis of ideology: an interpretation of mother child talk. In T. Threadgold, E. Grosz, G. Kress and M. A. K. Halliday (eds) *Semiotics Ideology Language.* Sydney: Sydney Association for Studies in Society and Culture (Sydney Studies in Society and Culture Volume 3).
Hasan, R. (1986b) The implications of semantic distance for language in education. In A. Abbi (ed.) *Studies in Bilingualism.* New Delhi: Bahri Publications.
Hasan, R. (1987a) Directions from structuralism. In N. Fabb, D. Attridge, A. Durant and C. MacCabe (eds) *The Linguistics of Writing: arguments between language and literature* 103–22. Manchester: Manchester University Press.
Hasan, R. (1987b) The grammarian's dream: lexis as most delicate grammar, in M. A. K. Halliday and R. P. Fawcett (eds) *New Developments in Systemic Linguistics.* London: Pinter.
Hasan, R. (1988) Language in the process of socialisation: home and school. In J. Oldenburg, T. van Leeuwen and L. Gerot (eds) *Language and Socialisation: home and school.* (Proceedings from the Working Conference on Language in Education, 17–21 November 1986). North Ryde, NSW: Macquarie University. To be reprinted in Volume 2 of Collected Works of R. Hasan.
Hasan, R. (1989) Semantic variation and sociolinguistics. *Australian Journal of Linguistics* 9(2): 221–76.
Hasan, R. (1991) Questions as a mode of learning in everyday talk. In T. Lê and M. McCausland (eds) *Language Education: interaction and development* 70–119. Launceston: University of Tasmania.
Hasan, R. (1992/2005) Speech genre, semiotic mediation and the development of higher mental functions. In M. A. K. Halliday and F. C. C. Peng (eds) *Language Sciences.* Special Issue: Current Research in Functional Grammar, Discourse and Computational Linguistics with a Foundation in Systemic Theory, Volume 14(4): 489–528. [Chapter 3, this volume]
Hasan, R. (1992a) Rationality in everyday talk: from process to system. In Jan Svartvik (ed.) *Directions in Corpus Linguistics: proceedings of Nobel Symposium 82, Stockholm, 4–8 August 1991* 257–307. Berlin: Walter de Gruyter.

Hasan, R. (1992b) Meaning in sociolinguistic theory. In K. Bolton and H. Kwok (eds) *Sociolinguistics Today: international perspectives* 80–119. London: Routledge.

Hasan, R. (1993) Contexts for meaning. In J. E. Alatis (ed.) *Language, Communication and Social Meaning*, GURT 1992 79–103 Washington, DC: Georgetown University Press.

Hasan, R. (1995a) The conception of context in text. In P. H. Fries and M. Gregory (eds) *Discourse in Society: systemic functional perspectives* (*Meaning and Choice in Language: Studies for Michael Halliday*). Norwood NJ: Ablex.

Hasan, R. (1995b) On social conditions for semiotic mediation: the genesis of mind in society. In A. R. Sadovnik (ed.) *Knowledge and Pedagogy: the sociology of Basil Bernstein* 171–196. Norwood, NJ: Ablex.

Hasan, R. (1996a) Literacy, everyday talk and society. In R. Hasan and G. Williams (eds) *Literacy in Society* 377–424. London: Longman.

Hasan, R. (1996b) Semantic networks: a tool for the analysis of meaning. In C. Cloran, D. Butt and G. Williams (eds) *Ways of Saying, Ways of Meaning: selected papers of R. Hasan*. London: Cassell.

Hasan, R. (1996c) The ontogenesis of ideology: an interpretation of mother child talk. In C. Cloran, D. Butt and G. Williams (eds) *Ways of Saying, Ways of Meaning: selected papers of R. Hasan*. London: Cassell. [Chapter 10, this volume]

Hasan, R. (1998) Educating the language teacher: a social semiotic approach. In B. Asker (ed.) *Teaching Language and Culture: building Hong Kong on education*. Hong Kong: Addison Wesley Longman.

Hasan, R. (1999a) Society, language and the mind: the meta-dialogism of Basil Bernstein's theory. In F. Christie (ed.) *Pedagogy and the Shaping of Consciousness: linguistic and social processes*. London: Cassell. [Chapter 1, this volume]

Hasan, R. (1999b) Speaking with reference to context. In M. Ghadessy (ed.) *Text and Context in Functional Linguistics* 219–328. Amsterdam: John Benjamins.

Hasan, R. (1999c) The disempowerment game: Bourdieu and language in literacy. *Linguistics and Education* 10(1): 25–87. [Chapter 11, this volume]

Hasan, R. (2000b) The uses of talk. In S. Sarangi and M. Coulthard (ed.) *Discourse in Social Life* 28–47. London: Pearson Education.

Hasan, R. (2001a) The ontogenesis of decontextualised language: some achievements of classification and framing. In A. Morais, I. Neves, B. Davies, H. Daniels (eds) *Towards a Sociology of Pedagogy: the contribution of Basil Bernstein to Research*. New York: Peter Lang.

Hasan, R. (2001b) Wherefore context? The place of context in the system and process of language. In R. Shaozeng, W. Guthrie, I. W. Ronald Fong (eds) *Grammar and Discourse: Proceedings of the International Conference on Discourse Analysis* 1–21. Macau: Universidad de Macau.

Hasan, R. (2002) Semiotic mediation and mental development in pluralistic societies: some implications for tomorrow's schooling. In G. Wells and G. Claxton (eds) *Learning for Life in the 21st Century: socio-cultural perspectives on the future of education.* Oxford: Blackwell. [Chapter 7, this volume]

Hasan, R. (2004) Reading picture reading: a study in ideology and inference. In J. Foley (ed.) *Functional Perspectives on Education and Discourse.* London: Continuum. [Chapter 9, this volume]

Hasan, R. and Cloran, C. (1990) A sociolinguistic interpretation of everyday talk between mothers and children. In M. A. K. Halliday, J. Gibbon and Howard Nicholas (eds) *Learning, Keeping and Using Language Volume 1: selected papers from the 8th World Congress of Applied Linguistics, Sydney 16–21 August 1987* 67–100. Amsterdam: Benjamins.

Hawkins, P. R. (1969) Social class, the nominal group and reference. *Language and Speech* 12 and reprinted in this volume.

Hickman, M. (ed.) (1987) *Social and Functional Approaches to Language and Thought.* New York: Academic Press.

Hjelmslev, L. (1961) *Prolegomena to a Theory of Language.* Revised English edition, translated by F. J. Whitfield. Madison: University of Wisconsin Press (Danish original: Copenhagen, 1943).

Hoggart, R. (1957) *The Uses of Literacy.* London: Chatto and Windus.

Holland, J. (1981) Social class and orientations to meanings. *Sociology* 15(1): 1–8.

Hymes, D. (1962) The ethnography of speaking. In T. Gladwin and W. C. Sturtevant (eds) *Anthropology and Human Behaviour.* Washington, DC: Anthropological Society of Washington.

Hymes, D. (1967) Models of the interaction of language and social setting. *Journal of Social Issues* 23(2): 8–28.

Jenkins, Richard (1992) *Pierre Bourdieu.* London: Routledge.

John, V. P. (1972) Styles of learning - styles of teaching: reflections on the education of Navajo children. In C. B. Cazden, V. P. John and D. Hymes (eds) *Functions of Language in the Classroom.* New York: Teachers College Press.

Katz, J. J. and J. A. Fodor (1968) The structure of a semantic theory. In J. A. Fodor and J. J. Katz (eds) *The Structure of Language: readings in the philosophy of language.* Englewood Cliffs, NJ: Prentice-Hall.

Kress, G. and Hodge, R. (1979) *Language as Ideology.* London: Routledge & Kegan Paul.

Kress G. and van Leeuwen, T. (1990) *Reading Images.* Geelong, Vic: Deakin University Press.

Kress, G. and van Leeuwen, T. (1996) *Reading Images: the grammar of visual design.* London: Routledge.

Labov, W. (1969) The logic of non-standard English. *Georgetown Monographs on Language and Linguistics,* Volume 22. Washington, DC: Georgetown University Press.

Labov, W. (1972) *Sociolinguistic Patterns.* Oxford: Basil Blackwell.

Langendoen, D. T. (1968) *The London School of Linguistics: a study of the linguistic theories of B. Malinowski and J. R. Firth.* Cambridge, MA: MIT Press (MIT Research Monograph No 46).

Lave, J. (1997) What's special about experiments as contexts for thinking. In
M. Cole, Y. Engeström and O. Vasquez (eds) *Mind, Culture and Activity.*
Cambridge: Cambridge University Press.
Lee, B. (1987) Recontextualizing Vygotsky. In M. Hickman (ed.) *Social and
Functional Approaches to Language and Thought.* New York: Academic Press.
Lee, P. (1996) *The Whorf Theory Complex: a critical reconstruction.* Amsterdam:
Benjamins.
Lemke, J. L. (1984) *Semiotics and Education.* Toronto Semiotic Circle Monographs,
Working Papers and Pre-publications 1984.2. Toronto: Victoria University.
Lemke, J. L. (1990) *Talking Science: language, learning and values.* Norwood, NJ:
Ablex.
Lemke, J. L. (1992) Interpersonal meaning in discourse: value orientation. In M.
Davies and L. Ravelli (eds) *Advances in Systemic Linguistics: recent theory and
practice.* London: Frances Pinter.
Lemke, J. L. (1993) Discourse, dynamics and social change. In M. A. K. Halliday
(ed.) *Language as Cultural Dynamic*, Special Issue of Cultural Dynamics,
Volume 6(1–2): 243–75.
Lemke, J. L. (1995) *Textual Politics: discourse and social dynamics.* London: Taylor
and Francis.
Lemke, J. L. (2002) Becoming the village: education across lives. In G. Wells and G.
Claxton (eds) *Learning for Life in the 21st Century: socio-cultural perspectives
on the future of education.* Oxford: Blackwell.
Leontiev, A. N. (1978) *Activity, Consciousness and Personality.* Englewood Cliffs
NJ: Prentice Hall.
Lewontin, R. (2000) *The Triple Helix: gene, organism, environment.* Cambridge,
MA: Harvard University Press.
LiPuma, E. (1993) Culture and the concept of culture in a theory of practice. In
C. Calhoun, E. LiPuma and M. Postone (eds) *Bourdieu: critical perspectives.*
Oxford: Polity.
Lucy, J. A. (1985) Whorf's view of the linguistic mediation of thought. In E. Mertz
and R. J. Parmentier (eds) *Semiotic Mediation: sociocultural and psychological
perspectives.* New York: Academic Press.
Luke, A. (1996) Genres of power? Literacy education and the production of capital.
In R. Hasan and G. Williams (eds) *Literacy in Society.* London: Longman.
308–38.
Luria, A. R. (1976) *Cognitive Development: its cultural and social foundations*
(translated by M. Lopez-Morillas and L. Solotaroff, edited by M. Cole).
Cambridge, MA: Harvard University Press.
Lyons, J. (1966) Firth's theory of meaning. In C. E. Bazell, J. C. Catford, M. A. K.
Halliday and R. H. Robins (eds) *In Memory of J. R. Firth.* London: Longmans.
Macken-Horarik, M. (1996) Literacy and learning across the curriculum: toward a
model of register for secondary school teachers. In R. Hasan and G. Williams
(eds) *Literacy in Society.* London: Longman.
Malinowski, B. (1923) The problem of meaning in primitive languages. In
Supplement 1 to C. K. Ogden and I. A. Richards (eds) *The Meaning of Meaning.*
London: Kegan Paul; 8th edition: New York: Harcourt Brace & World.
Malinowski, B. (1935) *Coral Gardens and Their Magic*, Vol. 2. London: Allen &
Unwin.

Malinowski, B. (1935a) An ethnographic theory of language. *Coral Gardens and their Magic,* Volume 2, Part IV. London: Allen and Unwin; New York: American Book Co.
Markova, I. (1990) Introduction. In I. Markova and K. Foppa (eds) *The Dynamics of Dialogue.* New York: Harvester Wheatsheaf.
Marshall, G, Newby, H., Rose, R. and Vogler, C. (1988) *Social Class in Modern Britain.* London: Hutchinson.
Martin, J. R. (1985a) Process and text: two aspects of human semiosis. In J. D. Benson and W. S. Greaves (eds) *Systemic Perspectives on Discourse,* Volume 1. Norwood, NJ: Ablex.
Martin, J. R. (1985b) *Factual Writing: exploring and challenging social reality.* Geelong,Vic: Deakin University Press.
Martin, J. R. (1986) Intervening in the process of writing development. In C. Painter and J. R. Martin (eds) *Writing to Mean: teaching genres across the curriculum,* Occasional Paper 9. Applied Linguistic Association of Australia.
Martin, J. R. (1991) Intrinsic functionality: implications for contextual theory. *Social Semiotics* 1(1): 99–162.
Martin, J. R. (1992) *English Text: system and structure.* Amsterdam: John Benjamins.
Martin, J. R. (1993) Life as a noun: arresting the universe in science and humanities. In M. A. K. Halliday and J. R. Martin (eds) *Writing Science: literacy and discursive power.* London: The Falmer Press.
Martin, J. R. and Painter, C. (eds) (1986) *Writing to Mean: teaching genres across the curriculum.* Occasional Paper 9. Applied Linguistic Association of Australia.
Martin, J. and Peters, P. (1984) On the analysis of exposition. In R. Hasan (ed.) *Discourse on Discourse.* Applied Linguistics Association of Australia (Occasional Paper No 7).
Marx, K. (1975) Preface to a contribution to the critique of political economy. In *Karl Marx, Early Writings.* Harmondsworth: Penguins.
Marx, K. (1976) *Selected Writings in Sociology and Social Philosophy.* Edited by T. B. Bottomore and M. Rubel. Harmondsworth: Penguin.
Marx, K. and Engels, F. (1947) *The German Ideology.* Translated and edited by C. J. Arthur. London: Lawrence & Wishart.
Matthiessen, C. (1992) Interpreting the textual metafunction. In M. Davies and L. Ravelli (eds) *Advances in Systemic Linguistics: recent theory and practice.* London: Frances Pinter.
Matthiessen, C. (1993) The Object of study in cognitive science in relation to its construal and enactment in language. In M. A. K. Halliday (ed.) *Language as Cultural Dynamic.* Special Issue of *Cultural Dynamics* 6(1–2): 187–242.
Matthiessen, C. (1995) *Lexicogrammatical Cartography: English systems.* Tokyo: International Language Sciences Publishers.
Matthiessen, C. (1997) Construing processes of consciousness: from the commonsense model to the uncommonsense model of cognitive science. In J. R. Martin and R. Veel (eds) *Reading Science: critical and functional perspectives on discourse of science.* London: Routledge.
Matthiessen, C. and Nesbitt, C. (1996) On the idea of theory-neutral descriptions. In R. Hasan, C. Cloran and D. G. Butt (eds) *Functional Descriptions.*

McLellan, D. (1975) *Marx. Fontana Modern Masters Series*. Glasgow: Fontana/Collins.
Mead, G. H. (1934) *Mind, Self and Society*. Edited by C. W. Morris. Chicago: University of Chicago Press.
Mehan, H. (1979) *Learning Lessons: social organization in the classroom*. Cambridge, MA: Harvard University Press.
Mercer, N. (2002) Developing dialogues. In G. Wells and G. Claxton (eds) *Learning for Life in the 21st Century: socio-cultural perspectives on the future of education*. Oxford: Blackwell.
Mertz, E. and Parmentier, R. (eds) (1985) *Semiotic Mediation: sociocultural and psychological perspectives*. New York: Academic Press.
Minick, N. (1997) The early history of the Vygotskian school: the relationship between mind and activity. In M. Cole, Y. Engeström and O. Vasquez (eds) *Mind, Culture and Activity: seminal papers from the Laboratory of Comparative Human Cognition*. Cambridge: Cambridge University Press.
Morais, A., Neves, I., Davies, B. and Daniels, H. (eds) (2001) *Towards a Sociology of Pedagogy: the contribution of Basil Bernstein to research*. New York: Peter Lang.
Muller, J., Davies, B. and Morais, A. (eds) (2004) *Reading Bernstein, Researching Bernstein*. London: Routledge Falmer.
Newson, J. (1978) Dialogue and development. In A. Lock (ed.) *Action, Gesture and Symbol: the emergence of language*. New York: Academic Press.
Olson, D. R. (1977) From utterance to text: the bias of language in speech and writing. *Harvard Educational Review* 47(3): 257–81.
Painter, C. (1984) *Into the Mother Tongue: a case study in early language development*. London: Frances Pinter.
Painter, C. (1989) Learning language: a functional view of language development. In R. Hasan and J. R. Martin (eds) *Language Development: learning language, learning culture. Meaning and Choice in Language: studies for Michael Halliday*. Norwood, NJ: Ablex.
Painter, C. (1996) The development of language as a resource for thinking: a linguistic view of learning. In R. Hasan and G. Williams (eds) *Literacy in Society*. London: Addison Wesley Longman.
Painter, C. (1999) *Learning through Language in Early Childhood*. London: Continuum.
Painter, C. and Martin, J. R. 1986 (eds) *Writing to Mean: teaching genres across the curriculum*. Occasional Papers No 9. Applied Linguistics Association of Australia.
Phillips, S. U. (1972) Participant structures and communicative competence: warm springs children in community and classroom. In B. Courtney, V. Cazden, P. John and D. Hymes (eds) *Functions of Language in the Classroom*. New York: Teachers College Press.
Piaget, J. (1924) *Le Jugement et le Raisonnement chez l'Enfant*. Paris: Delachaux et Niestlé.
Pike, K. L. (1954) *Language in Relation to a Unified Theory of the Structure of Human Behaviour*, Part I, (prelim edition). Glendale, California: SIL.
Pinker, S. (1994) *The Language Instinct*. New York: William Morrow.
Popper, K. R. (1957) *The Poverty of Historicism*. London: Routledge & Kegan Paul.

Popper, K. R. (1972) *Objective knowledge: an evolutionary approach*. Oxford: Clarendon.
Popper, K. R. (1979a) *Objective Knowledge: an evolutionary approach*. Revised edition. Oxford: Clarendon Press.
Popper, K. R. (1979b) Two faces of common sense: an argument for common-sense realism and against the commonsense theory of knowledge. *Objective Knowledge: an evolutionary approach*. Revised edition. Oxford: The Clarendon Press.
Poulantzas, N. (1975) *Classes in Contemporary Capitalism*. London: New Left Books.
Robbins, D. (1991) *The Work of Pierre Bourdieu*. Buckingham: Open University Press.
Robinson, W. P. (1973) Where do children's answers come from? In B. Bernstein (ed.) *Class, Codes and Control Vol. 2. Applied Studies towards a Sociology of Language*. London: Routledge & Kegan Paul.
Robinson, W. P. and Rackstraw, S. J. (1972) *A Question of Answers*. London: Routledge & Kegan Paul.
Rosenau, P. M. (1991) *Post-Modernism and the Social Sciences: insights, inroads and intrusions*. Princeton, NJ: Princeton University Press.
Rothery, J. (1996) Making changes: developing an educational linguistics. In R. Hasan and G. Williams (eds) *Literacy in Society*. London: Longman.
Russell, B. (1940) *An Inquiry into Meaning and Truth*. London: Allen and Unwin.
Sadovnik, A. R. (ed.) (1995) *Knowledge and Pedagogy: the sociology of Basil Bernstein*. Norwood, NJ: Ablex.
Sapir, E. (1921) *Language: an introduction to the study of speech*. New York: Harcourt, Brace and Co.
Scase, R. (1992) *Class*. Buckingham: Open University Press.
Searle, J. R. (1969) *Speech Acts: an essay in the philosophy of language*. London: Cambridge University Press.
Sharp, R. (1981) *Knowledge, Ideology and the Politics of Schooling*. London: Routledge & Kegan Paul.
Shotter, J. (1978) The cultural context of communication studies: theoretical and methodological issues. In A. Lock (ed.) *Action, Gesture and Symbol: the emergence of language*. New York: Academic Press.
Sinclair, McH. J. and M. Coulthard (1975) *Towards an Analysis of Discourse: the English used by teachers and pupils*. London: Oxford University Press.
Taylor, G. (1968) *Language and Learning: deep structure in a chemical text*. Unpublished M. Litt. thesis, University of Edinburgh.
Thibault, P. J. (1991) *Social Semiotic as Praxis: text, social meaning making and Nabakov's Ada'*. Minneapolis: University of Minnesota Press.
Thibault, P. J. (1997) *Re-reading Saussure: the dynamics of sign in social life*. London: Routledge.
Thibault, P. J. (2004) *Brain, Mind and the Signifying Body: an ecosocial semiotic theory*. London: Continuum.
Thibault, P. J. (2005) The interpersonal gateway to the meaning of mind: unifying the inter- and intraorganism perspective on language. In R. Hasan, J. Webster, C. M. I. M. Matthiessen (eds) *Continuing Discourse on Language*. London: Equinox.

Thompson, J. B. (1991) Editor's introduction' to *Language and Symbolic Power* by P. Bourdieu (edited by J. B. Thompson). Cambridge: Polity Press.

Todorov, T. (1984) *Mikhail Bakhtin: the dialogical principle* (translated by Wlad Godzich). Manchester: Manchester University Press.

Torr, J. (1997) *From Child Tongue to Mother Tongue: a case study of language development in the first two and a half years*. Nottingham: Department of English Studies, Nottingham University [Monographs in Systemic Linguistics No 9].

Trevarthen, C. (1977) Descriptive analyses of infant communicative behaviour. In H. R. Schaffer (ed.) *Studies in Mother-Infant Interaction*. New York: Academic Press.

Treverarthen, C. (1979) Communication and cooperation in early infancy: a description of primary intersubjectivity. In M. Bullowa (ed.) *Before Speech: the beginning of interpersonal communication*. London: Cambridge University Press.

Turner, G. J. (1973) Social class and children's language of control at age five and seven. In Bernstein, B. (ed.) *Class, Codes and Control Volume 2: Applied Studies towards a Sociology of Language*. London: Routledge & Kegan Paul

van Leeuwen, T. and Humphrey, S. (1996) On learning to look through a geographer's eyes. In R. Hasan and G. Williams (eds) *Literacy in Society*. London: Longman.

Veel, R. and Coffin, C. (1996) Learning to think like an historian: the language of secondary school history. In R. Hasan and G. Williams (eds) *Literacy in Society*. London: Longman.

Ventola, E. (1984) The dynamics of genre. *Nottingham Linguistic Circular* 13, 103–24.

Ventola, E. (1987) *The Structure of Social Interaction: a systemic approach to the semiotics of service encounters*. London: Frances Pinter.

Vološinov, V. N. (1973/1986) *Marxism and the Philosophy of Language* (translated by Ladislav Matejka and I. R. Titunik). Cambridge, MA: Harvard University Press. First published in 1973 by Seminar Press.

Vygotsky, L. S. (1962) *Thought and Language* (translated and edited by Eugenia Hanfmann and Gertrude Vakar). Cambridge MA: Harvard University Press.

Vygotsky, L. S. (1971) *The Psychology of Art*. Cambridge MA: MIT Press.

Vygotsky, L. S. (1978) *Mind in Society: the development of higher psychological processes* (edited by M. Cole, V. John-Steiner, S. Scribner and E. Souberman). Cambridge, MA: Harvard University Press.

Vygotsky, L. S. (1981) The genesis of higher mental functions. In J. V. Wertsch (ed.) *The Concept of Activity in Soviet Psychology*. Armonk, NY: M. E. Sharp.

Wacquant, Loïc J. D. (1993) Bourdieu in America: notes on the transatlantic importation of social theory. In Craig Calhoun, Edward LiPuma and Moishe Postone (eds) *Bourdieu: critical perspectives*. Oxford: Polity.

Wearing, B. (1984) *The Ideology of Motherhood*. Sydney: Allen & Unwin.

Weekly, E. and Wyatt, A. J. (1907) *The Tutorial French Grammar*. 2nd edition. London: W. B. Clive.

Weiner, J. E. and Labov, W. (1983) Constraints on the agentless passive. *Australian Journal of Linguistics,* 19(1): 29–58.

Wells, G. (1980) Apprenticeship in meaning. In K. E. Nelson (ed.) *Children's Language*, Volume 2 45–126. New York: Gardner Press.

Wells, G. (2002) Enquiry as an orientation for learning: teaching and teacher education. In G. Wells and G. Claxton (eds) *Learning for Life in the 21st Century: socio-cultural perspectives on the future of education*. Oxford: Blackwell.
Wertsch, J. V. (ed.) (1981) *The Concept of Activity in Soviet Psychology*. Armonk NY: M. E. Sharpe.
Wertsch, J. V. (ed.) (1985a) *Culture, Communication and Cognition: Vygotskian perspectives*. Cambridge: Cambridge University Press.
Wertsch, J. V. (1985b) *Vygotsky and the Social Formation of Mind*. Cambridge, MA: Harvard University Press.
Wertsch, J. V. (1985c) The semiotic mediation of mental life: L. S. Vygotsky and M. M. Bakhtin. In E. Mertz and R. A. Parmentier (ed.) *Semiotic Mediation: sociocultural and psychological perspectives*. New York: Academic Press.
Wertsch, J. V. (1990) Dialogue and dialogism in a socio-cultural approach to mind. In I. Markova and K. Foppa (eds) *The Dynamics of Dialogue*. New York: Harvester.
Wertsch, J. V. (1991) *Voices of the Mind: a socio-cultural approach to mediated action*. Cambridge, MA: Harvard University Press.
Wertsch, J. V. and Hickman, M. (1987) Problem solving in social interaction: a microgenetic analysis. In M. Hickman (ed.) *Social and Functional Approaches to Language and Thought*. New York: Academic Press.
Whorf, B. L. (1956) *Language, Thought and Reality: selected writings of Benjamin Lee Whorf* (edited and introduced by J. B. Carroll). Cambridge, MA: The MIT Press.
Williams, G. (1995) *Joint Book-Reading and Literacy Pedagogy: a socio-semantic interpretation*. Unpublished PhD dissertation. School of English, Linguistics & Media, Macquarie University (Available as CORE Volume 1(19):3 and Volume 2(20):1).
Williams, G. (1999) The pedagogic device and the production of pedagogic discourse: a case example in early literacy education. In F. Christie (ed.) *Pedagogy and the Shaping of Consciousness: linguistic and social processes* 123–55. London: Cassell.
Williams, G. (2001) Literacy pedagogy prior to schooling: relations between social positioning and semantic variation. In A. Morais, I. Neves, B. Davies and H. Daniels (eds) *Towards a Sociology of Pedagogy: the contribution of Basil Bernstein to research*. New York: Peter Lang.
Williams, G. and Lukin, A. (2004) (eds) *The Development of Language: functional perspectives on species and individuals*. London: Continuum.
Wittgenstein, L. (1953) *Philosophical Investigations* (translated by G. E. M. Anscombe). Oxford: Basil Blackwell. Second edition in 1958.
Wright, E. O. (1985) *Classes*. London: Verso.

Index

Abercrombie, D. 316
accent(s) 24, 297, 309, 317–8, 325, 332, 354
acculturated/acculturation 40–1, 47, 74, 108, 148–9
adult(s) 19, 58, 81–2, 105, 113, 121, 139, 142, 147, 149, 201, 257–8, 260, 269
affective 142, 144, 162, 166–7, 172
ambiguity 168–70, 183, 273
anthropology 285, 289, 365
anthropological(ly) 47, 144, 278, 285, 365
anthropologist(s) 34, 139, 175, 359–60
aphorisms/aphoristic 201, 208
articulatory 296–8, 304
Atkinson, P. 53, 66–7
Austin, J.L. 34, 301
autistic 139, 141, 156
Bakhtin, M. 68–9, 83–98, 101–3, 121, 128, 145
Bakhtinian 38, 69, 83–4, 91, 98
Bateson, G. 122, 234, 240
Bernstein, B. 3–5, 7–10, 12–5, 15, 17–47, 50–3, 55–67, 69, 78, 98, 101–2, 104, 107, 110, 117, 120–38, 145, 147–58, 171–5, 188, 193, 201, 211, 215–9, 221, 223–7, 231, 233–4, 239–40, 245–6, 250–4, 268–70, 273, 276, 279, 295, 309, 316, 318, 323–4, 326, 328, 333, 336, 339, 341–2, 344, 346–7
biogenetic(ally) 5, 58, 71, 75, 81, 105, 107–8, 113–4, 117, 128, 131, 342
biological(ly) 8, 20, 51, 58, 71, 73, 75, 106, 109, 112–4, 117, 129, 131–2, 134, 160, 173–4, 215, 229, 286–7, 342
Bourdieu, P. 4, 9, 11, 17, 47, 56, 63, 67, 134, 275–336, 337–53
brain 7–9, 12–5, 57, 75, 107, 213, 215, 238, 261, 286–7, 350
Brandis, W. 166, 171
Butt, D. 17, 82, 121, 255, 257, 270, 306, 312
Cartesian(s) 75, 113, 133

child/children 18–9, 24–5, 32, 36, 38–41, 45, 57–8, 62, 65, 74, 81, 102, 109–13, 123, 135, 139–43, 148–50, 153, 158–9, 166, 172–4, 193–4, 198, 200–6, 209–14, 217–27, 231–3, 237–69, 274, 318–9, 323–7, 345
Chomsky, N. 17, 38, 51, 174, 253, 257, 270, 275, 281, 284, 286–7, 299, 302, 334, 342, 353
Chouliaraki, L. 340, 343–4, 346–8
Christie, F. 13, 233, 326
class 22–3, 43–5, 53, 67, 82, 97, 105, 121–4, 148, 151, 163, 171, 180, 216, 232, 236–7, 241, 243, 245–6, 253, 255, 261, 283, 287, 291–2, 296–7, 303, 307–8, 317–25
    -based 44, 320
    relations 22, 36, 54–9, 61, 123–4, 250
classroom 29–30, 82–3, 120, 158, 182, 206, 208, 213–4, 232–41, 249, 252–5, 276, 278, 322–6, 332, 352
    discourse 82, 158, 232–5, 239–41, 249, 252–5
    practices 158, 213, 276, 278, 332
clause(s) 37, 180, 183–5, 242, 311
Claxton, G. 196, 209, 211, 214
Cloran, C. 15, 36, 38, 44, 46, 58, 63, 65, 82, 121, 153, 156, 209–10, 214, 217–8, 221–2, 232, 245, 252–7, 318, 326
code(s) 15, 18, 23–31, 36–7, 43–6, 53–4, 58–9, 79, 97, 100, 102, 117, 123–8, 160–93, 215–8, 221–7, 250, 254, 288, 347, 351–2
    elaborated 30, 165, 168, 171, 187–8, 221, 223, 227
    restricted 26, 154, 167, 169–71, 183, 187, 223
    -correlating 189
    -regulated 24, 37, 40, 152–3
    theory 15, 36, 41, 44, 53, 58, 60–5, 150–8, 216–7, 223, 225
co-genetic 337, 341, 347
cognition 9, 18, 33, 39, 107–8, 147, 249
cognitive 57, 79, 109, 111, 117, 120, 127, 135, 152, 214, 231, 353

communication 14, 19, 23–39, 42, 48–9, 54–5, 59–60, 81, 83–91, 94, 96–7, 100–4, 122–6, 139–43, 149, 151–9, 169, 172–6, 184–5, 191, 206, 215–7, 231–2, 239–40, 250–3, 267–72, 300
community 6, 53, 61, 74, 77, 85, 94, 97, 99–102, 112, 115, 119, 121–4, 145, 149, 162–4, 167, 172–3, 186, 191, 196–201, 209, 222, 234, 251–2, 256–8, 264, 267, 284, 286–8, 295, 308, 316, 327, 341, 346
  language 17, 87, 163, 177, 251
  speech 82, 99, 121, 138, 162, 164, 172, 177, 271, 287, 306
competence 29, 45, 174, 191, 213, 234, 284, 286–7, 292, 294, 299, 302–3, 325–6, 330, 351, 353, 368
conflict 124, 248, 254, 275, 279
consciousness 4–7, 10–13, 15–6, 18, 20, 22–5, 29, 31, 39–40, 42, 52–3, 66–7, 74–5, 78–80, 82–3, 93–8, 100–102, 113, 117–9, 121–3, 125–6, 130–2, 135, 150–1, 155–8, 206, 213, 215–7, 227, 231, 233, 239–40, 250, 262, 269, 272, 276, 295–6, 318, 320, 322, 324, 336, 338, 341, 345–6, 348
  human 5, 15, 24, 40, 52, 57–8, 66, 83, 97–8, 100, 104–5, 119, 122–3, 128, 131–2, 143, 148, 150, 155, 216, 278, 282, 329, 345
control 25–7, 38, 42, 48, 67, 71–2, 75–6, 105, 109–10, 114, 132–3, 137, 156, 172, 175, 181, 184–7, 191, 211–2, 247–50, 253–5, 273, 281, 302, 316, 332–3, 335
  power and 27, 31, 55, 57, 101–2, 125, 151, 211, 218
  principles of 22–3, 25–6, 31, 36, 53–5, 59, 122–3, 125, 151, 215, 218, 250
conversation 37–8, 139, 159, 184, 201, 218, 221, 255, 257–8, 260
Coulthard, M. 233, 237
culture(-al) 5, 7, 12, 14, 16–7, 21–2, 28, 39–42, 45, 47, 57–8, 65, 67, 74, 103, 110, 112–3, 131, 134–5, 143, 146, 149, 152, 167, 189, 195–202, 206–9, 211–2, 214, 216, 231, 234–5, 259, 269–70, 282, 305, 342, 347

cultural activity(-ies) 146, 149, 195–9, 200, 206–8, 209, 214
  community 198, 209
  reproduction 21–2, 206, 347, 355
  transmission 45, 189
Deacon, T. 134, 215, 252
denotation 300, 306, 341
development 3, 5–7, 9–10, 15, 17, 19, 28, 30, 38, 40–2, 50, 52, 65–6, 68, 70–81, 90, 105, 108–122, 125, 127–8, 131–5, 139–43, 146, 148–9, 155, 158, 194–7, 199, 211–6, 235, 262, 276, 278, 282, 325–7, 333, 337
  of higher mental
function(s) 57, 68, 70, 73–4, 113, 115, 345
  biological 73, 112, 134
  cognitive 109, 111, 120, 127, 231
  cultural 40, 57
  historical 76, 109, 114
  intellectual 112, 116, 341
  language 139–40, 149, 289, 318, 329
  literacy 323, 325–6
  mental 7, 66, 70–1, 73, 81, 84, 108, 113, 116, 118–9, 121, 131–2, 139–41, 149, 194–5, 197, 199, 201, 203, 205, 207, 209, 211, 213, 249
  psychological 70, 76, 108, 114
dialect(s) 44, 97, 157–8, 160, 162–5, 169, 171–2, 176–7, 186, 191–2, 213, 287, 293–8, 316–7, 336
dialectic 5, 14, 20, 33, 42, 55, 57, 60, 64, 66, 122, 128, 156, 216, 276, 279, 307, 310–11, 317, 324, 333, 342, 347
dialectical 59, 76, 92, 114, 123, 294, 319
dialogue 8, 11, 13, 19, 36, 49–50, 52, 57–8, 60, 64, 66, 88–90, 198, 207, 210, 214, 253–4, 263, 265, 341, 348–9
discourse 3–7, 11, 14–6, 19, 26–42, 46–7, 53, 55–6, 58–60, 64, 66–7, 81–5, 91, 97, 101–2, 120, 125–7, 134–9, 145–9, 152–8, 177–86, 194, 196–8, 200–6, 209–18, 221–7, 238–55, 268, 277–80, 284–5, 288, 291–2, 298–313, 318–32, 337–40, 343–5, 348, 351
  academic 106, 280, 332
  classroom 82, 158, 232–3, 239–41, 249, 252–5
  horizontal 30, 155, 339
  instructional 29, 41, 231–4, 239

pedagogic 27–9, 31, 46, 81, 102, 104, 120, 148, 153–4, 213, 221, 225, 233
  regulative 29, 234, 239
  specialized 158, 200, 212–3, 337
  vertical 30
  written 184, 298
Durkheim, E. 26, 267, 282
education 3, 7, 15, 21, 27–9, 31, 33, 41, 77, 115, 148, 158, 163–4, 171, 173, 195–6, 213, 230, 232–3, 240, 252, 255, 257, 275–8, 281–2, 321–3, 325–8, 331–6, 352
educational 3, 6, 24–31, 41, 46, 81, 120, 131, 158, 173, 196, 201, 208, 213, 233–5, 238, 241, 252–3, 281, 294–5, 302, 321, 323, 325–7, 330
  sociology 278–9, 295
  success 6, 81, 120, 327
  system 28, 30–1, 41, 46, 120, 158, 173, 213, 241, 253, 281, 294, 323
  transmission(s) 26, 355
egalitarian 17, 41, 158, 195
egocentric 139–40
endotropic 9–10, 19, 51–2
English 169, 218, 242–3, 271, 288, 298, 302, 334
epistemology 344, 346
evolution 9, 11, 51–2, 66, 75–6, 105, 107, 114–8, 155–6, 235, 271, 276, 305, 309, 335, 337–8, 341, 347
exotropic 10–4, 18–9, 32, 51–6, 66–7, 130, 155
experiential 140–2, 144, 146–7, 149
explanatory 26, 35, 58, 84, 101, 106, 111, 113, 157–8, 161, 172, 215, 291
extra-linguistic 63, 80, 91, 162–5, 185–6, 188, 190, 298, 311
Fairclough, N. 340, 343–50
Firth, J.R. 10, 17, 34, 38, 43, 56, 62, 67, 81, 86, 92, 134, 144, 161–2, 175, 192, 223, 251, 274, 282–89, 291–3, 312, 333–4
formalism 8, 278–9, 344
formalist 34, 103, 276, 278, 286, 289, 299–300, 302–7, 310, 317, 343–5
French 288, 335
functional 14, 19, 21, 34, 36, 43, 50, 55, 62, 69, 136, 148, 188, 217–8, 291–3, 301, 305, 307, 310, 313, 315–6, 318, 320, 338, 340, 347–9

linguistics 14, 19, 34, 43, 55, 136, 338, 347–9
  semantics 310, 313, 315–6, 318
genetic 19, 70, 74, 107–9, 114, 118, 228
genetically 74, 78, 117, 135, 141, 287
genre(s) 12, 28, 35, 69, 83–93, 96, 100, 145, 180, 234, 298–9, 326–7, 349
German 92, 288
gesture 110, 140, 228, 270, 331
grammar(s) 16, 24, 36, 63–5, 91, 94–5, 141, 143–4, 147–8, 161, 173, 191–2, 217, 292–3, 297, 301–4, 306, 310, 315–6, 333, 335–6, 341, 345, 350
grammatical 84, 90, 136, 154, 180, 191, 216, 218, 245, 272
Gumperz, J. 47, 289
Halliday, M. A. K. 8, 10, 12–5, 17–20, 24, 34–6, 43–5, 47, 49–50, 60, 62, 64–7, 69, 81, 83, 91–2, 95, 99–100, 104–5, 120, 122, 125–7, 129–30, 134–5, 138, 140–2, 148–9, 154–6, 162, 175–6, 178, 180, 183–5, 193, 215–6, 218, 226, 228, 240, 245, 251, 255, 268, 270–1, 274, 285–6, 289, 305, 309–10, 312, 318, 322, 325–6, 332–3, 335–6
Hjelmslev, L. 8, 48, 52, 66–7, 134, 271, 274, 283, 310–11, 335
Hymes, D. 47, 289, 317
ideational 95, 142, 147–8, 278
ideology (-ies) 19, 23, 26–7, 29, 33, 42, 44–5, 58–9, 61–3, 94, 97, 105, 118, 125, 148, 152, 158–9, 228–9, 239, 250, 252, 256–7, 259, 261–3, 265, 267–74, 281–2, 312, 325, 336, 345, 348
individuality 75, 89, 90, 92
infant 139–40, 173, 192, 251
innate 78, 117, 286–7
intellect 72, 111, 113, 116, 132, 135, 142, 235, 261, 267, 323
intelligence 5, 24, 79, 112, 116, 118, 135, 230–1, 304, 336
interpersonal 15, 80, 87, 95, 102–4, 110, 112, 119, 141–2, 144, 146, 148–9, 166–8, 222, 225–6, 251, 278, 339
intersubjective 38, 57, 94, 205, 250
intertextuality 38, 50, 83–4, 97, 100, 102
intonation 91, 143–4
langue 34, 69, 92, 162, 174, 274, 282–90, 293, 308, 324, 334–5, 341

learner(s) 28, 41, 102, 158, 196, 240, 252, 321–2, 326, 336
learning 5, 15, 25, 28, 31–2, 41, 46, 62, 81, 102, 106, 115, 123, 135, 149–50, 153, 158, 173–4, 191, 194, 196–7, 206, 213–27, 231, 234–5, 239–40, 249, 251, 255, 257, 259, 276–7, 318, 321–4, 336
van Leeuwen, T. 14, 298
lexical 84, 176, 190, 216, 227, 296, 298, 301, 306, 316, 345
lexicogrammar 15, 35, 43, 63, 92, 100, 155–6, 245, 272, 310–7, 343–4, 347–8
lexicogrammatical(ly) 6, 43, 63, 92, 218, 242, 270–4, 310–2, 315, 320
lexicon 91, 144, 161, 164, 173, 180–3, 192, 293, 303, 306, 308, 310, 322, 345, 350
lexis 167, 171, 175, 193, 363
linguist(s) 4–5, 7, 9, 12, 19, 24, 33–4, 36–9, 43, 45, 47, 49, 62, 65, 67–8, 88, 92, 142, 144, 148, 151, 154, 161, 163, 172, 175, 183, 217, 223, 251, 254, 270, 274–5, 278–93, 296–8, 300–5, 307, 310, 315–7, 322, 331, 333–4, 338–9, 344–5, 347–52
listener(s) 62, 87, 95, 120, 185, 240, 283, 336
literacy 2, 44, 77, 115, 156, 214, 234, 254, 275–8, 281, 321–32, 336, 338–9, 349, 352
literary 96, 145, 186, 298, 342
Luria, A. R. 24, 46, 58, 69, 75, 77–81, 99, 102, 113, 115–8, 121, 126–8, 136, 147, 153–4, 230–2, 240, 249–50, 252
Malinowski, B. 17, 34, 56, 81, 116, 139, 144, 147, 269, 286, 289, 312
Markova, I. 75, 305
Martin, J. 15, 35, 38, 47, 65, 69, 91–2, 104, 272, 323, 326, 333–4, 336
Marx, K. 6, 42, 53, 67–8, 71, 74, 78, 101, 104, 113, 116, 128, 133, 148, 256, 309, 329, 336
Marxist 5, 40, 42, 44, 47, 122, 127, 148
material
 action/activity 199–200, 202, 208, 273
 base 27, 60, 101, 105, 126
 conditions 42, 78, 101, 107
 situational setting 180, 218–9

Matthiessen, C. M. I. M. 8, 15, 17, 24, 50, 62, 64, 92, 95, 215, 255, 336
meaning 5–7, 9, 13–5, 24–5, 34–5, 37, 39, 43–4, 60, 63–5, 67, 81–2, 85, 95, 97, 100–1, 103–5, 107, 112, 119–20, 125, 127–8, 134, 139, 142–8, 154–5, 157–8, 161–2, 166–7, 170–9, 182, 184–5, 187–8, 190–3, 194, 201, 203, 206, 215–27, 242–53, 272, 274, 276, 277, 285–6, 298–301, 305–23, 326, 329, 332–6, 345–6, 352
 linguistic 128, 143–7, 301, 306, 309–13
 ways of 5, 13, 24, 44, 105, 107, 127, 158, 217, 251, 253, 316–20, 326
(semiotic) mediation 6–7, 17–20, 24, 40–1, 47, 58, 61, 68–74, 76–81, 83–4, 88, 96, 99–104, 106–8, 110–13, 115–7, 119–23, 126–39, 142, 145–55, 158, 194–201, 203, 205–7, 209, 211, 213, 216, 227, 282, 345
mediator(s) 112, 136–8, 149, 151–4
mental 3, 5–10, 13–4, 19–20, 24, 51, 66, 68–84, 102, 104–22, 131–43, 194–7, 201–7, 215, 222–3, 231–2, 258, 336, 345
 action/activity(ies) 6, 70, 73, 76, 83, 108–12, 114, 117, 127, 131–2, 134, 141–2, 147, 197, 232
 development 7, 66, 70–1, 73, 81, 84, 108, 113, 116, 118–9, 121, 131–2, 139–41, 149, 158, 194, 201, 249
 disposition(s) 13, 112–3, 148, 152, 158, 196–7, 202, 206, 212–3
 function(s) 6–7, 24, 57–8, 68–74, 76–7, 80–2, 84, 96, 99, 104–5, 108–13, 115–21, 127, 131–4, 137–8, 142, 146–9, 156, 194–5, 207, 226, 314
 life 20, 42, 135, 138, 156
 state 37–8, 202–5, 223
message 65, 125–6, 143, 156, 171, 185, 188, 190–1, 203–4, 214, 222, 224, 227, 235, 239–41, 243–5, 255, 282, 298, 313, 325, 333, 352
metadialogue 11, 19, 49–50, 52, 59, 61, 64
modality 6, 60, 67, 136–8, 145, 150, 154–5, 183, 195, 272
modalities 9–10, 12–6, 29–30, 32–3, 39, 42, 56–7, 67, 73, 112, 134, 156, 194–5, 209, 221, 277, 296, 298, 347

mothers 19, 36, 38, 65, 140, 159, 184, 198, 202–6, 210–11, 214, 217–9, 221, 225–6, 253, 255, 257, 259, 260–7
negotiation 158, 196, 206, 242, 244
ontogenesis 131, 139, 141, 159, 209, 212, 256, 267, 269
ontogenetic 15, 70, 108, 131
phonology 15, 64, 144, 148, 161, 167, 171, 175, 193, 299, 303, 308, 311, 347–8
phonological 176, 274, 296–8, 311–2, 316, 319–20, 336, 347
Piaget 5, 133, 139, 141
Pike, K. L. 17, 47, 161, 175
pronunciation 294, 296–7, 304, 308, 328, 332
prosodic 15, 304
protolanguage 62
protolinguistic 141–2, 226
psychology 17, 19–21, 33, 45, 68–9, 76, 114, 129, 133, 135, 148, 194, 282
psychological 25, 57, 62, 68, 70, 72–8, 86, 102, 108–9, 111–2, 114, 116, 123, 132–5, 143, 148, 150, 172
register 15, 65, 157–8, 160–1, 176–80, 182–86, 189–93, 104, 308–9, 317–19, 326–7, 347
rhetorical 65, 93, 298, 308
Robbins, D. 338–43, 345, 348, 350–3
role-system(s) 186–9
roles 23, 165, 177, 179–83, 185–6, 266, 272
Russian 40, 68, 230
de Saussure, F. 26, 34, 45, 55, 64, 67, 69, 92, 94, 134, 145, 162, 271, 274–5, 281–7, 289, 305, 310, 315, 321, 324, 333–6, 339–41, 343, 350, 353
school(s) 29, 41, 72, 111, 132, 158, 173, 182, 193–4, 203, 206, 209, 213, 227, 231–2, 234, 236–8, 240, 247, 249, 252–3, 255, 260, 266, 294, 332–6, 345
schooling 29, 77, 115, 147–8, 158, 194, 209, 213, 232–3, 235, 238, 240, 322
science 8, 15, 17, 96, 127, 286, 291–2, 315–6, 322, 343
sciences 5, 8–9, 30, 180, 280, 284, 290, 308, 314, 333, 339, 345
scientific 9, 68, 70, 80, 88–89, 96, 104, 108, 111–2, 196, 286, 352

semantic(s) 15, 24, 35–6, 43–4, 60, 63–5, 90–1, 97, 103–4, 126, 136, 144, 149, 151, 153–8, 165, 167, 169–71, 175, 179–80, 183, 189–91, 193, 202, 205–6, 217–9, 222–7, 232, 245–7, 249, 252–3, 255, 270, 272–3, 285, 299, 301, 303, 306–7, 309–20, 322, 326, 333, 341, 344
analysis 154–5, 219, 253, 255
component(s) 167, 175, 179–80, 183, 189–90
feature(s) 126, 202, 205, 223–6, 245, 320
level 167, 169, 175, 223, 310, 319
network(s) 65, 154, 219, 222–3
potential 63, 270, 311, 314
variation 15, 36, 65, 126, 232, 252, 319–20, 322, 326
semiosis 14–6, 20, 61, 73–4, 77, 98, 105, 107, 112, 119, 126, 128, 135, 154, 156, 215–6, 339
semiotic(s) 5–7, 9–20, 24, 33, 39–41, 47, 52–4, 58–61, 64–7, 97, 156, 159, 214, 234, 251, 269–70, 275–9, 281–2, 285, 287, 293, 298, 305–7, 312, 314–5, 317, 319, 321, 323, 333, 337–8, 342–8
mediation 6–7, 17, 19–20, 24, 40–1, 47, 58, 61, 68–71, 73–81, 83–4, 88, 96, 99–104, 106–8, 111–3, 115–7, 119–23, 126–9, 130–1, 133–9, 142, 145–55, 194–203, 205–7, 209, 211, 213, 216, 227, 282, 345
modalities 9–10, 13–4, 16, 33, 67, 73, 112, 134, 195, 209, 298
semologic(al) 305, 311–7, 320–2, 329
signifier(s) 63–4, 134, 294, 300, 307, 310–2, 316, 320, 335, 346
Sinclair, Molt. J. 233, 237
situation
context of 14, 17, 33, 64, 277
social 85–8, 91–2, 98, 314
situation-type 177–85
socialisation 21, 102, 166, 171, 218
socialising contexts 166–8, 172, 188

sociogenesis 13, 73, 75, 82, 99, 104–5, 110, 113, 118, 121, 128, 131, 138, 141, 145–8, 150, 194
sociogenetic 15, 20, 76, 78, 81, 107–8, 110–11, 117, 121–2, 128–9, 132–3, 139, 155, 231, 305
sociolinguistic(s) 7, 34, 44, 49, 160–1, 172, 174, 192–3, 198, 254, 280, 296, 316, 340
sociology 13, 18–23, 26–33, 45–6, 49, 56, 58, 67, 69, 122, 127, 129, 149–52, 155, 172, 174, 192, 194, 276, 278–80, 282, 285, 292, 295, 308, 315–7, 322, 324, 331–4, 337–8, 342
  of language 23, 285
  of pedagogy 22, 27–32, 151
speech
  communication 87–9, 91
  community 82, 99, 121, 138, 162, 164, 172, 177, 271, 287, 306
  fellowship 17, 38, 56, 251, 254
  genre 69, 83–8, 91, 145
  process 83, 88, 90–2, 94–6
  systems 25, 62, 102, 123, 150, 227
structuralism 282, 287, 344, 346
structuralist 284, 289
syllogism(s) 79–80, 117–8, 230–1
syllogistic 77, 79–81, 115, 117–8
symbolic 4, 22, 30–1, 42, 54, 61, 81, 111, 177, 190–1, 193, 215, 218, 284, 294–5, 300, 303, 309, 319, 325, 333, 340, 350
syntax 11, 19, 43, 50–3, 56, 60, 130, 144–5, 151, 161, 164, 167, 171, 175, 182–4, 193, 270, 301, 304, 308, 310, 322
syntactic 176, 184, 216, 227, 295, 328
systemic 14, 19, 34–5, 43, 50, 55, 62, 69, 120, 136, 145, 175, 217–8, 291–3, 301, 305, 313, 316, 338, 343, 347–9
text 14, 35–6, 39, 55, 60, 65, 83, 91–2, 95, 103, 120, 145–7, 179–85, 188–90, 192, 199–200, 259, 275, 281, 283, 285, 310, 335–6, 347, 351
textual 36, 65, 95, 142, 148, 190, 278, 351
Thibault, P. J. 15, 306, 334, 346
transmit 59, 124, 250
transmitted 159, 177, 257, 267, 296, 329, 342

universal 80, 102, 108, 118, 138, 198, 203, 209, 229, 231, 271, 287, 290, 293, 314
Urdu 272, 334, 341
utterance(s) 14, 45, 84–98, 141, 143, 161–2, 201, 254, 258, 273
Uzbekistan, Uzbek 58, 77–8, 81–2, 99, 102, 115–8, 147, 153, 230
variation
  code 157, 186–9, 193
  linguistic 293, 297, 309, 316–8, 334–5, 340
  register 178, 184, 186, 189, 319, 326, 347
  semantic 15, 36, 65, 126, 232, 252, 319–20, 322, 326
  systematic 58, 65, 216, 218, 225, 317
Ventola, E. 35, 91
verbal
  action 199–201, 208–9, 214
  consciousness 94–5, 97
  interaction 11, 74, 80, 83–4, 88, 90, 94, 97, 103–4, 112, 162, 167, 169, 182, 188
verbal-logical 79, 118, 230
  semiosis 74, 77, 98, 112, 126
Vygotsky, L. S. 5–7, 10–3, 17–20, 24, 40–1, 46, 57–8, 61, 66, 68–77, 80–1, 83–4, 86, 96, 98–9, 102, 104, 105–16, 118–22, 127–50, 152, 154–6, 194–6, 226–7, 231, 240, 314, 326, 333, 336, 345–6
Vygotskian 24, 41, 69, 76, 99, 114, 119, 128, 131, 134, 137, 145–6, 149, 195, 278
Wertsch, J. V. 69–72, 74, 80, 82–4, 108, 110–11, 113, 121, 132, 136, 138, 145–6, 153, 194–5, 231
Whorf, B. L. 5–7, 10, 12–3, 17, 39, 41, 46, 105, 122, 134, 144, 147, 161, 175, 264, 269–72, 311, 320, 335–6, 346
Whorfian 24, 78, 100, 117, 172, 270
Wittgenstein, L. 5, 122, 310, 313, 335–6
working-class(es) 23–4, 43–5, 171, 232, 245–9